Anya von Bremzen has been many things: as a child in the Soviet Union, she was the granddaughter of the former head of Soviet intelligence, and thus a bona fide member of the *nomenklatura*; she was also the daughter of a disaffected dissident; a child actress; a piano prodigy. Then, because of political repressions in Brezhnev-era Russia, she and her mother became émigrés, to America. Eventually, when an injury ended her piano career, she reinvented herself as one of the most accomplished food writers of her generation: the author of five acclaimed cookbooks, the recipient of three James Beard awards, and a contributing editor at *Travel + Leisure* magazine. Anya's articles have also appeared in *The New Yorker*, *Food & Wine*, *Saveur*, and the *Los Angeles Times*. She divides her time between New York City and Istanbul.

Acclaim for *Mastering the Art of Soviet Cooking*:

'Heartbreakingly poignant and laugh-out-loud funny. This is an important book, a must read!'   Heston Blumenthal

'The culinary memoir has lately evolved into a genre of its own . . . But Anya von Bremzen is a better writer than most of the genre's practitioners, as this delectable book, which tells the story of post-revolutionary Russia through the prism of one family's meals, amply demonstrates . . . von Bremzen moves artfully between historical longshots . . . and intimate details. The descriptions of meals are delightful'   Sara Wheeler, *New York Times*

'This poignant memoir is an education in the richness of eastern European cuisine, and the story of Soviet communism, through the lens of family experience'   *Observer*

'I don't think there's ever been a book quite like this; I couldn't put it down. Warm, smart and completely engaging . . . this is a book you won't forget'   Ruth Reichl, author of *Tender at the Bone*

'You will read few better books about food, family, exile or the Soviet tragedy – and none, I'll bet, which combines all those themes this magically. Funny, angry, ingenious and moving' A. D. Miller, author of *Snowdrops*

'A monumental but deeply human book that reads like a great Russian novel, filled with dark humor and nostalgia. It opens up an entire universe, teaching us about the many deep meanings of food: cultural, political, social, historical, personal. It is also an utterly magical journey into a rich, mysterious land of totalitarian tyranny, and a portrait of a courageous, passionate people' Ferran Adria

'Von Bremzen has conjured up the Proustian aromas of her Soviet life for her enjoyable "foodoir" . . . perceptive and funny on the subtleties of life under Soviet rule and in exile'   Charlotte Hobson, *Spectator*

'By turns funny, tragic and nostalgic, this is a wonderful, fascinating volume, which puts a human face on the grim pages of the history books' *The Lady*

'Moving and darkly comic' Niki Segnit, *Sunday Times*

'Wry, provocative, genre-busting' *Wall Street Journal*

'Absorbing . . . a social history of the Soviet Union cast through the prism of food' *Jewish Chronicle*

'Rollicking and heartrending' *Time*

'Vastly entertaining . . . A real treat' *Woman & Home*

'One-of-a-kind . . . Breathtaking feats of raconteurial skill . . . *Mastering the Art of Soviet Cooking* is not only a magic tablecloth, it's a magic carpet that revisits the roads and lanes of the former *Soyuz*, surveying the tales of hardship and hardwon joys of von Bremzen's relatives and the Russian people' Liesl Schillinger, *The Daily Beast*

'Through a kaleidoscopic mix of family life, politics, history, and jokes, von Bremzen evokes in her book a whole Sovict-era world of deprivation and delight' *Tablet*

'A delicious, intelligent book. When I read it, I can taste the food but also the melancholy, tragedy, and absurdity that went into every bit of pastry and borscht' Gary Shteyngart

'A rich, zesty history of family life in the USSR' *Entertainment Weekly*

'Much more a work of family memory than a practical cookbook or a historical survey . . . in which colours, textures and aromas open into often gut-wrenching recollections' *Times Literary Supplement*

'Celebrated food writer von Bremzen pulls back the curtain on Soviet life in this sweeping, multigenerational memoir' *Publishers Weekly*

'Most Westerners imagine Stalinist Russia as a food desert . . . Although this view has plenty of truth, it lacks nuance and humanity, as von Bremzen reveals so eloquently in this memoir . . . [von Bremzen] shows the personal side of Soviet life, recounting the terror of war and secret police as well as the power of human resilience' *Booklist*

'Turns a bittersweet eye and an intelligent heart on Soviet history through food . . . Beautifully told' *Los Angeles Times*

'Von Bremzen knows how to tell a story – poignant, funny but never lacking' *Chicago Tribune*

'An ambitious food memoir that is also a meticulously researched history of the Soviet Union . . . a meditation on culinary nostalgia' Julia Moskin, *New York Times*

'A painstakingly researched and beautifully written cultural history but also the best kind of memoir . . . A breathtaking balancing act . . . von Bremzen is as much a virtuoso in her writing as her mother is in her cooking' *New York Review of Books*

'My heart gladdened at the sight of Anya von Bremzen's book, This is history at a personal level, the kitchen table' Martin Cruz Smith, *Wall Street Journal*

'[Von Bremzen] is a profoundly gifted writer, able to lace information with observation, observation with wit . . . [this book] feels rather like a novel, richly populated and filled with deft dialogue, yet it's also crammed full of history' *LA Weekly*

'One of the most unexpectedly pleasurable reads this year. Beyond the innately voyeuristic thrill of reading about the details of Soviet life, *Mastering the Art of Soviet Cooking* is funny, intimate, evocative and rueful' *Kirkus Reviews*

Mastering the Art of Soviet Cooking

ANYA VON BREMZEN

BLACK SWAN

TRANSWORLD PUBLISHERS
61–63 Uxbridge Road, London W5 5SA
A Random House Group Company
www.transworldbooks.co.uk

MASTERING THE ART OF SOVIET COOKING
A BLACK SWAN BOOK: 9780552777476

First published in Great Britain
in 2013 by Doubleday
an imprint of Transworld Publishers
Black Swan edition published 2014

Selected recipes originally appeared, in somewhat different form, in *Saveur* and
Food & Wine magazines. *Please to the Table* by Anya von Bremzen and John
Welchman (New York: Workman Publishing Company, 1990), and in *The
Greatest Dishes!* by Anya von Bremzen (New York: William Morrow, 2004).

Photograph on opening page for Part IV courtesy of John Welchman.

A CIP catalogue record for this book
is available from the British Library.

Addresses for Random House Group Ltd companies outside the UK
can be found at: www.randomhouse.co.uk
The Random House Group Ltd Reg. No. 954009

The Random House Group Limited supports the Forest Stewardship Council®
(FSC®), the leading international forest-certification organisation. Our books
carrying the FSC label are printed on FSC®-certified paper. FSC is the only
forest-certification scheme supported by the leading environmental
organisations, including Greenpeace. Our paper procurement
policy can be found at www.randomhouse.co.uk/environment

Typeset in 11/14pt Requiem by Falcon Oast Graphic Art Ltd.
Printed and bound by CPI Group (UK) Ltd, Croydon, CR0 4YY.

2 4 6 8 10 9 7 5 3 1

For Larisa

CONTENTS

POISONED MADELEINES

Whenever my mother and I cook together, she tells me her dreams. So rich and intense is Mom's dream life, she's given to cataloging and historicizing it: brooding black-and-white visions from her Stalinist childhood; sleek cold war thrillers laced with KGB spooks; melodramas starring duty-crushed lovers.

In a nod, I suppose, to her Iron Curtain past, Mother gets trapped in a lot of her dreams – although now, at seventy-nine years of age and after nearly four American decades, she tends to get trapped in pretty cool places. Deep, for example, in a maze-like, art-filled palace, one much resembling the Metropolitan Museum of Art, where, having retired as a schoolteacher, she works as a docent. In this dream's Technicolor finale, an orange balloon rescues Mom from her labyrinth and deposits her at the museum's sumptuous café. Whereupon she gorges on cream puffs.

But it's one dream of hers from long ago, one I remember her telling me of many times, that's most emblematic. Here she is, skinny, short-haired, tiptoeing into my bedroom as I awake to the hopeless darkness of a Soviet socialist winter. We're in our minuscule flat in a shoddy Khrushchev-issue stained-concrete prefab on the outskirts of Moscow. It's

1968; I am five. Soviet tanks have just rolled into Prague, my dad has abandoned us recently, and we've moved here from a Kafka-esque communal apartment near the Kremlin where eighteen families shared one kitchen. Mom, in her robe with faded blue cornflowers, sits on my bed, presses a reassuring kiss to my forehead. But in her eyes I see such *toska* (that peculiarly Russian ache of the soul), such desperate longing, I know right away she's been visited once more by *that* dream.

'Listen, listen, Anyuta,' she murmurs. 'Yet again I'm transformed into a *lastochka* (a swallow) . . . I escape from Russia, flying across the Soviet border, and somehow no one asks me for documents. And suddenly I'm in Paris! *In Paris!* I circle over the ocher-colored streets, I recognize them from Utrillo paintings. On a tiny rue – it's called 'Street of a Cat Who Fishes' – I notice an enchanting café. I speed down to the impossibly colorful awning, I'm dizzy from the delicious smell of the food, everything inside me is aching to taste it, to join the people inside . . .'

At this point my mother always woke up. Always on the wrong side of the entrance. Always ravenous, overwhelmed by yearning for a world beyond the border she was never destined to see. By nostalgia for flavors that would forever elude her.

All happy food memories are alike; all unhappy food memories are unhappy after their own fashion.

Mom and I both grew up within a triumphalist, scarlet-blazed fairy tale of socialist abundance and glorious harvests. Our experiences, though, featured no happy kitchens enveloped in an idyllic haze of vanilla, no kindly matriarchs setting golden holiday roasts on the table. Tea cakes rich in bourgeois butter? I do have such a memory . . . It's of Mom reading Proust aloud in our Khrushchevian slum; me utterly bored by the Frenchman's sensory reveries but besotted with the idea of the real, edible cookie. *What did it taste like, that exotic capitalist madeleine?* I desperately wanted to know.

Inevitably, a story about Soviet food is a chronicle of longing, of unrequited desire. So what happens when some of your most intense culinary memories involve foods you hadn't actually tasted? Memories of imaginings, of received histories; feverish collective yearning produced by seventy years of geopolitical isolation and scarcity . . .

Until recently I didn't talk about such memories much. Asked why I write about food, I'd just rattle off my well-rehearsed story. How my mother and I emigrated from Moscow without my father in 1974 – stateless refugees with no winter coats and no right of return. How, after I graduated from Juilliard, my piano career was cut short in the late eighties by a wrist injury. And how, searching for a new start, I fell into food, almost by accident, really. And I never looked back. Following my first cookbook, *Please to the Table*, about the cuisines of the former USSR, nice things kept happening: exciting magazine stories, more cookbooks, awards, almost two decades of travel and memorable meals.

Here's what I rarely mentioned: scribbled skull-and-bones warnings affixed to pots in my grandmother's communal apartment kitchen, where comrade residents pilfered one another's soup meat. The afternoons of me desperately gagging on caviar at my kindergarten for the offspring of the Central Committee – gagging because along with the elite Party fish eggs I felt I was ingesting the very ideology my anti-Soviet mom couldn't stomach. Nor did I mention the girls' bathroom at School 110, where I, a nine-year-old fledgling black marketeer in a scratchy brown uniform, charged my Soviet classmates five kopeks to touch the bottle of Coca-Cola that friends had brought us from the mythical *zagranitsa* (abroad). Nor my present-day impulse to steal every last croissant from the splendid free breakfast buffets at the lovely hotels where I often stay for my work.

What would be the point of confessing my constant feeling of inhabiting two parallel food universes: one where degustation menus at places like Per Se or Noma are routine; the other where a simple banana—a once-a-year treat back in the USSR—still holds an almost talismanic sway over my psyche?

The stories I've kept to myself are the stuff of this book. Ultimately, they're why I *really* write about food. But they aren't just my stories. For any ex-citizen of a three-hundred-million-strong Soviet superpower, food is never a mere individual matter. In 1917 bread riots sparked the overthrow of the czar, and, seventy-four years later, catastrophic food shortages helped push Gorbachev's floundering empire into the dustbin. In between, seven million people perished from hunger during Stalin's collectivization; four million more starved to death during Hitler's war. Even in calmer times, under Khrushchev and Brezhnev, the daily drama of putting a meal on the table trumped most other concerns. Across eleven time zones the collective socialist fate of standing in food lines united comrades from the Union's fifteen ethnic republics. Food was an abiding theme of Soviet political history, permeating every nook and cranny of our collective unconscious. Food brought us together in obsessive Soviet hospitality rituals – *more* herring, *more* Doctor's Kolbasa—and in our shared envy and spite for the privileged few, the grifters and Party hacks with their access to better kolbasa (sausage). Food anchored the domestic realities of our totalitarian state, supplying a shimmer of desire to a life that was mostly drab, sometimes absurdly comical, on occasion unbearably tragic, but just as often naively optimistic and joyous. Food, as one academic has noted, defined how Russians endured the present, imagined the future, and connected to their past.

That past is now gone. Vanished after the Soviet Union's collapse. In place of our 'Socialist Homeland' there are cultural ruins, a vast archaeological site of a Soviet Atlantis. But we're not ready to let go of this rubble. Toppled head-less statues of leaders, songbooks and candy wrappers, once-scarlet Young Pioneer scarves, triangular Soviet milk cartons blackened with grime—we cling to these fragments. Unlike the melancholy ruins that fueled the Romantics' nostalgia for an idealized past, ours are pieces of our physical homes, of the lives we once lived. For us they're still freighted with meaning: historical, political, personal. And almost always ambiguous.

I started my own collection of socialist fragments in 1974, weeks into our Philadelphia life. Mom instantly fell for *Amerika*. Me? Huddled on our bony refugee sofa I read Chekhov's *Three Sisters* and whimpered along with the characters: 'To Moscow . . . to Moscow.' My childhood fantasies of capitalist delicacies crashed against our first meal at the Robin Hood Diner. I choked on the cloying fluff of American coleslaw, stared in shock at the Day-Glo that is Velveeta. At home, while my mother gleefully slapped Oscar Mayer bologna onto alien Wonder Bread, I pined for the fragrant bricks of Moscow sourdough rye and the stale reek of cheapo Krakovskaya kolbasa. I'm pretty sure I'd lost my sense of taste those first Philadelphia months. Because depleted of political pathos, hospitality, that heroic aura of scarcity, food didn't seem much of anything anymore.

Like a raggedy orphan, I paced our apartment, repeating to myself our sardonic Soviet *defitsit* (shortage) jokes. 'Would you slice one hundred grams of kolbasa?' asks a man in a store. 'Bring the kolbasa and we'll slice,' answers the salesgirl. Or 'Why are you emigrating?' 'Coz I'm sick of celebrations,' says the Jew. 'Bought toilet paper – celebration; bought kolbasa – more celebrating.'

In Philadelphia, no one celebrated Oscar Mayer bologna.

To revive my taste buds I began playing a game in my head. Picturing myself at a dacha (country cottage) surrounded by prickly gooseberry shrubs, I'd mentally preserve and pickle the tastes and smells of my Soviet socialist past in an imaginary three-liter jar of memory. In went the Order of Lenin Red October chocolate bars with a mirthful kid on the wrapper. In went the scarlet-wrapped Bolshevik Factory Jubilee Biscuits, the ones that dissolved so poignantly when dipped in tea from a yellow packet adorned with an elephant. In my mind's eye I unwrapped the foil from the squishy rectangles of Friendship Cheese. Paused to dig an imaginary aluminum fork into the industrial breading of the six-kopek meat patties named after Stalin's food supply commissar.

There was, however, an ideological cloud darkening my nostalgia exercise. The Friendship Cheese, the kolbasa, the chocolates – all were produced by the reviled Party-state we'd fled. Recalling Mom's Proust recitations, I've come up with a phrase to describe them. *Poisoned madeleines*.

This is my 'poisoned madeleine' memoir. It was my mother, my frequent co-conspirator in the kitchen and my conduit to our past, who suggested the means to convey this epic disjunction, this unruly collision of collectivist myths and personal antimyths. We would reconstruct every decade of Soviet history – from the prequel 1910s to the postscript present day – through the prism of food. Together, we'd embark on a year-long journey unlike any other: eating and cooking our way through decade after decade of Soviet life, using her kitchen and dining room as a time machine and an incubator of memories. Memories of wartime rationing cards and grotesque shared kitchens in communal apartments. Of Lenin's bloody grain requisitioning and Stalin's table manners. Of Khrushchev's kitchen debates and Gorbachev's disastrous antialcohol policies. Of food as the focal point of our everyday lives, and – despite all the deprivations and shortages – of compulsive hospitality and poignant, improbable feasts.

PART I

FEASTS, FAMINES, FABLES

My maternal grandparents, Liza and Naum Frumkin, circa 1929

CHAPTER ONE

✯

1910s: THE LAST DAYS OF THE CZARS

My mother is expecting guests.

In just a few hours in this sweltering July heat wave, eight people will show up for an extravagant czarist-era dinner at her small Queens apartment. But her kitchen resembles a building site. Pots tower and teeter in the sink; the food processor and blender drone on in unison. In a shiny bowl on Mom's green faux-granite counter, a porous blob of yeast dough seems weirdly alive. I'm pretty sure it's breathing. Unfazed, Mother simultaneously blends, sautés, keeps an eye on Chris Matthews on MSNBC, and chatters away on her cordless phone. At this moment she suggests a plump modern-day elf, multitasking away in her orange Indian housedress.

Ever since I can remember, my mother has cooked like this, phone tucked under her chin. Of course, back in Brezhnev's Moscow in the seventies when I was a kid, the idea of an 'extravagant czarist dinner' would have provoked sardonic laughter. And the cord of our antediluvian black Soviet *telefon* was so traitorously twisted, I once tripped on it while carrying a platter of Mom's lamb pilaf to the low three-legged table in the cluttered space where my parents did their living, sleeping, and entertaining.

Right now, as one of Mom's ancient émigré friends fills her ear with cultural gossip, that pilaf episode returns to me in cinematic slow motion. Masses of yellow rice cascade onto our Armenian carpet. Biddy, my two-month-old puppy, greedily laps up every grain, her eyes and tongue swelling shockingly in an instant allergic reaction to lamb fat. I howl, fearing for Biddy's life. My father berates Mom for her phone habits.

Mom managed to rescue the disaster with her usual flair, dotty and determined. By the time guests arrived – with an extra four non-sober comrades – she'd conjured up a tasty fantasia from two pounds of the proletarian wurst called *sosiski*. These she'd cut into petal-like shapes, splayed in a skillet, and fried up with eggs. Her creation landed at table under provocative blood-red squiggles of ketchup, that decadent capitalist condiment. For dessert: Mom's equally spontaneous apple cake. 'Guest-at-the-doorstep apple charlotte,' she dubbed it.

Guests! They never stopped crowding Mom's doorstep, whether at our apartment in the center of Moscow or at the boxy immigrant dwelling in Philadelphia where she and I landed in 1974. Guests overrun her current home in New York, squatting for weeks, eating her out of the house, borrowing money and books. Every so often I Google 'compulsive hospitality syndrome.' But there's no cure. Not for Mom the old Russian adage 'An uninvited guest is worse than an invading Tatar.' *Her* parents' house was just like this, her sister's even more so.

Tonight's dinner, however, is different. It will mark our

archival adieu to classic Russian cuisine. For such an important occasion Mom has agreed to keep the invitees to just eight after I slyly quoted a line from a Roman scholar and satirist: 'The number of dinner guests should be more than the Graces and less than the Muses.' Mom's quasi-religious respect for culture trumps even her passion for guests. Who is she to disagree with the ancients?

And so, on this diabolically torrid late afternoon in Queens, the two of us are sweating over a decadent feast set in the imagined 1910s – Russia's Silver Age, artistically speaking. The evening will mark our hail and farewell to a grandiose decade of Moscow gastronomy. To a food culture that flourished at the start of the twentieth century and disappeared abruptly when the 1917 revolution transformed Russian cuisine and culture into *Soviet* cuisine and culture – the only version we knew.

Mom and I have not taken the occasion lightly.

The horseradish and lemon vodkas that I've been steeping for days are chilling in their cut-crystal carafes. The caviar glistens. We've even gone to the absurd trouble of brewing our own kvass, a folkloric beverage from fermented black bread that's these days mostly just mass-produced fizz. Who knows? Besides communing with our ancestral stomachs, this might be our last chance on this culinary journey to eat *really well*.

'The burbot liver – *what* to do about the burbot liver?' Mom laments, finally off the phone.

Noticing how poignantly scratched her knuckles are from assorted gratings, I reply, for the umpteenth time, that burbot, noble member of the freshwater cod family so fetishized by pre-revolutionary Russian gourmands, is nowhere to be had in Jackson Heights, Queens. Frustrated sighing. As always, my pragmatism interferes with Mom's dreaming and scheming. And let's not even mention *víziga*, the desiccated dorsal cord of a sturgeon. Burbot liver was the czarist foie gras, *víziga* its shark's fin. Chances of finding either in any zip code hereabouts? Not slim – none.

But still, we've made progress.

Several test runs for crispy brains in brown butter have yielded smashing results. And despite the state of Mom's kitchen, and the homey, crepuscular clutter of her book-laden apartment, her dining table is a thing of great beauty. Crystal goblets preen on the floral, antique-looking table-cloth. Pale blue hydrangeas in an art nouveau pitcher I found at a flea market in Buenos Aires bestow a subtle fin-de-siècle opulence.

I unpack the cargo of plastic containers and bottles I've lugged over from my house two blocks away. Since Mom's galley kitchen is far too small for two cooks, much smaller than an aristocrat's broom closet, I've already brewed the kvass and prepared the trimmings for an anachronistic chilled fish and greens soup called *botvínya*. I was also designated steeper of vodkas and executer of Guriev kasha, a dessert loaded with deep historical meaning and a whole pound of home-candied nuts. Mom has taken charge of the main course and the array of *zakuski*, or appetizers.

A look at the clock and she gasps. 'The *kulebiaka* dough! Check it!'

I check it. Still rising, still bubbling. I give it a bang to deflate – and the tang of fermenting yeast tickles my nostrils, evoking a fleeting collective memory. Or a memory of a received memory. I pinch off a piece of dough and hand it to Mom to assess. She gives me a shrug as if to say, 'You're the cookbook writer.'

But I'm glad I let her take charge of the kulebiaka. This extravagant Russian fish pie, this history lesson in a pastry case, will be the pièce de résistance of our banquet tonight.

'The kulebiaka must make your mouth water, it must lie before you, naked, shameless, a temptation. You wink at it, you cut off a sizeable slice, and you let your fingers just play over it . . . You eat it, the butter drips from it like tears, and the filling is fat, juicy, rich with eggs, giblets, onions . . .'

So waxed Anton Pavlovich Chekhov in his little fiction 'The Siren,' which Mom and I have been salivating over during our preparations, just as we first did back in our unglorious socialist pasts. It wasn't only us Soviet-born who fixated on food. Chekhov's satiric encomium to outsize Slavic appetite is a lover's rapturous fantasy. Sometimes it seems that for nineteenth-century Russian writers, food was what landscape (or maybe class?) was for the English. Or war for the Germans, love for the French – a subject encompassing the great themes of comedy, tragedy, ecstasy, and doom. Or perhaps, as the contemporary author Tatyana Tolstaya suggests, the 'orgiastic gorging' of Russian authors was a compensation for literary taboos on eroticism. One must note, too, alas, Russian writers' peculiarly *Russian* propensity for moralizing. Rosy hams, amber fish broths, blini as plump as 'the shoulder of a merchant's daughter' (Chekhov again), such literary deliciousness often serves an ulterior agenda of exposing gluttons as spiritually bankrupt philistines – or lethargic losers such as the alpha glutton Oblomov. Is this a moral trap? I keep asking myself. Are we enticed to salivate at these lines so we'll end up feeling guilty?

But it's hard not to salivate. Chekhov, Pushkin, Tolstoy – they all devote some of their most fetching pages to the gastronomical. As for Mom's beloved Nikolai Gogol, the author of *Dead Souls* anointed the stomach the body's 'most noble' organ. Besotted with eating both on and off the page – sour cherry dumplings from his Ukrainian childhood, pastas from his sojourns in Rome – scrawny Gogol could polish off a gargantuan dinner and start right in again. While traveling he sometimes even churned his own butter. 'The belly is the belle of his stories, the nose is their beau,' declared Nabokov. In 1852, just short of his forty-third birthday, in the throes of religious mania and gastrointestinal torments, Nikolai Vasilievich committed a slow suicide rich in Gogolian irony: *he refused to eat.* Yes, a complicated, even tortured, relationship with food has long been a hallmark of our national character.

According to one scholarly count, no less than eighty-six kinds of edibles appear in *Dead Souls*, Gogol's chronicle of a grifter's circuit from dinner to dinner in the vast Russian countryside. Despairing over not being able to scale the heights of the novel's first volume, poor wretched Gogol burned most of the second. What survives includes the most famous literary ode to kulebiaka – replete with a virtual recipe.

'Make a four-cornered kulebiaka,' instructs Petukh, a spiritually bankrupt glutton who made it through the flames. And then:

'In one corner put the cheeks and dried spine of a sturgeon, in another put some buckwheat, and some mushrooms and onion, and some soft fish roe, and brains, and something else as well. . . As for the underneath . . . see that it's baked so that it's quite . . . well not done to the point of crumbling but so that it will melt in the mouth like snow and not make any crunching sound.

Petukh smacked his lips as he spoke.'

Generations of Russians have smacked their own lips at this passage. Historians, though, suspect that this chimerical 'four-cornered' kulebiaka might have been a Gogolian fiction. So what then of the genuine article, which is normally oblong and layered?

To telescope quickly: kulebiaka descends from the archaic Slavic *pirog* (filled pie). Humbly born, they say, in the 1600s, it had by its turn-of-the-twentieth-century heyday evolved into a regal golden-brown case fancifully decorated with cut-out designs. Concealed within: aromatic layers of fish and *viziga*, a cornucopia of forest-picked mushrooms, and butter-splashed buckwheat or rice, all the tiers separated by thin crepes called *blinchiki* – to soak up the juices.

Mom and I argued over every other dish on our menu. But on this we agreed: without kulebiaka, there could be no proper Silver Age Moscow repast.

When my mother, Larisa (Lara, Larochka) Frumkina – Frumkin in English – was growing up in the 1930s high Stalinist Moscow, the idea of a decadent czarist-era banquet constituted exactly what it would in the Brezhnevian seventies: laughable blue cheese from the moon. *Sosiski* were Mom's favorite food. I was hooked on them too, though Mom claims that the sosiski of my childhood couldn't hold a candle to the juicy Stalinist article. Why do these proletarian franks remain the madeleine of every *Homo sovieticus*? Because besides sosiski with canned peas and *kotleti* (minced meat patties) with kasha, cabbage-intensive soups, mayoladen salads, and watery fruit *kompot* for dessert – there wasn't all that much to eat in the Land of the Soviets.

Unless, of course, you were privileged. In our joyous classless society, this all-important matter of privilege has nagged at me since my early childhood.

I first glimpsed – or rather *heard* – the world of privileged food consumption during my first three years of life, at the grotesque communal Moscow apartment into which I was born in 1963. The apartment sat so close to the Kremlin, we could practically hear the midnight chimes of the giant clock on the Spassky Tower. There was another sound too, keeping us up: the roaring *BLARGHHH* of our neighbor Misha puking his guts out. Misha, you see, was a food store manager with a proprietary attitude toward the socialist food supply, likely a black market millionaire who shared our communal lair only for fear that flaunting his wealth would attract the unwanted attention of the anti-embezzlement authorities. Misha and Musya, his blond, big-bosomed wife, lived out a Mature Socialist version of bygone decadence. Night after night they dined out at Moscow's few proper restaurants (accessible to party bigwigs, foreigners, and comrades with illegal rubles), dropping the equivalent of Mom's monthly salary on meals that Misha couldn't even keep in his stomach.

When the pair stayed home, they ate unspeakable delicacies – batter-fried chicken tenders, for instance – prepared for them by the loving hands of Musya's mom, Baba Mila, she a blubbery former peasant with one eye, four – or was it six? – gold front teeth, and a healthy contempt for the nonprivileged.

'So, making kotleti today,' Mila would say in the kitchen we all shared, fixing her monocular gaze on the misshapen patties in Mom's chipped aluminum skillet. 'Muuuuusya!' she'd holler to her daughter. 'Larisa's making kotleti!'

'Good appetite, Larochka!' (Musya was fond of my mom.)

'Muuusya! Would *you* eat kotleti?'

'Me? Never!'

'Aha! You see?' And Mila would wag a swollen finger at Mom.

One day my tiny underfed mom couldn't restrain herself. Back from work, tired and ravenous, she pilfered a chicken nugget from a tray Mila had left in the kitchen. The next day I watched as, red-faced and teary-eyed, she knocked on Misha's door to confess her theft.

'The chicken?' cackled Mila, and I still recall being struck by how her twenty-four-karat mouth glinted in the dim hall light. 'Help yourself anytime – *we dump that shit anyway.*'

And so it was that about once a week we got to eat shit destined for the economic criminal's garbage. To us, it tasted pretty ambrosial.

In 1970, into the eleventh year of their on-and-off marriage, my parents got back together after a four-year separation and we moved to an apartment in the Arbat. And kulebiaka entered my life. Here, in Moscow's most aristocratic old neighborhood, I was shooed out of the house to buy the pie in its Soviet incarnation at the take-out store attached to Praga, a restaurant famed 'before historical materialism' (that's ironic Sovietese for 'distant past') for its plate-size *rasstegai* pies with two fillings: sturgeon and sterlet.

Even in the dog days of Brezhnev, Praga was fairly dripping with *klass* – a fancy *restoran* where Misha types groped peroxide blondes while a band blasted, and third-world diplomats hosted receptions in a series of ornate private rooms.

'Car of Angola's ambassador to the door!'

This was music to my seven-year-old ears.

If I loitered outside Praga intently enough, if my young smile and '*Khello, khau yoo laik Moskou?*' were sufficiently charming, a friendly diplomat might toss me a five-pack of Juicy Fruit. The next day, in the girls' bathroom, aided by ruler and penknife, I would sell off the gum, millimeter by millimeter, to favored classmates. Even a chewed-up blob of Juicy Fruit had some value, say a kopek or two, as long as you didn't masticate more than five times, leaving some of that floral Wrigley magic for the next masticator to savor. Our teacher's grave warnings that sharing capitalist gum causes syphilis only added to the illegal thrill of it all.

I loved everything about shopping at Praga. Loved skipping over the surges of brown melted snow and sawdust that comrade janitors gleefully swept right over the customers' feet. Loved inhaling the signature scent of stale pork fat, *peregar* (hangover breath), and the sickly sweet top notes of Red Moscow perfume. Loved Tyotya Grusha (Aunt Pear), Praga's potato-nosed saleslady, clacking away on her abacus with savage force. Once, guided by some profound late socialist instinct, I shared with Grusha a five-pack of Juicy Fruit. She snatched it without even a thank-you, but from then on she always made sure to reserve a kulebiaka for me. 'Here, you loudmouthed infection,' she'd say, also slipping me a slab of raisin-studded poundcake under the counter.

And this is how I came to appreciate the importance of black marketeering, *blat* (connections), and bribery. I was now inching my own way toward privilege.

Wearing shiny black rubber galoshes over my *valenki* (felt boots) and a coat made of 'mouse fur' (in the words of my dad), I toted the Pravda-wrapped kulebiaka back to our family table, usually taking the long way home – past onion-domed churches now serving as warehouses, past gracious cream and green neoclassical facades scrawled with the unprintable slang that Russians call *mat*. I felt like Moscow belonged to me on those walks; along its frozen streetscape I was a flaneur flush with illicit cash. On Kalinin Prospect, the modernist grand boulevard that dissected the old neighborhood, I'd pull off my mittens in the unbearable cold to count out twenty icy kopeks for the blue-coated lady with her frosty zinc ice cream box. It was almost violent, the shock of pain on my teeth as I sank them into the waffle cup of vanilla *plombir* with a cream rosette, its concrete-like hardness defying the flat wooden scooping spoon. Left of Praga, the Arbatskaya metro station rose, star-shaped and maroon and art deco, harboring its squad of clunky gray *gazirovka* (soda) machines. One kopek for unflavored; three kopeks for a squirt of aromatic thick yellow syrup. Scoring the soda: a matter of anxious uncertainty. Not because soda or syrup ran out, but because *alkogoliks* were forever stealing the twelve-sided beveled drinking glass – that Soviet domestic icon. If, miraculously, the drunks had left the glass behind, I thrilled in pressing it hard upside down on the machine's slatted tray to watch the powerful water jet rinse the glass of alcoholic saliva. Who even needed the soda?

Deeper into Old Arbat, at the Konservi store with its friezes of socialist fruit cornucopias, I'd pause for my ritual twelve-kopek glass of sugary birch-tree juice dispensed from conical vintage glass vats with spigots. Then, sucking on a dirty icicle, I'd just wander off on a whim, lost in a delta of narrow side streets that weaved and twisted like braids, each bearing a name of the trade it once supported: Tablecloth Lane, Bread Alley. Back then, before capitalism disfigured Moscow's old center with billboards and neons and antihistorical historicist mansions, some Arbat streets did retain a certain nineteenth-century purity.

At home I usually found Mom in the kitchen, big black receiver under her chin, cooking while discussing a new play or a book with a girlfriend. Dad struck a languid Oblomovian pose on the couch, playing cards with himself, sipping cold tea from his orange cup with white polka-dots. 'And how was your walk?' Mother always wanted to know. 'Did you remember to stop by the house on Povarskaya Street where Natasha from *War and Peace* lived?' At the mention of Tolstoy, the Juicy Fruit in my pocket would congeal into a guilty yellow lump on my conscience. Natasha Rostova and my mom – they were so poetic, so gullible. And I? What was I but a crass mini-Misha? Dad usually came to the rescue: 'So, let's have the kulebiaka. Or did Praga run out?' For *me*, I wanted to reply, Praga never runs out! But it seemed wise not to boast of my special *blat* with Aunt Grusha, the saleslady, in the presence of my sweet innocent mother.

Eating kulebiaka on Sundays was our nod to a family ritual – even if the pie I'd deposit on the kitchen table of our five-hundred-square-foot two-room apartment shared only the name with the horn of plenty orgiastically celebrated by Gogol and Chekhov. More *bulka* (white bread-roll) than *pirog*, late-socialist kulebiaka was a modest rectangle of yeast dough, true to Soviet form concealing a barely there layer of boiled ground meat or cabbage. It now occurs to me that our Sunday kulebiaka from Praga expressed the frugality of our lives as neatly as the grandiose version captured czarist excess. We liked our version just fine. The yeast dough was tasty, especially with Mom's thin vegetarian borscht, and somehow the whole package was just suggestive enough to inspire feverish fantasies about pre-revolutionary Russian cuisine, so intimately familiar to us from books, and so unattainable.

Dreaming about food, I already knew, was just as rewarding as eating.

✳ ✳ ✳

For my tenth birthday my parents gave me *Moscow and Muscovites*, a book by Vladimir Giliarovsky, darling of fin-de-siècle Moscow, who covered city affairs for several local newspapers. Combining a Dickensian eye with the racy style of a tabloid journalist, plus a dash of Zola-esque naturalism, Giliarovsky offered in *Moscow and Muscovites* an entertaining, if exhausting, panorama of our city at the turn of the century.

As a kid, I cut straight to the porn – the dining-out parts. During the twentieth century's opening decade, Moscow's restaurant scene approached a kind of Slavophilic ideal. Unlike the then-capital St. Petersburg – regarded as pompous, bureaucratic, and quintessentially foreign – Moscow worked hard to live up to its moniker 'bread-and-salty' (hospitable) – a merchant city at heart, uncorrupted by the phony veneer of European manners and foods. In St. Petersburg you dressed up to nibble tiny portions of foie gras and oysters at a French restaurant. In Moscow you gorged, unabashedly, obliviously, orgiastically at a *traktir*, a vernacular Russian tavern. Originally of working-class origins, Moscow's best *traktirs* in Giliarovsky's days welcomed everyone: posh nobles and meek provincial landowners, loud-voiced actors from Moscow Art Theater, and merchants clinching the million-ruble deals that fueled this whole Slavophilic restaurant boom. You'd never see such a social cocktail in cold, classist St. Petersburg.

Stomach growling, I stayed up nights devouring Giliarovsky. From him I learned that the airiest blini were served at Egorov's *traktir*, baked in a special stove that stood in the middle of the dining room. That at Lopashov *traktir*, run by a bearded, gruff Old Believer, the city's plumpest *pelmeni* – dumplings filled with meat, fish, or fruit in a bubbly rosé champagne sauce – were lapped up with folkloric wooden spoons by Siberian gold-mining merchants. That grand dukes from St. Petersburg endured the four-hundred-mile train journey southeast just to eat at Testov, Moscow's most celebrated *traktir*. Testov was famed for its suckling pigs that the owner reared at his dacha ('like his own children,' except for the restraints around their trotters to prevent them from resisting being force-fed for plumpness); its three-hundred-pound sturgeons and sterlets transported live from the Volga; and Guriev kasha, a fanciful baked semolina sweet layered with candied nuts and slightly burnt cream skins, served in individual skillets.

And kulebiaka. The most obscenely decadent kulebiaka in town.

Offered under the special name of Baidakov's Pie (nobody really knew who this Baidakov was) and ordered days in advance, Testov's golden-cased tour de force was the creation of its 350-pound chef named Lyonechka. Among other things, Lyonechka was notorious for his habit of drinking *shchi* (cabbage soup) mixed with frozen champagne as a hangover remedy. His kulebiaka was a twelve-tiered skyscraper, starting with the ground floor of burbot liver and topped with layers of fish, meat, game, mushrooms, and rice, all wrapped in dough, up, up, up to a penthouse of calf's brains in brown butter.

And then it all came crashing down.

In just a bony fistful of years, classical Russian food culture vanished, almost without a trace. The country's nationalistic euphoria on entering World War I in 1914 collapsed under nonstop disasters presided over by the 'last of the Romanovs': clueless, autocratic czar Nicholas II and Alexandra, his reactionary, hysterical German-born wife. Imperial Russia went lurching toward breakdown and starvation. Golden pies, suckling pigs? In 1917 the insurgent Bolsheviks' banners demanded simply the most basic of staples – *khleb* (bread) – along with land (beleaguered peasants were 80 percent of Russia's population) and an end to the ruinous war. On the evening of October 25, hours before the coup by Lenin and his tiny cadre, ministers of Kerensky's foundering provisional government, which replaced the czar after the popular revolution of February 1917, dined finely at the Winter Palace: soup, artichokes, and fish. A doomed meal all around.

With rationing already in force, the Bolsheviks quickly introduced a harsher system of class-based food allotments. Heavy manual laborers became the new privileged; Testov's fancy diners plunged down the totem pole. Grigory Zinoviev, the head of local government in Petrograd (ex–St. Petersburg), announced rations for the bourgeoisie thusly: 'We shall give them one ounce a day so they won't forget the smell of bread.' He added with relish: 'But if we must go over to milled straw, then we shall put the bourgeoisie on it first of all.'

The country, engulfed now by civil war, was rushed toward a full-blown, and catastrophic, centralized communist model. War Communism (it was given that temporary-sounding tag *after* the fact) ran from mid-1918 through early 1921, when Lenin abandoned it for a more mixed economic approach. But from that time until the Soviet Union's very end, food was to be not just a matter of chronic uncertainty but a stark tool of political and social control. To use a Russian phrase, *knut i prianík*: whip and gingerbread.

There was scarce gingerbread at this point.

Strikes in Petrograd in 1919 protested the taste (or lack thereof) of the new Soviet diet. Even revolutionary bigwigs at the city's Smolny canteen subsisted on vile herring soup and gluey millet. At the Kremlin in Moscow, the new seat of government, the situation was so awful that the famously ascetic Lenin – Mr. Stale Bread and Weak Tea, who ate mostly at home – ordered several investigations into why the Kremlyovka (Kremlin canteen) served such inedible stuff. Here's what the investigation found: the cooks couldn't actually cook. Most pre-revolutionary chefs, waiters, and other food types had been fired as part of the massive reorganization of labor, and the new ones had been hired from other professions to avoid using 'czarist cadres.' 'Iron Felix' Dzerzhinsky, the dread founding maestro of Soviet terror, was besieged by requests from Kremlin staffers for towels for the Kremlyovka kitchens. Also aprons and jackets for cooks. Mrs. Trotsky kept asking for tea strainers. In vain.

Part of the Kremlyovka's troubles sprang from another of War Communism's policies: having declared itself the sole purveyor and marketer of food, and setter of food prices, the Kremlin was not supposed to procure from private sources. And yet. The black market that immediately sprang up became – and remained – a defining and permanent fixture of Soviet life. Lenin might have railed against petty speculators called *meshochniki* (bagmen), the private individuals who braved Dzerzhinsky's Cheka (secret police) roving patrols to bring back foodstuffs from the countryside, often for their own starving families. But in fact most of the calories consumed in Russia's cities during this dire period were supplied by such illegal operators. In the winter of 1919–20, they supplied as much as 75 percent of the food consumed, maybe more. By War Communism's end, an estimated 200,000 bagmen were riding the rails in the breadbasket of the Ukraine.

War Communism showed an especially harsh face to the peasantry. An emphatically urban party, the Bolsheviks had little grasp of peasant realities, despite all the hammer-and-sickle imagery and early nods toward land distribution. To combat drastic grain shortages – blamed on speculative withholding – Lenin called down a 'food dictatorship' and a 'crusade for bread.' Armed detachments stalked the countryside, confiscating 'surpluses' to feed the Red Army and the hungry, traumatically shrunken cities. This was the hated *prodrazverstka* (grain requisitioning) – a preview of the greater horrors to come under Stalin. There was more. To incite Marxist class warfare in villages, the poorest peasants were stirred up against their better-off kind, the so-called kulaks ('tight-fisted ones') – vile bourgeois-like objects of Bolshevik venom. 'Hang (hang without fail, so the people see) no fewer than one hundred known kulaks, rich men, bloodsuckers,' Lenin instructed provincial leaders in 1918. Though as Zinoviev later noted: 'We are fond of describing any peasant who has enough to eat as a kulak.'

And so was launched a swelling, unevenly matched war by the radicalized, industrialized cities – the minority – to bring to heel the conservative, religion-saturated, profoundly mistrustful countryside – the vast majority. Who were never truly fervent Bolshevik supporters.

Agriculture under War Communism plummeted. By 1920, grain output was down to only 60 percent of pre-World War I levels, when Russia had been a significant exporter.

It goes without saying that the concept of cuisine went out the window in those ferocious times. The very notion of pleasure from flavorsome food was reviled as capitalist degeneracy. Mayakovsky, brazen poet of the revolution, sicced his jeering muses on gourmet fancies:

Eat your pineapples, gobble your grouse
Your last day is coming, you bourgeois louse!

Food was fuel for survival and socialist labor. Food was a weapon of class struggle. Anything that smacked of Testov's brand of lipsmacking – kulebiaka would be a buttery bull's-eye – constituted a reactionary attack on the world being born. Some czarist *traktirs* and restaurants were shuttered and looted; others were nationalized and turned into public canteens with the utopian goal of serving new kinds of foods, supposedly futuristic and rational, to the newly *Soviet* masses.

Not until two decades later, following the abolition of yet another wave of rationing policies, did the state support efforts to seek out old professional chefs and revive some traditional recipes, at least in print. It was part of a whole new Soviet Cuisine project courtesy of Stalin's food-supply commissariat. A few czarist dishes came peeping back, tricked out in Soviet duds, right then and later.

But the bona fide, layered fish kulebiaka, darling of yore, resurfaced only in Putin's Moscow, at resurrect-the-Romanovs restaurants, ordered up by oligarch types clinching oil deals.

Mom and I have our own later history with kulebiaka.

After we emigrated to America in 1974, refugees arriving

in Philadelphia with two tiny suitcases, Mom supported us by cleaning houses. Miraculously, she managed to save up for our first frugal visit to Paris two years later. The French capital I found haughty and underwhelming. Mom, on the other hand, was euphoric. Her decades-long Soviet dream had finally been realized, never mind the stale *saucissons* we fed on all week. On our last night she decided to splurge at a candlelit smoky bistro in the sixteenth arrondissement. And there it was! The most expensive dish on the menu – our fish-filled kulebiaka! That is, in its French incarnation, coulibiac – one of the handful of à la russe dishes to have made the journey from Russia in the mainly one-way nineteenth-century gastronomic traffic. Nervously counting our handful of tourist francs, we bit into this coulibiac with tongue-tingled anticipation and were instantly rewarded by the buttery puff pastry that shattered so pleasingly at the touch of the fork. The lovely coral pink of the salmon seemed to wink at us – scornfully? – from the opened pie on the plate as if to suggest France's gastronomic noblesse oblige. The Gauls, they just couldn't help being smug. We took a second bite, expecting total surrender. But something – wait, wait – was wrong. *Messieurs-dames!* Where did you hide the dusky wild mushrooms, the dilled rice, the *blinchiki* to soak up all those Slavic juices? What of the magically controlled blend of tastes? This French coulibiac, we concluded, was a fraud: saumon en croute masquerading as Russian. We paid the bill to the sneering garçon, unexpectedly wistful for our kulebiaka from Praga and the still-unfulfilled yearnings it had inspired.

It was back in Philadelphia that we finally found that elusive holy grail of Russian high cuisine – courtesy of some White Russian émigrés who'd escaped just before and after the revolution. These gray-haired folk had arrived via Paris or Berlin or Shanghai with noble Russian names out of novels – Golitsyn, Volkonsky. They grew black currants and Nabokovian lilacs in the gardens of their small houses outside Philadelphia or New York. Occasionally they'd attend balls – balls! To them, we escapees from the barbaric Imperium were a mild curiosity. Their conversations with Mother went something like this:

'Where did you weather the revolution?'

Mom: 'I was born in 1934.'

'What do the Soviets think about Kerensky?'

Mom: 'They don't think of him much.'

'I heard there've been major changes in Russia since 1917.'

Mom: 'Er . . . that's right.'

'Is it really true that at the races you now can't bet on more than one horse?'

The Russian we spoke seemed from a different planet. Here we were, with our self-consciously ironic appropriations of Sovietese, our twenty-seven shades of sarcasm injected into one simple word – *comrade*, say, or *homeland*. Talking to people who addressed us as *dushechka* (little soul) in pure, lilting, innocent Russian. Despite this cultural abyss, we cherished every moment at these people's generous tables. Boy, they could cook! Suckling pig stuffed with kasha, wickedly rich Easter molds redolent of vanilla, the Chekhovian blini plumper than 'the shoulder of a merchant's daughter' – we tasted it all. Mom approached our dining sessions with an ethnographer's zeal and a notebook. Examining the recipes later, she'd practically weep.

'Flour, milk, yeast, we had all those in Moscow. Why, why, couldn't I ever make blini like this?'

One day, an old lady, a Smolianka – a graduate of the prestigious St. Petersburg Smolny Institute for Young Women, where culinary skills were de rigueur – invited us over for kulebiaka. This was the moment we had been waiting for. As the pie baked, we chatted with an old countess with a name too grand to even pronounce. The countess recounted how hard she cried, back in 1914, when she received a diamond necklace as a birthday gift from her father. Apparently she had really wanted a puppy. The kulebiaka arrived. Our hearts raced. Here it was, the true, genuine kulebiaka – 'naked, shameless, a temptation.' The mushrooms, the *blinchiki*, even *víziga*, that gelatinous dried sturgeon spine our hostess had unearthed somewhere in deepest Chinatown – all were drenched in splashes of butter inside a beautifully decorated yeast pastry mantle.

As I ate, Tolstoy's *Anna Karenina* flashed into my mind. Because after some three hundred pages describing Vronsky's passion for Anna, his endless pursuits, all her tortured denials, the consummation of their affair is allotted only one sentence. And so it was for us and the consummate kulebiaka. We ate; the pie was more than delicious; we were satisfied. Happily, nobody leapt under a train. And yet . . . assessing the kulebiaka and studying our hostess's recipe later at home, Mom started scribbling over it furiously, crossing things out, shaking her head, muttering, '*Ne nashe*' – not ours. I'm pretty sure I know what she meant. Dried sturgeon spine? Who were we kidding? Whether we liked it or not, we were Soviets, not Russians. In place of the sturgeon, defrosted cod would do just fine.

It took us another three decades to develop a kulebiaka recipe to call our own – one that hinted at Russia's turn-of-the-century excess, with a soupçon of that snooty French elegance, while staying true to our frugal past.

But that recipe just wouldn't do for our 1910s feast tonight.

We needed to conjure up the real deal, the classic.

My mother is finally rolling out her kulebiaka dough, maneuvering intently on a dime-size oasis of kitchen counter. I inhale the sweetish tang of fermented yeast once again and try to plumb my unconscious for some collective historical taste memory. No dice. There's no yeast in my DNA. No heirloom pie recipes passed down by generations of women in the yellowing pages of family notebooks, scribbled in pre-revolutionary Russian orthography. My two grandmothers were emancipated New Soviet women, meaning they barely baked, wouldn't be caught dead cooking 'czarist.' Curious and passionate about food all her life, Mom herself only became serious about baking after we emigrated. In the USSR she relied on a dough called *na skoruyu ruku* ('flick of a hand'), a version involving little kneading and no rising. It was a recipe she'd had to teach *her* mother. My paternal babushka, Alla, simply wasn't interested. She was a war widow and Soviet career woman whose idea of dinner was a box of frozen dumplings. 'Why should I *bake*,' she told Mother indignantly, 'when I can be reading a book?' 'What, a *detektiv*,' Mom snorted. It was a pointed snort. Russia's top spy thriller writer, the Soviet version of John le Carré, was Grandma's secret lover.

Peering into the kitchen, I prod Mom for any scraps of pre-revolutionary-style baking memories she might retain. She pauses, then nods. '*Da*, listen!' There were these old ladies when she was a child. They were strikingly different from the usual bloblike proletarian babushkas. 'I remember their hair,' says Mom, almost dreamily. 'Aristocratically simple. And the resentment and resignation on their ghostly faces. Something so sad and tragic. Perhaps they had grown up in mansions with servants. Now they were ending their days as kitchen slaves for their own Stalin-loving families.'

My mom talks like that.

'And their *food*?' I keep prodding. She ponders again. 'Their blini, their pirozhki (filled pastries), their *pirogs* . . . somehow they seemed airier, fluffier . . .' She shrugs. More she can't really articulate. Flour, yeast, butter. Much like their counterparts who had fled Bolshevik Russia, Mom's Moscow old ladies possessed the magic of yeast. And that magic was lost to us.

And that was the rub of tonight's project. Of the flavor of the layered Silver Age kulebiaka we had at least an inkling. But the botvinya and the Guriev kasha dessert, my responsibilities – they were total conundrums. Neither I nor Mom had a clue how they were meant to taste.

There was a further problem: the stress and time required to prepare a czarist table extravaganza.

Over an entire day and most of the night preceding our guests' arrival, I sweated – and sweated – over my share of the meal. Have you ever tried making Guriev kasha during one of the worst New York heat waves in memory?

Thank you, Count Dmitry Guriev, you gourmandizing early-nineteenth-century Russian minister of finance, for the labor-intensive dessert bearing your name. Though actually by most accounts it was a serf chef named Zakhar Kuzmin who first concocted this particular kasha (*kasha* being the Russian word for almost any grain preparation both dry and porridgy). Guriev tasted the sweet at somebody's palace, summoned Kuzmin to the table, and gave him a kiss. Then he bought said serf-chef and his family.

Here is how Kuzmin's infernal inspiration is realized. Make a sweetened farina-like semolina kasha, called manna kasha in Russian. Then in a pan or skillet layer this manna with homemade candied nuts, and berries, and with plenty of *penki*, the rich, faintly burnished skins that form on cream when it's baked. Getting a hint of the labor required? For one panful of kasha, you need at least fifteen *penki*.

So for hour after hour I opened and closed the door of a 450-degree oven to skim off the cream skins. By two a.m. my kitchen throbbed like a furnace. Chained to the oven door, drenched in sweat, I was ready to assault palaces, smash Fabergé eggs. I cursed the Romanovs! I cheered the Russian Revolution!

'Send your maid to the cellar.' That charming instruction kicked off many of the recipes in the best surviving (and Rabelaisian) source of pre-revolutionary Russian recipes, *A Gift to Young Housewives* by Elena Molokhovets. How my heart went out to that suffering maid! Serfdom might have been abolished in Russia in 1861, but under the Romanovs the peasants – and, later, the industrial workers – continued to live like subhumans. Haute bourgeois housewives gorged on amber fish broths, rosy hams, and live sterlets, while their domestics had to make do with *tyuria* (a porridgy soup made with stale bread and water), kvass, and bowlfuls of buckwheat groats. Yes, the revolution was necessary. But why, I pondered in my furnace kitchen, why did things have to go so terribly wrong? Woozy from the heat, I brooded on alternative histories:

Suppose Kerensky's provisional government had managed to stay in power?

Or suppose instead of Stalin, Trotsky had taken over from Lenin?

Or suppose—

Suddenly I realized I'd forgotten to skim off new *penki*. I wrenched open the oven. The cream had transformed into cascades of white sputtering lava covering every inside inch with scorched white goo. I'd need a whole cadre of serfs to clean it all off. I screamed in despair.

Somehow, at last, at five a.m., I was done. A version of Guriev kasha, no doubt ersatz, sat cooling in my fridge under a layer of foil. Falling asleep, I recalled how at the storming of the Winter Palace thirsty, violent mobs ransacked the Romanovs' wine cellar, reportedly the largest and the best-stocked in the world. I congratulated them across the century, from the bottom of my heart.

Unlike me, my septuagenarian mom actually relishes late-night kitchen heroics. And her political thinking is much clearer than mine. Yes, she loathes the Romanovs. But she despises the Bolsheviks even more. Plus she had no reason for pondering alternative histories; she was sailing along smoothly with her kulebiaka project.

Her dough, loaded with butter and sour cream, had risen beautifully. The fish, the dilled rice, the dusky wild mushrooms, the thin *blinchiki* for the filling layers, had all come out juicy and tasty. Only now, two hours before the party, right before constructing the pie, does Mom suddenly experience distress.

'Anyut, tell me,' she says. 'What's the point of the *blinchiki*? Filling dough with more dough!'

I blink blearily. Ah, the mysteries of the czarist stomach. 'Maybe excess is the point?' I suggest meekly.

Mom shrugs. She goes ahead and arranges the filling and its antimush *blinchiki* into a majestic bulk. Not quite a Testov-style skyscraper, but a fine structure indeed. We decorate the pie together with fanciful cut-out designs before popping it into the oven. I'm proud of Mom. As we fan ourselves, our hearts race in anticipation, much like they did for our encounter decades ago with that true kulebiaka chez White Russian émigrés.

But the botvinya still hangs over me like a sword of doom.

A huge summer hit at Giliarovsky's Moscow *traktirs*, this chilled kvass and fish potage – a weird hybrid of soup, beverage, fish dish, and salad – confounded most foreigners who encountered it. 'Horrible mélange! Chaos of indigestion!' pronounced *All the Year Round*, Charles Dickens's Victorian periodical. Me, I'm a foreigner to botvinya myself. On the evening's table I set out a soup tureen filled with my homemade kvass and cooked greens (*botva* means vegetable tops), spiked with a horseradish sauce. Beside it, serving bowls of diced cucumbers, scallions, and dill. In the middle: a festive platter with poached salmon and shrimp (my stand-in for Slavic crayfish tails).

You eat the botvinya by mixing all the elements in your soup bowl – to which you add, please, ice. *A Gift to Young Housewives* also recommends a splash of chilled champagne. Ah yes, booze! To drown out the promised 'chaos of indigestion,' I'll pour my horseradish vodka.

'Fish and kvass?' says my mother. '*Foo.*' (Russian for *eek.*)

'*Aga* (Yeah),' I agree.

'*Foo,*' she insists. ''Cause you know how I hate poached salmon.'

Mom harbors a competitive streak in the kitchen. I get the feeling she secretly wants my botvinya to fail.

★ ★ ★

'You've made what? A real botvinya? Homemade kvass?'

Our first guests, Sasha and Ira Genis, eyeball Mom's table, incredulous. Mom hands them the welcome *kalach*, a traditional bread shaped like a purse. Their eyes grow wider.

Sasha (the diminutive of Alexander) is a freewheeling émigré essayist and cultural critic, something of a legend in Russia, where his radio broadcasts are adored by millions. He's a serious gourmet, too. Dinners at the Genis home in New Jersey feature mushrooms gathered under a Siberian moon and smoked lamprey eels smuggled from Latvia.

Mom's face blossoms with pride as Sasha confesses that, in his whole life, he's never tasted botvinya and tiered kulebiaka.

'And Guriev kasha?' he cries. 'Does it really *exist* outside literature?'

Suddenly all the guests are here, crowding Mom's tiny

foyer, kissing hello three times, handing over bouquets and bottles. At table, we are: a documentary filmmaker, Andrei, and his wife, Toma, sexy in her slinky, low-cut cocktail frock; my South African-born partner, Barry; and 'distinguished American guests' – a couple from Brooklyn, both in the culture business.

'A proper fin-de-siècle *traktir* setting,' Mom expounds to the Brooklynites in her museum-docent tones, 'should be a blend of art nouveau and Russian folkloric.' The Brooklynites nod respectfully.

Zakuski devoured, first vodkas downed, everyone addresses my botvinya. Mom barely touches hers, wrinkling her nose at the salmon. I both like the botvinya and don't: it tastes utterly alien.

And then, gasp, Mom carries out her kulebiaka. A choral whoop goes up. She cuts into the layers, releasing fishy, mushroomy steam into the candlelight. Slowly, bite by bite, I savor the voluptuousness of the dough-upon-dough Slavic excess. The fluffy layers put me in the mind of luxurious Oblomovian sloth, of collapsing into a huge feather bed. I think I finally get the point of the *blinchiki*. They're like marbling in a steak.

Sasha Genis raises his vodka glass to Larisa. 'This is the most patriotic meal of my life!' he enthuses. 'Putin should be taking note!'

His toast puzzles me. More, it perplexes, touching on what I've been turning over in my mind. Patriotic about what? The hated czarist regime? The repressive State we fled decades ago? Or some collective ur-memory of a cuisine never rightfully ours? Back in the USSR, *patriotism* was a dirty word in our dissident circles. And for that matter, what of our supposed *Russianness*? At table we're a typical pan-Soviet émigré crew. Andrei is a Ukrainian Jew; his wife, Toma, is Russian; both are from Kiev. Although the Genises hail from Riga, they're not Latvian. Mom, also Jewish, was born in Odessa and lived in Murmansk and Leningrad before moving to Moscow. I'm the only born Muscovite among us.

My ruminations on patriotism are drowned out by more toasts. Mom's air conditioner chugs and strains; the toasts grow more ironic, more Soviet, more 'ours' . . .

What was going on in the Russia we're bidding adieu to here, in the year 1910? our Brooklyn culturati are asking. 'Well, Chekhov has been dead for six years,' answers Sasha. 'Tolstoy has just died at a remote railway station.'

'His strange death a major cultural milestone,' Mother chimes in, not to be outdone. 'It caused a massive media frenzy.'

In 1913, I add myself, revisiting my patriotism theme, the tone-deaf Czar Nicholas II created a minor public relations disaster by serving a Frenchified menu at the banquet celebrating three hundred years of the Romanov dynasty. *Potage a tortue* – definitely not patriotic.

Cautiously I dig my spoon now into my Guriev kasha. Rich yet light, with a texture somewhere between pudding and torte, it tastes like a celestial version of my dreaded kindergarten breakfast farina. The guests giggle at my three a.m. *penki* fiasco.

And then it's suddenly time for au revoirs. To Mom, to me, to czarist excess. The Genises head off down the hallway to the elevator. Suddenly Sasha comes running back.

'*Devochki* (Girls)! The kulebiaka, I just have to say again: wow! Inserting blini into yeast pastry!? Unreal.'

Maybe I do understand Sasha's brand of patriotism and nostalgia. It's patriotism for that nineteenth-century Russian idea of Culture with a capital C – an idea, and an ideal, that we ex-Soviets from Ukraine and Moscow and Latvia have never abandoned. They still stir us, those memories of savoring orgiastic descriptions of edibles in Chekhov and Gogol while dunking stale socialist pies into penitentiary-style soups.

I want to ask Mom what she thinks of all this, but she looks too exhausted. And sweaty. I have a feeling she's welcoming the seven and a half decades of frugal Soviet eating ahead of us.

CHAPTER TWO

✷

1920S: LENIN'S CAKE

When I was four, I developed a troubling fascination with Lenin. With Dedushka (Grandpa) Lenin, as the leader of the world proletariat was known to us Soviet kids.

For a grandfather, Vladimir Ilyich was distressingly odd. I puzzled over how he could be immortal – 'more alive than all the living,' per Mayakovsky – and yet be so clearly, blatantly dead. Puzzling too how Lenin was simultaneously the curly-haired baby Volodya on the star-shaped Octobrists badge of first-graders and yet a very old *dedushka* with a tufty triangular beard, unpleasantly bald under his inescapable flat cap. Everyone raved about how honest he was, how smart and courageous; how his revolution saved Russia from backwardness. But doubts nagged at me. That cheesy proletarian cap (who ever wore such a thing?) and that perpetual sly squint, just a bit smirky – they made him not entirely trustworthy. And how come *alkogolíks* sometimes kicked his stony statues, mumbling 'Fucking syphilitic'? And what awesome revolutionary, even if bald, would marry Nadezhda Konstantinovna Krupskaya, who resembled a misshapen tea cozy?

I decided the only way to resolve these mysteries would

be to visit the mausoleum in Red Square where Vladimir Ilyich – dead? alive? – resided. But a visit to the *mavzoley* wasn't so easy. True, it stood just a short distance from my grandma Alla's communal apartment, where I was born. All I had to do was walk out of her house, then follow the block-long facade of GUM department store into Red Square. But here you encountered the *mausoleum line*. It was longer than the lines at GUM for Polish pantyhose and Rumanian ski boots combined. No matter how early I'd trudge over, thousands would already be there in a mile-long orderly file. Returning in the afternoon, I'd see the same people, still waiting, the bright enthusiasm of a socialist morning now faded from their glum, tired faces. It was then I began to understand that rituals required sacrifice.

But the foremost obstacle between me and Lenin's *mavzoley* was my mother's dogged anti-Soviet hostility. When I started kindergarten, where instructive mausoleum field trips were frequent, she forbade me from going, warning the teachers that I threw up on buses (true enough). On class trip days the kindergarten became eerily peaceful – just me and cleaners and cooks. I had instructions to sit in the Lenin Corner and draw the mausoleum and its bald occupant. The red and black stone ziggurat of the low little building – that I could reproduce perfectly. But the mysterious interior? All I came up with was a big table around which my kindergarten mates and Dedushka Lenin were having tea. On the table I always drew apple cake. All Soviet children knew of Lenin's fondness for apple cake. Even more, we knew how child-Lenin once secretly gobbled up the apple peels after his mom baked such a cake. But the future leader owned up to his crime. He bravely confessed it to his mother! This was the moral. We all had to grow up honest like Lenin.

Actually, the person who knew all about Lenin and the mausoleum was my father, Sergei.

In the seventies, Dad worked at an inconspicuous two-story gray mansion near the Moscow Zoo on the Garden Ring, discreetly accessed through a courtyard. Most passersby had no clue that this was the Ministry of Health's Mausoleum Research Lab, where the best and brightest of science – some 150 people in many departments—toiled to keep Lenin looking his immortal best under the bulletproof glass of his sarcophagus. The hand-washing and sterilizing of his outfit, of his underwear, shirts, vests, and polka-dot ties, were strictly supervised at the lab, too, by a certain zaftig comrade named Anna Mikhailovna. A physics of color guy, Dad manned the *kolorimeter*, monitoring changes in the hue of Lenin's dead skin. (In his seven years there, there weren't any.)

Dad and those of his rank of course were never allowed near the 'object' itself. That required top security clear-ance. Mere mortal researchers practiced on 'biological structures' – cadavers embalmed in the exact same glycerin and potassium acetate solution as the star of the show. There were twenty-six practice stiffs in all, each with its own name. Dad's was 'Kostya,' a criminal dead from asphyx-iation and unclaimed by relatives. On Dad's first day his new colleagues watched cackling as he nearly fainted at a display of severed heads. It was a pretty gruesome, over-the-top place, the lab. Embalmed limbs and fetuses bobbed in the basement bathtubs. But my father quickly got used to the work. In fact, he came to quite like it, he says. Because it was classified as dangerous to employees' health, the job brought delightful perks. Shortened work hours, a free daily carton of milk, and, best of all, a generous monthly allotment of purest, highest-grade *spirt* (ethyl alcohol). In his reports, Dad noted the alcohol's use for cleaning 'optical spheres,' but he often came home with the robust smell of mausoleum spirits on his breath. Behold Soviet science.

★ ★ ★

I was sufficiently older and smarter by the time of my father's necro-employment that Lenin no longer bewitched and bothered me. But certain curiosities linger even today, such as:

What did Lenin and his fellow Bolshevik revolutionaries actually eat?

Mom, on the other hand, has no such curiosity. 'Over *my* dead body!' she almost bellows at my suggestion that we reproduce some Lenin-esque menus. Although she does chuckle when I mention Dad's pet cadaver. Her own memory of his mausoleum days is just the alcohol breath, and she doesn't find that one amusing.

Mom has her own notions of how the 1920s should be dealt with gastronomically. Rightly, she characterizes the decade as a fractured chaos of contradictory utopian experiments and concessionary schemes leading nowhere – all forgotten once Stalin's leaden hand fell in the thirties.

'For us today,' she propounds, ever the culture vulture,

'the Soviet twenties are really remembered for the writers. And the avant-garde art – the Maleviches, Rodchenkos, and Tatlins on museum walls all over the world!'

So besides digging into family history for her grandmother's gefilte fish recipe, Mom assigns herself the task of leafing through art albums to troll for food references.

And I'm left to tackle Lenin. Dedushka Lenin.

From my kindergarten nanny, Zoya Petrovna, I knew that her dear Vladimir Ilyich Ulyanov was born in 1870, some 430 miles from the Kremlin, in the provincial Volga town of Simbirsk. Volodya (the diminutive of Vladimir) was the smart, boisterous third child of six in a large and happy family. At the cozy Ulyanov homestead there were musical evenings, tea in the garden gazebo, gooseberry bushes for the kids to raid. Mom Maria – a teacher of Germanic and Jewish descent – cooked stolid Russo-Germanic fare. The family enjoyed *Arme Rítter* ('poor knights,' a German French toast) and lots of *buterbrodi*, the open-faced sandwiches that would become staples of our Soviet diets. About the proverbial apple cake reliable scholarly sources are silent, alas.

The Ulyanovs' idyll ended when Volodya was sixteen. His father died from a brain hemorrhage. The next year his older brother Alexander was arrested and hanged for conspiring to assassinate the czar. Most historians see Alexander's fate as the trauma that radicalized the future Bolshevik leader. They also acknowledge the influence of Alexander's favorite book, *Chto delat'?* or *What Is to Be Done?* In

1902 Vladimir Ilyich borrowed the title for a revolutionary pamphlet he signed using for the first time his adopted name: Lenin.

The original was penned in 1863 by an imprisoned socialist, Nikolai Chernyshevsky, and is widely acknowledged as some of the most god-awful writing ever spawned under the northern sun. A didactic political tract shoehorned into a breathtakingly inept novel, it gasses on and on about free love and a communal utopia populated by a 'new kind' of people. Writers as disparate as Nabokov and Dostoyevsky mocked it. And yet, for future Bolsheviks (Mensheviks too) the novel wasn't just inspirational gospel; it was a practical guide to actually reaching utopia.

Vera Pavlovna, the book's free-loving do-goodnik heroine, inspired Russian feminists to open labor cooperatives for poor women. And Rakhmetov, its Superman of a revolutionary, became the model for angry young men aspiring to transform Russia. Half Slavic secular saint, half Enlightenment rationalist, this Rakhmetov was ascetic, ruthlessly pragmatic, and disciplined, yet possessed of a Russian bleeding heart for the underprivileged. He abstained from booze and sex and grabbed his forty winks on a bed of nails to toughen up – a detail gleefully recalled by any former Soviet teen who slogged through a ninth-grade composition on *What Is to Be Done?*

And to eat?

For Rakhmetov, an oddball 'boxer's' diet sufficed: raw meat, for strength; some plain black bread; and whichever humble fare was available (apples, fine; fancy apricots, *nyet*).

As I reread *Chto delat'?* now, this stern menu for heroes

strikes me as very significant. Rooted in mid-nineteenth-century Russian liberal thought, culinary austerity – not to say nihilism – was indeed the hallmark of the era's flesh-and-blood radicals and utopians. The father of Russian populism, Alexander Herzen – Chernyshevsky's idol, admiration alas unreturned – had condemned the European petite bourgeoisie's desire for 'a piece of chicken in the cabbage soup of every little man.' Tolstoy preached vegetarianism. Petr Kropotkin, the anarchist prince, avowed '*tea* and *bread*, some milk . . . a thin slice of meat cooked over a spirit lamp.' And when Vera Zasulich, a venerated Marxist firebrand, was hungry, she snipped off pieces of wretchedly done meat with scissors.

True to the model, Lenin qua Lenin ate humbly. Conveniently, his wife, Krupskaya, was a lousy cook. On the famous 'sealed' train headed for Petrograd's Finland Station in 1917, Lenin made do with a sandwich and a stale bread roll. During their previous decade of European exile, the Bolshevik first couple, though not poor, dined like grad students on bread, soups, and potatoes at cheap boardinghouses and proletarian neighborhood joints. When she did cook, Krupskaya burned her stews ('roasts,' Lenin called them ironically). She even made 'roast' out of oatmeal, though she could prepare eggs a dozen ways. But she needn't have bothered: Lenin, she reported later, 'pretty submissively ate everything given to him.' Apparently Lenin didn't even mind horsemeat. Occasionally his mother would send parcels of Volga treats – caviar, smoked fish – from Simbirsk. But she died in 1916. So there were no such treats in 1918 when her son and daughter-in-law moved into the Kremlin, by the wall of which I would later brood over the endless line for the mausoleum.

✶ ✶ ✶

Ascetic food mores à la Rakhmetov carried over, it might be said, into the new Bolshevik state's approach to collective nutrition. Food equaled utilitarian fuel, pure and simple. The new Soviet citizen was to be liberated from fussy dining and other such distractions from his grand modernizing project.

Novy sovetsky chelovek. The New Soviet Man!

This communal socialist prototype stood at the very heart of Lenin and company's enterprise. A radically transforming society required a radically different membership: productive, selfless, strong, unemotional, rational – ready to sacrifice all to the socialist cause. Not letting any kind of biological determinism stand in their way, the Bolsheviks held that, with proper finagling, the Russian body and mind could be reshaped and rewired. Early visions of such Rakhmetovian comrade-molding were a goony hybrid of hyper-rational science, sociology, and utopian thinking.

'Man,' enthused Trotsky (who'd read *What Is to Be Done?* with 'ecstatic love'), 'will make it his purpose to . . . raise his instincts to the heights of consciousness . . . to create a higher social biologic tongue type, or, if you please, a superman.'

A prime crucible for the new Soviet identity was *byt* (everyday life and its mores) – to be remade as *novy byt* (the new lifestyle). A deeply Russian concept, this *byt* business, difficult to translate. Not merely everyday life in the Western sense, it traditionally signified the metaphysical weight of the daily grind, the existentially depleting cares of material living. The Bolsheviks meant to eliminate the problem. In Marxian terms, material life determined consciousness. Consequently, *novy byt* – everyday life modernized, socialized, collectivized, *ideologized* – would serve as a critical arena and engine of man's transformation. Indeed, the turbulent twenties marked the beginning of our state's relentless intrusion into every aspect of the Soviet daily experience – from hygiene to housekeeping, from education to eating, from sleeping to sex. Exact ideologies and aesthetics would vary through the decades, but not the state's meddling.

'Bolshevism has abolished private life,' wrote the cultural critic Walter Benjamin after his melancholy 1927 visit to Moscow.

The abolition started with housing. Right after October 1917, Lenin drafted a decree expropriating and partitioning single-family dwellings. And so were born our unbeloved Soviet *kommunalki* – communal apartments with shared kitchens and bathrooms. Under the Bolsheviks, comforting words such as *house* and *apartment* were quickly replaced by *zhilploshchad'*, chilling bureaucratese for 'dwelling space.' The official allowance – nine square meters ·per person, or rather, per statistical unit – was assigned by the Housing Committee, an all-powerful institution that threw together strangers – often class enemies – into conditions far more intimate than those of nuclear families in the West. An environment engineered for totalitarian social control.

Such was the domicile near Red Square where I spent the first three years of my life. It was, I'm sad to report, not the blissful communal utopia envisaged in the hallowed pages of *What Is to Be Done?* Sadder still, by the seventies, the would-be socialist ubermensch had shrunk to *Homo sovieticus:* cynical, disillusioned, wholly fixated on kolbasa, and yes, Herzen's petit bourgeois chicken.

Naturally, the Bolshevik reframing of *byt* ensnared the family stove. Despite the mammoth challenge of feeding the civil-war-ravaged country, the traditional domestic kitchen was branded as ideologically reactionary, and down-right ineffectual. 'When each family eats by itself,' warned a publication titled *Down with the Private Kitchen*, 'scientifically sound nutrition is out of the question.'

State dining facilities were to be the new hearth – the public cauldron replacing the household pot, in the phrase of one Central Committee economist. Such communal catering not only allowed the state to manage scarce resources, but also turned eating into a politically engaged process. 'The *stolovaya* [public canteen] is the forge,' declared the head of the union in charge of public dining, 'where Soviet *byt* and society will be . . . created.' Communal cafeterias, agreed Lenin, were invaluable 'shoots' of communism, living examples of its practice.

By 1921 thousands of Soviet citizens were dining in public. By all accounts these *stolovayas* were ghastly affairs – scarier even than those of my Mature Socialist childhood with their piercing reek of stewed cabbage and some Aunt Klava flailing a filthy cleaning rag under my nose as I gagged on the three-course set lunch, with its inevitable ending of desolate-brown dried fruit compote or a starchy liquid jelly called *kissel*.

Kissel would have appeared ambrosial back in the twenties. Workers were fed soup with rotten sauerkraut, unidentified meat (horse?), gluey millet, and endless *vobla*, the petrified dried Caspian roach fish. And yet . . . thanks to the didactic ambitions of *novy byt*, many canteens offered reading rooms, chess, and lectures on the merits of hand-washing, thorough chewing, and proletarian hygiene. A few model *stolovayas* even had musical accompaniment and fresh flowers on white tablecloths.

Mostly though, the New Soviet slogans and schemes brought rats, scurvy, and filth.

There were rats and scurvy inside the Kremlin as well.

Following Lenin's self-abnegating example, the Bolshevik elite overworked and under-ate. At meetings of the Council of People's Commissars, comrades fainted from ill-ness and hunger. As the flames of civil war guttered, the victorious socialist state came staggering into the century's third decade 'never so exhausted, so worn out,' to quote Lenin. An overwhelming roster of crises demanded solution. War Communism and its 'food dictatorship' had proved catastrophic. Grain production was down; in February of 1921, a drastic cut in food rations in Petrograd set off major strikes. At the end of that month, the sailors at Kronstadt Fortress – whose guns had helped to launch the October Revolution – rose against Bolshevik authoritarianism. The mutiny was savagely suppressed, but it reverberated all over the country. In a countryside still seething from the violent forced grain requisition, peasants revolted in every corner.

What was to be done?

Lenin's pragmatic shock remedy was NEP – the New Economic Policy. Beginning in mid-1921, grain requisition was replaced by tax in kind. And then the bombshell: small-scale private trade was permitted alongside the state's control of the economy's 'looming heights.' It was a radical leap backward from the Party ideal, a desperate tack to nourish frail socialism through petty capitalism. And it was done even as the utopian New Soviet Man program pushed ahead in contradictory, competitive parallel.

Such were the Soviet twenties.

Despite the policy turnabout, famine struck southeastern Russia in late 1921. Five million people were dead before the horrors subsided the next year. But between this famine and the one that would follow under Stalin, the NEP's seven years lit up a frenzied, carnal entr'acte, a Russian version of Germany's sulfurous Weimar. Conveniently, the *nepachi* (NEPmen) made a perfect ideological enemy for the ascetic Bolsheviks. Instantly – and enduringly – they were demonized as fat, homegrown bourgeois bandits, feasting on weakened, virtuous socialist flesh.

And yet for all its bad rap, NEP helped tremendously. A reviving peasant economy began feeding the cities; in 1923 practically all Russia's bread was supplied by private sources. Petrograd papers were gleefully reporting oranges – oranges! – to be had around town.

For a few years the country more or less *ate*.

★ ★ ★

Images of gluttonous conmen aside, most NEP businesses were no more than market stands or carts. This was the era of pop-up soup counters, blini stalls, and lemonade hawkers. Also of canteens run out of citizens' homes – especially Jewish homes, according to Russia's top culinary historian, William Pokhlebkin.

Checking in on Mom and her twenties research, I find her immersed in reconstructing the menu of one such canteen. It's in NEP-era Odessa as she imagines it, half a decade before she was born.

The focus of my mother's imagining is one sprawling room in Odessa's smokestack factory neighborhood of Peresyp. Owner? Her maternal grandmother, Maria Brokhvis, the best cook in all of Peresyp. To make ends meet, Maria offers a public table. And there's a regular customer, dining right now. Barely in his twenties, with dark hair already starting to recede but with lively, ironic eyes and dazzling white teeth that make him a natural with the ladies. Often he comes here straight from work in his suave blue naval uniform. He's new to Odessa, to his posting in the Black Sea naval intelligence. Naum Solomonovich Frumkin is his name, and he will be my mother's father.

Naum pays lavish attention to Maria Brokhvis's chopped herring and prodigious stuffed chicken. But his eye is really for Liza, the second of Maria and Yankel Brokhvis's three daughters. There she is in the corner, an architectural student running gray, serious eyes over her drafting board. Ash blond, petite and athletic, with a finely shaped nose, Liza has no time for Naum. He suggests a stroll along the seaside cliffs, hints at his feelings. Not interested.

But how could she ever say *nyet* to tickets to Odessa's celebrated, glorious opera house? Like everyone in town, Liza is crazy for opera, and tonight it's *Rigoletto* – her favorite.

Naum proposes right after *Rigoletto*. And is turned down flat. She must finish her studies, Liza informs him indignantly. Enough with his 'amorous nonsense'!

So Naum, the crafty intelligence officer, turns his focus to the parents at whose table he dines. How could Maria and Yankel refuse such a fine young New Soviet Man for their pretty *komsomolochka* (Communist youth)?

How indeed?

Naum and Liza would be happily married for sixty-one years. Their first daughter, Larisa, was born in Odessa in 1934.

'So you see,' Mom says grandly, 'I owe my birth to NEP's petty capitalism!'

The enduring union of my grandparents, on the other hand, owed nothing to cooking. Like Lenin's Krupskaya, Grandma Liza had scant passion for her stove; and just like Dedushka Lenin, my grandpa Naum submissively ate whatever was on his plate. Occasionally, Liza would make fish meatballs from frozen cod, awkwardly invoking her mother Maria's *real* Jewish gefilte fish. She even made noises to us about some-day making the actual stuff – but she never did. In our 'anti-Zionist' State of the seventies, gefilte fish was an unpatriotic commodity. And Babushka Liza was the wife of a longtime Communist intelligence chief.

But I did encounter real gefilte fish as a kid – in Odessa, in fact, the city of my grandparents' Bolshevik-NEP courtship more than forty years before. And it shook my young self, I recall again now, with the meaning of our Soviet Jewishness. A Jewishness so drastically redefined for my mother's and my generations by the fervent Bolshevik identity policies forged in the 1920s.

That first taste of gefilte fish in Odessa still torments me, here across the years in Queens.

'Ah, Odessa, the pearl by the sea,' goes the song. Brought into being by Catherine the Great, this rollicking polyglot port on the Black Sea was by the nineteenth century one of the fastest-growing cities in Europe; its streets remain a riot of French and Italian Empire-style architecture, full of fantastical flourishes.

Ah, the Odessa of my young Augusts! The barbaric southern sun withered the chestnut trees. The packed tram to Langeron Beach smelled thickly of overheated socialist flesh, crayfish bait, and boiled eggs, that sine qua non of Soviet beach picnics. We stayed with Tamara, Grandma Liza's deaf, retired older sister, formerly an important local judge. Tamara's daughter, Dina, had a round doll's face perched on a hippo's body; she worked as an economist. Dina's son, Senka, had no neck and no manners. Dina's husband, Arnold, the taxi driver, told jokes. Loudly – how else?

'Whatsa difference between Karl Marx and Dina?' he'd roar. 'Marx was an economist, our Dina's a *senior* economist! HA HA HA!!'

'Stop nauseating already into everyone's ears!' Dina would bellow back.

This was how they talked in Odessa.

In the morning I awoke – appetiteless – to the *tuk-tuk-tuk* of Dina's dull chopping knife. Other *tuk-tuk-tuk*s echoed from neighborhood windows. Odessa women greeted the day by making *sininkie*, 'little blue ones,' local jargon for eggplants. Then they prepared stuffed peppers, and then *sheika*, a whole stuffed chicken that took hours to make. Lastly they fried – fried everything in sight. Odessa food seemed different from our Moscow fare: greasier, fishier, with enough garlic to stun a tramful of vampires. But it didn't seem particularly *Jewish* to me; after all, black bread and *salo* (pork fatback) was Judge Tamara's favorite sandwich.

Then one day I was dispatched on an errand to the house of some distant relations in the ramshackle Jewish neighborhood of Moldovanka. They lived in an airless room crowded with objects and odors and dust of many generations. In the kitchen I was greeted by three garrulous women with clunky gold earrings and fire-engine-red hair. Two were named Tamara just like my great-aunt; the third was Dora. The Tamaras were whacking a monstrous pike against the table – 'to loosen its skin so it comes off like a stocking.' They paused to smother me with noisy, blustery kisses, to ply me with buttermilk, vanilla wafers, and honeycake. Then I was instructed to sit and watch 'true Jewish food' being prepared.

One Tamara filleted the fish; the other chopped the flesh with a flat-bladed knife, complaining about her withered arm. Dora grated onions, theatrically wiping away tears. Reduced to a coarse oily paste and blended with onion, carrots, and bread, the fish was stuffed back into the skin and sewn up with thick twine as red as the cooks' hair.

It would boil now for three whole hours. Of course I must stay! Could I grate horseradish? Did I know the meaning of Shabbos? What, I hadn't heard of the pogroms? More wafers, buttermilk?

Suffocating from fish fumes, August heat, and the onslaught of entreaties and questions, I mumbled some excuse and ran out, gasping for air. I'm sure the ladies were hurt, mystified. For some time afterward, with a mixture of curiosity and alienation, I kept wondering about the taste of that fish. Then, back in Moscow, it dawned on me:

On that August day in Odessa, I had run away from my Jewishness.

I suppose you can't blame a late-Soviet big-city kid for fleeing the primal shock of gefilte fish. As thoroughly gentrified Moscow Jews, we didn't know from seders or matzo balls. Jewishness was simply the loaded *pyaty punkt* (Entry 5) in the Soviet internal passport. Mandated in 1932, two years before my mother was born, Entry 5 stated your *ethnicity*: 'Russian, Uzbek, Tatar . . . Jew.' Especially when coupled with an undesirable surname, 'Jew' was the equivalent of a yellow star in the toxic atmosphere of the Brezhnev era. Yes, we were intensely aware of our difference as Jews – and ignorant of the religious and cultural backstory. Of course we ate pork fat. We loved it.

The sense that I'd fled my Jewishness in Odessa added painful new pressure to the dilemma I would face at sixteen. That's when each Soviet citizen first got an internal passport – the single most crucial identity document. As a child of mixed ethnicities – Jewish mom, Russian dad – I'd be allowed to select either for Entry 5. This choice-to-come weighed like a stone on my nine-year-old soul. Would I pick difficult honor and side with the outcasts, thereby dramatically reducing my college and job opportunities? Or would I take the easy road of being 'Russian'? Our emigration rescued me from the dilemma, but the unmade choice haunts me to this day. What would I have done?

In the early 1920s, hundreds of thousands of Jews made their own choice – without anguish they renounced Judaism for Bolshevism.

One such Jewish convert was Mom's Grandpa Yankel. He too became a New Soviet Man, albeit a short, potbellied, docile one. But he was a fanatical proletarian nevertheless, a blacksmith who under Stalin would become a decorated Hero of Socialist Labor.

Yankel came to Odessa in the early 1900s from a shtetl in the Pale of Settlement – the zone where since 1772 the Russian Empire's Jews had been confined. Though within the Pale, the port of Odessa was a thriving melting pot of Greeks, Italians, Ukrainians, and Russians as well as Jews. Here Yankel married Maria, began to flourish. And then in 1905, he returned from the disastrous Russo-Japanese War to something unspeakable. Over four October days, street mobs killed and mutilated hundreds in an orgy of anti-Jewish atrocities. Yankel and Maria's firstborn, a baby boy, was murdered in front of them.

The civil war revived the pogrom of 1905 with anti-Semitic marauding by counterrevolutionary Whites. The Red Army – commanded by one Lev Bronstein, better known as Leon Trotsky – vehemently denounced the violence. Jews flocked to the Reds. Too old for combat now, Yankel cheered from the side-lines.

At first the revolution was good to the Jews. The official birth of the USSR in 1922 brought them rights and opportunities unprecedented in Russia's history. Anti-Semitism became a state crime; the Pale was dismantled. Jews could rise through the bureaucratic and cultural ranks. At the start of the decade Jews made up one fifth of the Party's Central Committee.

But there was a catch.

Like the Russian Empire before it, the Soviet Union was vast and dizzyingly multiethnic. For the Bolsheviks the ethnic or 'nationalities' issue was fraught. In Marxist terms, nationalism was reactionary. Yet not only did ethnic minorities exist, but their oppression under the czar made them ripe for the socialist cause. So Lenin, along with the early Bolshevik nationalities commissar, Stalin, an ethnic Georgian, contrived a policy of linguistic, cultural, and territorial autonomy for ethnic minorities – in a Soviet format – until international socialism came about and nationalities became superfluous.

The USSR, in the words of the historian Terry Martin, became the world's first affirmative-action empire.

The catch for Jews? Jewishness was now defined in strictly *ethno-national* terms. The Talmud had no place in building the Radiant Future. Reforming and modernizing the so-called 'Jewish Street' fell to the Yevsektsii, the Jewish sections of the Communist Party. They worked savvily. Religious rituals were initially semitolerated – in Sovietized form. Passover? Well, if you must. Except the *Soviet*

Haggadah substituted the words 'October Revolution' for
'God.'

In 1920s Odessa, the Soviet supporters Yankel and Maria
Brokhvis continued to light candles on Shabbos at their
one-room flat in Peresyp – but without mentioning God.
Maria saw no wrong in gathering their three daughters
around Friday table; she was a proud Jew. As the terrible
times of the 1921 famine gave way to NEP's relative bounty,
she shopped every week at Odessa's boisterous Privoz
market for the pike for her famous gefilte fish. It was her
second daughter Liza's favorite. Maria made challah bread
too, and *forshmak* (chopped herring), and bean tzimmes, and
crumbly pastries filled with the black prune jam she cooked
over a primus stove in the courtyard.

Then one Friday Liza returned from school and sat
at the Shabbos table staring down at the floor, lips pursed,
not touching a thing. She was fourteen years old and had
just joined the Komsomol, the youth division of the
Communist Party. After dinner she rose and declared:
'Mother, your fish is vile *religious* food. I will never eat it
again!'

And that was it for the Brokhvis family's Friday gefilte
fish. Deep in her heart, Maria understood that the New
Soviet Generation knew better.

I had no idea about any of this. Not the baby dead in the
pogrom, not Grandma Liza's ban on Maria's religious food.
Only when Mom and I were in her kitchen making our
gefilte tribute to Maria did I find out.

Suddenly I understood why Grandma Liza had looked

pensive and hesitant whenever she mentioned the dish. She too had run from her Jewishness back in Odessa. To her credit, Liza, who was blond and not remotely Semitic-looking, became enraged, proclaiming herself Jewish, if ever anyone made an anti-Semitic remark. Granddad Naum . . . not so much. About his family past Mom knows almost nothing – only that his people were shtetl Zionists and that Naum ran away from home as a teen, lied about his age to join the Red Army, and never looked back.

In Jackson Heights, Mom and I are both ecumenical cul-turalists. We light menorahs next to our Christmas trees. We bake Russian Easter kulich cake and make ersatz gefilte fish balls for Passover. But our gefilte fish this time was different – *real Jewish food*. We skinned a whole pike, hand-minced the flesh, cried grating the onion, sewed the fish mince inside the skin, and cooked the whole reconstituted beast for three hours.

The labor was vast, but for me it was a small way of atoning for that August day in Odessa.

★ ★ ★

Returning to twenties Bolshevik policies, I reflected again on how kitchen labor, particularly the kind at Maria's politically equivocal NEP home canteen, got so little respect in the New Soviet vision. Partly this was pragmatic. Freeing women from the household pot was a matter of lofty principle, but it was also meant to push them into the larger workforce, perhaps even into the army of political agitators.

I haven't mentioned her yet, this New Soviet Woman.

Admittedly a lesser star than the New Soviet Man, she was still decidedly not a housewife-cook. She was a liberated *proletarka* (female proletarian) – co-builder of the road to utopia, co-defender of the Communist International, avid reader of *Rabotnitsa* (*Female Worker*), an enthusiastic participant in public life.

Not for her the domestic toil that 'crushes and degrades women' (Lenin's words). Not for her nursery drudgery, so 'barbarously unproductive, petty, nerve-racking, stultifying' (Lenin again). No, under socialism, society would assume all such burdens, eventually eradicating the nuclear family. 'The real emancipation of women, real communism, will begin,' predicted Lenin in 1919, 'only where and when an all-out struggle begins . . . against . . . petty . . . housekeeping.'

In one of my favorite Soviet posters, a fierce New Soviet *proletarka* makes like a herald angel under the slogan DOWN WITH KITCHEN SLAVERY, rendered in striking avant-garde typography. She's grinning down at an aproned female beleaguered by suds, dishes, laundry, and cobwebs. The red-clad *proletarka* opens wide a door to a light-flooded vision of New Soviet *byt*. Behold a multistoried Futurist edifice housing a public canteen, a kitchen-factory, and a nursery school, all crowned with a workers' club.

The engine for turning such utopian Bolshevik feminist visions into reality was the Zhenotdel, literally 'women's department.' Founded in 1919 as an organ of the Party's Central Committee, the Zhenotdel and its branches fought for – and helped win – crucial reforms in childcare, contraception, and marriage. They proselytized, recruited, and educated. The first head of Zhenotdel was the charismatic

Inessa Armand – Paris-born, strikingly glamorous, and by many accounts more than simply a 'comrade' to Lenin (Krupskaya being strikingly *not* glamorous). Ravaged by overwork, Armand died of cholera in 1920, desperately mourned by Vladimir Ilyich. The Zhenotdel mantle then passed to Alexandra Kollontai, who was perhaps *too* charismatic. Kollontai stands out as one of communism's most dashing characters. A free-love apostle and scandalous practitioner of such (the likely model for Garbo's Ninotchka), Kollontai essentially regarded the nuclear family as an inefficient use of labor, food, and fuel. Wife as homebody-cook outraged her.

'The separation of marriage from kitchen,' preached Kollontai, 'is a reform no less important than the separation of church and state.'

In our family, we had our own Kollontai.

As Russian families go, mine represented a rich sampling of the pre-Soviet national pot. Mom's people came from the Ukrainian shtetl. Dad's paternal ancestors were Germanic aristocracy who married Caspian merchants' daughters. And Dad's mom, my extravagant and extravagantly beloved grandmother Alla, was raised by a fiery agitator for women's rights in remote Central Asia.

When I was little, Alla cooked very infrequently, but when she bothered, she produced minor masterpieces. I particularly remember the stew my mom inherited from her and cooks to this day. It's an Uzbek stew. A stew of burnished-brown lamb and potatoes enlivened with an angry dusting of paprika, crushed coriander seeds, and the faintly medicinal funk of *zíra*, the Uzbek wild cumin. 'From my childhood in Ferghana!' Alla would blurt over the dish, then add, 'From a person very dear to me . . .' And then the subject was closed. But I knew whom she meant.

Alla Nikolaevna Aksentovich, my grandmother, was born a month before the October Revolution in what was still called Turkestan, as czarist maps labeled Central Asia. She was an out-of-wedlock baby, orphaned early and adopted by her maternal grandmother, Anna Alexeevna, who was a Bolshevik feminist in a very rough place to be one.

Turkestan. Muslim, scorchingly hot, vaster than modern India, much of it desert. One of the czars' last colonial conquests, it was subjugated only in the 1860s. A decade later, Anna Alexeevna was born in the fertile Ferghana valley, Silk Road country from which the Russian Empire pumped cotton – as would the Soviet Empire, even more mercilessly. The lone photo we have of her, taken years later and elsewhere, shows Anna with a sturdy round Slavic face and high cheekbones. Her father was a Ural Cossack, definitely no supporter of Reds. In 1918, when she was already forty, a midwife by training, she defied him and joined the Communist Party. By 1924, she and little orphaned Alla were in Tashkent, the capital of the new republic of Uzbekistan. The Soviets by then had carved up Central Asia into five socialist 'national' entities. Anna Alexeevna was the new deputy head of the 'agitation' department of the Central Asian Bureau of the Central Committee.

There was much agitating to be done.

The civil war thereabouts had dragged on for extra years, Reds pitched against the *basmachi* (Muslim insurgents). With victory came — as elsewhere — staggering challenges. Unlike the Jews, Uzbeks weren't easy converts to the Bolshevik cause. If Russia itself lacked the strict Marxian preconditions for communism — namely, advanced capitalism — agrarian former Turkestan, with its religious and clan structures, was downright feudal. How does one build socialism without a proletariat? The answer was women. Subjugated by husbands, clergy, and ruling chiefs, the women of Central Asia were 'the most oppressed of the oppressed and the most enslaved of the enslaved,' as Lenin put it.

So the Soviets switched their rallying cry from class struggle and ethno-nationalism to gender. In the 'women of the Orient' they found their 'surrogate proletariat,' their battering ram for social and cultural change.

Anna Alexeevna and her fellow Zhenotdel missionaries toiled against the *kalym* (bride fee) and under-age marriage, against polygamy and female seclusion and segregation. Most dramatically, they battled the most literal form of seclusion: the veil. In public Muslim women had to wear a *paranji*, a long, ponderous robe, and a *chachvan*, a veil. But veil sounds so flimsy. Imagine instead a massive, primeval head-to-knee shroud of horsehair, with no openings for eyes or mouth.

'The best revolutionary actions,' Kollontai reportedly once pronounced, 'are pure drama.' Anna Alexeevna and the feminists had their coup de théâtre: The veil had to go! Few Soviet revolutionary actions were more sensational than the *hujum* (onslaught), the Central Asian campaign of unveiling.

March 8, 1927: International Women's Day. In Uzbek cities veiled women go tramping en masse, escorted by police. Bands and native orchestras play. Stages set up on public squares swarm with flowers. There are fiery speeches by Zhenotdelki. Poems. Anna is on Tashkent's main stage no doubt when the courageous first ones step up, pull off their horsehair mobile prisons, and fling them into bonfires. Thousands are inspired to do the same then and there – ten thousand veils are reportedly cast off on this day. Unveiled women surge through the streets shouting revolutionary slogans. Everyone sings. An astounding moment.

The backlash was wrathful and immediate.

Trapped between Lenin and Allah, Moscow and Mecca, the unveiled became social outcasts. Many redonned the paranji. Many others were raped and murdered by traditionalist males or their families, their mutilated bodies displayed in villages. Zhenotdel activists were threatened and killed. The firestorm lasted for years.

By decade's end the radical theatrics of unveiling were abandoned. And all over the country the Zhenotdeli were being dismantled because Stalin pronounced the 'women's question' *solved*. By the midthirties, traditional family values were back, with divorce discouraged, abortions and homosexuality banned. On propaganda posters the Soviet Woman had a new look: maternal, full-figured, and 'feminine.' And for the rest of the USSR's existence, female comrades were expected to carry on their shoulders the infamous 'double burden' of wage labor and housework.

✳ ✳ ✳

And my great-great-grandmother, the New Soviet feminist?

In 1931 Anna Alexeevna moved with the teenage Alla to Moscow, to follow her boss Isaak Zelensky. A longtime Party stalwart, Zelensky was one of the engineers of War Communism's grain requisitioning; he'd been brought back now to the capital from Central Asia to run the state's consumer cooperatives. In 1937, in the midst of the purges, Zelensky was arrested. A year later he was in the dock with Bolshevik luminary Nikolai Bukharin at Stalin's most notorious show trial. As ex-head of cooperative food suppliers, Zelensky breathtakingly 'confessed' to sabotage, including the spoiling of fifty trainloads of eggs bound for Moscow, and the ruining of butter shipments by adding nails and glass.

He was promptly shot and deleted from Soviet history.

A year later my great-great-grandmother Anna was arrested as Zelensky's co-conspirator and also deleted from history. From our *family* history, by my grandma Alla, who destroyed all photographs of her and stopped mentioning her name. Then one day, after the end of World War II, shaking with fear, Alla opened a letter from the gulag, from Kolyma in furthest Siberia. With blood-chilling precision, Anna Alexeevna had detailed the tortures she'd been subjected to and pleaded with the granddaughter she'd adopted and raised to inform Comrade Stalin. Like millions of victims, she was convinced the Supreme Leader knew nothing of the horrors going on in the prison camps. In my dad's various retellings, Alla immediately burned the letter, flushed it down the communal apartment toilet, or ate it.

Only when drunk, very drunk, and much later, when I

was a child, would Alla chase her shot glass of vodka with herring and crocodile tears and bellow how her grandma Anna Alexeevna had been stripped naked in minus-forty-degree weather, beaten in the cellars of the secret police's Lubyanka Prison, kept from sleep for weeks. Then Dad would whisper to me the inheritance story. How Anna Alexeevna had been released in 1948 at the age of seventy, without a right of return to Moscow, and had lived in the Siberian city of Magadan. How Alla never visited her, not once. How Anna died in 1953, a few months before Stalin.

So imagine Alla's surprise when in the mail arrived a death certificate; the photo of her grandmother, the only one that remains, taken in the gulag; and a money order for a whopping ten thousand rubles, most likely Anna Alexeevna's hoardings from performing black market abortions in the prison camps.

Alla and Sergei burned through the inheritance at Moscow's best restaurants. Alla favored the soaring dining room at the Moskva Hotel, fancying it for its green malachite columns and famously tender lamb riblets – and not, incidentally, because the mustachioed maestro of the gulags had liked to celebrate his birthdays there. Dad spent his gulag money at Aragvi, the Georgian hot spot on Gorky Street, again not because it was a favorite of Stalin's last chief of secret police, Lavrenty Beria. It was just that the iron rings of Soviet life overlapped with all others.

With the rest of Anna Alexeevna's rubles Alla bought a pair of suits for Sergei, which he wore for two decades. Also two blankets under which I slept when I stayed at Alla's kommunalka near the mausoleum as a kid. They were wondrous blankets, one green, the other blue: feather-light and exquisitely silky-soft.

And there it was: two Chinese silk coverlets, two fancy suits, and a dish of Uzbek lamb – the only legacy of a Bolshevik feminist with her round, high-cheekboned Slavic face, a fierce crusader for women's rights in the early days who helped in the assault, so dramatic, so ill-conceived, against the horsehair veil. And then disappeared.

★ ★ ★

The radical Bolshevik identity policies expanded rights for women, for Jews, for even the most obscure ethnic minorities, be they Buryat, Chuvash, or Karakalpak.

But one category of the disempowered got pushed off into the shadows of the Radiant Future, treated as an incorrigible menace. They happened to be 80 percent of the population, the ones feeding Russia. The peasants.

The 'half-savage, stupid, ponderous people of the Russian villages,' as Maxim Gorky, village-born himself, called them in 1920.

'Avaricious, bloated, and bestial,' as Lenin termed them – specifically the kulaks, whose proportion was small, but whose name made an easily spread ideological tar.

The NEP offered a temporary lull in the ongoing conflict between town and country, but by the end of 1927, a full-blown grain crisis erupted once more.

Cue the cunning Georgian: Iosif Vissarionovich Dzhugashvili.

Stalin, as he was known (his Bolshevik pseudonym derived from 'steel'), had since 1922 been the Party's general secretary — a supposedly inconsequential post by which he'd maneuvered to be Lenin's successor. (Trotsky, his chief rival, thought him slow-witted. It was brilliant, arrogant Trotsky, however, who was banished in 1929, and who had an ice ax driven into his skull in 1940.)

The 1927 grain crisis arose partly from fears of war — of an attack by Britain or some other vile capitalist power — that seized the country that year. Panic hoarding flared; peasants shied from selling grain to the state at low prices. Raising these prices might well have solved things. Instead, crying sabotage, the government turned again to repression and violence. On a notorious 1928 trip to Siberia, Stalin personally supervised coercive requisitioning. As his hench-man Molotov later explained: 'To survive, the State needed grain. Otherwise it would crack up. So we pumped away.'

The NEP market approach was effectively dead. About to replace it was Stalin's final solution to the 'peasant problem' — the problem of a reliable supply of cheap grain.

In 1929 the Soviet Union wrenched into Veliky Perelom (The Great Turn). As embodied in the first Five-Year Plan, this fantastically, fanatically ambitious project aimed to industrialize the country full throttle — at the expense of everything else. Long-backward Russia was to be trans-formed into 'a country of metal, an automobilizing country, a tractorized country,' in Stalin's booming phrases. Rationing reappeared, privileging industrial workers and leaving poorer peasants to fend for themselves.

The first thing to be rationed was bread. 'The struggle for bread,' growled Stalin, with an echo of Lenin, 'is the struggle for socialism.' Meaning the Soviet State would brook no more trouble from its 80 percent.

The furies of collectivization and 'dekulakization' were unleashed now on the countryside. Up to ten million kulaks (that toxically elastic term) were thrown off their land, either killed or shipped to prison-labor settlements known after 1930 as the gulags, where great numbers died. The rest of the peasant households were forced onto kolkhozes (giant collective farms overseen by the state), from which the industrial engine could be dependably fed (or at least that was the idea). Peasants resisted this 'second serfdom' by force, destroying their livestock on a catastrophic scale. By 1931 more than twelve million peasants had fled to the towns. In 1933 the country's breadbasket, the fertile Ukraine, would plunge into man-made famine – one of the great tragedies of the twentieth century. Roads were blocked, peasants forbidden to leave, reports of the ongoing devastation suppressed. A dead peasant mother's dribble of milk on her emaciated infant's lips had a name: 'the buds of the socialist spring.' Out of the estimated seven million who died in the Soviet famine, some three million perished in the Ukraine.

From these horrors Soviet agriculture would never recover.

✱ ✱ ✱

By this point Lenin had been dead for almost ten years.

Dead – but not buried.

Following his long, mysterious illness (the 'syphilis' whispers of many decades have lately reintrigued historians) Lenin expired in effective isolation on January 21, 1924. Stalin, a seminarian in his youth, understood the power of relics and was one of the early proponents of keeping the cadaver 'alive.' At a 1923 Politburo session he'd already proposed that 'contemporary science' offered a possibility of preserving the body, at least temporarily. Some Bolsheviks howled at the reek of deification. Krupskaya objected too, but nobody asked her.

From January 27 on, Lenin's body lay in state at the unheated Hall of Columns in Moscow. The weather was so bitter that the palm trees laid on inside for the funeral froze. An icy fog hung over Red Square; mourners were treated for frostbite. But the cold helped preserve the 'mournee' for a while.

The idea to replace the temporary embalmment with something eternal apparently arose spontaneously among the Funeral Commission – swiftly renamed the Immortalization Commission. Refrigeration was being mulled over, but as the weather warmed the body deteriorated, and the Commission panicked. Enter Boris Zbarsky, a self-promoting biochemist, and Vladimir Vorobyev, a gifted provincial pathologist. The pair proposed a radical embalming method. Miraculously, their wild gambit worked. Even a reluctant Krupskaya later told Zbarsky: 'I'm getting older and he looks just the same.'

So the USSR had a New Soviet Eternal Man. Proof in the flesh that Soviet science could defeat even the grave. Socialist reshaping of humanity, it seemed, had soared beyond wildest imagining – far beyond a new everyday life. The antireligious Bolshevik of Bolsheviks, who had ordered clergy murdered and churches destroyed, was now a living relic, immortal in the manner of Orthodox saints.

From August 1924 on, the miraculous Object No. 1 (as it

would later be code-named) preened for Red Square crowds inside a temporary wooden shrine created by the Constructivist architect Alexei Shchusev. Shchusev would go on to build the permanent mausoleum, the now iconic ziggurat of red, gray, and black stone the inner sanctum of which I was so desperate to penetrate as a child. The *mavzoley* was unveiled in 1930, but without particular fanfare. By then the USSR had a successor-God, one who was relegating Lenin to hazy Holy Spirit status.

Lenin, incidentally, transmigrated from this distant, idealized Spirithood into warm and fuzzy *dedushka*-hood during the Brezhnevian phase of his cult. That's when the didactic cake stories became popular, along with that silly iconographic cap on his bald head – asserting Ilyich's modest, friendly, proletarian nature.

The country would by then be wary of God-like personality cults.

PART II

LARISA

The Frumkin family: Yulia, Liza, Sashka, Naum, Larisa, and Liza's father, Dedushka Yankel, in 1943

CHAPTER THREE

1930s: THANK YOU, COMRADE STALIN, FOR OUR HAPPY CHILDHOOD

Like most Soviet kids of her time, my mother was raised on stories by Arkady Gaidar. Gaidar's tales are suffused with a patriotic romanticism that doesn't ring insincere even today. They fairly brim with positive characters – characters who know that the true meaning of happiness is 'to live honestly, toil hard, and deeply love and protect that vast fortunate land called The Soviet Country.' Mom was particularly struck by a story titled 'The Blue Cup.' After overcoming a spell of conflict, a young family sits under a tree ripe with cherries on a late-summer night (spring and summer, one ironic critic remarked, being the only two seasons permissible in socialist realism). A golden moon glows overhead. A train rumbles past in the distance. The main character sums things up, closing the story: 'And life, comrades, was good . . . entirely good.'

This phrase filled my five-year-old mother with alienation and dread.

To this day she can't really explain why. Her parents, youthful, striving, and faithful to the State, exemplified Gaidarian virtues and the Stalinist vision of glamour. Liza, her mother, was a champion gymnast, an architect, and a painter of sweet watercolors. Naum, her father, possessed a radiant smile and a high, honest forehead to go along with his spiffy naval caps, which smelled of the foreign cologne he brought back from frequent trips abroad. If Mom and her younger sister, Yulia, were good, Naum would let them pin his shiny badges on their dresses and dance in front of the mirror. On his rare days off he'd take them to the Park of Culture and Relaxation named after Gorky.

Mother had a second father, of course. Like her kindergarten classmates, she began each school day gazing up at a special poster and thanking him for her joyous, glorious childhood. On the poster the youthfully middle-aged Genius of Humanity and Best Friend of All Children was smiling under the black wings of his mustaches. In his arms a beautiful little girl also smiled. With her dark hair cut in a bowl shape, the girl reminded Mom of herself, only with Asiatic features. She was the legendary Gelya (short for Engelsina, from Friedrich Engels) Markizova. Daughter of a commissar from the Buryat-Mongol region, she came to the Kremlin with a delegation and handed a bouquet of flowers to the Supreme Leader, whereupon he lifted her in his arms, warming her with his amused, benevolent gaze. Cameras flashed. After appearing on the front page of *Izvestia*, the photograph became one of the decade's iconic images. It was reproduced on millions of posters, in paintings and sculptures. Gelya was the living embodiment of every Soviet child's dream.

Comrade Stalin kept a watchful eye over Mom and her family, she was sure of that. And yet a pall hung over her. Life, she suspected, was not 'entirely good.' In place of big bright Soviet happiness, my mother's heart often filled with *toska*, a word for which there is no English equivalent. 'At its deepest and most painful,' explains Vladimir Nabokov, 'toska is a sensation of great spiritual anguish . . .. At less morbid levels it is a dull ache of the soul.'

When Mom heard cheerful choruses on the radio, she imagined squalid people singing drunkenly around a putrid-smelling barrel of pickles. Sometimes she'd refuse to go out into the street, frightened of the black public loudspeakers broadcasting the glories of the Five-Year Plan. Many things about Moscow made her feel scared and small. At the Revolution Square station of the new metro, she ran as quickly as she could past bronze statues of athletic figures with rifles and pneumatic drills. No use. Night after night she was haunted by nightmares of these statues coming alive and tossing her mother into a blazing furnace, like the one in the mural at the Komsomolskaya station.

Perhaps she had such dreams because the parents of other children were disappearing.

There were many things my mother didn't know, couldn't have known, at the time. She didn't know that Arkady Gaidar, beloved writer for the young, had brutally murdered civilians, including women and children, as a Red commander during the civil war. She didn't know that one year after that bouquet at the Kremlin, Gelya Markizova's father was accused of a plot against Stalin and executed –

just one of an estimated twelve to twenty million victims of Stalin. Gelya's mother perished as well. The poster child for a happy Stalinist childhood was deported and raised in an orphanage.

Darkness. The unyielding blackness of Arctic winter in Murmansk is my mother's earliest memory. She was born in sunny Odessa, a barely alive five-pound preemie bundled in wads of coarse cotton. Her father was then sent to Russia's extreme northwest to head the intelligence unit of the newly formed Northern Flotilla. The year was the relatively benign 1934. The harvest was decent. Collectivization's famines and horrors were slowly subsiding. Ration cards were being phased out, first for bread and sugar, then meat.

Myska – childspeak for 'little mouse' – was Mother's very first word, because mice scurried along the exposed wires above her bed in the tiny room she shared with her sister and parents. Thinking back on those days, Mother imagines herself as a mouse, burrowing through some dark, sinister tunnel of early consciousness. She remembers the thunderous crunch of Murmansk's snow under their horse-drawn sled, the salty taste of blood in her mouth after the icicles she liked to lick stuck to her tongue.

Leningrad, where Naum was transferred in 1937, was a thousand kilometers south but still on the chill sixtieth degree of north latitude. Its darkness was different, though. Russia's former imperial capital suggested various conjugations of gray: the steely reflection off the Neva River, with its somber granite embankments; the dull aluminum of the grease-filmed kasha bowls at Mother's nursery school. In place of mice there were rats – the reason Uncle Vasya, their communal apartment neighbor, was missing half his nose. Too bad Mom's name rhymed with *krysa* (rat). 'Larisa-krysa, Larisa-krysa,' children taunted her in the courtyard. Liza occasionally took the girls to see museums and palaces in the center of town. Their melancholy neoclassical grandeur contrasted starkly with the web of bleak alcoholic alleys near their apartment. Mother was inconsolable when a drunk trampled and ruined her brand-new galoshes, so shiny and black, so red inside.

Bleak too was the mood in the city. Three years earlier, Leningrad's charismatic Communist boss Sergei Kirov had been shot down in the corridors of the Smolny Institute, local Party headquarters, by a disgruntled ex-Party functionary. His killing signaled the prologue to the years of paranoia, midnight knocks on the door, denunciations, witch hunts for 'enemies of the people,' and mass slaughter that would come to be known as the Great Terror of 1937–38. Stalin's suspected involvement in Kirov's murder has never been proved. But the Friend of All Children was quick to seize the moment. After planting a sorrowful kiss on Kirov's brow at his operatic show funeral, Stalin unleashed an opening paroxysm of violence against his own political enemies. The show trials would follow. The charge of conspiracy to kill Kirov was used until 1938; it offered one of the key justifications of terror among the grab bag of crimes against the Soviet State and betrayals thereof. Thousands were arrested without cause and shipped to the gulags or killed. Moscow staged the most notorious trials (including the trial of Zelensky, my great-great-grandmother Anna Alexeevna's boss), but Leningrad's suffering was possibly deeper still. By 1937 the former capital had been ravaged by deportations and executions. It was Stalin's vendetta against the city he hated, the locals whispered. Indeed, after Kirov's coffin left Leningrad for Moscow, the Great Leader never set foot by the Neva again.

I look at a picture of my mother from that time. She has an upturned nose, a bob of black hair, wary, defiant eyes. She's laughing, but in her laughter there seems to lurk a shadow. In constructing the narrative of her childhood, Mother likes to portray herself as Dissident-Born, a young prodigy of distress, instinctively at odds with the land of happy children of Stalin. A thousand times I've heard her tales of constantly running away from summer camps and health sanatoria. Of how she finally escaped to America as an adult and at last stopped running.

But to when and what, exactly, does she trace the origins of her childhood *toska*? I've always wanted to know. And now I learn about one particular wintry day.

It's still pitch-black outside when Liza yanks Larisa from her blanket cocoon. 'Hurry hurry, we have to get there by six for the start,' she urges, blowing furiously on Mom's farina to cool it. On the sled ride wet snow cakes Mother's face; the tubercular Baltic chill pierces right through her limbs still heavy with slumber. Despite the early hour she hears marching songs in the distance, sees people hurrying somewhere.

Why is this? Her stomach tightens with alarm and foreboding. A sick worm of fear comes alive; it keeps gnawing at her intestines as she finally reaches a thronged hall inside a building decked out with life-size posters of Great Comrade Stalin. Her parents push through the crowds toward officials bellowing greetings on loud-speakers behind a long table covered with *kumach*, the crimson calico of the Soviet flag. The march music turns deafening. Her parents fill out some papers and momentarily she loses them in the commotion. 'They're voting!' a woman in the crowd cries, handing Mom a red baby-size flag – on this day, December 12, 1937. *Voting.* It's a new word. It stems from *golos*, or 'voice.' Could her parents be screaming for her? She starts to scream too, but her shrieks are drowned out by song.

'*Shiroka strana moya rodnaya*' ('O vast is my country!'), the people are singing. '*There's no other country where a man breathes more freely.*' Swept up in the collective elation, Mom inhales as deep as she can, filling her lungs with what she will always describe as 'that smell' – the Soviet institutional odor of dusty folders, *karbolka* cleaner, woolen coats, and feet stewing in rubber galoshes, which will haunt her all her adult life in the USSR, at offices, schools, political meetings, at work. Her parents find her at last. They are beaming with pride, laugh at her anguish.

By evening Mom is happy again. On the family's afternoon stroll, Leningrad's vast squares look dazzling, decked out in red slogans and posters. Tiny lights outline the buildings in the early dusk. And now on their way to Uncle Dima's house Naum is promising that they will see the *salut* from his balcony. What's *salut*? Why on the balcony? 'Just wait, you'll see!' says Naum.

Mom's excited to be visiting Uncle Dima Babkin. He isn't really her uncle; he's her dad's tall, bald naval boss. In his high-ceilinged apartment, he has a rosy-cheeked baby and twin girls a little older than Mom, and, always, a never-ending supply of sugary *podushechki* candies. When they arrive, the family is celebrating full-throttle. Bottles burst open with a loud popping of corks; toasts are drunk to Russia's historic election and to the arrival of Uncle Dima's elderly father from Moscow. 'Vast is my country,' sing the children, dancing around the baby's crib, which Uncle Dima's wife has filled with sweet raisin rusks. Any minute Aunt Rita, Dima's sister, will arrive with her famous cake called Napoleon.

Uncle Dima's whole building is, in fact, celebrating Election Day; neighbors stream in and out, borrowing chairs, carrying treats.

'Aunt Rita? Napoleon?' scream the children constantly darting up to the door.

There is a short, harsh buzz of the doorbell – but instead of cake Mom sees three men in long coats by the entrance. How come they don't bring tangerines or pirozhki, she wonders? Why haven't they shaken the snow off their felt *valenki* boots before entering – as every polite Russian must do?

'We're looking for Babkin!' barks one of the men.

'Which Babkin?' Uncle Dima's wife asks with an uncertain smile. 'Father or son?'

The men look confused for a moment. 'Well . . . both – sure, why not?' they say, and they shrug. 'Both.' They almost giggle.

The silence that follows, and the smile that's turned

strangely petrified on Uncle Dima's wife's face, reawakens the worm in Mom's stomach. As if in slow motion, she watches Uncle Dima and his old father go off with the men. To her relief, the family's babushka orders the children onto the balcony to see the *salut*. Outside, the black night erupts in glitter. Fiery thrills shoot through Mom's body with each new soaring, thundering explosion of fireworks. Green! Red! Blue! – blooming in the sky like giant, sparkling, jubilant bouquets. But when she goes back inside she is startled to see Uncle Dima's wife splayed out on the couch, panting. And the house is filled with the sweet-rotten odor of valerian drops. And silence – that dead, scary silence.

Arrests to the popping of corks, horror in the next room from happiness, fear emblazoned with fireworks and pageantry – this was the split reality, the collective schizophrenia of the 1930s. Venom-spitting news accounts of the show trials of 'fascist dogs of the Trotskyite-Zinovievite gang' ran beside editorials gushing over crepe de chine dresses at 'model department stores' and the 'blizzards of confetti' at park carnivals.

People sang. Sometimes they sang on their way to the firing squad, chanting 'O Vast Is My Country,' a tune used as a station signal for Radio Moscow even during my youth. Featured in *Circus*, a Hollywood-style musical comedy, 'O Vast Is My Country' was composed to celebrate Stalin's new 1936 constitution, heralded as 'the world's most democratic.' On paper it even restored voting rights to the formerly disenfranchised classes (kulaks, children of priests). Except now arrests were not so much class-based as guided by regional quotas affecting every stratum of the society.

Chronicles of Stalin's terror have naturally shaped the narrative of the era. They dominate so completely, one can forgive Westerners for imagining the Soviet thirties as one vast gray prison camp, its numbed inhabitants cogs in the machinery of the State that promoted itself solely through murder, torture, and denunciation. This vision, however, doesn't convey the totalizing scope of the Stalinist civilization. A hypnotic popular culture, the State's buoyant consumer goods drive, and a never-ending barrage of public celebrations – all stoked a mesmerizing sense of building a Radiant Future en masse.

Those who didn't perish or disappear into the gulags were often swallowed up in the spectacle of totalitarian joy. Milan Kundera describes it as 'collective lyrical delirium.' Visiting Russia in 1936, André Gide couldn't stop marveling at the children he saw, 'radiant with health and happiness,' and the 'joyous ardor' of park-goers.

When I think of the Stalinist State, which I knew only as a banished ghost, these are the images that come to my mind: Nadezhda Mandelstam's description of her husband, the poet Osip Mandelstam, being led away to the sounds of a Hawaiian guitar in a neighbor's apartment. Anna Akhmatova's unbearably tragic poem 'Requiem' (dedicated to the victims of purges) juxtaposed with the indomitable cheer of Volga-Volga, an infectiously kitsch celluloid musical comedy of the time. Alexander Solzhenitsyn's account of the voronki (black Mariahs), prison transports disguised as brightly painted comestibles trucks, their sides eventually featuring ads for Sovetskoye brand champagne with a laughing girl.

The frenzy of industrialization of the first Five-Year Plan (1928–32) had bulldozed and gang-marched a rural society into something resembling modernity – even as officials suppressed details of the millions of deaths from famines brought on by collectivization. In 1931, more than four million peasant refugees flooded the overwhelmed cities. The state needed something to show for all the upheavals. And so in 1935 Stalin uttered one of his most famous pronouncements.

'Life has gotten better, comrades, life has gotten more cheerful,' he declared at the first conference of Stakhanovites, those celebrated over-fulfillers of socialist labor quotas, whose new movement emulated the uber-miner Alexei Stakhanov, famed for hewing 102 tons of coal in *one* workshift. 'And when life is happier, work is more effective,' Stalin added.

After the speech, reported one participant, the Leader of Progressive Mankind joined all in a song from the wildly popular screen farce *Jolly Fellows,* released weeks after Kirov's murder. The Genius of Humanity liked music, and occasionally even edited song lyrics himself. He had personally instigated Soviet movie musical comedy by expounding to director Grigory Alexandrov – former assistant to Sergei Eisenstein in Hollywood – on the need for fun and cheer in the arts. The melodies and mirth that exploded onto Soviet screens in the late thirties were the socialist realist answer to Hollywood's dream factory. Instead of Astaire and Rogers, dashing shepherds burst into song and gutsy girl weavers achieved fairy-tale Stakhanovite apotheoses. 'Better than a month's vacation,' pronounced Stalin after seeing *Jolly Fellows,* which was Alexandrov's jazzy, madcap debut. The Leader saw the director's 1938 musical *Volga-Volga* more than a hundred times. Never mind that the main cameraman had been arrested during filming and executed, and the screenwriter had written the lines in exile.

Quoted on posters and in the press and, of course, set to music, Stalin's 'life is happier' mantra established the tonality for the second half of the decade. It was more than just talk. In a fairly drastic redrawing of Bolshevik values, the State ditched the utopian asceticism of the twenties and encouraged a communist version of bourgeois life. The Radiant Future was arriving, citizens were told. Material rewards – offered for outstanding productivity and political loyalty – were the palpable proof. Promises of prosperity and abundance invaded public discourse so thoroughly, they shimmered like magical incantations in the collective psyche. Stakhanovite superworkers boasted in the pages of *Pravda* and *Izvestia* about how many rubles they earned. They stood beaming beside their new furniture sets and gramophones – rewards for 'joyous socialist labor.' Anything capitalism could do for hardworking folk, went the message, socialism could do better – and happier.

The masses even got to pop a cork on occasion. Scant years after the paroxysms of the first Five-Year Plan, Stalin turned his thoughts to reviving Russia's fledgling, prerevolutionary champagne industry, centered by the Black Sea near the Crimea. Sovetskoye Shampanskoye became a frothy emblem of Stalin's directive, in his words 'an important sign . . . of the good life.' Garbo's Ninotchka may have cooed about only knowing bubbly from newsreels. But by the thirties' end Soviet fizzy, mass-produced in pressurized reservoir vats, would be embraced by the Soviet common man. It could even be found on tap in stores.

Alongside abundance and prosperity, the third pillar of Stalin's new cultural edifice was *kulturnost'* (culturedness). Hence, Soviet citizens – many of them formerly illiterate – were exhorted to civilize themselves. From table manners to tangos, from perfume to Pushkin, from tasseled lampshades to *Swan Lake*, the activities and mores reviled by the earlier Bolsheviks as bourgeois contamination were embraced as part of the new *Homo sovieticus*. If a member of the *nomenklatura* (Communist political elite) showed up at a meeting in his trophy silk pajamas and carrying a chocolate bar, it just went to show that socialism was doing swell. The teetotaler Vyacheslav Molotov, the Soviet premier, took tango lessons. His imperious wife, Polina Zhemchuzhina, delivered perfume to the masses in her role as chairman of the cosmetics trust. The food supply commissariat established and codified a Soviet cuisine canon.

Russia's annus horribilus of 1937, which closed with the carnivalesque December election festivities, was launched with a lavish New Year's Day *yolka* (fir tree) party for kids at the Kremlin. The tubby comedian Mikhail Garkavi played Ded Moroz (Grandfather Frost), the Russian answer to Santa. Banned by the Bolsheviks for ten years as religious obscurantism, New Year's fetes – and fir trees – had just returned from the political cold with the Great Leader's approval, at the initiative of one Pavel Postyshev. This man whom Soviet children could thank for their new winter gaiety was also one of the chief engineers of the Ukrainian famine; he himself would be shot a year later. Still wearing his long, flowing Ded Moroz robe and white beard, Garkavi appeared later that New Year's Day at a Stakhanovite ball attended by Stalin. 'All are strictly cautioned to leave their sadness outside,' joshed a placard inside the ballroom. Garkavi popped a cork of Sovetskoye Shampanskoye. The tradition is still going strong to this day, even if the brand is being eclipsed by Dom Perignon.

When Mom was five and Yulia was four they moved to Moscow. It was 1939. The country was celebrating Stalin's sixtieth birthday, and Naum his promotion – to the 'Capital of the New World,' to Headquarters.

Mom still had her bouts of *toska*, but life did get a bit better in Moscow. A little jollier, you could say.

For one thing, Moscow wasn't dark. Their ninth-floor apartment boasted an airy panorama of shingled old city roofs from the window. It was still a communal apartment, to be shared with shrill, dumpling-like Dora and her henpecked husband. But it had new plywood furniture, and it had gas – gas! – in place of their Leningrad *burzhuíka* (bourgeois) coal-burning stove, which always ran out of fuel by morning, leaving a veil of frost on the walls.

Best of all was the building itself. Constructed the year before in the fashionable Stalinist Empire style – a bulky mash-up of deco and neoclassical – it resembled an organ, or perhaps musical staves, its vertical lines zooming up from an imposing ground-floor loggia. The musical reference was not accidental. Neither were the extra-thick walls (such a boon in this era of eavesdropping). The house was created as a co-op for the Union of Soviet Composers, with a small quota of apartments for the military. Songs poured out of the open windows the summer Mother moved in.

I always get goose bumps thinking of my five-year-old mom living among the George Gershwins and Irving Berlins of the socialist order. They were the people whose buoyant, jubilant marches I still sing in the shower. Along with generations of Russians, I've got them under my skin – which of course was the plan. 'Mass song' was a vital tool in molding the new Soviet consciousness. Song set the romantic-heroic tone of the era. Song fused individual with *kollektiv*, comrade with State. It carried the spirit of sunny, victorious optimism into every choking communal apartment, glorifying labor, entrenching ideology – all in catchy tunes you couldn't stop humming.

Mom didn't actually share the collective zest for mass song. But there was no escaping the iron grip of Ninka, her new best chum in the building. Daughter of a Jewish symphonist and an Armenian pianist, brash and imperious Ninka had raven-black eyebrows and fingertips callused from violin lessons. She appointed herself Mom's musical instructor.

'*We're eternally warmed … by the sun-ny Stalinist glor-y!*' C'mon, haven't you memorized the words yet?' she'd demand.

'*Reason gave us steel wings for arms,*' she'd continue, trying another popular tune, wincing at Mom's off-key attempts to keep up. '*And a fiery motor instead of a heart.*'

'People had mechanical parts in their bodies?' asked Mom.

'The song celebrates Stalin's Falcons!'

'What are Stalin's Falcons?'

'Our Soviet Aviators – clueless dimwit!'

In good weather Ninka conducted her tutorials on the building fire escape. 'Ooh . . . the brothers Pokrass!' she'd swoon, pointing at two men passing below, one lanky, the other plump and short, both with big frizzy hair that sat like hats on their heads. Didn't Mom know their song 'The Three Tankmen'? From the film *Tractor Drivers*? Mom couldn't admit to Ninka she hadn't yet seen real *kino*. With perfect pitch (she did truly have a golden ear), Ninka chanted another 'very important' Pokrass work. '*Bustling! Mighty! Invincible!* My country. My Moscow. You *are my true beloved!*' In my own childhood this was the song Mom always turned off when it played on the radio. The radio played it a lot.

Ninka's musical bullying was tiresome. But at least now Mom could sing along at the parades Naum zealously attended whenever he returned to Moscow from his mysterious, vaguely explained absences. The parades . . . well, they were deafening, overwhelming. And what of all those small kids perched on their dads' shoulders, shouting, 'Look, *papochka*, what a scary mustache!' when they saw Comrade Stalin? Eyes stark with fear, papa would clap a big, unclean hand over his kid's mouth. Naum never had to muzzle Larisa or Yulia. He was dashing and funny, his squarish nails were immaculate, and he had a privileged view of the Leadership's podium from his special Red Square parade bench. 'Comrade – are you Stalin's Falcon?' Mom would ask in a small, polite voice whenever an aviator she'd recognize from newspaper photos shook Naum's hand.

And so it went. May Day. Constitution Day. Revolution

Day. Thunderous welcomes for aviators and polar explorers. Citizens marched; their children sucked sticky ruby-red Kremlin Star lollipops. Meanwhile, just outside the city, on one busy day alone in 1938, 562 'enemies of the people' were shot and dumped in trenches by the NKVD, the secret police, at its Butovo firing range. There were many thousands more. The German historian Karl Schlögel sums up the atmosphere of the times in his description of Red Square. 'Everything converges: a ticker-tape parade and a plebiscite on killing, the atmosphere of a folk festival and the thirst for revenge, a rollicking carnival and orgies of hate. Red Square . . . at once fairground and gallows.'

I was born in Moscow. The seventies capital of my childhood seemed as familiar and comforting to me as a pair of old slippers. Mother's anti-Soviet zeal assured I never trooped in a single parade in my life, never once peered at Lenin's cosmeticized corpse at his Red Square mausoleum.

But often I lie awake nights imagining Mom, a tiny, reluctantly choral protagonist in the mythology of high Stalinist Moscow. The city of her childhood was engulfed in newcomers – from the upwardly mobile *nomenklatura* like Naum to dispossessed victims of collectivization fleeing the countryside. Pharaonic construction works boomed nonstop. Avenues became behemoths ten lanes wide, historic churches were turned to rubble, from vast pits rose socialist public magnificences. '*Bustling. Mighty. Invincible.*' How overwhelming the 'Heart of the Socialist Homeland' must have seemed to an alienated, sad child.

Sometimes I picture Mom clutching Liza's hand on the escalator sinking 130 feet below ground into the electrified blaze of the palatial, newly built Moscow Metro. What did Larisa make of the lofty stained glass and acres of steel and colored granite – of more marble than had been used by all the czars? Did her neck hurt from gazing up at the Mayakovskaya station's soaring subterranean cupolas, with their mosaics of parachutists and gymnasts and Red Army planes pirouetting against baroque blue skies? Were they really so nightmarish, those eighty-two life-size bronze statues half crouching under the rhythmic arches of the Revolution Square station? Didn't they produce in Mom the stunned awe of a medieval child at Chartres?

Looking back, ever-dissident Mom wavers about the metro, one minute gushing, the next bashing it as vile propaganda.

But about the All-Union Agricultural Exhibition she is unequivocal.

'In September 1939, at six years of age,' she says, 'I saw earthly paradise!'

On a crisp autumn morning in the northern part of Moscow, young Larisa and her family strolled into Eden through monumental entry arches crowned by Vera Mukhina's triumphant sculpture *The Worker and the Kolkhoz Woman*. They passed into a wide alley of dancing fountains and on toward an eighty-foot statue of Stalin. Stakhanovite growers told them tales of their achievements in the Sugarbeet Pavilion. At the marbled courtyard of the star-shaped Uzbekistan Pavilion, dark, round-faced women with myriad braids flowing from their embroidered skullcaps dispensed green tea and puffy round breads. Uzbeks, Tajiks, Tatars! Never had Mother suspected that such a riot of physiognomies and ethnic costumes existed.

Designed as a microcosm of the Soviet Empire's glories, the Exhibition's sprawling six hundred acres showcased exotic USSR republics and feats in practically every agricultural realm from dairy farming to rabbit breeding. The republics' pavilions were fabulously decorated in 'native' styles – 'national in form, socialist in content,' as Stalin, Father of All Nations, prescribed. Inside Armenia's pink limestone edifice Mom rushed over to a giant aquarium where mountain trout nosed and flitted. At Georgia's Orientalist headquarters, she and Yulia brazenly grabbed at tangerines on a low branch in a subtropical garden where persimmon trees flowered and palms swayed. Soon it all became one dazzling blur. Model socialist hen eggs. Pink prizewinning pigs. Everything more beautiful, more 'real' than life. The mini-fields sprouted perfect rye, wheat, and barley. Mom recalled her bullying pal Ninka's favorite song: 'We were born to turn fairy tale into reality.' A very true song, thought Mom, tonguing the chocolate shell off her Eskimo pie as they toured the mini-kolkhoz replete with a culture club and a maternity ward.

My poor dissident mother: in moments of candor she admits to this day that her vision of ideal love is walking arm in arm amid the splendiferous gardens of the Georgia Pavilion. But what inflamed her imagination the most was the food. If she closes her eyes, she claims to smell the musky striped *adjui* melons at the Uzbek Pavilion; taste the crunch of red Kazakh apples that were sometimes the size of those Uzbek melons – thank you, Grandpa Michurin, the Soviet miracle plant breeder whose motto was 'We cannot wait for favors from Nature; our task is to take them from her.'

It was as if my mother had discovered a world beyond the universe of parades and blaring loudspeakers and institutional smells. The discovery sparked a fascination with food that has animated her all her life.

'Finish your bouillon. Have another kotleta.' Liza's admonitions now sounded inviting, caressing. They whispered to Mom of a different, far more intimate happiness than Comrade Stalin's collective ideals. And when Naum was at the table, life seemed particularly cheerful. With him there, Liza reached with special abandon into the box hung outside their window – Stalin-era refrigeration – for their *nomenklatura* food parcels wrapped in blue paper.

Out came a rosy bologna called Doctor's Kolbasa. Or sosiski, Mom's favorite frankfurters. Boiled taut, they squirted salty juice into your mouth when you bit into them, and they tasted particularly good with sweet gray-green peas from a can. Stores didn't usually carry those cans. For them Mom and Liza had to trudge to an unmarked depot guarded by an unsmiling man. Naum was 'attached' to such a depot store – as were many Moscow bigwigs. The babushka working the lift, on the other hand, wasn't attached. Mom could tell this from her sad lunch of rotten-smelling boiled eggs sprinkled with salt she kept in little foldings of *Pravda*.

When visitors came, Liza made fish suspended in glistening aspic and canapes with frilly mayonnaise borders. The guests – men in dressy naval suits, women with bright red lips – brought with them the crisp fall air and candies with names like Happy Childhood and Soviet North Pole. A momentous event was the gift of a dinner service with golden borders around tiny pink flowers, replacing their mismatched chipped plates and cups. The same high-ranking naval officer who brought the service gave Liza a book.

The Book of Tasty and Healthy Food was hefty, with a somber parsley-green cover. Opening it, Mom gasped at the trove of fantastical photos . . . of tables crowded with silver and crystal, of platters of beef decorated with tomato rosettes, of boxes of chocolates and wedges of frilly cake posed amid elaborate tea sets. The images roused the same euphoria Mom had felt at the agricultural exhibition. They conjured up *skatert' samobranka*, an enchanted tablecloth from a Russian folk fairy tale that covered itself with food at the snap of a finger. Mom thought again about Ninka's song. Liza could even turn this fairy tale into reality, it seemed. She said the book contained recipes, and the dinner sets pictured were identical to the new one they'd been given.

Fish. Juices. *Konservi* (conserves). One day Mom shocked Liza by announcing that she could now read the words in the book. And the book, and the labels of the packaged foods in their house – many of these delicious things often contained an exotic word: *Mi-ko-yan*. Was it a kind of *sosiski*? Or perhaps *kotleti* – not the uninspired homemade meat patties, but the trim store-bought ones that fried up to a fabulous greasy crunch. 'Mi-ko-yan,' said Mom to herself when Liza was cooking a dinner for guests, and scrupulously comparing her table setting to the photographs in the parsley-green book. In those moments life seemed good to my mother. Yes, entirely good.

Mikoyan – first name Anastas, patronymic Ivanovich – was a petite Bolshevik from Armenia with a hawk nose angling over a mustache trimmer and more dapper than that of his fellow son of the Caucasus, Stalin. His gait was quick and determined, his gaze unsettlingly sharp. But petitioners in his office would on occasion be offered an orange. Fellow Kremlinites also knew that Anastas Ivanovich grew an exotic, some might say extravagant vegetable called asparagus at his dacha. Anastas Mikoyan was the *narkom* (people's commissar) of the Soviet food industry. If writers were 'engineers of the human soul' (per Comrade Stalin), then Mikoyan was the engineer of the Soviet palate and gullet.

Three years before Mom got hooked on sosiski made by the Mikoyan Meat Processing Plant and opened the green cookbook he'd sponsored, the *narkom* had his suitcases packed for a Crimean vacation. It was a holiday he'd long promised his wife, Ashkhen, and their five sons. He dropped by the Kremlin to say goodbye to his boss and old comrade, whom he addressed with ty, the familiar intimate form of 'you.'

'Why don't you go instead to America,' Stalin proposed unexpectedly. 'It, too, will be a pleasant vacation; besides, we need to research the American food industry. The best of what you discover,' he declared, 'we'll transplant here.'

Mikoyan gauged the Supreme Leader's mood: the proposal was impromptu but serious. Even so, he demurred: 'I've promised Ashkhen a holiday.' Mikoyan was famously family-minded.

Stalin must have been in good spirits.

'Take Ashkhen with you,' he suggested.

Who knows how Soviet food would have tasted had Stalin not allowed the *narkom*'s wife to join her husband. Had the Mikoyans sunned themselves on the Black Sea instead.

One wonders too how the Armenian managed for so long to retain Stalin's favor while other Politburo members were 'liquidated' or saw their wives off to the gulags. 'Anastas seems more interested in cheese varieties than in Marxism and Leninism,' Stalin would quip without reproach. Perhaps this escape into the world of sosiski, kolbasa, and condensed milk was Mikoyan's secret of survival. Formerly ascetic in the old Bolshevik manner, Stalin by now was developing quite a palate himself.

Mikoyan and his foodie squad landed in New York on the SS *Normandie* on a sweltering August morning in 1936. In their stopover in Germany they had drawn giggles with their identical new 'European-style' outfits. For two months the Soviet expedition covered 12,000 miles of America by car and train, coast to coast. They toured fish, ice cream, and frozen fruit plants. They inspected production of mayonnaise, beer, and 'inflated seeds' (Mikoyan-speak for popcorn). They studied corrugated cardboard and metal jar lids. Wisconsin dairies, Chicago slaughterhouses, California fruit farms – not exactly the holiday Ashkhen had been promised. They ate intently at self-service cafeterias. ('Here,' noted Mikoyan, 'was a format born out of the bowels of capitalism but most suited to communism.') They studied Macy's display strategies – models for the trend-setting department stores that would emerge in Moscow by the end of the decade.

In Detroit, Henry Ford told Mikoyan not to waste time

on meat production. 'Meat's bad for you,' he insisted. Soviet workers should eat vegetables, soy products, and fruit. The Armenian *narkom* found Ford most peculiar.

Urbane but unsmiling, Mikoyan could barely restrain himself in his rather dull late-life memoirs from gushing about the wonders of his American trip. Here was the efficient industrialized society for Stalinist Russia to emulate. Was it flash freezing or mechanized cow milking (take *that*, Stakhanovite milkmaids) that impressed him more? Maybe the fruit juices? True, Russia didn't have enough oranges, but Mikoyan dreamed of turning tomato juice into a Soviet national drink. (Mission accomplished: in my school days I gagged on the red stuff.) The ever-practical *narkom* showed no ideological qualms about adopting techniques and mass standardization from the capitalist West. These were the internationalist Soviet thirties, before World War II unleashed Stalinist xenophobia. Unlike evil, devious Britain, the United States was considered a semifriendly competitor – though having American relatives could still land you in the gulag.

Perhaps what struck Mikoyan most was the American guy at a stainless-steel griddle who swiftly cooked a curious-looking kotleta, which he inserted into a split white bun, then flourished with pickles and dabs of red sauce. 'For a busy man it is very convenient,' marveled Mikoyan. Didn't Soviet workers deserve this efficient, cheap, filling snack on their parades, their outings to Parks of Culture and Relaxation?

Mikoyan plunked down Stalin-approved scarce hard currency for twenty-two American hamburger grills, with the capacity to turn out two million orders a day. Burger production launched in select major cities, to some acclaim. But World War II intervened; the bun got lost in the shuffle. Soviet food planning settled instead for a take-out kotleta, unsandwiched.

'So that's it?' I gasped, reading Mikoyan's memoirs.

'So that's it?' gasped Mother when I passed her the book.

Our mythic all-Soviet store-bought kotleta – the lump-in-the-throat nostalgic treat from five generations of childhoods. *That's* what it was? An ersatz burger that mislaid its bun? Mikoyan's account of the origins of Soviet ice cream further wounded what was left of my food patriotism. *Morozhennoye* – our national pride? The hard-as-rock *plombir* with its seductive cream rosette I licked at thirty below zero? The Eskimos on a stick from Mom's childhood outings? Yup, all the result of Yankee technology, imported by Mikoyan. The savvy Armenian even coveted Coca-Cola but couldn't wangle the syrup recipe. As for sosiski and kolbasa, those other ur-Soviet food icons . . . they were German sausages that, in Mikoyan's words, 'changed their citizenship.' So much for our ideologically charged native madeleines.

Mikoyan returned from America loaded with samples, information, and brand-new wardrobes for himself and his wife. The Mickey Mouse pens he carried home for his sons were promptly stolen at the boys' school for Politburo offspring.

Given Russia's still rudimentary consumer conditions, the *narkom* was able to introduce a surprising number of American novelties – from mass-produced ice cream (hitherto made by hand) to *kornfleks* to the concept of prepackaged foods. A 1937 newspaper ad even urged Soviets to embrace a 'spicy aromatic condiment' that 'every American housewife keeps in her cupboard.' Ketchup! Occasionally Stalin objected. Russian winters were long, he said, and there was no need to produce the GE-style home fridges that Mikoyan wanted. What's more, heavy-industry factories were preoccupied with defense orders. So until the end of the war Soviets made do with a box outside the window.

Stalin took great personal interest in Mikoyan's business. The Leader took great personal interest in many things. When he wasn't busy signing execution orders or censoring books or screening *Volga-Volga*, the Standardbearer of Communism opined on fish ('Why don't we sell live fish like they did in the old days?') or Soviet champagne. A fan of sweet bubbles, he wanted to ban brut production whole-sale, but here Mikoyan held firm. Suds? Indeed. Mikoyan recalls how with his bloodthirsty henchmen Molotov and Kaganovich, Stalin fingered, sniffed, and critiqued trial soap bars, deciding which should go into production. 'Our comrade Stalin has a boundless resource of wisdom,' gushed Mikoyan of the soap venture. Clearly, the bathing habits of Homo sovieticus were a matter of great national concern.

An obsessive micromanager himself, Mikoyan taste-tested each new food product, approved all recipes and label designs, okayed punishments for wreckers and saboteurs. Stalin's directive for happiness, abundance, and cheer loomed large. 'Since life has gotten better,' wrote Mikoyan in a report, 'we need to produce more aromatic high-quality cigarettes.' In a speech: 'What kind of cheerful life can we have if there's a shortage of beer and liqueurs?' Period food industry trade magazines portray their workers practically agog with joy and enthusiasm. Inspired by Stalin's credo, they'd even staged an amateur theater pro-duction called *Abundance*, featuring singing sausages. One of the comrades playing a sausage recalled using the Stanislavsky method to interpret her role.

Or picture this. May Day. The Mikoyan Meat Plant procession parades toward Red Square under the portrait of the mustachioed Armenian and a festive panel of children with flowers beneath the slogan THANK YOU COMRADE STALIN FOR OUR HAPPY CHILDHOODS. Banners em-blazoned with sosiski, kolbasa, and bacon wave alongside – emblems of Soviet-issue smoked goodness.

One pauses at the grotesquery of such scenes in this most murderous decade of a political regime in which abundance would remain a myth for another half-century. For those not attached to privileged stores – in the thirties and later – shortages of basic essentials were the grinding reality. And yet – Mom's elderly friends remember equally vividly the prewar chocolates and champagne, the caviar and smoked fish magically materializing in stores before holidays.

In 1937 Mikoyan's favorite Red October Chocolate Factory produced more than five hundred kinds of confections, his meat plant close to 150 kinds of sausages. True, these were mainly available at flagship stores in larger cities. (Moscow, with 2 percent of the population, got 40 percent of the country's meat allocation.) True, basics were often neglected in favor of luxury items; the champagne, chocolates, and smoked sturgeon all served as shining political symbols, furthering the illusion that czarist indulgences were now accessible to the masses. And yet in his push to create a socialist consumer culture – based on

Western models, ironically – and to democratize certain foodstuffs, Mikoyan delivered moments of happiness to the common folk. A pink slice of kolbasa on a slab of dark bread, Eskimo on a stick at a fair – in the era of terror these small tokens had an existential savor.

On Stalin's death in 1953, the secret police chief Beria was executed and Molotov was effectively exiled to outer Mongolia. But Mikoyan prospered. His ability to side with winners matched his uncanny managerial skills. He backed Stalin against Trotsky, then denounced Stalin's legacy and rose to the lofty post of Supreme Soviet chairman under Khrushchev. He voted for Khrushchev's ouster and retained Brezhnev's favor, tactfully retiring in 1965. Thirteen years later, he died of old age.

A jingle summed up his career: 'From Ilyich to Ilyich [Lenin's and Brezhnev's shared patronymic] without *infarkt* [heart attack] and *paralich* [stroke].'

More resilient still were his kolbasa and sosiski. Just like my mother, when I was growing up I thought Mikoyan was the brand name of a kotleta. To our minds he was the Red Aunt Jemima or Chef Boyardee. The Mikoyan meat plant remains operational. These days it produces actual hamburgers.

In the seventies, when Soviet Jews began emigrating, many packed Mikoyan's hefty cookbook in their paltry forty-pound baggage. *The Book of Tasty and Healthy Food* had become a totalitarian *Joy of Cooking* – a kitchen bible so cherished, people lugged it with them even as they fled the State that published it. But the book didn't keep its original parsley-green cover for long. Its color – physical and political – kept changing with each new regime and edition: a dozen editions in all, more than eight million copies in print, and still selling. Most iconic and politicized is the 1952 version, which I will revisit later.

Mom, though, left her copy behind. The tattered volume that had taught her and her mother good socialist house-keeping was by then ideologically radioactive to her. She even despised the gaudy photos with the Soviet food industry logos meant to drive home the idea that the State was our sole provider.

In the fall of 2010, I presented my mother with an original 1939 edition of Mikoyan's masterwork. She flinched. Then she fell for it – hard. 'Drab, dreary recipes,' she'd grumble while cooking up a storm from the book and matching her table settings in Queens to the ones in the photos as her mother had done in Moscow seventy years before. She piped mayonnaise borders onto 'Stalinist-Baroque' crab salads. She carved tomato rosettes, trapped fish in aspic, and fashioned kotleti from meat, carrots, cabbage, and beets. Every night she telephoned friends, roaring at the book's introduction, its vaunting invocations of 'man-kind's centuries-old dream of building a communist society . . . of an abundant, happy, and joyous life.'

'I'm *not* nostalgic!' she would correct me. 'I just like old cookbooks, and this one, wow, a real antique!'

Then: 'Anyuta, what do they call that syndrome . . . when victims fall for their tormentors?'

Followed by: '*You* dragged me into this!'

Finally: 'So what, I like *all* foods.'

But never an admission of sentiment.

* * *

One blustery Saturday night Mom's elderly friends gather for a thirties-style dinner around her table set with ornamental cut-crystal bowls and bottles of sickly sweet Sovetskoye Shampanskoye.

At first, the ladies recall their Stalinist childhoods with the guarded detachment of people who've long entombed their pasts. But with each new toast, fragments of horror and happiness tumble out, intermingled. They talk of the period's dread silence, the morbid paralysis of families of the newly arrested, and in the same breath they remember the noise.

'Living in the thirties was like being inside a giant metal forge,' says Inna. 'Incessant drumbeats and songs, street loudspeakers, radios blasting behind every door.'

'It was feast in a time of plague,' declares another friend, Lena, quoting the title of Pushkin's play. 'You were happy each new day you weren't arrested. Happy to simply smell tangerines in your house!'

'My father had murdered Kirov,' announces Musya, an octogenarian former Leningrader, in a clear, spirited voice. 'I was convinced of this as a child. Why else would he and my uncle silently pass notes to each other at dinner?'

Did she think of denouncing him? asks Inna.

Musya vehemently shakes her head. 'We Leningraders hated Stalin!' she retorts. 'Before anyone else in the country, *we knew*.' When Musya's uncle was arrested, men in long coats showed up and confiscated her family's furniture. Sometime afterward Musya recognized their chairs and sideboard at a secondhand shop. She jumped with joy, hugging and stroking the plush blue upholstery. Her mother just yanked her away. 'I lost my innocence at that moment,' says Musya.

'I remained innocent – I knew nothing until Stalin died,' Katya confesses. A vivacious former translator near ninety who still smokes and swears like a sailor, Katya grew up – 'a true Soviet child' – in provincial Ukraine. Happiness to her meant the clean, toasty smell in the house when her mom ironed the pleats on her parade skirts. And singing along with the crowds.

'I too knew nothing about Stalin's crimes,' Inna puts in ever so quietly, nervously stroking her immaculate chignon. 'But I hated him for taking my mother away.' What she means is that her fanatical mother devoted her every breath to the Party. 'On the day she noticed me, hugged me, and promised to mend my socks, I went to bed the most euphoric child on the planet,' Inna tells us. Her mother never did mend the socks. When she was forced to relinquish her Party ID card because Inna was emigrating, 'she howled like an animal.'

The ladies finish their champagne and Mom's Soviet-style truffles and prepare to depart. 'Living under Stalin,' Inna reflects at the door, 'we censored our thoughts, terrified when anything bad crossed our minds. Then when he died, we kept on censoring, purging any traces of happiness from our childhoods.' Everyone nods.

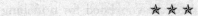

The autumn cold of 1939 ended Mom's fire escape music lessons. She and her pal Ninka found a different occupation: helping older kids in the building chase spies. All children in paranoid Russia played at chasing spies. Anyone could be a suspect. The lift lady, for instance, with her single odd metal coat button. Comrades wearing glasses, or fedora hats instead of proletarian caps.

Along twisting lanes, through dim *podvorotni* (deep archways), into silent, half-hidden courtyards – Mom and the gang pursued would-be evil betrayers of *Rodina* (Homeland). Mom liked the *podvorotni*. They smelled, not unpleasantly, of piss and decaying fall leaves. Under one of them a babushka in a tatty beret stood hawking an old doll. Forty whole rubles she was asking. Unlike the usual bald, grinning Soviet toy babies, this doll had flaxen hair, a frayed velvet dress, and melancholy eyes out of a tragic Hans Christian Andersen tale. In late November Naum relented; at home Mom inhaled the doll's musty mystery. The next morning Naum went away on a trip.

December brought soft, flaky snowfalls, the resinous aroma of fir trees, and invasions of gruff out-of-towners in stores. New Year's festivities were still new to Soviets. Some simply hung their trees with walnuts in tinfoil; Liza propped a bright Kremlin star on top of their tree and bought presents for Larisa and Yulia. Mom only wanted things for her doll. There was no news from Naum, and Liza's face had assumed a grim, absent expression. Silently she stood in lines for toy washboards and miniature versions of the dinner sets depicted in Mikoyan's parsley-green cookbook.

Every day Mom consulted the cookbook for dollhouse

decoration. Every day Liza perused its pages, churning out panfuls of kotleti and trays of cottage cheese *korzhiki* (biscuits). Uncharacteristically, she baked elaborate dried apricot pies – listening intently to the rattle of the approaching elevator. But it was usually Dora or the composers next door. Ninka and the Pokrass children ate most of the pies – their cheerful chewing filling Mom's heart with *toska*.

For New Year's Eve Liza draped a brand-new tablecloth over the table. It was deep red like a theater curtain, as plush as a teddy bear's cheek. Naum didn't come home to admire it. The Sovetskoye champagne stood unopened as fireworks exploded above the Kremlin clock.

'*Nichevo, mozhet nichevo.*' (Nothing, maybe it's nothing.) Their neighbor Dora had been whispering this lately to Liza while Mom hid under the table chewing on the tablecloth tassels.

'*Nichevo, nichevo,*' Mom whispered to her doll, licking tears off her face. The doll's eyes said that she understood everything: the worm of despair in Mom's stomach, the mystery of her father's absence, her gnawing suspicion that the Radiant Future was passing them by. Stroking and braiding the doll's flaxen hair, Mom desperately wanted at least to make her silent friend's life happy, abundant, and cheerful. She had an inspiration. With Liza out of sight, she reached for her scissors. The first piece of tablecloth she cut off didn't fit, so she kept cutting more: for the doll's tablecloth, for her toy bedspread. When Mom was done the doll's house was draped in red velvet, golden tassels lining its floor.

Seeing Mom's handiwork, Liza flailed a dishrag at her, but without her usual vigor. That day, and for days after, she kept looking for the key to Naum's desk. She was trying to decide if now was the time to read Larisa and Yulia the letter he had written and locked in a drawer. The letter that urged his children to love him, love their mother, and love their *Rodina* – no matter what might suddenly have happened to him.

CHAPTER FOUR

✶

1940s: OF BULLETS AND BREAD

On the weekend of June 21, 1941, in honor of the official arrival of summer, Liza finally switched from listless hot winter borscht to the chilled summer version. Tangy and sweet, the soup was alive with the crunch and vitality of the season's first cucumbers and radishes. Following a short cold spell, Saturday's weather was heartbreakingly lovely. Sun beamed on the lipstick-red tulips and dressy white lilies at the Pushkin Square flower beds; petunias scented the Boulevard Ring. Girls in their light graduation dresses floated past couples embracing on the Moskva River embankment. Summer plans, stolen kisses, blue and white cans of Mikoyan's condensed milk packed for the dacha. Even the babushkas who hawked fizzy water with cherry syrup at parks somehow looked decades younger. The happiness in the air was palpable, stirring. Or so it seemed to my mother on her Saturday stroll with Yulia and their father.

Naum was back with them – for a brief while at least. Ever since his alarming disappearance in 1939, when Liza thought him arrested or dead, his absences had gotten more prolonged and frequent. One morning Liza sat on the narrow cot that Mom shared with Yulia and explained Papa's job.

'Soviet spy?' Mom squealed with glee.

'Nyet, nyet! *Razvedchik* (intelligence worker).'

That too sounded thrilling. To protect their dad's secrets from enemies of the people, Mom and Yulia took to stealthily eating his papers. They'd tear them into confetti, soak them in milk, and dutifully chew, handful by handful. This felt heroic – until Naum threw a fit after they swallowed his *sberkassa* (savings bank) documents.

The girls now learned to put the names of foreign countries to his absences; they learned where their presents were coming from. The Russo-Finnish war of that winter in 1940 – a hapless bloodbath that sent Russians home badly mauled but with a strategic chunk of the chilly Ladoga Lake – yielded Larisa and Yulia a festive tin box of Finnish butter cookies. Bright yellow neck scarves of fine flimsy cotton were the girls' trophies from the ugly Soviet occupation of Estonia in July of 1940. From Naum's intelligence missions in Stockholm came sky-blue princess coats with fur trim. Scandinavia and the Baltic were Naum's specialties. He never mentioned the ugliness.

There were six of them now sharing two communal rooms in the house of composers. Liza's widowed dad from Odessa was living with them, snoring in the living room where the girls slept. Dedushka Yankel was obliging and doleful. A retired old Jewish communist shock-worker (pre-Stakhanovite uberlaborer), he hated the Talmud and detested the Bible. Mom liked to tug at the wispy clumps of hair on his temples as he sat in the kitchen copying *The Short*

Course of the History of the All-Union Communist Party into his notebook over and over and over. He knew it by heart, Stalin's Party catechism.

Sashka, their new baby brother, was noisier. Liza had him in May while Naum was in Sweden, and her heart nearly broke in the maternity ward when she saw the nurse carry a huge bouquet of pink roses to some other lucky new *mamochka*. 'For you,' said the nurse, smiling. 'Look out the window.' Below, Naum waved and grinned. Since the baby was born he hadn't left Moscow.

Sashka wasn't crying and Dedushka wasn't snoring late on Saturday, June 21. Still, Mom couldn't sleep. Perhaps she was overexcited at the prospect of seeing the famous chimp Mickey at the Moscow Circus the next day. Or maybe it was the thunderstorm that broke the still, airless sky after ten. Waking up often from her uneasy slumber, Mom noticed Naum in the room, crouched by his Latvian VEF shortwave radio. The radio's flashing green light and the non-Russian voices – *Hello . . . Bee Bee See* – finally lulled my mother to sleep.

Naum had his ear to the radio, fists clenched. Damn VEF! Were it not for the sleeping girls he'd have smashed it to pieces. It was shortly after dawn on Sunday. A static-crackly foreign voice had announced what he and his superiors had been warning about for months with desperate near certainty. His small suitcase had been packed for a week. Why wasn't headquarters calling? Why did he have to crouch by the whining, buzzing radio for information when intelligence had been so overwhelming, when he himself had reported menacing activity at the new Soviet-Baltic border for more than a year? Top-level defense profession-als had been aghast at the TASS news agency statement of June 14, which dismissed as base rumor the possibility of attack by Russia's Non-Aggression Treaty cosigner – Nazi Germany. But the directive for the TASS pronouncement had come from the Vozhd (Leader) himself. Certain top commanders left for vacations; others went to the opera.

Meanwhile, early the previous evening, a small, somber group had gathered nervously in Stalin's Kremlin office. Among those present was Naum's uberboss, naval commissar Admiral Kuznetsov. He'd brought along Captain Mikhail Vorontsov, a longtime acquaintance of Granddad's (and his direct boss some months later). Vorontsov had just landed from Berlin, where he was Soviet naval attaché. Hitler would invade at any hour, he warned. Stalin had been hearing these kinds of detailed alarms for months. He rejected them with contempt, even fury. Tellingly, the meet-ing started without his new chief of military staff, General Georgy Zhukov.

The signs, however, were too ominous to dismiss. The Dictator was noticeably agitated. General Zhukov rang at around eight p.m. from the defense commissariat: a German defector had crossed the border to warn that the attack would start at dawn. After midnight he rang again: another defector said likewise. Stalin grudgingly allowed a High Alert to be issued – with the bewildering caution not to respond to German 'provocations.' He also ordered the latest defector shot as a disinformer.

At his dacha the Leader, an insomniac usually, must have slept deeply that night. Because Zhukov was kept waiting on the line for a full three minutes when he telephoned just after dawn.

'The Germans are bombing our cities!' Zhukov announced.

Heavy breathing on the other end of the line.

'Do you understand what I'm saying?' asked Zhukov.

Upon returning to the Kremlin, Stalin appeared subdued, even depressed, his pockmarked face haggard. Refusing to address the nation himself, he delegated it to Molotov, who was then foreign commissar and stuttered badly. Hitler's Operation Barbarossa, the largest invasion in the history of warfare, comprising more than three million German troops augmented by Axis forces, and ranging from the Baltic to the Black Sea, had been allowed to commence in effective surprise.

In the early light of June 22, lying in bed with her eyes half closed, Larisa saw her father pull her mother to his chest with a force she'd never witnessed before. The embrace – desperate, carnal – told her that the circus was off even before Naum's one-word announcement: *war*.

At midday they all stood among panicked crowds under the black, saucer-shaped public loudspeakers.

'Citizens of the Soviet Union! . . . Today, at four a.m. . . . German troops . . . have attacked our, um um, country . . . despite . . . a treaty of non-aggression . . .'

Mercifully, Comrade Molotov didn't stutter as much as usual. But his halting speech was that of a clerk struggling through an arcane document. 'Our cause is just. The enemy will be beaten,' concluded the world's worst public speaker.

'What does *perfidious* mean?' asked children all over

Moscow. What happened to Stalin? wondered their parents, joining the stampedes for salt and matches at stores.

At two p.m. that afternoon, amid the wrenching chaos of departures at the Leningradsky railway station, Mother couldn't help but admire Naum's spiffy gray civilian suit.

'Please, please, take off that hat!' Liza yelled, running after his train. 'It makes you look Jewish – the Germans will kill you.'

The Father of all Nations finally spoke on July 3.

'Comrades! Citizens! Brothers and sisters! I am addressing *you*, my friends!'

It was a moving speech. The brothers and sisters line went down in history as possibly the only time Stalin called out to Russians in such an ungodlike familial fashion. Stalin had been even less godlike in private, though that was not known until years after his death.

'Lenin left us a great legacy and we shitted it away,' the Vozhd had blurted dismally a few days before his speech, after a frantic session at the defense commissariat where the ruthless General Zhukov had fled the room sobbing.

Indeed. By the time Stalin spoke to the nation, the Germans had swept some four hundred miles into Soviet territory along three fronts. By late October they counted three million Russian POWs. The tidal roar of the Wehrmacht with its onrushing Panzer tanks, Luftwaffe overhead, and SS rear guard would not begin to be turned until Stalingrad, a year and a half away.

After Naum's departure, though, life in Moscow seemed to Mom almost normal. Except that it wasn't. People carried home masks resembling sinister elephant trunks. Women with red swollen eyes clutched the hands of their husbands and sons all the way to conscription points. Dedushka Yankel glued X-shaped strips of tape on the windows and covered them with dark curtains, as officially required. The wails of the air raid sirens awoke in Mom the familiar sensations of alarm and *toska*, but now with an edge of adrenaline. *Strakh* (fear) was more tolerable somehow than *toska*. Falling asleep fully clothed, a rucksack packed with water and food by her bed for the frantic run to the bomb shelter – it was terrifying and just a little bit thrilling.

In the dark, freshly plastered shelter beneath the house of composers, familiar faces were fewer with each air raid. Loudspeakers urged remaining Muscovites to evacuate. 'Nonsense,' Liza kept murmuring. 'Haven't they said the war's almost over? Why go?' Following one particularly long mid-August night on the concrete shelter floor, they came back to the house. Liza opened the curtains. Her hollow scream still rings in Mother's ears after seventy years.

The entire panorama of shingled Moscow roofs Mom so loved stood in flames in the gray morning light.

The telephone call came at seven a.m. The evacuation riverboat was leaving that day. Someone from Naum's head-quarters could collect them in a couple of hours.

Liza stood in the living room, lost. Scattered around her were the cotton parcels and pillowcases she'd been distractedly stuffing. She was five feet tall, as thin as a teenager at thirty-one years of age, still exhausted from childbirth, fragile and indecisive by nature.

Sergei's baritone jolted her out of her stupor. He was their driver. Everything ready? One glance at Liza's flimsy parcels sent him into a tornado of packing.

'Your winter coats. Where are they?'

'Winter? *Please*, the war will be over by then!'

'Whose clothes are these?'

'My husband's – but don't touch them. He doesn't need them – he's fighting.'

Sergei now swung open the *sunduk* in the hallway. It was a lightweight blue trunk that had once belonged to an aunt who'd fled long ago to America, where she ran a chicken farm. It still held her stuff. The smell of mothballs wafted into the air as Sergei wrenched out Aunt Clara's old petticoats and filled the blue *sunduk* with Naum's dandyish suits, his dazzling white shirts, and the ties he wore on his intelligence missions. Dedushka's old sheepskin coat. Liza's fuzzy Orenburg shawl. The girls' *valenki* boots. Done packing, Sergei picked up both girls at once and tickled them with his breath. He had a wide smile and honest Slavic blue eyes. He also had a raging case of TB he'd pass on to the children.

The building manager came to seal off the apartment per regulations. Approaching the riverboat station, Liza screamed: they'd forgotten little Sashka. Sergei raced back to the house while the family waited on board, sick with anxiety. Smiling broadly, Sergei made it back with the baby.

✫ ✫ ✫

'But is he lucky?' Napoleon famously asked when promoting a general.

The good fortune of Naum Solomonovich Frumkin, my grandfather, was the stuff of family lore. He was, in that regard, a Bonapartian whiz. 'Dedushka,' my older cousin Masha would plead, tugging at the three gold stars on his old uniform shoulder boards, 'tell how your car was bombed and you escaped without even a scratch!' Or she'd ask to hear about the time when he had been adrift in freezing waters, hanging on for life – to a mine. Which 'forgot' to explode!

Everyone's favorite was the day they finally came to arrest him. True to his luck, Naum was away, sick in the hospital. Oh, and the date was March 5, 1953. The day Stalin died. The beginning of the end of the repressions.

After joining the RKKA (Workers and Peasants Red Army) in 1921, Granddad went into intelligence in 1931. For the two prewar years he had a perilous job recruiting and coordinating agents abroad. Yet this international cloak-and-dagger – and later even the hazards of combat – seemed to Naum like afternoons in the park compared to the perils from within. Between 1937 and 1941, purges utterly ravaged the leadership of the Soviet military and in particular of GRU, its intelligence branch. GRU's director-ship became a blood-soaked revolving door; five of its chiefs were executed in the four years leading up to Hitler's attack. A domino effect then took down the heads of departments and branches, liquidating the top GRU cadres almost entirely.

In this harrowing, half-paralyzed environment, Naum in 1939 became a section head himself, supervising spies for the naval commissariat in Moscow. In a sense, my fortunate grandfather was a beneficiary of the *chistki* (cleansings), swiftly moving up the career ladder from fleet to fleet, fill-ing the empty desks of the purged. But he was also a target, his own arrest lurking outside every window. 'I developed eyes in the back of my head,' Naum the retired spy would tell anyone willing to listen. Tailed by the NKVD (secret police) almost continuously, he perfected the art of vanishing into courtyards, of jumping onto fast-moving trolleys. He knew the drill: training spies was part of his job. When the stress got to him, he fantasized about wheeling on his shadowers, demanding to their faces: 'Either arrest me or stop following me!'

My grandfather was a vain man. He esteemed his power to charm. To explain his improbable survival, he often mentioned an NKVD comrade called Georgadze, the officer in charge of signing arrest warrants for lieutenant colonels (each rank was assigned its own man, according to Naum). Apparently, this Georgadze fell under Granddad's spell at a gathering. Naum imagined Georgadze deliberately overlooked or 'misplaced' his arrest papers. Mainly, though, Granddad would shrug. *Gospozha udacha*, Lady Luck – she was quite charmed by him too.

Stalin's intelligence decimations had left the Red Army hierarchy 'without eyes and ears,' as one insider put it, on the eve of war. But here was the paradox: by June 22 the Vozhd had been flooded with ongoing, extremely precise details of the looming Nazi attack. A major font of these warnings – all scoffed at by Stalin – was someone whom Naum, the pro charmer, never could stop talking about.

Meet playboy Richard Sorge (code name Ramzai): philanderer, drunkard, and, in the words of John le Carré, 'the spy to end spies.' 'The most formidable spy in history,' agreed Ian Fleming. '*Unwiderstehliche*' (irresistible), marveled one of his main dupes, the German ambassador to Japan. With his cover as a Nazi journalist in Tokyo starting in 1933, the half-German, half-Russian Sorge and his ring of false-front cohorts steadily passed top-level Japanese and German secrets to GRU headquarters in Moscow. (Larisa particularly recalls Japan specialists as guests at their apartment in 1939 and 1940.) Incredibly, Sorge's detailed alarms about the exact onset of Operation Barbarossa, up to its very preceding hours, only roused Stalin's scorn. 'A shit,' the Vozhd dismissed him, according to one commentator, 'who has set himself up with some small factories and brothels in Japan.'

Stalin was even less cordial to another accurate warning, from code name Starshina at the Nazi Air Ministry less than a week before Hitler's onslaught. This 'source,' sneered the Great Strategist of the Revolution, signaling contempt with quotation marks, should be *sent to his fucking mother*.

Why the delusional ignorance, the vitriol? Stalin's rejection of the intelligence continues to foment countless theories among historians, both Western and Russian. But it deserves noting that Hitler orchestrated a disinformation campaign fine-tuned to Stalin's suspicions of capitalist Britain and Churchill, and to the Vozhd's faith that Germany would *never* attack during hostilities with England – the supposed German dread of a two-front war. In May 1941 Hitler even wrote a very nice personal letter to Stalin to calm his unease, pledging 'his word as a foreign leader.' He went so far as to ask Stalin not to give in to any border provocations by unruly Nazi generals! As Solzhenitsyn later suggested, the ogre of the Kremlin, who trusted no one, somehow trusted the monster of Berchtesgaden.

In his memoirs General Zhukov later sensationally (and rather improbably) asserted that the defense commissariat never saw the crucial bulletins Stalin received from Soviet foreign spies. As for Sorge, who had stayed away from Russia, fearing the purges, he was unmasked and arrested in Tokyo in the fall of 1941. The Japanese wanted to exchange him, but Stalin replied he'd never heard of him. Sorge was hanged in 1944, on the holiday of the October Revolution. He had the ultimate lousy luck: he depended on Stalin.

For his part, Naum always claimed that *he* saw Sorge's urgent alerts.

Still, this hardly prepared him for what was about to unfold in the north.

On the morning of June 22, when Grandma ran waving after his train, Naum was bound for Tallinn, the Estonian capital. The Baltic Fleet headquarters had moved there the previous summer after the USSR occupied the three Baltic states.

Like stranded ducks, the Baltic ports almost immediately began falling to the German onslaught.

By late August the Nazis were closing on Tallinn. The Baltic Fleet under Naum's old boss Admiral Tributs was ordered, frantically and at the last minute, to evacuate through the Gulf of Finland to Kronstadt near Leningrad, the fleet's former traditional base. Red Army units and civilians were packed aboard. Tallinn often gets called the Soviet Dunkirk. Except it was an all-out disaster – one of the gravest naval fiascos in warfare history. Despite being the fleet's intelligence chief, Naum supervised a ship's scuttling under shellfire to block Tallinn's harbor as the residue of Soviet smoke screens drifted murkily overhead. He was one of the last out. Some two hundred Russian vessels tried to run a 150-nautical-mile gauntlet through heavily mined waters, with no air protection against German and Finnish onslaughts. The result was apocalyptic. The waves resounded with explosions and Russian screams, with desperate choruses of 'The Internationale' and the gun flashes of suicides as ships sank. More than sixty Soviet vessels were lost, and at least 12,000 people drowned. Naum made it to Kronstadt with only four other survivors from his scuttling mission. His own luck had held, but he was badly shaken.

By fall, the juggernaut of Operation Barbarossa pounded at Leningrad's gates. On September 8, Shlisselburg, a strategically important town nearby on Lake Ladoga, fell to the Germans. Russia's second-largest city was now completely cut off by land: no transport, no provisions, no fuel. It was the start of *blokada*, the Siege of Leningrad, which would last a mythic nine hundred days. Stalin was furious. He'd only learned the Shlisselburg news from a German communiqué; Marshal Kliment (Klim) Voroshilov, Leningrad's bumbling commander, had been too scared to tell him. The Vozhd rushed General Zhukov north with a terse note for Voroshilov: he was fired. Zhukov was taking over. Klim bade stoic farewells to his aides, assuming he would be shot. (Somehow he wasn't.)

On September 22 Naum stood in Zhukov's office at the Smolny in Leningrad. The general seemed even more abrupt and severe than usual, pacing with his arm behind his back. A bold, brutal campaigner, Georgy Konstantinovich was notoriously callous with the lives of his men. He cleared minefields by sending troops attacking across them. The cheapness of Russian blood fueled the future marshal's combat strategy.

Zhukov ordered Naum to lead an amphibious recon-naissance mission as part of a counterattack on Shlisselburg, to try to break the Nazi encirclement. Immediately.

Naum quickly calculated. Zero time for preparations. Boats for the counterattack in wretched shape. Number of men: grossly inadequate. His troops were to include 125 naval school cadets – mere kids. Granddad had recently delivered an address to them. He remembered one eager boy: dark-haired, small, with pensive eyes and crooked teeth, a pimply face.

Despite his survival instinct, almost despite himself, Naum blurted out his objections.

A bolt of rage familiar to everyone under Zhukov's command flashed in the general's eyes. His bullmastiff jaw tightened.

'We'll execute you for this,' Zhukov snarled quietly. 'You have your orders!'

Orders were orders, even if suicidal.

High winds on Lake Ladoga postponed the counterattack the first night. The second night three boats overturned, drowning two men, and the operation was aborted. The main force's commander was arrested on the spot and sent to the gulag. The third night Naum and his scouting party were able to land, though the main force still couldn't. Granddad and his men had to wade two kilometers through chest-high, ice-cold water. With their radio soaked, they were unable to relay reconnaissance but managed some sabotage before fighting their way back to Soviet lines the following night, losing four men.

The main assault force was ordered to try yet again the day after. It was obliterated in the shallows by the Germans.

But Russian blood was cheap; that was the ongoing lesson from Zhukov, who would be anointed the great architect of the Soviet victory to come, then brutally demoted by Stalin (saved from arrest by a heart attack), repromoted by Khrushchev, then demoted again.

Back from his mission, Naum lay semiconscious, wheezing and grunting. The acute pneumonia he'd contracted from his forty-eight drenched hours could finish him, he knew, here in this anonymous hospital bed. Or he could perish in another 'meat-grinder' like Shlisselburg – the best death, since his kids would remember him as a hero. Zhukov's firing squad was the most agonizing scenario. Families of 'enemies of the people' were usually exiled, or worse; their children grew up in orphanages, branding their fathers as betrayers of Homeland. This last possibility deprived Naum of sleep. It pierced like a red-hot iron. For several years now he'd been writing to his kids almost daily, letters composed mostly in his head, but some actually written and left in locked drawers.

Only one of those letters was ever opened in front of Larisa, Yulia, and Sashka. Three sentences jabbed out there on that hospital bed: '*Liza, teach the children to throw grenades. Make sure they remember their papa. He loved them so.*'

✶ ✶ ✶

These lines reached Liza at the end of 1941 in a seven-hundred-square-foot room on the second floor of a crumbling warehouse. She, the children, and Dedushka Yankel shared the room with six other families evacuated from Moscow. The September journey, during which Nazi Messerschmitt fighters circled low over their riverboat, had brought them here, to the relative safety of Ulyanovsk, an old Volga town with muddy streets and folkloric carved wooden shutters.

'Look, look, Jews!' pale-blond street kids greeted them upon arrival.

'We are *not* Jews,' Mother corrected them. 'We are from Moscow.'

Now, several months into their stay, Liza had barely unpacked Aunt Clara's blue *sunduk*. Why bother? Peace, she still believed, would surely come any day. She attended to their makeshift existence while Dedushka Yankel dug trenches – and sometimes potatoes – outside the city, both his fingers and the potatoes harder and blacker as the earth froze. The five of them slept and did most of their living on two striped mattresses pushed together on the room's cement floor. Beyond the flimsy curtain partition a sound tormented them around the clock: the piercing shriek of a toddler slightly older than Sashka. The boy was barely nursed, barely touched by Katya, his mother, who disappeared all day to return after midnight with nylon negligee and Coty perfume. '*Prostitutka* and black marketeer' everyone in the room said, taking turns holding and rocking the inconsolable child, who wouldn't eat.

Katya wasn't home when the boy stopped crying. The next day Larisa watched in solemn exultation as a small sheet-wrapped bundle was carried out the door. She knew exactly what had happened: death had been her constant obsession ever since she'd read about a little frozen match girl in a Hans Christian Andersen tale.

Death. It was in the wail of Dasha their neighbor when she unfolded the triangular letter from the front, the official notification known as a *pokhoronka*, or funeral letter. Death came every day from the radio where the Voice announced it, in numbers so catastrophic, they baffled a child who could barely count over one hundred.

'*Vnimaniye, govorit Moskva!*' (Attention, Moscow speaking!) the Voice always began. The dramatic, sonorous baritone that awed and hypnotized not just my mother but the whole country belonged to Yuri Levitan, a bespectacled Jewish tailor's son. Russia's top radio man delivered most of his broadcasts – some 60,000 throughout the war – not from Moscow but from cities hundreds of miles away, to which radio staff had been evacuated. Such was Levitan's power, Hitler marked him as a personal enemy. A whopping 250,000 reichsmarks was offered for his head.

Reading aloud soldiers' letters home, the Voice conjured tender, intimate chords. Reporting the fall of each new city as the Germans advanced, it turned slow and grave, chanting out and accenting each syllable. *Go-vo-rit Mos-kva.*

More frightening still was a song on the radio. '*Arise, our vast country. Arise to mortal battle. With dark fascist forces, with the accursed horde!*' After a blood-chilling staccato opening, the vast choral refrain gathered force and crescendoed in a massive wave of sheer terror.

The song was playing when Liza opened Naum's letter from the Baltic, hand-delivered by his red-haired young adjutant, Kolya.

'*Liza, teach the children to throw grenades . . .*'

There was a parcel as well, of raisins and rock-hard prunes for the kids. 'Naum, he's *fine* . . .' Kolya assured them.

The letter's jolting past tense and Kolya's averted gaze told Liza otherwise. And there was something else. A paper slipped out of the parcel. Kolya leapt to tear it up and throw it in the trash. Liza spent half the night assembling the pieces into a photo of a brunette in a nurse's cap. *To my dear Naum*, read the inscription. And that's how my petite grandmother, who was terrified even of mice, decided to leave the children with Dedushka and start north, north toward besieged Leningrad – to claim her husband.

Heading up past Moscow, Liza was already pushing her own version of Naum's improbable luck. Late for a military chopper, she could only watch helplessly as it took off – and exploded in the air, struck by a bomb. A train carried her now through snowy wastes in the direction of Leningrad. The entire way a general held Liza's hand, crying. She reminded him of his daughter, who'd just starved to death in the Siege. The train reached Kobona, a village on the span of Lake Lagoda's frigid southeastern shore still in Russian hands. A makeshift hospital had been set up for evacuees from Peter the Great's imperial city, which Hitler meant to raze to the ground. The emaciated arrivals, mostly women and children, were given half a liter of warm water and spoonfuls of gruel. Some ate and instantly died, their dystrophied bodies unable to handle the food. I can only imagine my grandmother confronting all this with her characteristic half daze, half denial. In the years to come, she would rarely discuss her own feelings, modestly deferring instead to the collective narrative of the Leningrad tragedy.

The lone route in and out of blockaded Leningrad lay across twenty perilous miles of windswept snow-covered lake ice to the opposite shore – through enemy fire. This was the legendary Doroga Zhizni, the Road of Life, a route desperately improvised by authorities and meteorologists in the second month of the Siege as temperatures sank and the lake froze over. This first terrible winter – the coldest in decades – and the two following, trucks laboring over the Road of Life carried the only supplies into a city where rations fell to four ounces of ersatz bread a day, and vintage parquet floors and precious rare books were burned as fuel in the minus-thirty-degree cold. The besieged ate sweetened soil around a sugar warehouse bombed by the Germans, and papier-mâché bookbinding, even jelly made out of softened carpenter glue – not to mention far more gruesome stuff. More than fifty thousand people perished in December 1941 alone.

On their two daily runs along the Road of Life, exhausted drivers fought sleep by hanging a metal pot from the cab ceiling, which rattled and hit them on the head. German shells and bombs fell constantly. Often the ice caved in. Liza rode on a truck on top of a flour sack. In the open back, wind-whipped snow, like an icy sandstorm, lashed her face.

All my grandmother possessed was a special pass and an official letter asking for assistance. Reaching besieged, frozen Leningrad at last, she had no idea how or where to find Naum. At city naval headquarters, harried men in uniform kept shrugging, waving her off.

Naum Solomovich Frumkin? Baltic intelligence chief? Could be *anywhere*.

Finally the desperation in Liza's gray eyes moved a staffer to suggest she try Baltic Fleet headquarters at Kronstadt – nineteen miles away, in the Gulf of Finland. As it happened, a naval *glisser*, an ice-gliding hovercraft, was going there shortly. In fact a driver was about to take someone to the glisser that very minute. If Liza rushed . . .

My grandmother made the hovercraft, too weak and shaken to even hope. Someone brought her to the onboard cafeteria to scrounge for something to eat. A group of naval commanders was sitting at a table. And among them, who else? Naum. Smiling (of course), smelling of cologne. Lucky as ever, he had survived pneumonia and then escaped Zhukov's execution threat by reporting the Shlisselburg mission to Voroshilov, who still retained a seat on the Soviet High Command – going around Zhukov, essentially. Instead of a firing squad, Naum got a medal.

'I SAW WAR, I SAW DEATH, I SAW BULLETS AND BLOOD!' Grandma would yell years later. 'There I was, scratched up, starving, braids flying . . . and there *he* is, flashing his idiotic white teeth at me!'

'Lizochka!' Granddad famously greeted my grandma. 'And what brings *you* here?'

✷ ✷ ✷

The tale of finding Naum on the *glisser* has always been among my grandmother's wartime chestnuts. My cousin Masha and I preferred the one about Liza returning to the family in Ulyanovsk and finding Larisa burning with scarlet fever. Every evening Grandma would trudge miles through the snow to the hospital carrying potato peel pancakes for Larochka. Until one night, caught in a blizzard, she fell through a snow slope into a trench and couldn't climb out.

'I dozed half frozen inside the trench, leaning on some

hardened tree trunks,' she'd tell us repeatedly. 'At the morning's first light I realized that those 'tree trunks' were . . .'

Amputated arms and legs! Cousin Masha and I would squeal the punchline in unison.

Of her monthlong hospital stay Mother herself remembers only the pancakes. Indeed, in her mind food dominates all other wartime recollections. For instance, the ration during her first school year in Ulyanovsk. Lunch was at 11:15 during grand recess. From a smudgy zinc tray children were allotted one *bublik* and one *podushechka* each. *Bublik*: a flimsy chewy bagel scattered with poppy seeds. *Podushechka* (little pillow): a sugar-coated pebble, green, blue, or pink, the size of a fingernail, with a center of jam. Eating them together was a ritual, a sacrament really. You stuck the candy under your tongue and sat without breathing as a pool of sweetened saliva collected on the floor of your mouth. A cautious oral maneuvering delivered a stronger sweet rush and the sublime coarseness of sugar grains against the tip of your tongue. Dizzy with desire you pressed the *bublik* hard against your face and inhaled for a while. Then you spat out the candy into your hand and took the first careful bite of the *bublik*; it tasted like the greatest of pastries in your candy-sweet mouth. A bite of *bublik*, a lick of *podushechka*. The pleasure *had* to last the entire fifteen minutes of recess. The hardest part was putting off the rapturous moment when the surface of the *podushechka* cracked and jam began to ooze from inside. Some stoic classmates managed to spit out the half-eaten candy for younger siblings. Mom wasn't one of them.

My mother has impeccable manners, is ladylike in every respect. But to this day she eats like a starved wolf, a war survivor gobbling down her plate of food before other people at table have even touched their forks. Sometimes at posh restaurants I'm embarrassed by how she eats – then ashamed at myself for my shame. 'Mom, really, they say chewing properly is good for you,' I admonish her weakly. She usually glares. 'What do *you* know?' she retorts.

From her I do know that civilians distilled survival into one word: *kartochki*. They were printed on one large sheet of paper, these ration cards, a month's worth of square coupons with an official stamp, the recipient's name and signature, and a stern warning – CARDS NOT REPLACEABLE – because corruption and counterfeiting ran rampant. Lost your *kartochki*? Good luck surviving.

At seven years of age my mother was a *kartochki* veteran. She was the one dispatched to trade them at stores while Dedushka Yankel dug his trenches and Liza and Yulia minded baby Sashka. The most crucial *kartochki* were for *khleb* (bread). One morning long before opening time Larisa joined hundreds of puffy-eyed, red-nosed people outside the bakery door. She tried not to gulp and swallow cold air too hard when the bread truck arrived and two men carted the aromatic, thick-crusted dark bricks inside. Behind the counter severe women in splotchy blue robes over shapeless padded coats weighed each ration of bread to the last milligram. They stomped their feet to keep warm and wore fingerless gloves so they could easily snip off the right coupon.

As her turn in the line neared, Mom felt a slight panic. Back in the house a power outage had prevented her from sorting through the ration books. It was the first of the month. All the coupon sheets – for grain, sugar, bread, meat for each family member – sat folded in the pocket of the blue princess coat Naum had brought from Sweden. Now she could barely feel them there; she couldn't even feel her own hands from the cold.

Why did she put all the cards on the counter when her turn came? But how else to sift through the rationing sheets with people behind pushing and barking? Why panic so completely, so utterly at the invasion of arms? Arms, hands, mittens and gloves, smelly coat armpits, anxious breath. Fingers swarming the counter like tentacles – gnarled, blackened digits; gaunt fingers with white anemic nails; red swollen fingers. The *kartochki* were gone from the counter. The saleslady gave a bleak grin and a wag of a nail-bitten finger.

Standing outside the bread store, Mother imagined what she'd always imagined ever since she remembered imagining anything. She saw Naum coming back home. He'd be dressed in the gray civilian suit he wore at the station for Leningrad; she could almost smell the *lavanda* cologne on his cap. 'Lizochka, I'm home!' he would shout, peering at the thin, shoddy figures in the warehouse room. Then he'd spy them. Arms open, he'd rush over. And what would he find? Liza, Dedushka, and Sashka – and Larisa and Yulia, pale and majestically beautiful in their identical fur-trimmed princess coats. All silent and motionless on their striped mattress, like Katya's small baby. Dead, all of them.

Dead is what happened to people who lost their rationing cards on the first of the month. Dead from *golod* (starvation), from thirty whole days without kasha or bread or the tiny ration of milk for the baby. Would Naum wail like Dasha their neighbor did when she opened her funeral letter? Or would he find a new wife, one who didn't shriek and convulse in hysterics like Liza surely would when Larisa came home *without bread and without rationing cards*.

Going home wasn't an option. And so Mother went to the only place in the city where electricity always shone brightly and where a sprit of cozy, prosperous happiness wafted through every beautiful room. She went there often, to that traditional wooden two-story house up the street from their warehouse. She came to escape from the sight of her pitiful dedushka peeling warty potatoes, from the catastrophic Voice on the radio. The house was untouched by all this. Here the mother, Maria Alexandrovna, never yelled at her children. She played the grand piano while everyone had tea from a samovar in the living room. There were six kids in the house, but the apple of everyone's eye was a boy called Volodya. Larisa liked to examine his baby picture, a brim of blond curls fringing his high, stubborn forehead. As a student Volodya had a proud, focused expression and a shrewd direct gaze. He got the best grades in his class. He never lied to his parents. He fought for justice and truth. Volodya's attic bedroom with its patterned beige wallpaper was where Mom often sat daydreaming in the wooden chair between the boy's small, neat desk and his bookshelf filled with volumes by Pushkin, Turgenev, and Gogol. Lucky Volodya got to sleep alone in bed, unlike Larisa and Yulia. He had such a nifty map of the world on his wall. The green lamp on his desk was so hypnotic, so peaceful.

'*Devochka*, little girl, wake up, time to go.' Someone was clutching Larisa's shoulder, shaking her gently.

'The Lenin House Museum closes at five,' said the attendant.

Back at her own house Larisa sat with her arms closed around Liza, stroking the sharp shoulder blade under her mother's coarse woolen dress. They sat like this a long while. About the lost *kartochki* Liza said nothing. She remembered too well her own childhood loss of a ration in the twenties: a loaf of bread yanked out of her hand by a bearded giant who gorged on the entire half pound in front of her eyes.

Salvation came from Katya, of all people, the *prostitutka* and black marketeer.

'Liza, you fool – you have the *sunduk!*'

So every few days Liza and Katya went to the black market on the outskirts of Ulyanovsk to trade Naum's spiffy shirts, suits, and ties from inside the blue trunk. His best suit went for a sack of millet that they ate for the rest of the month. Millet for thin, watery breakfast gruel. Millet soup for lunch, flavored with herring heads. Best was millet baked for supper in a cast-iron pot inside the clay Russian stove in their warehouse. Russian war survivors fall into two categories: those who idolize millet and those who can't stand it. But they all agree: millet was life.

* * *

The Nazi invasion caught Stalin's Soviet Union with yet another food supply crisis looming. Two years of below-average harvests had combined with the drain of the 1940 war with Finland and mammoth defense spending. But if the Soviets had scant grain reserves, they had even scantier strategies for handling war-time supply problems.

The Reich, however, *had* a strategy: Hungerplan, the

'Hunger Plan.' Brainchild of corpulent, gourmandizing Hermann Göring and the Reich's Food Ministry, the Hunger Plan was possibly history's most sinister and cynical blueprint. The 'agricultural surplus' of the Ukraine – which the Nazis intended to capture immediately – would be diverted to feed only Wehrmacht soldiers and Germany's civilians. Thirty million Russians (a sixth of the population), mainly in cities, would be left without food. In other words: genocide by programmatic starvation.

By late fall of 1941, Hitler controlled half of the Soviet grain acreage. Crucially, however, he had not yet achieved the lightning victory he was so sure of. Despite staggering initial losses and blunders, the Soviet forces resisted. Moscow shuddered, bled, but didn't yield. Russian generals regrouped. Instead of swollen Ukrainian granaries and willing slave labor, the advancing Wehrmacht usually found only burnt crops and demolished farm equipment, as per Stalin's scorched earth policy. ('All valuable property, including non-ferrous metals, grain, and fuel which cannot be withdrawn, must without fail be destroyed,' instructed the Leader in early July.)

Then winter descended and it was the Germans whose poor planning was brutally exposed. Counting on three months of blitzkrieg at most, the Reich hadn't provided warm clothes to the men at its front. The war lasted four long years, much of the duration bitterly cold.

Soviet citizens got their first rationing cards in July of 1941. Average *kartochki* allotments, though symbolic and crucial, were nowhere near adequate for survival. Daily, it was only a bit more than a pound of bread; monthly, about four pounds of meat and under three pounds of flour or grain. Substitutions became the norm: honey for meat, rotten herring instead of sugar or butter. Under the slogan 'All for the Front, All for the Victory,' supplies and rail transport were prioritized for the Red Army, which often fought in a state of near-starvation. How did Stalin's state manage the food supply for civilians? By temporarily encouraging near-NEP conditions. Economic ideology was suspended and centralization loosened, meaning local authorities and citizens were left to fend for themselves. Schools and orphanages, trade unions and factories, all set up ad hoc green plots. Even in cities, people foraged, learning to digest birch buds, clover, pine needles, and tree bark. At the front, chronically hungry soldiers ate not just fallen horses but saddles and straps – anything made of leather that could be boiled for hours with some aromatic twigs to stun the tar smell.

'Naum's clothes and Aunt Clara's *sunduk* saved our lives!' Grandma Liza used to say, gravely nodding at the blue trunk still in her hallway during my childhood. Indeed. Markets of every shade from white (legal) to black (illegal) were central to daily survival. With rubles almost useless, food itself, bread especially, became currency.

Diaries from the Leningrad Siege leave bone-chilling details of the economics of starvation. *Ushanka* (flap hat) = four ounces of bread; men's galoshes = five ounces of bread; used samovar = two pounds of bread. Families hid the deaths of relatives so they could continue using the deceased's monthly bread *kartochki*. The cost of an individual grave = four and a half pounds of bread plus five hundred rubles.

Starvation was nowhere as horrifying, as extreme, as it

was in Leningrad, during those nine hundred days. But for any Russian who suffered hunger contractions at all, a wartime food glossary was etched in his or her memory:

Balanda: An anorexic sham 'soup.' Flavored with anything from a horse bone to herring tail. Thickened with crushed rusks or a handful of millet. Also a term used for gulag fodder.

Duranda: Hard cakes of linseed or other seed hulls left over from oil processing. Peacetime cattlefeed.

Kombizhir (literally 'combined fat'): Hydrogenated oil, usually rancid and greenish.

Khleb (bread): Heavy loaves, claylike inside. Baked from rye flour stretched out with oats or *duranda* and/or sawdust.

Tushonka (tinned pork): At the start of 1942 a new class of edibles began appearing in Russia. *Vtoroy front* ('second front') was the nickname for American lend-lease foodstuffs. The most coveted and iconic of Yankee delicacies was *tushonka* tinned in its fat in Iowa to exact Russian specifications. Tushonka far outlasted the war. Even during my childhood it was the cherished sine qua non of hiking trips and dacha summers.

Shokolad.

Of all the gifts that made their way from Naum during those days, one struck Mother right in the heart. It made her delirious. Not just because it was *shokolad* in war-torn Russia.

Not even because it tasted far better than the chalky American lend-lease stuff. No. It was because of the dark-eyed young man on the wrapper: prodigious of nose, young and steely of glare, with a gloriously embossed collar. The crush Mom developed on this chocolate hero was instant and hopeless. His swoony Orientalist name matched his fiery looks. *Mohammed Reza Pahlavi* – crowned shah of Iran in 1941 after his father was forced into exile by occupiers Soviet Union and Britain.

Oil. Petroleum was the reason the Frumkin children were getting Pahlavi Jr. chocolates.

The second summer of war marked the Soviet low ebb of the conflict: six million soldiers killed or captured, most of Ukraine occupied, Leningrad faltering under *blokada*, Moscow unfallen but vulnerable. As the Germans headed southeast, Naum had yet again been transferred, this time to Baku, the hot, windy, uneasily quiet capital of Soviet Azerbaijan. This vital Caucasian republic, bordering Iran on the Caspian Sea, pumped the majority of Russia's oil. It was oil Hitler coveted for himself. Launching Operation Blau at the Caucasus in June 1942, the Fuhrer aimed to take Baku by September. His overconfident generals presented him with an extravagantly frosted cake with a sign that said KASPISCHES MEER (Caspian Sea). Film footage shows Hitler smiling suavely as he takes the slice labeled BAKU. But the Luftwaffe left Baku alone: its vast petroleum infrastructure had to be delivered intact. The Fuhrer wanted to eat his cake but have it too.

Iran, meanwhile, occupied but still nominally neutral, simmered with international intrigue. Tehran was thick with German agents and operatives. Shuttling between

Baku and the Iranian capital, Naum was back in the familiar world of cloak-and-dagger. So highly classified was his work that he never confided its details to any of us — aside from bragging about having met the dashing young shah on the chocolates.

From Baku, Naum dispatched Ivan Ivanych, his intelligence aide, to Ulyanovsk to bring the family south. Gray-eyed and sinewy, Ivan looked the part of an elite GRU spy guy — lend-lease black leather coat, tall boots, a pistol, plus a mysterious attaché case he watched like a hawk. The journey to Baku lasted three nightmarish weeks, or maybe six, Mother can't remember. Mostly they bivouacked for days at train stations on layovers between hopelessly delayed, crawling *teplushki*, the wartime cattle freights overcrowded with orphaned children and wounded combatants whose bandages undulated with black swarms of lice. At one point Ivan dozed off on a station bench and someone snatched his attaché case. Mom watched the GRU hero chase down the culprit and whack him on the head with the butt of his gun. The police intervened, the attaché case sprang open, and to her utter astonishment, Mom saw watches — big clunky watches! — tumble out onto the pavement. Larisa was little, but not too little to smell a black marketeer, even though Granddad later insisted that the watches were 'crucial intelligence tools.' (Who knew?) For the final leg of the journey there was a boat at a filthy port in Turkmenistan where women in headscarves hawked quince and men with Turkic features rode atop camels. For several days everyone vomited crossing the Caspian during a storm.

Naum met the family on a pier in Baku with an armful of

tangerines. An oily Caspian darkness smothered the city. Mom could barely make out Naum's features, but the over-whelming aroma of citrus made her weep. The family was together again. Their luck had held.

Compared to hungry Ulyanovsk, Baku was a different planet, a lush Orientalist dreamscape similar to the magical pavilions Larisa had encountered at Moscow's agricultural exhibition back in prewar 1939. At the bazaars men with splendiferous mustaches not unlike Comrade Stalin's whistled at Liza as she bartered her bread rations for fuzzy porcelain-looking peaches, sun-dried figs threaded on strings, and tubs of Azeri yogurt, piercingly tart. There were swims in the polluted Caspian Sea; mouths and fingers stained from climbing mulberry trees. Local Caspian Flotilla dignitaries hosted rice pilaf feasts aboard destroyers and cruisers. Only the foul smell from the oil rigs marred Mother's happiness.

Once in a while Naum's family even got a taste – literally – of his intelligence work. A few of his 'boys' would haul a big table into the courtyard of the house where they shared one narrow closetlike room, but with a balcony and a view. On the table lay a sturgeon the size of a man, or a small whale. *Fishing* was the cover for Naum's spies in the Caspian. The sturgeon was split open, glistening caviar scooped from its belly. For weeks after, the family ate sturgeon pickled, brined, dried, and minced into kotleti. To this day Mother can't look at sturgeon or caviar, still riven, she says, by the guilt of eating those delicacies while the rest of the country was starving. During the entire eighteen months they spent by the Caspian, Mom couldn't shake the sense that she was hallucinating. She was dazed and overwhelmed by her family's luck – their improbable luck.

✳ ✳ ✳

By early 1943, Russia's luck, too, was changing at last. Hitler's lunge for the Caucasus oil fields had collapsed. It collapsed because it started so well that the Fuhrer split his forces to grab for another prize simultaneously: the strategic city on the Volga named after Stalin. The fate of the Reich was cast. Operation Blau (for the blue of the Caspian) was sucked into what the Germans now called the 'War of the Rats' in the freezing rubblescape of bombed-out Stalingrad. Over the course of more than six months, Hitler's forces, commanded by Field Marshal Paulus, were annihilated by the combined power of the Russian winter, hunger, and the Red Army under bloody Zhukov and General Vasily Chuikov. It was the first and the worst Nazi defeat since the beginning of Operation Barbarossa. Germans killed and wounded numbered some three-quarters of a million. The Russians suffered more than a million casualties (a figure that exceeds the total World War II losses for both the United States and Britain). But with Paulus's surrender in February 1943, the momentum had swung. Come May 1945, Zhukov and Chuikov's Red banner would wave over Berlin's ruins.

As for Naum, he stayed on in Baku even after Stalingrad and the passing of the Caucasus oil threat. In autumn of 1943 the Azeri capital became the hub of technical and logistical support for the Soviet presence at the Tehran Conference. Yalta and Potsdam might be more famous, but

Tehran was the grand rehearsal, the first time the 'Big Three' – Stalin, Roosevelt, and Churchill – came together around a table. Stalin himself arrived in Baku by train in November, from there flying to Tehran. The plane ride was another first: the phobic Wise Helmsman had never been airborne before.

On a notably balmy afternoon on November 29, mid-conference, the Big Three and their aides sat down to a white-tablecloth late lunch in the Soviet embassy's snug living room. Stalin was desperate for a second front in Europe, and the menu was part of his charm offensive. The lunch card featured zakuski (appetizers), clear bouillon with pirozhki, then steak followed by *plombir* ice cream. To drink: wines from the Caucasus, and the ever-indispensable Sovetskoye brand champagne, Stalin's pride. In Leningrad the Siege wouldn't be lifted for another two months yet, and close to a million had perished from hunger. In Tehran, as waiters passed around vodka, Armenian brandy, and vermouth, Marshal Stalin rose to offer a welcoming toast. No longer the abject gray-faced figure of June 1941, our Vozhd acted the part of the Nazi vanquisher of epic Stalingrad.

Not all the Soviet attendees showed Stalin's poise. The Vozhd's ravenous interpreter, Valentin Berezhkov, was caught with a mouthful of steak just as Churchill began to speak. There was awkward silence, tittering, laughter. Stalin's eyes flashed. 'Some place you found for a dinner,' he hissed at the hapless Berezhkov through clenched teeth.

'Look at you stuffing your face. What a disgrace!' (Berezhkov survived to record the incident, and the meal, in his memoirs.)

But mainly Stalin waxed gastronomic to his Allied invitees. He invoked the subtleties of his spicy native Georgian cooking. FDR revved up his own charm, praising the inky Caucasian wines and enthusing about Sovetskoye Shampanskoye – shouldn't this 'marvelous wine' be imported to the United States? A Pol Roger aficionado, Churchill tactfully chose to admire the Armenian brandy. No one mentioned the epidemic looting and black marketeering of American lend-lease food supplies, or that Soviet wine-bottling plants were mostly producing containers for Molotov cocktails. (Sovestkoye Shampanskoye? Among Russian troops this was the nickname for an explosive blond concoction of sulphur and phosphorus.)

To cap off the lunch, Stalin arranged for a pescatorial showstopper. Four stout uniformed men trailed by a pair of Filipino chefs trailed by a U.S. security guy carried in a giant fish, again as big as a man or a small whale. No, it wasn't one of Naum's spy-cover belugas, but a salmon freighted in from Russia.

'I want to present this to you, Mr. President,' Stalin announced.

'How wonderful! I'm touched by your attention,' said FDR graciously.

'No trouble at all,' said Stalin, just as graciously.

Reboarding his plane, the lunch host had what he wanted: a commitment to a European second front, Operation Overlord (D-Day), for early 1944; and the eastern slice of Poland as lawful property of the USSR.

Tastier pieces of European cake would follow at the Yalta Conference in February 1945. And a much fancier banquet proper. As the country still reeled from starvation, a grandiose Potemkin village resort was set up for the Big Three in the war-devastated Crimea in just under three weeks. Suddenly there appeared two service airports, lavish fountains, sixty-eight remodeled rooms across three czarist palaces, ten thousand plates, nine thousand pieces of silver-ware, and three kitchens fueled with masses of firewood magically transported along paralyzed railway networks. At the main feast? – white fish in champagne sauce, Central Asian quail pilaf, kebabs from the Caucasus – the host and soon-to-be Generalissimo was reported by attendees to be 'full of fun and good humor,' even 'smiling like a benign old man.' And why not? He'd gotten himself de facto the rest of Poland and the keys to most of post-war Eastern Europe.

'*Govorit Moskva*' – Moscow Speaking. Later that spring of 1945, the radio man Yuri Levitan made one of his most operatic announcements. In a steely, officious baritone, he announced that Soviet forces had concluded the destruction of Germany's Berlin divisions. 'Today, on the Second of May,' he continued, his voice rising, gathering force, 'they achieved total control . . . of the German capital . . . of the city . . . of BEAR-LEEEEEEEEEEEN!!!'

Without understanding Russian you might think he was a South American soccer commentator shouting out news of a goal. The iconic image of the Soviet Victory Banner on the roof of the Reichstag, however, is unambiguous.

On May 9, 1945, at 2:10 a.m., Levitan read the German Instrument of Surrender, and everything inside my mother froze. She couldn't help it. Dread and terror. She felt them, without fail, every time she heard Levitan's voice and the words 'Moscow Speaking.' It no longer mattered that for months now the Voice had been bringing *good* news, that following its announcements of the Soviet retaking of each new Russian city, fireworks and artillery salvos boomed through the center of Moscow, where the Frumkin family had been reunited for more than a year now. To this day the thought of Levitan's baritone paralyzes my mother.

Mom remembers as vividly the spontaneous, overwhelming outpouring of orgiastic relief and elation that swept the capital on May 9.

More than two million revelers streamed toward Moscow's old center. An undulating sea of red carnations and white snowdrops. Soldiers tossed into the air. Delirious people – hugging, kissing, dancing, losing their voices from shouting *OORAAAA* (hooray). That night powerful strobes flashed on the Kremlin's towers, illuminating the visage of Stalin, seemingly floating above Red Square, and the fireworks were extravagant: thirty blasts fired from one thousand mortars.

Among the celebrants was a reed-thin, six-foot-tall beauty with green sirenlike eyes and a hastily applied smear of red lipstick. She was in her late twenties, yanking along a recalcitrant eight-year-old boy. The louder everyone cheered, the harder the woman sobbed. Andrei Bremzen, her husband, my paternal grandfather, was one of the eight million men who didn't return from the front.

If one adds civilian deaths, the Great Patriotic War (as we officially called it) took 27 million lives, although some estimates are far higher. In Russia it left tragedy and devastation unprecedented in history, unfathomable in its scale. For four uninterrupted years war had camped on Soviet soil. There were 25 million citizens homeless, 1,700 towns and more than 70,000 villages reduced to rubble, an entire generation of men wiped out.

By war's end my mother was eleven, a bookish daydreamer with two thick black braids who'd graduated from Hans Christian Andersen to Hugo's *Les Misérables* in its mellifluous Russian translation. Really, any book permeated with romantic tragedy attracted my mother. The first post-war summer found her family at a cozy dacha on the outskirts of Pushkino, a town north of Moscow where Naum was now directing a spy-training academy. '*Counter*intelligence, *counter*intelligence!' Granddad kept correcting, brows furrowed, when anyone blurted out the 'spy' word. Later that year he'd be in Germany to debrief Hermann Goering amid the ruins at the Nurenberg Trials.

Swatting flies and picking at gooseberries, Mom read her sad books and contemplated what was happening to Russia. What to make of the crippled men now thronging stations, begging and playing the accordion? How to grieve for the fathers of her friends who hadn't come back? Strangely, no one else in her family shared these thoughts. Liza plunged herself into household chores; Naum, who anyway never really *talked* to the kids, was busy with his steely-eyed spy colleagues and their coiffed wives, who boasted of the furniture their husbands scored in Berlin. Yulia quoted Generalissimo Stalin so often now, it made Mother nauseated. And so Larisa started a diary. Carefully she selected a small book with glossy white pages and a gold-embossed cover, a prewar Scandinavian present from Naum. She dipped her pen in the inkpot and paused for so long that ink drops ruined the page and she had to tear it out.

'*Death,*' she then wrote, pressing hard on the pen so it squeaked. '*Death inevitably comes at the end of life. Sometimes a very short life.*' She thought a bit and continued. '*But if we are meant to die anyway, what should we do? How must we live that short hour between birth and death?*'

To these questions Mom had no answers, but simply writing them down she felt relief. She thought some more about such matters out on the grass by the house, sucking on a sweet clover petal as dragon-flies buzzed overhead.

'DEATH!! DEATH???' Liza's screams broke Mom's contemplation.

Liza pulled at Mom's braid, brandishing the notebook she'd just found on the table. 'We beat the Germans! Your father fought for your happiness! How *dare* you have such bad, silly thoughts. *Death!*' Liza ripped up the notebook and stormed back into the house. Mom lay on the grass looking at the shreds of paper around her. She felt too hollow even to cry. Her parents and the voices on the black public loudspeakers, she suddenly realized – they were one and the same. Her innermost thoughts were somehow all wrong and unclean, she was being told, and in her entire life she had never felt more alone.

CHAPTER FIVE

1950s: TASTY AND HEALTHY

In the prework hours of March 4, 1953, a time of year when mornings are still disagreeably dim and the icicles on roofs begin their thawing and refreezing act, classical music aficionados in Moscow woke up to a pleasant surprise. From early morning that day, instead of the usual Sovietica cheer, the radio was serving up a veritable banquet of symphonic and chamber delights in sad minor keys. Grieg, Borodin, Alexander Glazunov's most elegiac string quartet. It was when the radio's 'physical culture' lesson was replaced with yet another somber classical piece that people began to have *thoughts*.

'Someone in the Politburo kicked the bucket?'

The shocking announcement came around nine a.m.

'Comrade Stalin has suffered a brain hemorrhage . . . loss of consciousness. Paralysis of right arm and leg . . . loss of speech.'

Throughout that day a familiar baritone boomed on the airways. Declaiming medical bulletins of the beloved leader's declining condition, Yuri Levitan was back in combat mode. *Pulse. Breathing rate. Urinalyses*. The Voice infused such clinical details with the same melodrama with which it announced the retaking of Orel and Kursk from the Nazis, or the drops in prices immediately after the war.

'Over last night Comrade Stalin's condition has seriously *de-te-rio-ra-ted!*' announced Levitan next day, March 5. 'Despite medical and oxygen treatments, the Leader began Cheyne-Stokes *res-pi-ra-ti-on!*'

'Chain *what?*' citizens wondered.

Only doctors understood the fatal significance of this clinical term. And if said doctors had 'Jewish' as Entry 5 (their ethnicity) on their passports? Well, they must have felt their own death sentences lifting with Stalin's last, comatose breath. In his paranoid, sclerotic final years, the Generalissimo was outdoing himself with an utterly fantastical anti-Semitic purge known as the Doctors' Plot. Being a Jewish medic – Jewish anything, really – in those days signified all but certain doom. But now *Pravda* abruptly suspended its venomous news reports of the Doctors' Plot trial. And in the Lubyanka cellars where 'murderers in white coats' were being worked over, some torturers changed their line of questioning.

'What's Cheyne-Stokes?' they now demanded of their physician-victims.

By the time the media announced Stalin's condition on March 4, the Supreme Leader had been unconscious for several days. It had all begun late on the morning of March 1 when he didn't ask for his tea. Alarmed at the silence of motion detectors in his quarters, the staff at his Kuntsevo dacha proceeded to do exactly . . . nothing. Hours went by. Finally someone dared enter. The seventy-three-year-old Vozhd was found on the floor, his pajama pants soaked in urine. Comrade Lavrenty Beria's black ZIS sedan rolled up long after midnight. The secret police chief exhibited touching devotion to his beloved boss. 'Leave him alone, he's sleeping,' the pince-nezed executioner and rapist instructed, and left without calling an ambulance.

Medical types were finally allowed in the following morning. Shaking from fear, they diagnosed massive stroke. Suspecting he might have been Stalin's next victim, Comrade Beria had *reasons* for keeping assistance away. Ditto other Politburo intimates, including a sly, piglike secretary of the Moscow Party organization named Nikita Khrushchev. Whatever the Kremlin machinations, the pockmarked shoemaker's son né Iosif Dzhugashvili died around 9:50 p.m. on March 5, 1953.

He was gone.

The country was fatherless. Father of Nations-less.

Also Generalissimo-, Mountain Eagle-, Transformer of Nature-, Genius of Humanity-, Coryphaeus of Science-, Great Strategist of the Revolution-, Standard-bearer of Communism-, Grand Master of Bold Revolutionary Solutions and Decisive Turns-*less.*

The Best Friend of All Children, Pensioners, Nursing Mothers, Kolkhoz Workers, Hunters, Chess Players, Milkmaids, and Long-Distance Runners was no more.

He was gone.

The nation was Stalin-less.

In the sleety early March days right before Stalin's death, Larisa, dressed in perpetually leaking boots and a scratchy orange turtleneck under a gray pinafore dress, was navigating the cavernous bowels of INYAZ. This was the Moscow state institute of foreign languages, home to Kafka-esque corridors and an under-heated canteen with that eternal reek of stewed cabbage. Home to elderly multilingual professors: prime targets of Stalin's vicious campaign against 'rootless cosmopolitans.'

Closed vowels, open vowels. In her phonetics class my mother was sighing. *Land — Lend. Man — Men.* A Russian ear is deaf to such subtleties. Anyway, how to concentrate on vowels and the like when Comrade Stalin lay dying?

Irrespective of the Vozhd's condition, an English major at INYAZ didn't figure into Mom's idea of any Radiant Future. It was a dull, respectable career compromise, as her fervent dreams of the stage kept crashing. 'I probably lacked the talent,' Mom admits nowadays. 'And the looks.' Back then it seemed more, well, *dramatic* to blame her crushed hopes on a 'history of drama' exam at the fashionable GITIS theater academy. At her entrance orals, having memorized the official texts, Mom delivered the requisite critique of rootless cosmopolitanism to a pair of stately professors. Did they really grimace at her declaiming how art belongs to *narod*, the people? Why did they give her a *troíka*, a C, for her faultless textbook recitation? Only much later Mom realized, with great shame, that those two erudite connoisseurs of Renaissance drama were themselves being hounded and harassed for their 'unbridled, evil-minded cosmopolitanism.'

On March 6, as word of Stalin's passing spread, the INYAZ corridors echoed with sobs. Classes were canceled. Janitorial babushkas leaned on their mops, wailing over their buckets like pagan Slavs at a funeral. Mom's own eyes were dry but her teeth rattled and her limbs felt leaden under the historic weight of the news. On the tram home, commuters hunched on wooden seats in tense silence. Through the windows Mother watched funerary banners slowly rise across buildings. Workmen were plastering over the cheerful billboards advertising her favorite plays. She closed her eyes and saw blackness, a gaping void instead of a future.

Three days later, my mother, Liza, and Yulia set off for the funeral, but seeing the mobs on the streets, they turned back. My teenage dad persevered. Sergei, then sixteen and a bit of a street urchin, managed to hop forward on rooftops, thread through the epic bottleneck in Moscow's center, crawl under a barrier of official black Studebakers, squeeze past policemen atop panicked horses, and sneak into the neoclassic pomp of the Hall of Columns where Iosif Vissarionovich lay in state, gold buttons aglint on his gray Generalissimo uniform. Sergei's best friend, Platosha, wasn't so lucky, however: his skull was cracked in the infamous funeral stampede into Trubnaya Square. Nobody's sure of the exact number of fatalities, but at least several hundred mourners were trampled to death on March 9 in the monstrous surge to see Stalin's body. Even in his coffin, Stalin claimed victims.

Weeks after the funeral, Mom was still shaken. There were two things she just couldn't get over. The first was galoshes. Images of black galoshes strewn all over Moscow in the wake of the funeral, along with hats, mittens, scarves, fragments of coats. The second was unreality – the utter unreality of Levitan's health bulletins during Stalin's final days.

Urine. The Great Leader had urine? *Pulse? Respiration? Blood?*

Weren't those words she heard at the shabby neighborhood polyclinic?

Mom tried to imagine Stalin squatting on a toilet or having his blood drawn by someone with sweat stains under his arms from fear. But it didn't seem possible! And in the end how could Stalin do something as mundane, as mundanely human, as die?

When Stalin's passing finally began to sink in, Mom's bewilderment gave way to a different feeling: bitter and angry disappointment. *He* had left them – left *her*. *He* would never come to see her triumph in a play. Whether rehearsing for auditions, Mom realized, or picturing herself on the stage of the Moscow Art Theater in some socially meaningful Gorky production – she yearned for *his* approbation, *his* presence, *his* all-wise, discriminating blessing.

After Mom confided all this to me recently, I couldn't sleep. Larisa Naumovna Frumkina. The dissident heart who had always shielded me from Soviet contamination . . .

She wanted to be an actress for Stalin?

So here it was, then: the raw emotional grip of a totalitarian personality cult; that deep bond, hypnotic and intimate, between Stalin and his citizenry. Until now, I'd found this notion abstract. The State of my childhood had been a creaking geriatric machine run by a cartoonish Politburo that inspired nothing but vicious political humor. With the fossilized lump of Brezhnev as Leader, it was, at times, rather fun. But Mom's response to Stalin's death suddenly illuminated for me the power of his cult. Its insidious duality. On the one hand the Great Leader was a divinity unflawed by the banalities of human life. A historical force, transcendental, mysterious, and somehow existing out-side and above the wretched regime he'd created. At the same time, he was father figure to all – a kind, even cozily homely paterfamilias to the whole Soviet nation, a man who hugged kids on posters and attracted propaganda epithets like *prostoy* (simple), *blizky* (intimate), and *rodnoy*, an endearment reserved for the closest of kin, with the same etymology as the equally resonant *rodina* (homeland).

By the time Stalin died, Mother was no longer an alienated child; but neither was she a bumpkin or a brainwashed Komsomol (Communist Youth) hack. She was a hyperliterary nineteen-year-old, a worshipper of dissident cultural heroes like Shostakovich and Pasternak, appalled by their harassment – and all the while spouting anti-cosmopolitan vitriol. In short, she suffered from a full-blown case of that peculiar Stalinist split-consciousness.

'Look,' Mom explained, 'I was anti-Soviet from the time I was born – in my gut, in my heart. But in my head psycho-logically somehow . . . I guess I was a young Stalinist. But then after *he* died,' she concluded, 'my head became clear.'

✶ ✶ ✶

In certain dissident-leaning USSR circles there arose a tradition of celebrating March 5. Although de-Stalinization didn't take place overnight, for many, Stalin's deathday came to mark a watershed both historic and private; a symbolic moment when the blindfolds came off and one attained a new consciousness.

It so happened that March rolled along just as I was writing this chapter. In the spirit of these old dissident get-togethers, Mom decided that we should host our own deathday gathering. Again we turned to the cookbook my mother had fallen in love with at the age of five.

One sixth of the measured world, eleven time zones, fifteen ethnic republics. A population of nearly 300 million by the empire's end. This was the USSR. And in the best spirit of socialist communality, our polyglot behemoth Rodina shared one constitution, one social bureaucracy, one second-grade math curriculum – and one kitchen bible for all: *The Book of Tasty and Healthy Food*. Begotten in 1939, *Kniga* (The Book) was an encyclopedic cooking manual, sure. But with its didactic commentaries, ideological sermonizing, neo-Enlightenment scientific excursions, and lustrous photo spreads of Soviet production plants and domestic feasts, it offered more – a compete blueprint of joyous, abundant, cultured socialist living. I couldn't wait to revisit this socialist (un)realist landmark.

As a young woman, my mother learned to cook from the 1952 version. This was the iconic edition: bigger, better, *happier*, more politically virulent, with the monumental heft of those Stalinist neo-Gothic skyscrapers of the late forties and the somber-brown hard cover of a social science treatise. The appearance was meaningful. Cooking, it suggested, was no frivolous matter. No! Cooking, dear comrades, represented a collective utopian project: Self-Improvement and Acculturation Through Kitchen Labor.

You could also neatly follow post-war policy shifts by comparing the 1939 and 1952 editions of *The Book of Tasty and Healthy Food*.

In the late thirties, a Bolshevik internationalist rhetoric still held sway. This was the internationalism celebrated, for example, by the hit 1936 musical comedy film *Circus* of 'O Vast Is My Country' song fame. *Circus* trumpets the tale of Marion, a white American trapeze artist chased out of Kansas with her illegitimate mulatto baby. Marion winds up in Moscow. In the Land of the Soviets, she's not in Kansas anymore! Here she finds an entire nation eager to cuddle her kid, plus a hunky acrobat boyfriend. In a famous scene of the internationalist idyll, the renowned Yiddish actor Shloyme Mikhoels sings a lullaby to the African-American child.

That scene was later deleted. So was Mikhoels — assassinated in 1948 on Stalin's orders amid general anti-Semitic hysteria. America? Our former semifriendly (albeit racist) competitor was now fully demonized as an imperialist cold war foe. Consequently, xenophobia reigns in the 1952 *Kniga*. Gone is the 1939's Jewish *teiglach* recipe; vanished Kalmyk tea (Kalmyks being a Mongolic minority deported en masse for supposed Nazi collaboration). Canapés, croutons, consommés — the 1952 volume is purged of such 'rootless cosmopolitan' *froufrou*. Ditto *sendvichi*, *kornfleks*, and ketchup, those American delicacies snatched up by Mikoyan during his thirties trip to America.

In the next reprint, released in August 1953 . . . surprise! All quotations from Stalin have disappeared. In 1954, no Lavrenty Beria (he was executed in December 1953) — and so no more my favorite 1952 photo, of a pork factory in Azerbaijan named after him. *A pork factory in a Muslim republic, named after 'Stalin's butcher.'*

Kremlin winds shifted, commissars vanished, but the official Soviet myth of plenty persisted, and people clung to the magic tablecloth fairy tale. Who could resist the utopia of the socialist good life promoted so graphically in *Kniga*? Just look at the opening photo spread! Here are craggy oysters – oysters! – piled on a silver platter between bottles of Crimean and Georgian wines. Long-stemmed cut-crystal goblets tower over a glistening platter of fish in aspic. Sovetskoye brand bubbly chills in a bucket, its neck angling toward a majestic suckling pig. Meanwhile, the intro informs us, 'Capitalist states condemn working citizens to constant under-eating . . . and often to hungry death.'

The wrenching discrepancy between the abundance on the pages and its absence in shops made *Kniga*'s myth of plenty especially poignant. Long-suffering *Homo sovieticus* gobbled down the deception; long-suffering *H. sovieticus* had after all been weaned on socialist realism, an artistic doctrine that insisted on depicting reality 'in its revolutionary development' – past and present swallowed up by a triumphant projection of a Radiant Future. In socialist realist visions, kolkhoz maidens danced around cornucopic sheaves of wheat, mindless of famines; laboring weavers morphed into Party princesses through happy Stakhanovite toil. Socialist realism encircled like an enchanted mirror: the exhausted and hunger-gnawed in real life peered in and saw only their rosy future-transformed reflections.

Recently, I shared these musings with Mom. 'Huh?' she replied. Then she proceeded to tell me her own *Kniga* story.

December 1953, she said, was as frigid as any in Russia. The political climate, however, was warming. Gulag prisoners had already begun their return; Beria had just been executed. And Moscow's culturati were in an uproar over a piece in the literary magazine *Novy mir*. 'On Sincerity in Literature' the essay was called, by one Vladimir Pomerantsev, a legal investigator. It dared to bash socialist realism.

Larisa recalls that she was cooking her way through *The Book of Tasty and Healthy Food* when Yulia handed her the *Novy mír* conspiratorially wrapped in an issue of *Pravda*. In those days Mom cooked like a maniac. Her childhood suspicions of life not being 'entirely good' and the future not radiant had strengthened by now into a dull, aching conviction. Cooking relieved the ache somewhat. Into the meals she whipped up from scant edibles, she channeled all her disappointed theatrical yearnings. Her parent's multi-cornered, balconied kitchen offered a stage for a consoling illusion, that somehow she might cook her way out of the bleak Soviet grind.

The *Novy mír* sat on the white kitchen table as Mom assembled her favorite dish. It was a defrosted cod with potatoes in a fried mushroom sauce, all baked with a cap of mayo and cheapo processed cheese. The cod was Mom's *realist*-realist riff on a *Kniga* recipe. The scents of cheese, fish, and mushrooms had just started mingling when Mom, scanning the 'sincerity' article, came to the part about food. Overall, Pomerantsev was condemning socialist realist literature for its hypocritical 'varnishing of reality' – a phrase that would be much deployed in liberal attacks on cultural Stalinism. Pomerantsev singled out among the clichés the (fake) smell of delicious *pelmeni* (meat dumplings). He complained that even those writers who didn't set the table with phony roast goose and suckling pigs still removed 'the black bread' from the scene, airbrushing out foul factory canteens and dorms.

Mom leafed through her *Kniga* and suddenly laughed. Oysters? Champagne buckets? Fruit cornucopias spilling out of cut-crystal bowls? They positively glared with their hypocrisy now. 'Lies, lies, lies,' Mom said, stabbing her finger into the photo of the suckling pig. She slammed shut *The Book of Tasty and Healthy Food* and pulled her cod out of the oven. It was *her* dish, *her* creation stripped of the communal abundance myth – liberated from the Stalinist happiness project.

She never opened the *Kniga* again until I pushed it on her in New York.

✴ ✴ ✴

Prepping for our Stalin's Deathday dinner, Mom phoned constantly for my menu approval.

Her overarching concept, as usual, was maddeningly archival: to nail the cultural pastiche of late Stalinism. One dish *had* to capture the era's officious festive pomposity. We settled finally on a crab salad with its Stalinist-baroque decoration of chimerical anchovy strips (*never* seen in Moscow), coral crab legs, and parsley bouquets. Pompous and pastichey both.

As a nod to the pauperist intelligentsia youth of the emerging Thaw generation, Mom also planned on ultra-frugal pirozhki. The eggless pastry of flour, water, and one stick of *margarin* enjoyed a kind of viral popularity at the time.

This left us needing only an 'ethnic' dish.

Stalin's imperialist post-war policies treated Soviet minorities as inferior brothers of the great ethnic Russians (or downright enemies of the people, at times). So while the 1952 *Kniga* deigns to include a handful of token dishes from the republics, it folds them into an all-Soviet canon. Recipes for Ukrainian borscht, Georgian *kharcho* (a soup), and Armenian dolmas are offered with nary a mention of their national roots.

Mom rang a day later. 'To represent the ethnic republics,' she announced, unnaturally formal, 'I have selected . . . *chanakhi!*'

'No!' I protested. 'You can't – *it was Stalin's favorite dish!*'

'Oy,' Mom said, and hung up.

She called back. 'But I already bought lamb chops,' she bleated. She had also bought baby eggplants, ripe tomatoes and peppers, and lots of cilantro – in short, all the ingredients for the deliciously soupy clay-baked Georgian stew called chanakhi.

'But, Ma,' I reasoned, 'wouldn't it be weird to celebrate liberation from Stalin with his *personal favorite* dish?'

'Are you totally *sure*,' she wheedled, 'that it *was* his favorite dish?'

With a sigh I agreed to double check. I hung up and poured myself a stiff Spanish brandy. Grudgingly, I reexamined my researches.

'Stalin,' wrote the Yugoslav communist litterateur Milovan Djilas on encountering the Vozhd in the thirties, 'ate food in quantities that would have been enormous even for a much larger man. He usually chose meat . . . a sign of his mountain origins.' Describing meeting him again in 1945, Djilas gasped, 'Now he was positively gluttonous, as if afraid someone might snatch the food from under his nose.'

Stalin did most of his gluttonizing at his Kuntsevo dacha, not far from where I grew up, accompanied by his usual gang of invitees: Beria, Khrushchev, Molotov, and Mikoyan. The (non-refusable) invitations to dacha meals were spontaneous, the hours late.

'They were called *obedi* (lunches),' grumbled Molotov, 'but what kind of lunch is it at ten or eleven p.m.?'

There was a hominess to these nocturnal meals that suggested Stalin himself didn't much enjoy officious Stalinist pomp. A long table with massive carved legs was set in the dacha's wood-paneled dining room, which was unadorned save for a fireplace and a huge Persian carpet. Waiters presided over by round-faced Valechka – Stalin's loyal house-keeper and possible mistress – left food at one end of the table on heavy silver platters with lids, then vanished from sight. Soups sat on the side table. The murderous crew got up and helped themselves. Stalin's favorite Danube herring, always unsalted, and *stroganina* (shaved frozen raw fish) could be among the zakuski. Soups were traditional and Russian, such as *ukha* (fish broth) and meaty cabbage *shchi* cooked over several days. Grilled lamb riblets, poached quail, and, in-variably, plenty of fish for the main courses. It was Soviet-Eurasian fusion, the dacha cuisine: Slavic and Georgian.

I took a swallow of my Carlos I brandy.

At the dacha Stalin drank light Georgian wine – and, always, water from his favorite frosty, elongated carafe – and watched others get blotto on vodka. 'How many degrees below zero is it outside?' he enjoyed quizzing guests. For every degree they were off by, they'd have to drink a shot. Such dinnertime pranks enjoyed a long regal tradition in Russia. Peter the Great jolted diners with dwarfs springing from gi-ant pies. At his extravagant banquets, Ivan the Terrible, Stalin's role model, sent chalices of poisoned booze to out-of-favor boyars and watched them keel over. Stalin liked to make Humpty Dumpty-like Khrushchev squat and kick his heels in a Ukrainian gopak dance, or he'd roar as his henchmen pinned paper scribbled with the word *khui* (dick) to Nikita's rotund back. Mikoyan, ever practical, confessed to bringing extra pants to the dacha: tomatoes on chairs was a cherished dinner table hijink. (The tomatoes, incidentally, were grown on the dacha grounds.) Throughout this *Animal House* tomfoolery, Stalin sipped, 'perhaps waiting for us to untie our tongues,' wrote Mikoyan. These were men who, in their bloody hands, held the summary fate of one sixth of the world.

Ever the meticulous foodie, Mikoyan left us the best recollections of the Vozhd's dining mores. Apparently Stalin had a fondness for inventing new dishes for his chefs to perfect. One particular favorite was a certain 'part soup, part entree . . .'

Aha, I said to myself.

'In a big pot,' Mikoyan wrote, 'they'd mix eggplants, tomatoes, potatoes, black pepper, bay leaf, and pieces of unfatty lamb. It was served hot. They added cilantro . . . Stalin named it Aragvi.'

No, there could be no doubt: Mikoyan was describing a classic Georgian stew called *chankakhi*. Stalin must have dubbed it Aragvi after a Georgian river or a favored Moscow Georgian restaurant, or both.

I thought some more about Mikoyan. Seemingly bullet-proof for most of his career, by 1953 Stalin's old cohort, former food commissar, and now deputy chair of the Council of Ministers, had finally fallen into disfavor. The Vozhd trashed him and Molotov at Central Committee plenum; then the pair were left out of the Kuntsevo 'lunches.' Mikoyan must have counted his days. His son recalled that he kept a gun in his desk, a quick bullet being preferable to arrest, which would drag his big Armenian family with him. Anastas Ivanovich was a brutally calculating careerist. Yet, sitting at my desk with my brandy, I felt a pang of compassion.

The phone interrupted my ruminations.

'I've resolved the chanakhi dilemma!' my mother proudly announced. 'Before his death wasn't Stalin plotting a genocidal purge against Georgia?'

'Well, yes. I believe so,' I conceded, bewildered. This intended purge was less famous than the one against Jews. But indeed, Stalin seemed to have had ethnic cleansing in mind for his own Caucasian kin. More specifically, he was targeting Mingrelians, a subminority of which Beria was a proud son. This could well have been a convoluted move against Beria.

'Well then!' cried Mom. 'We can serve chanakhi as a tribute to the oppressed Georgians!'

★ ★ ★

'To Stalin's death!' hoots Katya after I've poured out the vodka. 'Let's clink!'

Inna is shocked.

'But, Katiush, it's a bad omen to clink for the dead!'

'*Exactly!* We must clink so the shit may rot in his grave!'

March 5 has arrived. Outside my mother's windows in Queens, rain hisses down as we celebrate the snuffing of Stalin's candle. Katya, Musya, Inna – the octogenarian ladies at Mom's table pick at the showy crab-salad platter amid fruit cornucopias and bottles of Sovetskoye bubbly. Sveta arrives last – slight, wan of face. Many moons ago, when she was a Moscow belle, the great poet Joseph Brodsky would stay with her on his visits from Leningrad. The thought touches me now.

'I *went*,' Sveta boasts, grinning, 'to Stalin's funeral!'

'Mishugina,' clucks Katya, making a 'crazy' sign with her finger. 'People were killed!'

As the monstrous funeral procession swelled and mourners got trampled, Sveta hung on to her school's flower wreath – all the way to the Hall of Columns.

'The lamb, a little tough, maybe?' says Musya, assessing Mother's chanakhi tribute to the oppressed Georgians. I pile insult on injury by slyly noting the connection to Stalin's dacha feasts. Mom flashes me a look. She leaves for the kitchen, shaking her head.

'Here we are, girls,' Inna muses. 'Arrests, repressions, denunciations . . . Been through *all that* . . . and still managed to keep our decency.'

Mom reappears with her intelligentsia-frugal pirozhki. 'So enough with Stalin already,' she implores. 'Can we move on to *ottepel*?'

✷ ✷ ✷

Less than a year after Stalin's death, Ilya Ehrenburg, a suave literary éminence grise, published a mediocre novella critiquing a socialist realist hack artist and a philistine Soviet factory boss. Or something like that; nobody now remembers the plot. But the title stuck, going on to define the era of liberalization and hope under Khrushchev.

Ottepel. Thaw.

By 1955, after an intense power struggle – Stalin hadn't designated any heir – Khrushchev was assuming full leadership of our Socialist Rodina. Except that nobody called the potbellied gap-toothed former metal worker Mountain

Eagle or Genius of Humanity. Father of All Nations? You must be kidding. Politely, they called him Nikita Sergeevich, or simply Nikita, a folkloric Slavic name that contrasted starkly with Stalin's aloof exotic Georgian otherness. But mostly comrades on the street called the new leader Khrushch (beetle), or Lisiy (the bald); later, Kukuruznik (Corn Man) for his ultimately self-destructive penchant for corn.

Referring to our leader with such familiar terms – that in itself was a tectonic shift.

'My elation was unforgettable, the early Thaw times – as intense as the fear during Stalin!' Inna leads off. She was working in those heady days at Moscow's Institute of Philosophy. 'Nobody worked or ate, we just talked and talked, smoked and smoked, to the point of passing out. What had happened to our country? How had we allowed it to happen? Would the new cult of *sincerity* change us?'

'*The Festival!*' Katya and Sveta squeal in unison. The memory has them leaping out of their seats.

If there was a main cultural jolt that launched the Thaw, it was 'the Festival.' In February 1956 Khrushchev made his epochal 'secret speech' denouncing Stalin. Seventeen months later, to show the world the miraculous transformation of Soviet society, Komsomol bosses with the Bald One's encouragement staged the Sixth International Youth Festival in the freshly de-Stalinized Russian capital.

For Muscovites that sweltering fortnight in July and August of 1957 was a consciousness-bending event.

'Festival? Nyet . . . *skazka* (a fairy tale)!' Sveta croons, her pallid face suddenly flushed.

Skazka indeed. A culture where a few years earlier the word *inostranets* (foreigner) meant 'spy' or 'enemy' had suddenly yanked open the Iron Curtain for a brief moment, letting in a flood tide of jeans, boogie-woogie, abstract art, and electric guitars. Never – never! – had Moscow seen such a spectacle. Two million giddy locals cheered the thirty thousand delegates from more than one hundred countries in the opening parade stretching along twelve miles. Buildings were painted, drunks disciplined, city squares and parks transformed into dance halls. Concerts, theater, art shows, the street as an orgy of spontaneous contact. That internationalist summer is credited with everything from spawning the dissident movement to fostering Jewish identity. (Jews flocked from all over the USSR to meet the Israeli delegation.) More than anything else perhaps was this: the first real spark of the all-powerful myth of *zagranitsa* – a loaded word meaning 'beyond the border' that would inflame, taunt, and titillate Soviet minds until the fall of the USSR.

And love, that picnic of love, the Khrushchevian Woodstock.

Sveta fell for a seven-foot-tall red-haired American. La bella Katya, translating for a delegation of Italian soccer players, had one of her inamoratos threaten suicide as they parted. In farewell, the distraught Romeo tossed her a package out of his hotel window.

'So I unwrap it at home,' cries Katya. 'Panties! *Transparent* blue panties!'

Mom's guests rock with laughter. 'Remember our Soviet underpants? Two colors only: purple or blue, knee length. Sadistic elastic!'

* * *

Larisa, too, fell in love with an International Youth Festival foreigner. And he with her.

Lucien was petite and deeply tanned, with chiseled features and dark, lively eyes. He wore a dapper short leather jacket and suede loafers so pristine and comfortable-looking, they instantly betrayed him as *ne nash* – 'not ours.' Born in Paris, raised on Corsica, Lucien ran a French lycée in the Moroccan town of Meknes, a cultural cocktail Mom found intoxicating. In my mother's cracked vinyl photo album, the fortnight's worth of pictures of him outnumber the ones of my dad three to one.

It was their mutual interest in Esperanto that brought the lovers together. Lucien sat next to Mom at the Festival's first Esperanto plenary session, and when two days later, under one of the behemoth Stalinist facades on Gorky Street, he put his arm around her, it seemed the most natural thing in the world. Lucien radiated charm and goodwill. In all her life Mom, then twenty-three, had never had a suitor who expressed his attraction with such disarming directness, such sweetness. Somehow her three words of Esperanto allowed her to communicate her innermost feelings to Lucien where Russian had failed her before.

Which makes sense. For all the Thaw talk of sincerity, Soviet Russian wasn't suited for goodwill or intimacy or, God knows, unselfconscious lyrical prattle. As our friend Sasha Genis the cultural critic wrote, the State had hijacked all the fine, meaningful words. *Friendship, homeland, happiness, love, future, consciousness, work* – these could only be bracketed with ironic quotation marks.

'Young lady, how about we go build Communism together'

178

went a popular pickup line in the metro. Girls found it hysterical.

Here's how the coyly convoluted Soviet mating ritual went: Igor meets Lida at a student dorm or party. They smoke on a windowsill. Igor needles Lida admiringly, she needles back coquettishly. Walking Lida home, Igor flaunts his knowledge of Hemingway, maybe mentions that he just happens to have sought-after tickets to the Italian film festival at the Udarnik Cinema. He lingers on her apartment landing. With studied nonchalance he mutters something about her *telefonchik* (ironic diminutive for phone number). After several weeks/months of mingy carnation offerings, aimless ambling along windswept boulevards, and heated groping in cat-piss-infested apartment lobbies, a consummation takes place. In some bushes crawling with ants if breezes are warm. Lida gets knocked up. If Igor is decent, they go to the ZAGS, the office that registers deaths and marriages. Their happily-ever-after involves moving into her or his family 'dwelling space,' which is overcrowded with a father who drinks, a mother who yells, a domineering war widow grandmother, and a pesky Young Pioneer brother. The Young Pioneer likes to spy on newly-weds having sex. From there, married life only gets jollier.

By the time I was nine, I already suspected that such nuptial bliss wasn't for me. I had a different plan, involving *zagranitsa*. A foreign husband would be my ticket out of this 'dismally-ever-after' to a glorious life filled with prestigious foreign commodities. More romantic by nature, Mom belonged as well to a generation more idealistic than mine. Her *zagranitsa* dreams did not feature hard-currency goods. Instead, into this single loaded term she distilled her desperate longing for world culture. Or, I should probably say,

World Culture. After the collapse of the Stalin cosmology and her drift away from her ur-Soviet parents, culture replaced everything else in her life. It became a private devotion.

When Lucien talked of Morocco, Mom imagined herself inside some electric Matissian dreamscape. His offhand mentions of visiting his grandmother in the French countryside fired up her Proustian reveries. She could almost touch the fine porcelain teacups in *la grand-mère*'s salon, hear her pearls rattling gently. Lucien's tiny gifts – such as a leather Moroccan change purse embossed with gold stars – were not mere commodities but totems of distant, mysterious freedoms. 'A souvenir from the free world to someone locked up in a prison cage,' she now puts it.

Marriage never came up between them. Lucien stayed for all of two weeks. But simply having the non-Russian softness of his palm against hers, Mom felt her lifelong alienation blossoming into a tangible shape, an articulated desire: to break physically free of Soviet reality. On the hot August day in 1957 when Lucien departed, giving her a volume of Zola's *Germinal* with a passionate Esperanto inscription, she knew that she too would leave. Until it happened, almost two decades later, Mom imagined that she existed in her own fourth dimension outside the Soviet time-space continuum.

'I was anti-Soviet,' she says. 'But at the same time a-Soviet: an *internal* émigré cocooned in my own private "cosmopolitan" microcosm.' Her own fairy tale.

To fill in a void left by Lucien and the Festival, Mom plunged back into cooking – but now her kitchen fantasies took a new tack. *The Book of Tasty and Healthy Food* had been retired in scorn. *Zagranitsa* was the new inspiration. What did this imaginary Elsewhere actually taste like? Mom hadn't a clue. While she could at least mentally savor the kulebiakas and botvinya so voluptuously cited by Chekhov and Gogol, Western dishes were mere names, undecoded signs from alternative domestic realities. The absence of recipes provided a certain enchantment; you could fill in these alien names with whatever flavors you chose.

Always stubbornly cheerful and good-natured about the paucity of ingredients in stores, Mom turned her parents' kitchen once more into a dreamer's home workshop. She may well have been the first woman in Moscow to make pizza, from a recipe 'adapted' from a contraband issue of *Family Circle* lent to her by a friend whose father once worked in America. Who cared if her 'pizza' bore a resemblance to a Russian meat *pirog*, only open-faced and smothered in ketchup and gratings of Sovetsky cheese? No ingredient, really, was too dreary for Mom to subject to a tasty experiment.

'Today I'll make pot-au-feu!' she'd announce brightly, eyeing a head of decaying cabbage. 'I read about it in Goethe – I think it's soup!'

'Tastes like your usual watery *shchi*,' her brother, Sashka, would mutter.

Mom disagreed. Just renaming a dish, she discovered, had a power to transfigure the flavor.

Every couple of weeks a letter from Lucien would arrive from Morocco. '*Mia kariga eta Lara* – my dearest little Lara,' he always began. 'My heart is wrenched,' he wrote after a year. 'Why doesn't *kariga* Lara answer me anymore?'

By then *kariga* Lara was madly in love with somebody else. Somebody named Sergei, somebody she thought looked uncannily like the French film heartthrob Alain Delon from

Rocco and His Brothers, which she'd seen at an Italian film festival.

✷ ✷ ✷

My mother and father met at the end of 1958. She was twenty-four; he was three years younger. My parents met in a line, and their romance blossomed in yet another line, which I guess makes me the fruit of the Soviet *defitsit* (shortage) economy with its ubiquitous queues.

Your average *Homo sovieticus* spent a third to half of his non-working time queuing for something. The *ochered'* (line) served as an existential footbridge across an abyss — the one between private desire and a collective availability dictated by the whims of centralized distribution. It was at once a means of ordering socialist reality; an adrenaline-jagged blood sport; and a particular Soviet *fate*, in the words of one sociologist. Or think of the *ochered'* as a metaphor for a citizen's life journey — starting on the queue at the birth registry office and ending on a waiting list for a decent funeral plot. I also like the notion of *ochered'* as 'quasi-surrogate for church' floated in an essay by Vladimir Sorokin, the postmodernist enfant terrible whose absurdist novel *The Queue* consists entirely of fragments of *ochered'* dialogue, a linguistic vernacular anchored by the long-suffering word *stoyat'* (to stand).

You stood? Yes, stood. Three hours. Got damaged ones. Wrong size.

Here's what the line wasn't: a gray inert nowhere. Imagine instead an all-Soviet public square, a hurly-burly where comrades traded gossip and insults, caught up with news left out of the newspapers, got into fistfights, or enacted comradely feats. In the thirties the NKVD had informers in queues to assess public moods, hurrying the intelligence straight to Stalin's brooding desk. Lines shaped opinions and bred ad hoc communities: citizens from all walks of life *standing*, united by probably the only truly collective authentic Soviet emotions: yearning and discontent (not to forget the unifying hostility toward war veterans and pregnant women, honored comrades allowed to get goods without a wait).

Some lines, Mom insists, could be fun, uplifting even. Such were the queues for cultural events in Thaw-era Moscow – culture being a *defitsit* commodity, like everything else. Thanks to Khruschev's parting of the Iron Curtain, Moscow was flooded with cultural exports back then. Scofield as Hamlet, Olivier as Othello, the legendary Gérard Philipe doing Corneille; Brecht's Berliner Ensemble led by his widow . . . Stokowsky, Balanchine, Bruno Walter – Mom devoured it all. And that's not counting domestic treasures: Shostakovich performing his piano quintet or the balletic comet Galina Ulanova. 'I stood in line so much, I had barely a moment to eat or inhale,' Mom likes to boast.

Like lines for cars and TV sets that could last months, years even, the Cultural Queue moved according to a particular logic and order. A whisper or a formal announcement of an upcoming tour set the wheel turning. A 'line elder' – a hyperactive high-culture priest – would spring into action by starting the *spisok* (list). Still an eternity away from the ticket sale, friends took turns guarding the box office, day in and day out, adding newcomers to the all-powerful *spisok*, assigning numbers. Many of Mom's friendships formed at the roll calls requiring everyone's presence. These resembled intelligentsia parties but were hosted on freezing sidewalks where the cold cracked your boots, or in gusty May when winds unleashed torrents of white poplar fluff.

'AHA! Here comes treacherous Frumkina!' cried Inna, the dark-haired 'line elder,' when Mom, once again, was unforgivably late for the French ballet roll call.

'AHA! Treacherous Frumkina!' mocked a stranger, so skinny, so young, with green liquid eyes offset by a vampiric pallor. Mother glared at him. But that night she kept thinking about how much he resembled Alain Delon.

In the end, the French ballet canceled. But Mom now kept noticing Sergei in different lines, finding herself more and more drawn to his shy cockiness, his spectral pallor, and most of all to his cultural queuing cred. In that department, Dad was a titan.

Sergei, my father, grew up neglected. Alla had him young, at nineteen. When he was a teenager, she was still stunning, a six-foot-tall bleached blonde war widow with a penchant for vodka, swearing, billiards, and cards, besides a busy career (city planning) and an even busier love life. During her assignations – married men usually – at their one room in a nightmarish communal apartment, Alla shooed Sergei out of the house. Dad spent most days on the streets anyway, a typical post-war fatherless youth, apathetic, cynical, disillusioned. One day he walked out of his squalid building and went rambling past the grand columned facade of the Bolshoi Theater with its chariot of Apollo rearing atop the Ionic portico. Dad was whistling. A five-ruble bill was in his pocket, a fat sum at the time, a gift from a rich uncle for

dad's fifteenth birthday. Sergei was strolling in sweet anticipation of how he could spend it when a scalper sidled up.

Five rubles for one fifty-kopek seat to Swan Lake at the
Bolshoi – tonight.

On a lark, Dad handed over the fiver. Mainly because
even though he passed the Bolshoi almost daily, he'd never
been inside. A massive red velvet curtain inlaid with myriad
tiny hammers and sickles rose slowly into the darkness. By
the time it went down and the lights came on, Dad was
hooked. Back in those days Moscow worshipped at the
exquisite feet of Galina Ulanova, the soaring sylph regarded
as the twentieth century's most heartbreakingly lyrical
ballerina. The entire performance Sergei felt as if he himself
were floating on air. And so Dad became a professional
Ulanova fan, seeing everything else at the Bolshoi and at the
Moscow Conservatory for good measure. He soon scalped
tickets himself. Dated long-necked swanettes from the
Bolshoi corps de ballet.

His science studies, meanwhile, passed in a blur. Arrogant
by nature, bored with mechanics and physics, he kept
dropping in and out of prestigious technical colleges. Right
before the exams in his final year, Alla was home after surgery
and she roped him into an intense three-day vodka-fueled
card game. Sergei never showed up for the exams, didn't
graduate, didn't care. The Cultural Queue was his life and his
drug. He did literal drugs, too, codeine mostly, hence his
vampyric complexion. Upon checking into a clinic, he was
advised by helpful Soviet doctors that the best way to kick a
drug habit was *to drink*. A lot. Which he did.

The day before ticket sales started, the Cultural Queue climaxed in a raucous marathon of actual standing all the way to the finish line. It could last twelve hours, sometimes eighteen, all-nighters that left Mom physically drained but charged with adrenaline. The final push! One morning at the end of May, Larisa and Sergei staggered from the box office window like a couple of triumphant zombies. Tickets to all five performances of Leonard Bernstein's New York Philharmonic, still months away, were nestled in their pockets. Mom bought a green-capped bottle of buttermilk and *kaloríynie bulchokí*, feathery buns studded with raisins, and they collapsed on the long, arching bench by the Great Hall of the Moscow Conservatory. Its neoclassical bulk gleamed custard-yellow in the morning sun. Mom and Dad kissed for the first time under the statue of a seated Tchaikovsky summoning his music. Men with lumpy briefcases were plodding to work. Burly women in kerchiefs hawked the season's first lilacs.

For a few weeks Larisa and Sergei were inseparable. Then he cooled. He behaved like a smug, mysterious cat, appearing and then vanishing, passionate one minute, listless and disengaged the next. By July he was gone. The cultural season was over. Days turned into weeks with no news of him, summer was passing, and Mom's insides twisted in a knot when someone whispered that Sergei was involved with Inna, the line elder. Inna with her glossy black hair, luminous skin, and a rich father.

All of Moscow, meanwhile, stood in another line, not as epic and devastating as the lines at Stalin's funeral, but as long and tedious as the *ochered'* at Lenin's mausoleum. They were standing to taste Pepsi-Cola at Sokolniki Park. Even my despondent mom was among them.

✳ ✳ ✳

Well before the official opening of the American National Exhibition, Muscovites streamed to Sokolniki in the north of the city to see what was up, or, rather, what was going up. Amid the raw greenery, U.S. construction workers were helping to erect Buckminster Fuller's spectacular geodesic dome, all thirty thousand golden, anodized aluminum square feet of it. Even the workers' colorful hard hats provoked wild curiosity.

To urban intelligentsia, *Ameríka*, imagined from novels and music and movies, loomed as a fervently desired mythical Other. Khrushchev, too, was obsessed with *Ameríka*. Nikita Sergeevich displayed the typical H. sovieticus mix of envy, fascination, resentment, and awe. (He would impetuously tour the United States later that year.) While 'churning out missiles like sausages,' as he liked to boast, the verbose, erratic premier simultaneously blathered on about 'peaceful co-existence,' promising to beat capitalist frenemy number one nonviolently – 'in all economic indicators.' *Dognat' i peregnat'* (catch up and overtake), this was called – the long-standing socialist slogan now recast to target the mighty Yanks. As in, 'Let's catch up and overtake America in dairy and beef production!' Comrades on the streets knew the score, though. 'We'd *better* not overtake,' went a popular wisecrack, 'or the Yanks will see our bare asses!' Less cynical Americans, meanwhile, stocked their shelters against Red ICBMs and had nightmares about brainwashing.

In such a heated context, Russia floated a temporizing gesture: a first-ever exchange of exhibitions of 'science, technology and culture.' The United States said yes. The Soviets went first. At the New York Coliseum in June 1959, three glistening Sputniks starred with their insectlike trailing filaments and a supporting cast heavy on models of power stations and rows of bulky chrome fridges.

A month later in Moscow, on about a third of the Soviets' budget, the Yanks retorted with consumerist dazzle – acre upon acre of it at Sokolniki Park. Almost eight hundred companies donated goods for the exhibit.

'What is this,' thundered Izvestia, 'a national exhibit of a great country or a branch of a department store?'

Cannily, it was both.

As a girl Mom had visited the socialist fairyland of the All-Union Agricultural Exhibition in Moscow. Now, exactly two decades later, just a mile or so away in Sokolniki, here she was in the Potemkin village of consumer capitalism. Which was more overwhelming? Mom usually giggles and rolls her eyes when I ask.

Inside Bucky's golden dome, seven giant screens positioned overhead by the designers Charles and Ray Eames flashed with their composite short film *Glimpses of the USA*. Mom stood open-mouthed, blinking hard as 2,200 still photos pulsed through a 'typical' workday and Sunday in suburban America, closing on a lingering image of flowers.

'*Nezabudki* . . .' Mom murmured along with the entranced crowd. 'Forget-me-nots.'

Beyond the dome waited an empire of household stuff in the Glass Pavilion. Inside stood a model apartment, outside, a model home. A Corvette and a Caddie enticed oglers. There were abstract expressionist paintings to puzzle over, a book exhibit to filch from, Disney's 360-degree Circarama travelogue of America to crane at. Fashion models ambled along runways while decadent jazz played and ever-smiling American guides answered all comers in fluent Russian. One of the guides was having a fling with Mom's close friend Radik. My mother couldn't get over this *amerikanka*'s non-Soviet directness and her fantastic big teeth.

In this setting, on press preview day, July 25, the spontaneous dialectic known as the Kitchen Debate erupted between Nikita and Nixon. Tension was still running high over the Western insistence on continued free access to West Berlin, surrounded as it was by East Germany. Khrushchev was agitated further by the U.S. Congress's renewal of its annual 'Captive Nations' Resolution to pray for Iron Curtain satellite countries. He carried a chip on his shoulder, vowing not to be overawed by America's vision of bounty. Nixon in turn hankered for the 1960 Republican presidential nomination. He had to look tough.

Cue the scenario at Sokolniki:

MODEL ON-SITE RCA TV STUDIO. MIDDAY.
Straw-hatted NK (Nikita Khrushchev) hectors RN (Richard Nixon) that Russia will soon surpass America in living standard. Waggles his fingers 'bye-bye' as if overtaking the U.S., guffaws for cameras.

PEPSI-COLA KIOSK. AFTERNOON.
RN leads NK over for a taste test of the sole product the U.S. has been permitted to give out as a sample. Pepsi will eventually be the first American consumer item available in the USSR. 'Very refreshing!' NK roars. Guzzles six Dixie cupfuls. Soviet men ask if Pepsi will get them drunk. Soviet women pronounce Russian kvass tastier. Some skeptical comrades

compare the smell to benzene – or shoe wax. Over the next six weeks 'disgusted' Soviets will gulp down three million cups. Country babushkas toting milk buckets will stand in line multiple times – to the point of fainting – to bring a taste of flat, warm *pepsíkola* back to the kolkhoz. Like everyone else, Mom will keep her Dixie cup as a relic for years.

SPLITNIK KITCHEN. SAME AFTERNOON.
NK and RN relock horns at GE's streamlined kitchen in the prefab tract house nicknamed 'Splitnik' (for the walkway put in for the show). Behold the sleek washing machine! The gleaming Frigidaire! The box of SOS soap pads!

NK (lying): You Americans think the Russian people will be astonished to see these things. The fact is, all our new houses have this kind of equipment.

RN (lying): We do not claim to astonish the Russian people.

In the debate's iconic photo, the accompanying throng includes the hawk-nosed Mikoyan, who had tried to wangle Coke's recipe back in the thirties, and a young bushy-browed bureaucrat, one Leonid Brezhnev.

RCA WHIRLPOOL MIRACLE KITCHEN. THAT EVENING.
After an early dinner and toasts with California wine, the debaters view a second, hyper-futuristic deluxe hearth. The dishwasher is movable and scoots on tracks. The robotic floor sweeper is remote-controlled.

NK (scoffing): Don't you have a machine that puts food in your mouth and pushes it down?

Secret polling later showed that Russians were equally unimpressed by the Miracle Kitchen. Voters rated it last. Jazz ranked first, along with Disney's Circarama. But so what? To U.S. minds the exhibition was its finest cold war propaganda action ever, and it was pronounced so.

My mom didn't vote in the poll. But to her surprise and dismay, she found herself among those underwhelmed by the kitchen. If anything, it left her feeling more lonely and down than before. She wanted to love the American exhibition, almost desperately she did. Had counted on it to be a vision of pure *zagranitsa*, to spirit her out of her socialist gloom, away from the deeper, more wounding gloom of her heartache. But for days afterward, she imagined cheery Yankee housewives trapped and frightened amid their sci-fi fridges and washing machines. She couldn't picture herself – ever – cooking her 'pot-au-feu' *shchi* in one of those blinding steel pots. This paradigm of happiness, fashioned from plastic tumblers, bright orange juice cartons, extravagantly frosted, unnaturally tall American layer cakes, seemed just as miserably phony as anything in the *Kniga*. It violated her intimate, private dream of *Amerika*. In any case, domestic bliss, whether socialist or capitalist, seemed more elusive than ever. She ate a slice of black bread with a raw onion ring now and then, that was all, and though it was August, buried herself under the scratchy beige woolen blanket with her blue-green volume of *Swann's Way*. The Soviets had stolen the lovely Russian term for 'companion' and 'fellow traveler' and fixed it to a glistening ball of metal hurtling through darkest space. Sputnik. Swann, suffering at Odette's infidelities, was Mom's *sputnik* in misery. There was still no word from Sergei.

* * *

And then on a dank September day, crossing a pedestrian underpass near the Bolshoi, she ran into him. Sergei looked pale, defenseless, and shivery. Larisa handed him three rubles; he seemed badly in need of a drink. He took it and walked off, gaze averted.

A few weeks later the doorbell rang at her parents' house in the Arbat. It was Sergei – returning the money, he said. Oh, and something else. 'I've been running into all these ballerinas,' he mumbled, 'so seductive and pretty in their bell skirts. But I have this short Jewish girl on my mind . . . *you are the one.*'

This is how my father proposed.

Mom should have slammed the door right then and locked it and dived back deep under the scratchy beige blanket and stayed there. Instead, she and Sergei formalized their love on a gray December afternoon in 1959, after three months of living together.

My parents' generation, the generation of the Thaw, scoffed at white dresses and bourgeois parties. Mom and Dad's uncivil non-ceremony took place at a drab ZAGS registry office near the Tretyakov Art Gallery. Outside, a wet snow was falling.

Under her shapeless coat with squirrel trim, Mom wore her usual blue hand-sewn poplin blouse. Sergei yet again looked pale and disheveled; he'd knocked back a hundred grams – rubbing alcohol, was it? – with buddies at work. But my parents' spirits were good. Everything amused them in the dingy reception area. Pimply sixteen-year-olds waiting for their very first Soviet internal passports. Non-sober families, and a war invalid with his accordion serenading nervous couples reemerging from their assembly-line knot-tying. On this occasion Mom didn't even mind the institutional smell of galoshes and acrid disinfectant that had nauseated her ever since her first elections in 1937.

A tiny head peeped out of the marriage hall area.

'Next couple!'

My parents passed through a vast hollow room beautified by a pair of forlorn chandeliers into a smaller room, this one bare save for a giant portrait of Lenin thrusting an arm out and squinting. The arm pointed conspicuously in the direction of the toilet. Behind a crimson-draped table sat a judge fringed by two dour clerks. The wide red ribbons draped across their gray-clad chests gave them the appearance of moving banners.

The judge cast a suspicious glance at Mom's homemade blouse. Her small face resembled a *vydra*'s (an otter's), squished below a towering hairdo.

'ON BEHALF OF THE RUSSIAN FEDERATION' – the *vydra*'s petite mouth suddenly boomed like a megaphone at a parade – 'WE CONGRATULATE THE . . .'

Mom clenched her jaw tight. She looked up at the ceiling, then over at squinting Lenin, then at Sergei, then exploded with hysterical laughter.

'STOP THIS DISGRACE, COMRADE BRIDE,' thundered the *vydra*, 'OR YOU WILL BE ESCORTED FROM HERE IMMEDIATELY!'

'DO YOU PROMISE TO RAISE YOUR

CHILDREN,' she resumed, 'IN THE BEST TRADITIONS OF MARXISM AND LENINISM?' Mom nodded, fighting the next eruption of laughter.

'RINGS!!!' shouted the *vydra*.

Mom and Dad had none.

'WITNESSES – WHERE ARE YOUR WITNESSES?'

Ditto the witnesses.

The *vydra* didn't bother with further felicitations. My parents didn't seem worthy of the customary wishes of good luck in creating a new socialist family.

'SIGN HERE, NOW!'

The *vydra* shoved a stack of documents across the red table.

Mom picked up the heavy blue fountain pen with a sharp, menacing metal tip. The vydra snatched it away and whacked it across my mother's knuckles.

'GROOM SIGNS FIRST!'

Three months after being assaulted with a fountain pen, Larisa moved into her mother-in-law's communal apartment, where eighteen families shared one kitchen.

PART III

ANYA

My mother and me the evening before we emigrated, 1974

CHAPTER SIX

✦

1960s: CORN, COMMUNISM, CAVIAR

The year I was born, 1963, is remembered by Russians for one of the worst crop failures in post-Stalinist history. War rationing still fresh in their memory, comrades found themselves back in breadlines with queue numbers scribbled on their hands in violet ink so indelible and so poisonous, the joke was that it infected your blood. All over Moscow adults enlisted schoolchildren to take their place in the line. For handing over as well the extra ration of bread they were allowed, some enterprising Young Pioneers made small fortunes charging ten kopeks per breadline.

Coarse and damp was the bread waiting at the end of the line. Not just damp, but often oozing weird greenish gunk: the flour had been stretched out with dried peas. Still, Moscow was hardly near starvation. In one of those savory ironies of socialist food distribution, some stores carried shrimp and crab from Vladivostok. But regular citizens didn't touch these exotic pink Far Eastern crustaceans out of the pompous pages of *Kníga*. Regular citizens hadn't a clue what shrimp were. People spat hardest at the fourteen-kopek cans of corn stacked up on store counters in

Giza-scaled pyramids. *All corn – no bread.* That was everyone's curse for Kukuruznik (Corn Man), the blabbering clown in the Kremlin who'd crowned this stupid, alien corn 'the new czarina of Russian fields.'

'What does the 1963 harvest look like?' went a popular joke. 'Like Khrushchev's hairdo (bald).'

Things were going badly for Nikita Sergeevich. After a stretch of prodigious economic boom and scientific achievement, his career was belly flopping. There was the bungled *Karíbsky krízis* (Russian for the Cuban missiles affair). His Virgin Lands scheme of planting grain en masse on the Central Asian steppes, promising initially, was ending in a cartoonish fiasco with millions of tons of topsoil simply blowing away. And his dairy and meat price hikes in 1962 had erupted in riots in the southern city of Novocherkassk. 'Khrushchev's flesh – for goulash!' railed a protest banner. The State responded with tanks, killing twenty-three rioters.

The massacre was concealed; but the Leader's *kukuruza* (corn) disaster could not be. Enthralled by a visiting Iowa farmer in 1955, the Bald One had introduced corn as the magic crop that would feed Russia's cattle. Corn was forced down human throats too. Khrushchev-look-alike chefs sang songs to the new corn in short propaganda films; animated rye and barley welcomed this new corn off the train in cartoons. 'The road to abundance is paved with *kukuruza!*' went a popular slogan. Maize was planted everywhere – while American instructions for proper seeding and care were everywhere ignored. After a couple of encouraging harvests, yields plunged. Wheat, neglected, grew in even shorter supply. Bread lines sprouted furiously.

In 1961 at the Twenty-Second Party Congress Khrushchev had promised true communism. Instead there was *kukuruza*. Russians could forgive many things, but the absence of wheat bread made them feel humiliated and angry. Wheat bread was symbolic, sacred. On induction into Komsomol, students were asked to name the price of bread. Woe to the politically retarded delinquent who blurted out 'thirteen kopeks.' The correct answer: 'Our Soviet bread is priceless.'

Capitalizing in part on this popular wrath, in October of 1964 a Kremlin clique forced Khrushchev from power. For a while papers talked about his 'subjectivism' and 'hare-brained scheming,' about the 'lost decade.' Then they stopped mentioning him. A previously obscure apparatchik named Leonid Brezhnev, now general secretary, ushered the USSR into a new era. Stagnation, the era was later dubbed. The age of cynicism and 'acquisitive socialism.' The age of bargains, contracts, and deals, of Brezhnev's-eyebrows jokes and Lenin Centennial anecdotes – of empty store shelves and connivingly stuffed fridges.

The dissolution of my parents' marriage mirrored Khrushchev's fall.

A product of the Thaw Era, Mom still retains tender feelings toward Kukuruznik. But she can't help blaming him and his corn and the breadlines for what happened with her and my father.

★ ★ ★

About a year before my mother's troubles began, she sat at a *pedsovet*, the pedagogical council of School No. 112, District 5.

Another meaningless 'agitational' propaganda meeting was about to begin. Mother felt queasy. The odor of sulfuric acid, potassium hydroxide, and teenage stress hormones hung in the air. The classroom they gathered in belonged to Comrade Belkin, the puffy-faced science teacher and font of communist consciousness.

For these endless, poisonous meetings Mom was partially to blame. She had spoken up at her very first 'agitational' session. Recently hired as the school's progressive young English teacher, she'd been eager to flaunt her dissident stripes. It was still the Thaw. *Sincerity* was the buzzword. Solzhenitsyn's anti-Stalinist *One Day in the Life of Ivan Denisovich* had just been published!

'Comrades!' my mother had begun in her best imitation Moscow Art Theater voice. 'What have we actually learned from this meeting? Why have we sat here listening to Comrade Belkin read aloud the entire political section of *Pravda*? Aren't piles of homework waiting? Don't some of us have hungry kids to go home to?'

At the last sentence Mom's oration trailed off. Nearing the Soviet grandmotherly age of thirty, she herself had no kid waiting hungrily. An ectopic pregnancy followed by barbaric Soviet gynecological care had left her in no shape to conceive, and 'home' was a dumpy single room she shared with her husband and mother-in-law in a bleak communal apartment.

Tak tak tak. 'So, so so,' said the troika: the Labor Union rep, the school's Party functionary, and Citizen Edelkin, the principal. *Tak tak tak*; they tapped their pencils in unison. 'Thanks for sharing your views, Comrade Frumkina.'

But the other teachers had been mesmerized by her

words. Mom caught their grateful, admiring glances. Shortly afterward a sign had appeared in the principal's office: FROM NOW ON: PROPAGANDA MEETINGS — COMPULSORY. The other teachers started avoiding my mother.

This new March session droned on and on. So much to discuss. Two Young Pioneers had been caught tying their scarlet scarves on a neighborhood cat. And what to do about Valya Maximova, the third-grader spied at gym class wearing a cross under her uniform? Confronted by responsible classmates, Valya had confessed: her babushka sometimes took her to church.

Valya's teacher waved Exhibit A, the confiscated cross, on its neck string as if dangling a dead mouse by the tail.

'That pesky babushka,' said the science teacher Belkin in a loud whisper. 'Under Stalin such types got twenty-five years.'

Stalin's corpse had recently been evicted from Lenin's mausoleum by Khrushchev, so as not to 'corrupt' that noblest of cadavers. Invoking the pockmarked Georgian was uncool. But instead of protesting, everyone turned and peered at Larisa. Some weeks before, sacrificing her own Sunday, she'd taken her pupils to a cemetery, where innocent Pioneers had been exposed to crosses galore. She regarded it as a cultural lesson, a way of lifting the Soviet taboo around death for the kids.

'Some Young Pioneers report that during the trip you mentioned *Jesus Christ*.'

Edelkin pronounced this as if Valya's religious babushka and Larisa were fellow opium pushers.

'Christianity is part of world culture,' Larisa protested.

Tak tak tak, went the troika.

Edelkin ended the meeting on an upbeat note. In the case of pupil Shurik Bogdanov there'd been serious progress. Poor Shurik Bogdanov – an A student, conscience of his class, and champion collector of scrap metal. Then he started getting Cs for 'behavior.' His distraught mother stormed into Edelkin's office and revealed the whole awful story: her husband had been cohabiting with a female colleague from his workplace. He intended to leave them. Poor young Shurik was traumatized.

'Could the Soviet school save a socialist family?' asked Edelkin with a dramatic flourish. Indeed, it could! The Party organization at Bogdanov père's workplace had been contacted, a public meeting called. Shurik's father and the female interloper had been instructed to cease their immoral cohabitation immediately.

'The father is now back in the family fold,' reported Edelkin, almost smirking with pride. Socialist values had triumphed. Would comrade teachers chip in for a bottle of Sovetskoye champagne for the couple?

Mom gasped for air as he finished. The chemical stench of the classroom, the intrusion of the *kollektiv* into some hapless comrade's love life, the bleakness of her own situation . . . Next thing she knew, the entire pedagogical council was fanning her with pages of *Pravda* and splashing her with cologne. She had fainted.

That week the doctor confirmed the impossible: she had fainted because she was with child. The troika at school suggested that she needn't bother to return after maternity leave.

My mother was pregnant, unemployed, and euphoric.

* * *

Mom remembers pregnancy as the happiest time of her life. She didn't understand why most Soviet mamas-to-be hid their bellies in shame under layers of baggy rags. Even at eight months she waddled down the street as if floating on air – belly forward. Inside her was a girl, she was sure of this. It was the girl she'd been dreaming about ever since she herself was a schoolgirl. The girl she imagined playing the piano, painting watercolors, learning languages in foreign countries, and – who knows? – maybe even riding a shiny brown Arabian horse on some verdant British estate. It was the girl she intended to guard like a tigress from the counterfeit Soviet happiness, from that rotten, demoralizing split-consciousness, from *toska*, the anguished, alienated anxiety of her own Stalinist childhood.

Apparently Mom also wanted to shield me from Sputnik and Yuri Gagarin and Belka and Strelka, the adorable black and white mutts who flew into space. My mother hated the *kosmos*; that preposterous futuristic final frontier of Soviet imperialism. At age five I was forced to hide my profound crush on Yuri Gagarin from her and weep in secret when the smiley *kosmonavt* died in a plane crash at the age of thirty-four. But I'm grateful Mom didn't name me Valentina, after Valentina Tereshkova, the first woman in space. I look nothing like Valentina. Mom named me instead after one of her favorite poems by Anna Akhmatova.

'*At baptism I was given a name – Anna, Sweetest of names for human lips or hearing.*'

Anna, Annushka, Anya, Anechka, the irreverent An'ka. The peasant-vernacular Anyuta and Anyuto-chka, Nyura and Nyurochka. Or Anetta, in a self-consciously ironic Russified French. Or the lovely and formal Anna Sergeevna (my name and patronymic) – straight out of Chekhov's 'The Lady with the Dog.' The inexhaustible stream of diminutive permutations of Anna, each with its own subtle semiotics, rolled sweetly off my mother's lips during pregnancy.

Her baby daydreams usually reached fever pitch in the food lines. Surrounded by disgruntled citizens muttering Khrushchev jokes, Mother drew up imaginary lists of the foods she would feed to her little Anyu-tik. Unattainable foods she knew only from her reading. *Omar*. Lobster. So noble-sounding, so foreign. Definitely pizza and pot-au-feu. And when the child was just old enough: Fleurie. Everyone swigged it in the novels of Hemingway, that most Russian of American writers. Yes, yes, definitely carafes of Fleurie, with snails dripping garlicky butter and parsley sauce. Followed by cakes from her beloved Proust. *Madlenki*, Mom called them in Russian, with the clumsy proprietary familiarity of someone who lived and breathed Proust but still thought madeleines were a species of jam-filled pirozhki.

Occasionally Mom would get lucky in the lines. She still talks of the day she victoriously lugged home five kilos – ten pounds – of *vobla* to last her the entire final trimester. Have I mentioned *vobla* before? It's the rock-hard, salt-encrusted dried Caspian roach fish. Rock-hard *vobla* sustained Russians through the revolutionary teens and twenties, the terrible thirties, the war-torn forties, the liberating fifties, and the rollicking sixties – until the Caspian was so depleted that in the stagnant seventies of my childhood *vobla* became a sought-after delicacy. *Vobla* brings out that particular Russian masochism; we love it because it's such a torment to eat. There's the violent whacking against a table to loosen the skin, followed by the furious yanking of the petrified leathery flesh off the skeleton. There's self-inflicted violence, too – a broken tooth here, a punctured gum there – all to savor that pungently salty, leathery strip of Soviet umami. *Vobla* was the last thing my mother ate before being rushed to Birthing House No. 4. This might explain why I'd happily trade all Hemingway's snails and Proust's cakes for a strip of petrified fish flesh.

From Birthing House No. 4 Mom brought home a jaundice-yellowed infant swaddled tight as a mummy into totalitarian submission. Awaiting her were the glories of Soviet socialist motherhood. Cribs as elegant as a beet harvester. Pacifiers made of industrial rubber you sterilized in a water bath for two hours while you hand-copied the entire volume of samizdat Dr. Spock. And *pelyonki* (diapers), twenty per day per Soviet child – not including nine flannel over-diapers, and a mountain of under-diapers fashioned from surgical gauze.

These scores of diapers couldn't simply be bought at a store. In an economy where every shred and scrap was recycled, all twenty *pelyonki* were made at home, by cutting up and hand-hemming old sheets. During the day Mom soaked them in cold water with suds from a brown smelly soap bar she grated until her knuckles bled. At night she scalded them in a four-gallon bucket on the stove of a communal apartment kitchen lacking hot water, then rinsed all twenty under an icy stream from the rusted communal tap until her arms were falling-off frozen. The weight of maternal love came down on me with full force when I learned that each morning she then *ironed* the twenty *pelyonki*. Mom claims that she loved me so much, she didn't mind the diaper routine, which I guess makes her a Soviet martyr to Motherhood. After she told me about it, I went to bed lamenting what a burden I'd been, being born.

This was Dad's sentiment, too.

Initially he rather enjoyed Soviet fatherhood. He helped with the *pelyonki*. Stood in breadlines after work. Arrived home 'tired but joyful,' to use a cherished socialist-realist cliché, with heavy, doughy bricks of rye inside his string bag. Together he and Mom bathed me in a zinc tub, adding disinfectant drops that tinted the water pink. But after three months, this life no longer seemed so rosy and pink to Dad. One night he didn't come home. Mom spent sleepless hours running to the single black telephone of the entire communal apartment at the far end of the endless unheated hallway. The phone was silent, as silent as the *alkogolík* Tsaritsin passed out by the kitchen. In the morning Mother put on the seductive lilac robe with tiny white checks, a gift from Clara, her American aunt, and she waited. She waited long enough to read me the entire volume of *Mother Goose* in both Russian and English. (Humpty Dumpty translates as 'Shaltai Baltai,' in case you're curious.)

A murky February dusk had already descended when Sergei returned. He had hangover breath and a look of aggressive guilt. It didn't make sense, him having a family, he announced from the threshold. 'This whole *baby* business . . .' He let it go at that. He had no real means to provide for the family, no energy to endure the breadlines, no real desire. He yanked off a quilted blanket covering the folding cot in the corner. Slowly, demonstratively, he unfolded the cot a safe distance from the marital bed and fell asleep right away. Mom says that he snored.

On occasion Sergei would come home after work, and reenter my mother's bed. Or sleep on the cot. Often he wouldn't come home for weeks. He never bathed me any-more but from time to time he'd pick me up and make goo-goo eyes. Mom's life went on — a wrenching, demoral-izing limbo that left her will broken and her heart always aching. In her wildest, most daring fantasies Larisa hoped for one thing now: a half-basement room of her own where she and I would have tea from colorful folkloric cups she'd once seen at a farm market. Happiness to her was those cups, those artisanal cups of her own.

Mom's purgatory lasted three years.

By the standards of the massive and perpetual housing crisis that pushed half the Soviet population into far more suffocating arrangements than ours, three years was a virtual fortnight. Anna Akhmatova, my genius namesake, was brought into a communal apartment at the Fountain House (formerly Sheremetev Palace) in Leningrad by her longtime lover, Nikolai Punin. His ex-wife lived with them. After the lovers' breakup, both Akhmatova and the ex-wife remained in the flat, with nowhere to go, while Punin brought home new lovers. Following Punin's arrest, Akhmatova continued to shuffle through a series of rooms at the same apartment (which now houses a tenderly curated museum). Memoirists recall how she and her ex-lover's ex-family all sat at the dinner table, not talking.

When Akhmatova's son came back from the gulag he slept on a *sunduk* (trunk) in the hallway. At the Fountain House Akhmatova spent almost thirty years.

I too slept on a *sunduk* in the drafty hallway of my grandparents' Arbat apartment when, in despair, Mom would run back to Naum and Liza. It was the same blue lightweight trunk that during the war saved Liza's family from starvation. My grandparents' two tiny rooms were already overcrowded with Mom's brother and my three-year-old cousin, whose mother had her own marital difficulties. So Mom slept on a cot in the kitchen or next to me in the hallway. In the archaeology of Soviet domestic artifacts, the *raskladushka* – a lightweight aluminum and khaki tarp folding cot on which entire lives had been spent – ranks, perhaps, as the most heartbreaking and the most metaphoric. It also damaged millions of backs.

My mother was fortunate to have her marriage collapse in 1964.

In the late fifties, the composer Dmitry Shostakovich, best known for epic symphonies, scored *Moskva, Cheryomushki*, a rollicking operetta pastiche satirizing the housing shortage. In 1962 it was turned into a film. Sasha and Masha, its young protagonists, have a marital crisis that is the inverse of my parents' mess: they're recently wed but forced by the dreaded 'housing issue' to live apart, each with his or her family. My favorite bit is the campy Technicolor dream sequence when Sasha and Masha go waltzing through their imaginary new digs – private digs! – singing '*Our* hallway, *our* window, *our* coat hanger . . . *Nashe, nashe, nashe: ours ours ours.*' In the film's socialist Hollywood ending, corrupt housing officials taste defeat and the lovers finally nest in their ugly new prefab flat – *nashe nashe!* – in the Cheryomushki district.

Cheryomushki in southwestern Moscow was, in fact, quite real, the country's first mass development of private apartments. Similar housing blocks went shooting up in the sprawl of other outlying *mikrorayoni* (micro-districts). They were the Bald One's low-cost revision of the Soviet domestic fairy tale: an escape from the hell of forced communality. At long last the nuclear family had a promise of privacy.

It's hard to overestimate the shift in consciousness and social relations brought about by this upsurge of new housing. Initiated by Khrushchev in the late fifties, the construction continued well beyond him, into the eighties. It was the country's biggest lifestyle transformation since the 1917 revolution, and represented probably the Bald One's greatest social achievement.

By 1964 close to half the population – almost 100 million people – had moved into the new, bare-bones units slapped up quick and shoddy from prefab concrete panels. Soviet stats boasted that the USSR was churning out more apartments per year than the USA, England, France, West Germany, Sweden, Holland, Belgium, and Switzerland combined. Who doesn't remember those endless housewarming bashes where we sat on the floor and ate herring off a newspaper, garnished with enticing whiffs of wallpaper glue? The prefabs put an end to the era of ornate, loftyceilinged, elite Stalinist housing. No longer just for *nomenklatura* and Stakhanovites, material well-being (such as it was) was now touted as a birthright for all. Khrushchev wanted to offer us a preview of the promise of full communism, shining bright *just beyond* Mature Socialism. And like Iosif Vissarionovich before him, Nikita Sergeevich bothered with the details. The Mustachioed One sniffed the soap. The Bald One tested and approved the standardized *unitaz* (toilet).

It was not large, this *unitaz*. Private dwellings were in no way meant to provoke bourgeois aspirations or rampant individualism. The vernacular name for the new prefabs, after all, was *khrushcheba*, a contraction of Khrushchev and *truscheba* (slum). What's more, the new egalitarian residential spirit expressed itself in crushing architectural uniformity. Boxlike elevatorless blocks, usually five stories high, held multiple tiny *dvushki* (two-roomers). Ceiling height: two and a half meters. Living room: fourteen square meters. Bed-room: always the same eight square meters. For cooking, eating, talking, guzzling vodka, sipping tea, chain-smoking, doing homework, telling political jokes, playing the seven-string Russian guitar, and generally *expressing* yourself, the now-legendary 'five-*metrovki*' – shorthand for the minuscule fifty-square-feet kitchens – fondly remembered later as incubators of free speech and dissent. The expression 'kitchen dissident' entered the lexicon from here. Dissidence was an unintended but profound consequence of Khrushchev's housing reforms.

The unrelenting sameness of the *khrushchebas* weighed heavily on the Soviet soul. 'Depressing, identical apartment buildings,' wrote Alexander Galich, a well-known bard and singer of the time, forced into exile. 'With identical roofs, windows, and entrances, identical official slogans posted on holidays, and identical obscenities scratched into the walls with nails and pencils. And these identical houses stand on identical streets with identical names: Communist Street, Trade Union Street, Peace Street, the Prospect of Cosmonauts, and the Prospect or Plaza of Lenin.'

Most of the above applied to the long-awaited new home we finally moved into in 1966. With a couple of major exceptions. Our street was called Davydkovskaya, not Lenin, Engels, Marx, or, God forbid, Mom's dreaded Gagarin. Full address: Davydkovskaya, House 3, Fraction 1, Structure 7. At first, yes, Mom and I wandered forever trying to find it among identical blocks surrounded by pools of mud. But the neighborhood – Davydkovo, part of the Kuntsevo district – wasn't depressing. It was rather charming, in fact. A former village in the western reaches of Moscow, it was a twenty-minute drive from the Kremlin along a wide, arrow-straight road. In former times Davydkovo was known for its bracing air and for the nightingales that sang from the banks of a fast-moving, shallow river called Setun'. A short walk from our Khrushchev slum rose a beautiful forest of fragrant tall pines. The pines shaded a massive green fence surrounding the closed-up dacha of a certain short, pockmarked Georgian, deceased for over a decade and rarely mentioned.

Mom swears we owed our *khrushcheba* joy to a ring and a miracle. It all began with a whisper – someone, somewhere, tipping her off to a waiting list for apartments that moved surprisingly swiftly. But there was a catch: the flat was a co-op requiring a major down payment. Which is where the ring and supposed miracle enter the picture. An art nouveau folly of dark-yellow gold in the shape of a graceful diamond-studded bouquet, the band was a post-war present to Liza from Naum, celebrating their survival. Babushka Liza lacked bourgeois instincts; I've always admired that about her. Having worn the ring once or twice, she tossed it into her sewing box. She was mending socks when Mom told her about the impossible down payment. The ring – so Mother swears – glinted at Liza with magical force. Miraculously a buyer materialized, offering the very seven hundred rubles (six monthly salaries) needed for the down payment. The entire family took it as an omen, and nobody was upset when they later learned that the ring was worth at least five times that price.

And so, here we were.

Our sauerkraut fermented under a wooden weight in *our* very *own* enameled bucket on *our* mini-balcony. From *our* windows hung *our* curtains, sewn by Mom from cheapo plaid beige and brown linen. *Our* shoe-box-size fridge, which Boris, the drunken plumber, had affixed to a wall because there was no space in the kitchen. The fridge beckoned like a private hanging garden of Babylon. Falling asleep every night in the privacy of her own four walls, my mother felt . . . Well, she felt she was still living in a Bolshevik communal utopia.

Our walls were cardboard *khruscheba* walls. Ukrainian Yulia next door wailed at her husband's philandering. Prim Andrei upstairs rehearsed plaintive double bass passages from Tchaikovsky's Sixth Symphony to the guttural ostinato of Uzbek arguments on the ground floor. The worst tormentors, Colonel Shvirkin and his chignoned wife, Nina, were quiet as mice, but such unacceptably paradisiacal smells of fried baby hen wafted from their kitchen that the entire building wanted to collectively lynch them.

My mother couldn't afford baby hens. After several years of maternity leave she still refused to rejoin the workforce. Relatives chided her, but she insisted she *had* to spend every second with her little Anyutik. And so we lived essentially on Dad's forty-five-ruble alimony, less than half of the pitiful Soviet monthly wage. Occasionally Mom added a pittance by giving an English lesson to Suren, an Armenian youth with fuzz on his lip and a melon-bosomed mother with fuzz on her lip. 'Larisa Naumovna! I understood *everything*!' Suren would bleat. 'Except this one strange word everywhere. *T-k-he?*' Which is the Russian pro-nunciation of *the*.

After utilities and transportation, Mother had thirty rubles left for food. Nowadays she recounts our ruble-a-day diet with glee. It's the same girlish giddiness that lights up her face whenever she describes cleaning houses for a living in our first year in America. In those early dissident days, poverty – or I should rather say pauperism – carried an air of romance, of defiance.

One Soviet ruble comprising one hundred kopeks; that crumpled beige note with a hammer and sickle encircled by an extravagant wheat wreath. Mom spent it wisely.

'Not *too* rotten please, please,' she beseeched the pug-faced anti-Semite Baba Manya, at the *dereviashka* (a little wooden one'), our basement vegetable store with its achingly familiar reek of Soviet decay. A discolored cabbage there set you back eight kopeks; likewise a kilo of carrots.

The potatoes were equally cheap and unwholesome. Mom filled our general grocery needs at the *stekliashka* ('a little glass one'), a generic nickname for glass and concrete sixties service constructions. The store lay across a scrappy ravine. On her way she nervously fingered her change. Thirty kopeks for a liter of milk, she was calculating, and a fifteen-kopek refund for the bottle. Thirty-two kopeks for ten eggs, three of them usually broken, which could last us a week.

A few coins remained for animal proteins from a store invitingly named the Home Kitchen. This was a lopsided wooden hut left over from Davydkovo's past as a village, a dystopian apparition that sat teetering in a garbage-strewn field. Whichever direction you came from you trudged through the garbage. It was like going into combat. Tall rubber boots; iodine in Mom's pocket in case a rusted can slashed through my footwear. In winter, alcoholics 'graffitied' the snow around the Home Kitchen with piss, spelling out the word *khui* (dick). Just so you know: pissing letters while under the influence requires great skill.

At the Home Kitchen, Mom handed over twenty-four kopeks for 125 grams of 'goulash' meat. The store also carried kotleti with a meat-to-filler ratio that recalled another Khrushchev-era joke. 'Where does the Bald One hide all the bread? Inside the kotleti.' Mom didn't buy them; we were poor but proud.

In our own five-meter home kitchen I assigned myself the task of inspecting the goulash and alerting Mom to its blemishes. The multicolored universe of imperfections contained in a single chunk of beef was endlessly fascinating to me. If the beef had been frozen, refrozen, and thawed again, the crosscuts offered an eye-pleasing contrast of bloody purple and gray. Sinew and fat practically shimmered with an ivory palette. The bluish spots on beef that had sat around for too long acquired a metallic glow; if the light hit them right you could see an actual rainbow. And the seal – how I loved the bright violet State seal of 'freshness' stamped on some lumps of flesh.

Trimming away imperfections reduced the four-ounce beef package by half, but Mom was resourceful. Perched on a white stool, I watched her slowly turn the handle of the awkward hand-cranked meat grinder she screwed onto the windowsill. My heart went out to her. In other families fixing the meat grinder in place was the husband's job. Mom's always wobbled in that defenseless feminine way. More often than not she ground the goulash with onions and bread into *frikadelki*, tiny meatballs she'd then float in a broth fortified by a naked soup bone. When a romantic mood struck her, she'd add cabbage and call the soup pot-au-feu, explaining how she'd read about this dish in Goethe. I rather preferred this Weimar pot-au-feu to the stew she prepared with the goulash and a frozen block of *guvetch*, the vitamin-rich vegetable mélange from Socialist Bulgaria with a slimy intervention of okra. I harbored a deep mistrust of Socialist Bulgaria.

On Sundays Mom invariably ran out of money, which is when she cracked eggs into the skillet over cubes of fried black sourdough bread. It was, I think, the most delicious and eloquent expression of pauperism.

We were happy together, Mom and I, inside our private idyll, so un-Soviet and intimate. She saved her kopeks to leave lovely, useless gifts on my bed every few days. A volume of Goethe's *Faust* in a purple binding, for instance.

(I was four years old.) Or a clunky weaving loom, which I never once used. For my fifth birthday, there was a recording, in Russian, of Oscar Wilde's *The Nightingale and the Rose*. It was just the two of us celebrating. Mom splurged and made roast duck stuffed with sauerkraut. She turned off the light, lit the candles, put on the record. A heartbreaking voice droned: 'The Nightingale pressed closer against the thorn . . . and a fierce pang of pain shot through her. Bitter, bitter was the pain, and wilder and wilder grew her song, for she sang of the Love that is perfected by Death.'

By the end of it I was hiccupping with birthday sobs.

I too lavished my mother with presents, usually paintings that tactfully avoided Soviet themes: nothing with a CCCP logo, no Yuri Gagarin grinning from his space helmet. I wasn't so blatant as my friend Kiril, whose entire painterly opus revolved around desirable East German toy railway sets. My artworks were subtler. I specialized in princesses, generic but always modeling feminine imported outfits and outsize nylon bows in their braids. My antimaterialist mom didn't budge. She continued to dress me in shabby boy's clothes and cut my hair in the shape of a bowl. She thought this looked charming.

'My Anyuta!' she'd coo to her friends. 'Doesn't she look just like Christopher Robin from my beloved E. H. Shepard illustrations?'

In my mind I devised excruciating tortures for Christopher Robin and Winnie the Pooh, but I didn't hold anything against Mom. As I said, we were happy together, basking in mutual adulation like besotted newly-weds in our *khruscheba* nest. Until Mom's compulsive hospitality syndrome went and interfered.

*** ★ ★ ★

The mud outside had dried, and fragrant May breezes rattled the skinny apple trees below our third-floor window when Oksana and Petya showed up on our doorstep.

Mom spotted them in the goulash line at the Home Kitchen and liked them immediately. She'd never seen them before, but overhearing their conversation filled her with compassion. The pair was temporarily homeless and intended to spend the night in the train station. Mom swiftly offered our house.

The doorbell rang the next day. There stood a man with a droopy mustache and bluish circles under his eyes. His entire lower half was obscured by a vast Saint Bernard.

'Meet Rex,' said Petya. 'Go ahead, hug him hello.'

It was like an invitation to cuddle a delivery truck. Overwhelmed by the dog, I hadn't noticed the boy lurking behind Petya. He was a pudgy teenager with a gloomy expression, a sickly complexion, and arms weighed down by two cages. The bigger cage contained a white owl. Inside the second cage, mice, also white, scurried and squeaked. 'Oleg,' said the gloomy boy. I couldn't tell whether it was his name or the owl's. 'Don't be afraid of the mice,' he said reassuringly. 'Oleg will soon eat them.'

Plodding steps on the concrete staircase below announced Oksana's arrival. She was out of breath and disheveled, a Jewish beauty with cascades of frizzy black hair falling wildly over a large glass box she hugged in her arms. 'A terrarium,' she panted. 'Ever seen a *real* terrarium?' I had, at the Moscow Zoological Park. But never a python slithering this close to my face. Igor, the serpent was called. Oleg and Igor, as if from a medieval Slavic epic.

'Igor and Oleg eat the same mice,' announced the boy, suddenly smiling.

Gogol's play *Inspector General* ends with a famous silent tableau called the 'mute scene.' At the news of the arrival of the real inspector general, the entire cast freezes in horror. This was approximately how Mom greeted the unexpected menagerie.

'You . . . you didn't mention you had a, um, son,' was all she could muster.

'Who, him? It's Oksana's bastard,' replied Petya, with a jovial wink.

For the following five months, living arrangements in our two-roomer were as follows: The gloomy youth lived on a cot in the five-meter kitchen. Big Rex, as the largest and most pedigreed member of our strange *kollektiv*, had the run of the premises, sometimes leaping onto the lightweight aluminum cot in my room where Mom now slept. For fear of being crushed by the canine truck, Mother stopped sleeping. Or perhaps she didn't sleep because Oksana and Petya, taking after their owl, led a mysterious nocturnal life-style. Most of the day they dozed away on Mom's ex-bed in the living room. At night they rumbled in and out of the kitchen, brewing tea and cursing when they bumped against the teenager's cot. 'Their tea,' as Mom called their brew, contained an entire packet of loose Georgian tea leaves for one mug of hot water.

My innocent mom. She had no idea that this was the hallucinogenic *chifir* that got inmates high in the gulags. She didn't know either that the grassy-sweet smell that now mingled in our apartment with the animal odors was *anasha*, a Central Asian hashish. Violent arguments followed the couple's intake of *anasha* and *chifir*. The whole building quaked from the pounding of neighbors on our walls, floor, and ceiling. The couple and the owl took turns disturbing the sleep of hardworking socialist households. The owl's guttural screeching curdled the blood.

But the biggest dilemma was getting in and out of the house. Because Igor the serpent lived in the hall-way. Anyone entering and exiting was treated to the sight of a python devouring albino mice procured by the youth from Medical Institute No. 2, where Oksana's cousin worked in a lab. I spent most of the five months barricaded inside my room. The only person who still visited us was the double bassist upstairs; he enjoyed borrowing Igor to frighten his mother-in-law. Baba Alla, my grandmother, schlepped her bags of chicken and other tasty tokens of grandmotherly love all the way to Davydkovo and left them down on the doorstep. Usually Rex ate the chicken.

It was Dad who finally ended all this. He missed having a family. Hinted that if Mom cleared the coast, he'd come stay, at least on weekends. My father was, and would remain, my mother's only true love. Oksana, Petya, Rex, Igor, Oleg, and the gloomy boy were exiled immediately, a sullen departing procession of people and cages and four thudding paws leaving behind a stench of zoo and hashish. Every flat surface of our brand-new dwelling space was scarred by burn rings from their kettle. I now acquired a semi-father in place of a python and an owl, one who delivered high-quality weekend offerings from a store called Dieta, a prestigious purveyor of cholesterol-laden items meant for the young and the infirm. Every Friday evening I listened impatiently for the turn of Dad's key in the door, leaping into the hallway to greet Dieta's buttermilk jellies and rich, crumbly cheese sticks. Recently Mom asked me whether I ever felt my father's abandonment. Flashing back to the cheese sticks and especially to the white, quivery, scallop-edged jellies, I had to say no.

Mom and I never did recover our intimate idyll. In 1961 the Supreme Soviet of the USSR had passed a law branding as 'parasites' any citizens who refused to engage in socially meaningful labor. Punishment: up to five years of exile or internment in camps. The law acquired some notoriety in the West in connection with Joseph Brodsky, the dissident poet convicted of parasitism and forced into international exile. Although she was still technically married, with a young child, and thus exempt from the law, Mom felt afraid and uneasy about not working. And so finally, on a brittle December day in 1968 when I was five years old, she re-engaged in socially meaningful labor. She began a job teaching English at the Ministry of Merchant Marines, and I went to my very first Soviet kindergarten. I don't remember all that much of the place, only that it was located across desolate train tracks from our *khrushcheba*, and that on my first morning there I soiled myself, I guess from separation anxiety, and for the entire day nobody attended to me. Mother discovered my shame on the way home. I still retain an image of her crying on the train tracks.

It never got any better. My fellow kindergarten inmates began falling ill from the spoiled meat in the borscht. Then on the bus Mother overheard my teacher instruct a younger colleague on how to reduce class sizes: 'Open the windows

– wide.' It was minus thirty degrees outside, and gusting.

Reluctantly, Mom turned to her father.

★ ★ ★

By the time I knew him, Colonel Naum Solomonovich Frumkin, my granddad the spy, looked nothing like the dapper, dark-eyed charmer we met in the 1940s chapter. Now long retired, Dedushka Naum had scant hair and heavy black-framed eyeglasses, and did morning calisthenics to patriotic songs. And he bellowed – he bellowed all day.

'I SALUTE YOU AND I CONGRATULATE YOU!!!!' he would thunder into the phone. 'My dear, esteemed Comrade . . . [insert name of appropriate admiral of Soviet fleet].'

It amazed me how Granddad always found reasons to congratulate somebody – until I discovered the squat tear-off calendar he kept by the phone. Each new page announced a fresh, bright Soviet day, a new joyous occasion. Aviation Day, Baltic Fleet Day, Transport Policeman's Day, Tank Driver's Day, Submarine Officer's Day. And let's not forget the all-out lollapalooza of Victory Day on May 9, which Granddad began observing with his customary barrage of salutations in April.

The bombastic Brezhnev-era myth of the Great Patriotic War and its cult of the veteran animated Dedushka's retirement. When he wasn't shouting felicitations, he was bustling about on some all-important veterans' business. Much of this bustle involved Richard Sorge, the half-German, half-Russian master spy we left two chapters ago, betrayed by Stalin, hanged in Tokyo, and long since forgotten – until a fluke led to his miraculous resurrection. In the early sixties the French made a feature film about Sorge's story and tried to sell it to Russia. The Soviet Ministry of Culture deemed the whole thing a malicious falsification, but Khrushchev's bodyguard tipped his boss off to the film. The Bald One demanded a screening.

'This is how all art should be made!' pronounced the excited Khrushchev when the lights came up. 'Even though it's fiction, I was on the edge of my seat.'

'Um . . . Nikita Sergeevich,' he was told, 'Sorge wasn't, um, fiction, he was, um, actual.' Khrushchev instantly rang the KGB. They confirmed both Richard Sorge's actuality and his intelligence record. Without further ado, Khrushchev anointed him a posthumous Hero of the Soviet Union and ordered that he be celebrated as Soviet Spy Number One.

Sorge books, Sorge scholars, long-lost Sorge relatives, Sorge films, Sorge buttons and postal stamps . . . Granddad was in the eye of this never-ending Sorgian typhoon. A few times I accompanied Dedushka Naum in his uniform and medals to his Sorge talks at rest homes or trade union concerts. Granddad was usually stuck on the entertainment program between an amateur folk songstress in a cornflower wreath wailing about the unrequited love of a factory girl, and, say, an amateur illusionist. People stayed for the cornflower lady, left to smoke when Naum came on, then returned to see the illusionist.

'Disgraceful! Nobody respects the veterans!' some bemedaled audience member would grumble. My palms would grow sweaty and my face would turn the color of summer tomatoes.

* * *

In approaching her father for help, Mother faced a moral dilemma.

Despite only narrowly escaping arrest during the Purges – to say nothing of General Zhukov's threat of execution for insubordination – Granddad remained an idealistic communist of the old Bolshevik school. Exploiting Party privileges for personal gain offended his principles; by *nomenklatura* (Communist elite) standards he and Grandma lived modestly. Mom's principles were offended for different reasons. This was 1968, the year Soviet tanks rolled into Prague, crushing all liberalizing hopes in a consolidation of Brezhnevian might. The Thaw was well over. Mother's anti-Soviet dissident zeal was at its peak, matching Granddad's fervent loyalty to the system. So explosive was their relationship, so profound her disgust for the State Granddad represented, that she with her sister and brother even threw out his archives. Among the things lost was an autographed edition of Mao Zedong's military writings and, yes, some significant Sorge memorabilia.

It goes without saying that Mother was loath to ask Granddad for any favors involving his Party *blat* (connections). But there was simply no other way to resolve my situation.

And so Mother swallowed her principles and pleaded with Granddad. He swallowed his principles and dialed a certain admiral's phone number.

The next day I was enrolled at the kindergarten for the offspring of the Central Committee of the USSR.

Upon hearing that the kindergarten's boarding setup meant

I'd be staying over Monday to Friday, day and night, I shrieked with a five-year-old's anguish. Mother herself looked ashen. She was relieved, yes, to save me from dysentery and pneumonia. But she would miss me crushingly.

And then there was the dreaded *nomenklatura* angle. The idea of a privileged Soviet caste and its coddled offspring enjoying politically incorrect delicacies was appalling to her. We spent half our lives queuing up for gristly goulash or tinned sprats. *They* dispatched their chauffeurs to 'closed supply depots' – those unmarked warehouses that dispensed sevruga and sturgeon and tongue, and instant coffee, that most elusive of luxuries. Or at least we imagined so. In a society that guaranteed equality for all, the dining mores of the ruling elite were concealed from the rest of us. To Mother and her dissident intelligentsia friends, *nomenklatura* flavors fairly reeked of complicity.

'Shhh about the food at the kindergarten,' Mother warned me as we trudged through the snow. 'And don't learn any Lenin songs.'

The Central Committee kindergarten, boxy and light-bricked, sat behind a tall wire enclosure in the thick, dark, resinous Kuntsevo woods. Close by, hidden behind a sixteen-foot green wooden fence, brooded Stalin's dacha. It was heavily guarded, mysterious, and had been locked up since he died there on March 5, 1953. Although the Brezhnev regime was making moves to rehabilitate him, in the popular imagination Stalin's name remained fraught, a semi-taboo. The entire neighborhood knew nevertheless that the tall pines had been put there in 1933 on personal orders from the nature-loving Generalissimo. His orders had brought about the hills surrounding the forest, too – so uncharacteristic of pancake-flat Moscow. *Did the dacha really have a secret underground bunker with a tunnel leading straight to the Kremlin?* everyone wondered. Kerchiefed babushkas hawking potatoes on roadsides whispered to customers that he had been poisoned by the Jews. Local alcoholics, meanwhile, didn't dare take their bottles into the woods, spooked by rumors of a restless mustachioed ghost, and by truer tales of uniformed comrades shooting at trespassers.

On the way to the kindergarten I wept uncontrollably, fearful of fences and ghosts (though secretly pleased, I admit, with the lyrical icicles that my tragic tears formed on my cheeks).

Inside, everything reeked of prosperity and just-baked pirozhki. The Lenin's Corner was particularly resplendent, with its white gladioli arrangements beneath Ulyanov family photos arranged like icons on a crimson velvet bulletin board. On a panoramic veranda facing the haunted woods, *nomenklatura* offspring snoozed al fresco, bundled like piglets in goose-feather sleeping bags. I had arrived during Dead Hour, Soviet for afternoon nap.

'Wake up, Future Communists!' the teacher cried, clapping her hands. She grinned slyly. 'It's fish-fat time!' I thought she meant fish oil, a bane in a brown bottle administered daily at all kindergartens with cubes of salt-rubbed black bread. Instead, a towering nanny named, I still recall, Zoya Petrovna approached me with a vast spoon of black caviar in her hand. It was my first encounter with sevruga eggs. They smelled metallic and fishy, like a rusty doorknob.

'Open wide . . . a spoonful for Lenin,' the elephantine

caretaker implored, pushing the spoon at my locked lips. 'For Rodina – for the Party!' she wheedled, her voice rising, fish eggs glistening right under my nose. I started to gag.

'You little bedbug!' she bellowed. 'Don't you dare throw up! Or I'll make you eat every drop of your puke!'

Between the two I chose caviar. But it didn't seem like much of an improvement on vomit.

It soon became apparent that I wasn't going to fit in, not at all. I had my estranged father's non-Russian name; my baggy hand-me-down Romanian coat; my nausea, which was constant; and my antiestablishment mother, who recklessly tried to shield me from indoctrination by forbidding me to read the beloved Soviet children's writer Arkady Gaidar or memorize Lenin hymns. I know Mother meant well, but really: what was she thinking, bringing me up as an ideological eyesore? Didn't she know that in the USSR 'happy' was, and always would remain, a mandatory modifier of 'childhood'? That for a sad-eyed kid like me, the kindergarten had an official term: 'non-friendly' – Soviet code for dangerously antisocial.

The intimate Proustian fantasies of my mother collided with the scarlet, trumpet-filled socialist epic of a shared Radiant Future, leaving me in a state of perpetual dazed alienation. My mom's desire to keep me from ever experiencing her Soviet split-consciousness resulted in my developing my own, reverse case. At home I dared not confess to her that I'd memorized the Lenin songs, by accident, simply by dint of hearing them so many times at rehearsals. Even to myself I could scarcely admit my enchantment with the forbidden red universe populated by the happy grandchildren of Lenin. '*Lenin is always with us*,' I sang softly into my pillow at home on weekends, cringing from shame. '*Lenin is always alive . . . In your each joyous day. Lenin is inside you, and inside me.*'

'Anyutik, we don't bring that *gadost*' (muck) home,' Mom said curtly when she overheard me one time.

Every weeknight at kindergarten, I was, of course, gripped by the opposite longing. Not daring to make even a peep in the fearsome presence of Zoya Petrovna, I noiselessly hummed Mom's favorite songs to myself. Like the Schubert one about Gretchen and her spinning wheel: '*My peace is gone, my heart is heavy, I will find it never and never more . . .*'

'On your right side – NOW! Arms straight, above the blanket!'

Like a sergeant inspecting her platoon, Zoya Petrovna surveyed the neat rows of beds in the dormitory to make sure we didn't engage in any individualistic, anti-Soviet activity. Scratching, for instance, or getting up to go to the bathroom. The right side suited me fine. This way I could peer out the window at the lights of the brand-new nine-story apartment block twinkling in the night's inky distance. The building was part of Brezhnev's slight improvement on the *khrushcheba* model: nine or thirteen stories instead of five, plus elevators and garbage chutes. I lay quietly humming my songs, mentally visiting the cozily lit domestic worlds where mothers poured tea into orange polka-dot cups before kissing their daughters good night. The women of my imagination always had my mother's short dark hair but not exactly her features. I stayed up for hours, counting and recounting the windows remaining illuminated. As each light was extinguished I felt a pang that gathered finally into a wave of lonely desolation when the building went altogether dark. The windows were lighthouses that shone to me from the world outside our tall wire fence.

In the mornings, more heartache. I didn't care much for my peers, but there was a blond, straight-nosed boy with expressive blue eyes, Victor, whose dad, also named Victor, was a famous TV personality. I didn't have the same heroic crush on little Victor as I had (furtively) on Yuri Gagarin. It was more like a sympathy, a bond of hidden mutual sadness. Victor and I barely spoke, but one time when I threw up and everyone teased me, he quickly touched my hair, to buck me up.

Victor had his own unfortunate issue: he wet his bed. In the morning, Zoya Petrovna would yank his blanket off and inspect the sheet, then tug him to his feet, pull down his white underpants, and drag him to the far end of the dormitory. She then lined up the rest of us to march past him. Each kid was instructed to slap the bed wetter's bare bottom. 'I hope *you* didn't slap him,' Mom would say, horrified by the story. But what could I do? As my turn approached, my heart pounded. I could neither disobey Zoya Petrovna nor be among Victor's abusers, as he stood there impassively, eyes glassy, with a strangely absent expression. I still remember my panic and the sight of his pale flesh as I mock raised my arm high, as if for a slap, then gently swiped my hand across his buttocks.

It astounded me how Victor could recover by breakfast and gleefully polish off his farina and tea. Me, I sat gagging at the white puddle of cereal on which squatted a cold yellow square of elite Vologda butter that refused to melt.

It was during mealtimes that my alienation gripped me

most profoundly. My struggles worsened with each new politically indigestible, delicious morsel I desperately wanted to eat but knew would horrify Mother. I threw up. I contemplated going on hunger strike, like a Tatar dissident she'd told me about. Then a desperate inspiration came to me. Next to my table was a radiator, an old-fashioned ridged one with enough of a gap to the wall to fit a whole week's worth of discarded provisions. And so, when no one was looking, I started dumping the Party elite delicacies behind it. First went the veal escalopes sauced with porcini mushrooms picked by our own young hands under fragrant Stalinist pines. Next, the macaroni, which unlike our coarse pasta at home was fine and white and lavished with gooey cheese imported from the glamorous (though occasionally not-so-friendly) homeland of Marshal Tito. Away went the prestigious cod liver pate, away went the wholesome, farm-fresh cottage cheese pudding with lingonberry *kissel*.

But the sweets served with our afternoon tea – those I couldn't bring myself to dispose of. In our happy classless society, candies were the most brutally clear signifiers of status. Sticky proletarian toffees called Iris-Kis-Kis and rock-hard rust-hued delights known as Crayfish Tails tormented the fillings of the masses. Of higher status and available only sporadically were chocolates like Little Bears in the North, with a picture of white bears on ice-blue wrappers. Ah, what a romantic candy the northern bear was! It spoke of the Arctic expanses our Soviet explorers were yet to conquer. And then there were Chocolate Rabbits, those big green-foil-wrapped white elephants of the socialist *defitsit* economy. Priced at nine rubles a kilo (a tenth of the average monthly salary), rabbits were always available, and utterly scorned for being so. Only traffic cops, flush from bribes, famously moronic and devoid of all taste, were enthusiastic consumers of them. 'Traffic cops buy their kids Chocolate Rabbits as payoff for forgetting to fetch them at kindergarten,' the saleslady in our local candy store used to say with a sneer.

Our kindergarten sweets were off this scale altogether. Like most Moscow candies, they were manufactured by the Red October Chocolate Factory, Mikoyan's pet confectionary. Only recently have I learned that Red October produced two versions of the sweets: one for the People, the other for the Party. *Nomenklatura* chocolates had the same names – Squirrel, Red Poppy, Hail to October – and wrappers that looked the same as those on their proletarian doubles. But they possessed a vastly superior flavor thanks to exalted ingredients. As a kindergartner I had no idea about any of this. I did know that our candies, hefty in weight and wrapped smartly in classy matte paper, exuded power and privilege. Unable to eat – or toss – something so status-laden, let alone imagine sharing it with my friends outside the fence, I stashed the sweets inside my underwear bag.

My food dumping went well until a smell began to rise from behind the radiator. First it was a disagreeable whiff, then a noxious stench that caused everyone to scream *foooo* and bolt away from the wall. It was Zoya Petrovna who discovered my decomposed pile. Mother was immediately summoned, with me, to the director's office. A small, sniffling woman, the kindergarten director had mothy hair pulled into a tight bun and the colorless Slavic features of a career *apparatchík*: in Mother's mind doubtless a high-ranking KGB informant. She was formidable despite her size. Once she'd attacked a flasher who loitered by our fenced-off playground, pounding him with her sharp-edged handbag. The flasher fled with a genuinely terrified expression.

'Your child, Comrade *Frum-kina*,' commenced the director, enunciating mother's Jewish surname with a meaningful curl of her lip, 'your child doesn't really belong to our *kollektiv* . . .' Was I being expelled from the Central Committee kindergarten? Was Mother going to lose her job – or worse? In a panic I rushed out to the dormitory and grabbed my precious underwear bag.

Mother brought me home on a sled, yanking it over the snow slopes with uncharacteristic aggression. I felt for her, a woman alone with no childcare. But then again, she had only herself to blame – raising me as a non-friendly kid, alienating me from the *kollektiv* – traumatizing my appetite with her dissident nonsense! Moodily, I pulled a candy out of my bag. It was called *ananas*. First I sucked on the crunchy chocolate shell, then slowly licked my way toward the center. The filling was so excruciatingly luscious with the synthetic-exotic flavor of pineapple, I shuddered. To mollify Mother, I decided to offer her the last remaining spectacular centimeter. I expected her to groan and topple into the snow, paralyzed with ecstasy and guilt by the taste. But she just absentmindedly chewed and kept pulling the sled.

The following Monday I was back among the Georgian's pines, gagging on caviar behind the tall wire kindergarten fence.

And Khrushchev? In his lonely, depressing retirement, he occupied himself with growing corn at his dacha.

CHAPTER SEVEN

1970s: MAYONNAISE OF MY HOMELAND

'Where does Homeland begin?'

So wondered a popular croonful tune of the seventies performed in that saccharine Mature Socialist tone that instantly infantilized the listener.

'With a picture in your alphabet book . . . That birch tree out in the fields?'

Russians of my mother's age, who spent most of their living hours standing in line, might insist that Rodina (Homeland) began with *avoska*. From the word *avos'* – 'with any luck' – this expandable mesh bag lay in wait in the pocket of every Russian, a stubborn handful of hope that *defitsit* Moroccan oranges or Baltic sprats might suddenly appear at some drab corner store. Our luck sack was a triumph of Soviet optimism and industrial strength. Inside the *avoska* you could practically fit a small tractor, and the sturdy cotton thread resisted even the sharp corners of the triangular milk cartons – yes, the blue and white leaky ones that dripped their accompaniment as you walked.

My generation, children of the Stagnation Era who now tend to dote on their Mature Socialist childhoods, might joke that Rodina began with their first black market jeans, or bootlegged Beatles LP. Or perhaps it began with the Young Pioneer parades where we sang Rodina songs, adding a nearly silent *U* in front of the *R*, which transformed the word into *urodina*: ugly hag.

That subversive hiccup before the *R* – this was the seventies. You could be disrespectful to Rodina and still enjoy four fun-filled August weeks at a Young Pioneers' camp – paid for by the State.

I, of course, experienced no such regime-sponsored enjoyment. My cruel mother wouldn't send me to camp, and she kept me home sick on that festive spring day in 1973 when our entire class was inducted into Young Pioneers. Never did I stand on Red Square making a five-finger salute to the clattering of drumbeats and the squawks of bugles. Never felt the garlicky breath of Vassa, our school's Pioneer leader, as she fumbled with the knot of the scarlet tie around my neck. Never solemnly swore to 'love Rodina, to live, learn, and struggle, as Lenin bequeathed, and as Communist Party teaches us.' Luckily, School 110 considered me a de facto Pioneer anyway and let me wear the tie, that small, sacred scrap of our Rodina's banner.

As for where Rodina *really* began ... Well, maybe it began, for all of us, with *salat Olivier*: with the colorful dice of cooked potatoes, carrots, pickles, hard-boiled eggs, peas, and some protein to taste, the lot smothered in a sharp, creamy dressing. *Apparatchiks*, impoverished pensioners, dissidents, tractor drivers, nuclear physicists – everyone across our eleven time zones relished salat Olivier, especially in the kitschy, mayonnaise-happy seventies. Borscht was banal; Uzbek pilaf or Georgian walnut chicken a little exotic, perhaps. But Olivier was just right, unfailingly festive and special on account of such *defitsit* items as canned Hungarian Globus-brand peas and tangy Soviet mayo, which was always in stores but never without a long line. Birthdays, engagements, dissertation-completion bashes, farewell parties for Jews who were emigrating (these sometimes felt like funeral wakes) – there was no special 'table' without salat Olivier.

And who doesn't remember big cut-crystal bowls of salat Olivier at New Year's celebrations where families gathered in front of their television sets waiting for the Kremlin clock to strike twelve, and for Dear Leonid Ilyich Brezhnev to adjust his reading glasses, rattle his medals, thunderously clear his throat, and then shuffle his papers in a desperate scramble to locate the first line of his New Year's address?

The first line was always the same: 'Dear Compatriots!'

✳ ✳ ✳

Nowadays Mom and I must have at least a thousand various salad recipes in our collective repertoire. I like Thai and Catalan. Mom has perfected the simple green salad, possibly the hardest one of all to master. Hers has toasted pine nuts and chewy dried cranberries to punctuate a shallot vinaigrette veiling impeccable lettuce leaves. It's as non-Russian as food ever gets. And salat Olivier? We don't make it often, and never idly, careful not to disturb its aura of festiveness. A precious heirloom of our non-idyllic socialist pasts, the Olivier recipe gets pulled out from the memory drawer to commemorate a particular moment in life.

One day Mom decides that it's time once again. Her

sister, Yulia, is coming to visit from Moscow. We will throw a party and Olivier will anchor the appetizer spread.

I arrive to help with the cooking. Mother's apartment, overheated as always, is permeated by the sweet, earthy smell of boiled root vegetables. In the dining nook off the kitchen, the potatoes and carrots sit, cooked in their skins – awaiting their transformation into salad. We peel, chop, chatter. As often happens in Mom's dining nook, time and space begin to blend and compress. A taste of a Lebanese pickle that uncannily resembles a Russian gherkin leads to a snippet from a Rodina song, which in turn rouses a political morality tale, or reawakens a recollection of a long-ago dream, of a fleeting pang of yearning.

Piling potato, carrot, and pickle fragments into a bowl, I think that Olivier could be a metaphor for a Soviet émigré's memory: urban legends and totalitarian myths, collective narratives and biographical facts, journeys home both real and imaginary – all loosely cemented with mayo.

We keep chopping, both now lost in our own thoughts.

I am seven when the grandest Olivier feast I can remember occurs. Tables are pushed together in a cavernous kitchen unevenly lit by greasy dangling bulbs. Potbellied men haul in chairs; women in splotched aprons dice and mince. A banquet is being prepared in a shared kitchen inside a long four-storied building on Kuybishev Lane, two minutes by foot from the Kremlin.

We're in the *kommunalka*, the communal apartment into which I was born. Where I heard Misha the black marketeer puke out his delicacies; where Dad's mother, Babushka Alla – Baballa, we call her – still lives; and where Mom spent three agonizing years after my birth until we moved out to Davydkovo.

We don't live in Davydkovo anymore, by the way. Before my first school year, Dad decided that he *did* want a family full time – but only if we moved to the center of Moscow. In a bureaucracy-defying maneuver, Mom finagled a dwelling swap between herself and her parents. Naum and Liza moved to our apartment, where bracing walks awaited among Stalinist pines, and we took over their central two-room flat in the Arbat, only one metro stop away from Baballa's *kommunalka* kitchen. Which is where we're crowded this evening.

I visit Baballa here every weekend, often staying overnight in her dank, high-ceilinged room. On our sleep-overs Grandma and I play cards and dine on no-fuss frozen dumplings followed by the 'Snowhite' meringue torte she has toted home from the elite canteen at Gosstroy, the State Construction Committee where she earns a whopping 260 rubles a month. I'm in awe of Baballa: her swagger with vodka and billiards, her three-tiered slang, her still-sexy looks. She's my playmate and role model, the one who pressured Mom to allow me to grow my hair long just like hers. Whenever construction workers whistle at her, I wink and whistle back proudly while she slanders the offenders in a voice roughened by a lifetime of Belomor cigarettes. Baballa is the world's coolest granny. But her *kommunalka* simultaneously fascinates me and scares me so much, I get butterflies in my stomach each time I visit.

✷ ✷ ✷

Bolshevism did away with private life, Walter Benjamin noted after his 1927 visit to Moscow. Describing a communal apartment, he wrote: 'One steps through the hall door – and into a little town.' It's a poignant image, Magrittian almost. Except that the 'town' in Baballa's apartment forty years later wasn't that little: more than fifty people jammed into eighteen rooms situated along a long narrow hallway. Unheated, with water-stained walls and no lights – the bulb was perpetually stolen and bartered by the *alkogolík* Tsaritsin – the hallway was a canyon of terror and peril for me. There you could catch pneumonia, fracture an ankle stumbling over the passed-out body of the self-same Tsaritsin – or worse. The *worst?* The ghoulish figure of demented old Mari Vanna, who meandered about in her torn once-white nightgown with a chamber pot in her hands. If she was feeling frisky she'd tilt it toward your feet.

I won't share details about the communal bathroom other than the fact that its three toilet cabins were separated by plywood, through which the peeper Vitalik liked to drill holes. Next to this peeper's gallery lay the shared kitchen.

Please note that there is no word for 'privacy' in Russian.

Fittingly, the kitchen of Baballa's apartment constituted a multifunctional public space, abustle with all manner of meaningful collective activities. Here were some of its functions:

AGORA: Glorious news of overfulfilled Five-Year Plans blasts from the transistor radio suspended above the stove. Neighbors discuss grave political issues. 'Motherfucking Jew-traitor Maya Spiro from room number six conspiring against the Soviet Union again.' MARKETPLACE: 'Na-taaaasha . . . Saaasha . . . Trade me an onion for half a cup of buckwheat?' BATHHOUSE: Over a kitchen sink women furtively rub black bread into their hair. Furtively, because while bread is believed to promote hair growth, it is also a sacred socialist treasure. Its misuse could be interpreted by other neighbors as unpatriotic. LEGAL CHAMBER: Comrades' Court tries neighbors for offenses, including but not limited to neglecting to turn off the kitchen lights. A more serious crime: stealing soup meat from the pots of your neighbors. In Baballa's rambling flat, the thief is a tiny, aristocratic-looking old lady whose mournful expression sometimes resolves into a beatific smile that seems glued to her face. To combat her theft, some neighbors hang skull-and-bones signs over their pots; others put padlocks on lids. LAUNDRY ROOM: As you enter the kitchen on a cold dark winter morning, half-frozen stockings swaying from clotheslines flagellate you in the face. Some neighbors get angry. The tall blond Vitalik grabs scissors and goes snip-snip-snip. If stockings were imported, a fistfight ensues. The communal apartment kitchen turns into an EXECUTION SQUARE.

People cooked, too, in communal kitchens; cooked greasy borscht, *shchi*, kotleti, and kasha. The petite fireball pensioner Valentina Petrovna, who babysat me sometimes, baked the world's most amazing pirozhki, seemingly out of thin air. Misha's mom, Baba Mila, fried succulent *defitsit* chicken tenders that Mother pilfered. Eating, however, was something neighbors did in the ideologically suspect privacy of their own rooms. In the entire memory of Baballa's apartment, that salat Olivier feast was the only exception.

The occasion was joyous indeed, exceeding the apartment's very bounds. A kitchen expansion on the floor above Baballa's!

Inside that kitchen, a door led to a tiny, bare, four-square-meter space that had been for years occupied by an old lady we all called Auntie Niusha. Miniature and birdlike, with sunken eyes, a sweet disposition, and a pervasive odor of formaldehyde, Auntie Niusha loved her job as a morgue attendant, loved sharing inspirational stories about washing cadavers. One day Niusha herself left this world. Not because neighbors added ground glass to her food to acquire her room, as sometimes happened in other communal apartments. Oh no no no – truly and genuinely! – Auntie Niusha died of natural causes.

Her death, everyone hoped, would result in a much-needed kitchen expansion. The *upravdom* (the building's manager) had other ideas. Although the apartment above Baballa's was already dangerously overcrowded even by the nine-meters-per-person standard, the *upravdom* instantly registered a new tenant in Auntie Niusha's room in exchange for a bribe. One evening people came home from work to find a notice from the Housing Committee. The next morning, it said, a new tenant would be claiming Auntie Niusha's dwelling space.

'Fuck the *upravdom*'s mother!' screamed the Tatar janitor.

'Over my dead body,' howled the Jewish expert in Sino-Soviet relations.

And so, in a feat of passionate and – for once – genuine *communality*, the communal apartment above Baballa's sprang into action. They performed their Stakhanovite labor in the night's slumbering darkness, so as not to attract the attention of informers on other floors.

By morning the door and walls had been brought down and the rubble trucked off. The entire expanded kitchen floor had been repainted, the seams between the kitchen and Auntie Niusha's former room sanded down and the space filled with kitchen furniture.

The kitchen was now four square meters larger. Not a trace of Niusha's dwelling space remained.

The *upravdom* arrived bright and early with a new tenant. The tenant was dangling keys to Auntie Niusha's room on a key ring shaped like Lenin's profile.

'Bastards! Motherfucking traitors of Rodina!' roared the *upravdom*. 'Where's the room?!' He started kicking the wall in front of which Auntie Niusha's room had stood.

Everyone went speechless with fear. It was after all illegal to alter a dwelling space. Only Octobrina stepped forward.

She was an exotic creature, this Octobrina. Of uncertain age, her fire-engine red hair always in rollers, her eyes wandering, her lips curled in a perpetual amorous smile. A not altogether unpleasant delusion possessed her. She was convinced both Stalin *and* Eisenhower were madly in love with her. '*He* sent me a cable to say "I miss you, my dove,"' she'd announce every morning in the line for a toilet. 'Who – Stalin or Eisenhower?' the *alkogolík* Tsaritsin would mutter grumpily.

'Room? What room?' Octobrina said, staring innocently and lasciviously straight into the *upravdom*'s eyes. 'Please leave, my dear, or I'll telephone Comrade Stalin this minute.' It was a good thing she didn't invoke Eisenhower. Or maybe she wasn't so mad after all.

Stalin had been dead for almost two decades. Still, the *upravdom* stepped back and instinctively shuddered. Then he sucked in his cheeks with great force and let out a blistering spit. Against the *kollektiv* he was powerless. Anyway, bribes for rooms – that wasn't exactly legal either.

That night the whole building threw a feast of celebration in the new kitchen. Herrings were whacked against the table to loosen their skins, then arranged on pristine sheets of fresh *Pravda*. Vodka flowed like the Don. Moonshine, too. In an act as communal as Auntie Niusha's room demolition, all four floors contributed to the construction of the salat Olivier. The Georgian family produced bunches of scallions – improbably in the middle of winter – to lend the salad a summery twang. Neighbors carted in boiled potatoes and carrots and pickles; and they dipped generously into their stashes of canned crabmeat and Doctor's Kolbasa. Special thanks went to our Misha, the food store manager with a proprietary attitude toward socialist property, for the *defitsit* peas and a whole case of mayonnaise. I can still picture Octobrina in her grime-fringed, formerly frilly housedress, piping mayonnaise flowers onto the salad with such abandon, you'd think both Joe and Ike were arriving for dinner. After a few bites of the Olivier salad I fell into a mayonnaise-lipped stupor.

I don't recall the exact taste, to be honest, but I assume it was pretty fab.

Now, in Mom's tiny kitchen in Queens, she doesn't share my nostalgic glow. '*Foo!* I've never had salat Olivier so laden and clunky as the one at Baballa's party,' she exclaims, still dicing the veggies into precise half-inch pieces for her more ethereal version. '*Who* mixes chicken, kolbasa, and crab?' Well, I can't blame her for having less than tantalizing memories of Baballa's apartment, where neighbors, straight to her face, called her *yevreechka* ('little kikette').

Like every Russian, Mom maintains her own firm ideas of a perfectly composed Olivier. And as with most Soviet dishes, the recipe's nuances expressed social belonging beyond one's personal flavor preferences. Soviets felt this acutely in the Stagnation years under Brezhnev. On the surface, the propaganda machine continued to spin out its creaking myths of bountiful harvest and collective identity; beneath, society was splintering into distinct, often opposing milieus, subcultures, and tightly knit networks of friends, each with its own coded vocabulary, cultural references, and political mindset – and, yes, recipes – that signaled how its members felt about the official discourse.

With salat Olivier, identity issues boiled down mainly to the choice of protein. Take for instance militant dissidents, the sort of folk who typed out samizdat and called Solzhenitsyn 'Isayich' (note the extremely coded, Slavic vernacular use of the patronymic instead of first and last names). Such people often expressed their culinary nihilism and their disdain for Brezhnev-era corruption and consumer goods worship by eschewing meat, fish, or fowl altogether in their Olivier. At the other end of the spectrum, fancy boiled tongue signified access to Party shops; while Doctor's Kolbasa, so idolized during the seventies, denoted a solidly blue-collar worldview. Mom's version – I'd call it arty bohemian – featured delicate crabmeat, along with a nonconformist crunch of fresh cucumbers and apples to 'freshen up' the Soviet taste of boiled vegetables.

But Mom's suddenly not so sure about my homespun semiotics.

'Eh? Whatever,' she says with a shrug. 'In the end didn't all the versions just taste like mayo?'

So they did! They tasted of the tangy, loose-textured Soviet Provansal brand mayo, manufactured for the first time in 1936 and taste-tested and approved by Stalin himself. Initially scarce, Provansal began to lubricate Soviet consciousness in the late sixties and early seventies, which is when salat Olivier took center stage at the table.

✳ ✳ ✳

Specifications of a totem: short, 250-gram, potbellied, and made of glass, with a tight-fitting lid. If, as Dostoyevsky supposedly said, all Russian literature comes out of Gogol's story 'The Overcoat,' then what Gogol's garment was to nineteenth-century Russian culture, the Provansal mayonnaise jar was to the domestic practices of Mature Socialism.

Our Brezhnevian days, so 'abundant,' 'friendly,' and 'happy,' were accompanied by a chronic and calamitous shortage of *tara*, the term for packaging and receptacles. Hence the deep bonds between people and their *avoskas*, into which salesladies would dump fish or meat – unwrapped, unless you brought along your own sheets of *Pravda*. Of this time too was the fetishistic adulation that comrades lavished on foreign-issue plastic bags – washing them tenderly with a fancy East German bath foam called Badoozan, hanging them to dry on the slipshod balcony, parading them at haute soirées the way modern fashionistas show off their Kelly bags.

Still, nothing matched the use – the reuse – value of the mayonnaise jar. I toted mayo jars full of nails, needles and threads, and other paraphernalia of socialist junior toil to my school 'Labor' classes. Both my babushkas sprouted scallions from onion bulbs in mayonnaise jars. My drunken Uncle Sashka used them as a) spittoons, b) ashtrays, and c) drinking vessels at certain unlovely canteens from which thoughtless comrades had pilfered the vodka glasses. When spring came and the first flowers perfumed Moscow air with romance, gangly students carried mayonnaise jars filled with lilies of the valley to their sweethearts. (Being short and delicate, lilies of the valley – and violets, too – were unjustly ignored by the Soviet flower vase industry, which favored tall, pompous blooms like gladioli.) And which H. *sovieticus*, strapped for cash three days before payday, hadn't stood in line to redeem a sackful of mayo jars for a handful of kopeks? Elaborate rituals sprang up around the act of glass redemption.

Finally, where would Soviet medicine be without this all-important receptacle?

COMRADES WOMEN, BRING YOUR PREGNANCY TEST SAMPLES IN MAYONNAISE JARS PREVIOUSLY SCALDED WITH BOILING WATER, instructed signs at gynecological clinics. And it wasn't just pregnant women: anyone having a urinalysis – routinely required for most polyclinic visits – had to deliver their specimen in the container from the tangy Provansal mayonnaise.

* * *

My poor mom. She was forced to contribute half her meager salary to the Soviet mayonnaise industry. My affliction was the reason.

The trouble began when I was eight. My life had actually turned fairly rosy by then. I excelled in second-grade Spanish at School 110, which my mom had also attended. I devotedly practiced piano for my weekly lessons at the prestigious Moscow Conservatory prep school near our Arbat house. I even acted in Soviet films on the side, not that my celluloid career was anything glamorous. Mainly it involved perspiring for hours in thick makeup and polyester costumes from fashion-forward Poland while waiting for an inebriated cinematographer to be fished out of a drunk tank. On the elaborate period set of Tolstoy's *Childhood*, however, the costumes were gauzy and gorgeous, and the cameraman was fairly sober. But there was another problem: the entire juvenile cast became disfigured by boils – caused, they said, by a viral mosquito gorging itself on young flesh within Ostankino TV Film Studios. The casting director herded the children to the Union of Cinematographers dermatologist. As the doc examined our boils, I decided to show him as well an oddly discolored patch on my right ankle that had been alarming Baballa.

The doctor sent me home with a note. On it was a single word, which sent Mom and Baballa rushing in past the bearded statue of Ilyich outside the Lenin Library.

'Scleroderma.'

I'm not sure exactly how the *Soviet Medical Encyclopedia* described it. But I do remember the conversation between

Mom and Dr. Sharapova, Moscow's most in-demand dermatologist, to whom she immediately hauled me.

Sharapova: 'Is Anechka an only child?'

Mom: 'Yes.'

Sharapova, in a treacly voice: 'Larisa Naumovna! You are young. There will be other children.'

Mom didn't want other children. Besides, her reproductive system had already been ravaged by socialist gynecology. So began our epic battle with scleroderma, which, it became quickly apparent, baffled and defied Soviet medics. Vitamin A and vitamin E; massage and physiotherapy; a ferociously expensive elite herbal goo called *moomiyo* used by Olympic athletes and cosmonauts; daily penicillin injections; weekly cortisone shots; mineral-rich mud from the gaudy and piratical Black Sea port of Odessa. All were deployed randomly, in hope of defeating this potentially fatal autoimmune disease – one that would most likely spread, so Mom was informed in whispers, from my leg to my vital internal organs, and shut them all down. We spent the next two years on a grinding merry-go-round of doctors, always clutching test samples in a trusted mayonnaise jar. While Mom endured yet more shrugs and compassionate frowns in their offices, I gaped at the public health posters in grimy hallways of dermatological clinics, which conveniently doubled as venereal wards.

RELIGION IS THE OPIATE OF THE PEOPLE. SHARING A COMMUNION CUP CAUSES SYPHILIS!

Gnawed-away chins, crumbled noses, cauliflower-like growths – the syphilitic faces on those posters are still etched in my memory. Syphilis terrified me far more than my scleroderma, since nobody had informed me about the 'fatal' part. About syphilis, however, I'd heard plenty from our homeroom teacher, a squat brunette with a clenched perm and a taste for corporal punishment. 'Syphilis is contracted by sharing chewed gum and accepting sweets from foreigners,' she never tired of proclaiming. Guilty of both, every day I'd examine my face in the mirror for cauliflower-like buds. In the meantime, my scleroderma kept creeping up my left leg. When one day the doctor noticed a fresh spot on my other leg, Mom plonked into a chair and covered her face with both hands.

Mom's other heartache was losing her friends.

Partly in response to Western pressure over human rights, partly to purge 'Zionist elements,' the 'compassionate' Soviet State began loosening the emigration quota for its Jews at the start of the seventies. By mid-decade about 100,000 had managed to leave. 'Reuniting with family in Israel' was the official qualification. Some Soviet Jews genuinely headed for their 'historic homeland.' The majority left on Israeli exit visas and then in Vienna, the first refugee transit point, declared their desire to immigrate elsewhere, to the New World mainly. These 'dropouts' were carted on to Rome to await American refugee visas.

Citing my illness, and her visceral hatred of Rodina, Mom herself began contemplating the move at the end of 1973.

A *vyzov* (invitation petition) from a chimerical great-uncle in Israel had been already secured. The paper with its suggestive red seal sat in Mom's underwear drawer as she pondered our future. Newspapers of the day freshly railed against the 'Zionist aggressors' (the Yom Kippur War had just ended). We attended clandestine Hebrew classes and endless farewell open houses for departing friends, their flats stripped down to bare yellow-stained mattresses. People squatted atop packed suitcases. Cried, smoked, guzzled vodka from mismatched borrowed mugs, scooped salat Olivier straight from the bowl. We left these gatherings loaded with practical tips – for example, *thoroughly lick* the stamps for your exit visa petition – and tantalizing snippets of news of the already departed. Lida's daughter was loving the kibbutz; Misha in Michigan had bought a used Pontiac, green with only two dents. At home I looked up Tella Veef and Sheekago on my globe as Mom weighed the pros and cons of Israel (honor) versus America (comfort, old friends, a renowned scleroderma expert).

I needed proper medical help. Dad evidently needed us out of his hair. He seemed bored once again with family life. '*Da, da,*' he'd agree, almost gleeful, whenever Mom brought up *zagranitsa*. 'Go, I might join you later once you are settled.'

And yet Mother kept stalling – torn between the dead-end 'here' and a future 'there' that she couldn't even begin to imagine.

Navsegda – forever. Emigrating without the right of return. It would be a kind of dying.

Our country's tragic shortage of *tara* was what tipped Mom finally toward the OVIR, the State Office of Visas and Registrations.

A luxurious late-spring day in 1974. The monumentalist capital of our Socialist Rodina was veiled in the yellow-green leafy crochet of its birch trees. But inside our regular grocery store, nuclear winter reigned. Besides the familiar rot, a greenish-white slime adhered to the beets; strange mutant growths sprouted on the potatoes. Normally oblivious to such things, my mother stormed off without her usual makings of soup, holding back tears. At the Three Piglets corner shop, an even grimmer landscape awaited: the counter was bare, save for bloodied hunks of unidentifiable flesh.

'Udder and whalemeat!' barked the button-nosed sales-girl. Her scowl was like frostbite.

With two mouths to feed, Mom swallowed hard and asked for a half kilo of each, trying not to look at the crimson trails left on the scale. 'Open your bag,' grunted the girl, shoving the purchase toward Mom. Mom informed her that she'd forgotten her *avoska*. Humbly, abjectly, she begged for some wrapping paper. 'A newspaper, *anything* – I'll pay you for it.'

'Citizen!' scolded the girl with her scowl. 'You think *everything* in our country can be bought and sold?'

Whereupon Mom exploded with everything she thought about the udder and whale and the salesgirl's scowl and our stinking bounteous Rodina. She took the meat anyway, bearing the lumps along home in her naked hands, forensic evidence of the State's remorseless assault on her dignity.

I was just back from school, practicing 'February' from Tchaikovsky's *The Seasons*, when Mom stormed in. She summoned me to the kitchen.

Her hands were still bloody. The conversation was brief.

She had had it with the USSR, she announced. She was finally ready to apply for an exit visa – but only if that was *my* earnest desire as well.

'If *you* want to stay,' she said, 'we will stay!'

Called away just like that from my Red October upright

piano to pronounce on our entire future, I shrugged. 'Okay, Mamulya,' I replied.

Zagranitsa would be an adventure, I added cheerily.

✳ ✳ ✳

To be honest, I only feigned a chipper nonchalance to appease Mom.

Personally I had no reason to emigrate, and no bitter grievances with our Rodina. Even my sickness wasn't that much of a drag, since the frightened doctors excused me from going to school whenever I wanted. I was now ten years of age, and my past as a sad-eyed bulimic was behind me. I was, at long last, enjoying a happy Mature Socialist childhood.

A couple of words about Mature Socialism.

My grandparents had idealistically embraced the regime, whereas the urban intelligentsia of my parents' Thaw generation of the sixties rejected it with equal fervor. We, the kids of *zastoi* (Stagnation), experienced a different relation with Rodina. As the first Soviet generation to grow up without ruptures and traumas – no purges, no war, no cathartic de-Stalinization, with its idealizing of sincerity – we belonged to an age when even cats on the street recognized the State's epic utopian project as farce. We, Brezhnev's grand-children, played *klassiki* (Russian hopscotch) on the ruins of idealism.

Happiness? Radiant Future?

In the cynical, consumerist seventies, these were embodied by the holy trinity of *kvartira* (apartment)-*mashina* (car)-dacha (country cottage). An imported sheepskin coat figured in too; so did *blat*, that all-enabling network of connection so scorned by Naum and Larisa. A popular Stagnation-era gag sums up what historians dub the Brezhnevian social contract. Six paradoxes of Mature Socialism: 1) There's no unemployment, but no one works; 2) no one works, but productivity goes up; 3) productivity goes up, but stores are empty; 4) stores are empty, but fridges are full; 5) fridges are full, but no one is satisfied; 6) no one is satisfied, but everyone votes yes.

In return for the 'yes' vote (at pseudoelections), the Kremlin gerontocracy kept commodity prices unchanged and guaranteed nominal social stability – steady employment that 'pretended to pay' while comrades 'pretended to work.' It also turned a semiblind eye to alternative economic and even cultural practices – as long as these didn't blatantly violate official norms. As one scholar notes, by socialism's twilight the only classes that took ideology at face value were professional Party activists and dissidents. They were an overwhelming minority. Everyone else eked out a daily life in the holes and crevices of the creaking machinery of power.

My own transformation from an alienated, shadow-eyed mess in my kindergarten days into a scheming, duplicitous junior *Homo sovieticus* occurred during Lenin's jubilee year. In 1970 beloved Vladimir Ilyich was turning an immortal one hundred inside his mausoleum, and Rodina was celebrating with such unrelenting kitsch pomp, all the force-fed rejoicing produced the reverse effect on the popular psyche.

Having just moved to the Arbat, smack in the center of Moscow, we were besieged by a never-ending stream of tea-guzzlers. In the airy, multicornered kitchen that once belonged to my grandparents, people came and went, eating us out of the house – and treating us to a feast of jubilee jokes. The 'commemorative Lenin products' series sent me into a paroxysm of private rejoicing. Items in the series:

Triple bed: 'Lenin Is with Us' (a ubiquitous State slogan)
Bonbon: Chocolate-dipped Lenins
Perfume: Scent of Ilyich
Body lotion: Lenin's cremains
Guidebook to Siberia: For those telling Lenin jokes!

My glee was so extravagant because my previous relations with Lenin had been so anguished. As Mom fought to exorcise him from my young mind, I furtively adored Ilyich at home, only to gag on him at the kindergarten, where Lenin-mania was crammed down my throat along with black caviar. The situation was tormenting, paralyzing; it had me throwing up almost daily. Until the populist carnival of jubilee humor liberated me from the schizophrenia of Lenin's conflicting presence. Laughter magically shrank the whole business. Imagining Lenin's squinty, beardy visage trapped inside a milk chocolate bonbon – instead of a raisin or cashew! – was somehow empowering. And how I delighted in seeing the local drunks slap a Lenin centennial ruble on a filthy liquor store counter, muttering: 'My pocket ain't no mausoleum. You ain't lying around in there for long.'

As I grew older, the symbology of our Rodina began to resemble not a fixed ideological landscape but a veritable kaleidoscope of shifting meanings and resonances. By the time I was in third grade and seriously playing around with the various significations of my Young Pioneer tie, I'd made further peace with Soviet split-consciousness. Rather than a debilitating scourge, it seemed like a healthy Mature Socialist mindset.

You didn't embrace or reject Power, I'd realized: you engaged and *negotiated*.

At school I was also busy chasing after the most crucial Mature Socialist commodity: social prestige. I accomplished this by forging my own deep relationship with the mythical *zagranitsa*. We lived, after all, in a Moscow district swarming with embassy foreigners. Shamelessly I stalked their children. Sheyda from Ankara, my very first target, became my best friend and I enjoyed weekly sleepovers at the Turkish embassy on Bolshaya Nikitskaya Street, the embassy row near my house. I got myself in, too, with Neema and Margaret, daughters of the ambassadors of Ghana and Sierra Leone, respectively. Ghana – what a world super-power! So I thought to myself, slipping past the dour guard and into a private elevator that deposited me right in the Ghanaian ambassador's sumptuous living room.

My life as diplomatic socialite left me flush with prestigious imported goods. Ballpoint pens, Donald Duck stickers, Smarties, Wrigley's Juicy Fruit, and Turkish Mabel gum with a picture of a beturbaned belle on a shimmery wrapper. Myself, I barely touched this stuff. Instead, in my own modest way I contributed to the massive Brezhnevian shadow economy. I sold, bartered, traded imports for services and favors. For three stale M&M's, Pavlik, the most glamorous boy at my school, two years my senior, slavishly carried my knapsack for a week. With profits from selling Juicy Fruit in a girls' bathroom at school, I treated myself to meals at House of Scholars, the elite Academy of Sciences clubhouse, where Mom sent me for dance lessons on Wednesdays. I skipped the silly ballet and made a beeline straight to the extravagantly marbled dining room. Once Mom came to pick me up early and the dance teacher reproachfully motioned her toward the restaurant. There I was, a proper black marketeer, at my regular corner table under a gilded mirror, enjoying a personal cocotte pan of wild mushroom 'julienne.'

A romantically mysterious illness, social prestige, a thriving black market career – to say nothing of hopscotch on the ruins of an ideology. This is what my mother proposed to take me away from. But I loved her. And so for her sake I said an insincere Brezhnevian 'yes' to her emigration plans.

✳ ✳ ✳

In May 1974, Mom resigned from her job to avoid compromising her colleagues and handed her emigration papers to an OVIR clerk. The clerk was an anti-Semitic Slav with a luridly ironic surname: Israeleva.

Mom was not optimistic. The big problem was Naum – him and his fancy 'intelligence worker' past. 'You'll never be allowed out!' thundered Dedushka, apoplectic at her announcement that she wanted to emigrate. He wasn't bluffing. Applicants with far fewer 'classified' relatives nevertheless joined the ranks of *otkazniki* (refuseniks), those bearded social outcasts (and dissident heroes) who were denied exit visas and thereafter led a blacklisted life with no work, no money, and a nonstop KGB tail. On the required 'parents' consent' form Mom had forged Naum's signature; when asked to describe his job, she put down a vague 'retired.'

I suppose OVIR was missing some teeth on its fine-toothed comb. In July, Mom and I came back from the polyclinic in the drenching rain to find Dad holding an opened OVIR envelope.

'September,' he blurted out. 'They say you're to leave by September!'

For once, Dad looked shaken. When the rain stopped he took me to an ugly, overlit shishkebab restaurant where a band blasted even at lunch. He told me not to forget him, to write. His unsardonic tone jolted me. Embarrassed by this sudden expression of fatherly sentiment, I silently wrestled with the tough, sinewy meat.

The next two months unfolded as a stagnant slog through red tape. How they tortured us pitiful would-be refugees! Lines to unregister from your 'dwelling space,' lines to notarize every legal scrap of your former life. And the money! In a final stroke of extortion and humiliation, the State charged a huge tariff to relinquish Soviet citizenship. All told, emigration expenses amounted to the equivalent of two years' salary. Mom scraped together the cash by selling art books sent by Marina, her school friend now in New York. This was a loan – she'd pay Marina back later in dollars.

Fra Angelico, Degas, Magritte: they financed our departure. 'Imagine, Anyutik!' Mom would exclaim, lugging the high-priced volumes to a dusty secondhand book shop. 'Soon – soon we will see the originals!'

The exit-visa process had transformed Mother, I noticed.

Anguished tears, sorrowful regrets – she wasn't interested. Her vision of departure was not so much a sad, extended farewell as a curt removal; an amputation, surgical and painless, of her forty years as a citizen of our glorious Rodina. *Amputation* might even be too grand: maybe she regarded her past as a Soviet wart that would simply fall off. Or imagined a quick death by injection and a resurrection in another future and dimension, the unimaginable *tam* (there) where she'd felt she belonged ever since Lucien of Meknes held her hand during the International Youth Festival. Even I, the cynical black marketeer in the family, couldn't fathom how a woman so delicate, who unfailingly wept at the exact same passage of *War and Peace*, and fainted – literally fainted – at my dad's infidelities could show such resolve in so tragic a circumstance. I don't think I saw Mother cry once.

This severing of the past included its physical remnants.

The spiteful Brezhnevian Rodina allowed us three suit-cases per person. Mom took two tiny ones for the both of us: a semisvelte black vinyl number and a misshapen eyesore resembling a swollen, decaying brick. Studiously she ignored the detailed 'to take' lists circulating among Jewish traitors to Rodina. Things for personal use; things to sell while at the transit points of Vienna and Rome. The latter included hand-crafted linens, Zenit cameras, *matryoshka* dolls, and wind-up toy chickens that apparently enjoyed enthusiastic demand at flea markets in the Eternal City. Also hammer-and-sickle souvenirs, for which sentimental Italian communists forked over decent lire.

And generally: 'Everything dear to you.'

Our mini-luggage held: one little blanket, two sets of cutlery, two bedding sets, two bowls with pink flowers made in Czechoslovakia, and by way of a 'dear object,' one terra-cotta Georgian flower vase of massive ugliness. We owned barely any clothes, and no boots; I had outgrown mine, and Mother's leaked badly. But she didn't forget an empty mayonnaise jar – the *tara* for my urinalysis. What if they didn't have suitable glassware at American clinics?

'Anything dear to *you*?' Mother asked.

I wasn't sure.

There was my collection of imported chocolate wrappers that I groomed and smoothed out with my thumb and kept inside Giliarovsky's *Moscow and Muscovites*. But why bother toting along these capitalist totems when I'd be residing where many, many more could be had? I adored Dedushka Naum's clanky medals, but he'd never part with them, and neither would customs allow them through.

To my surprise, I thought of my reviled school uniform. Brown, thigh-length, woolen and scratchy, worn under a black pinafore. The dress was dry-cleaned once a year, if at all. But every week, in a domestic ritual replayed across each of our eleven time zones, Soviet moms unstitched the white lace collar and cuffs and sewed on fresh ones. My mother always did this on Monday nights, simultaneously stitching and chattering away on her black *telefon*. We'd sit in my parents' room around the low three-legged Finnish table. Dad was usually gluing together the broken tape on his reel-to-reel *magnitofon*. I watched Vremya, the TV evening news. 'Turn it down,' Mother would hiss as Donbas metallurgical workers dutifully overfulfilled Five-Year Plans, and rye sprouted lavishly in the Ukraine, and bushy-browed Dear Leonid Ilyich Brezhnev locked in eternal embrace with bushy-cheeked Fidel.

The TV weather report, set to a bittersweet pop tune, would last an eternity. In Uzbekistan, a sunny twenty degrees centigrade. In Kamchatka, a snowstorm. Leningrad region, intermittent precipitation. Vast was our Socialist Rodina!

How could I ever confess to my parents that I felt secret pangs of pride at this vastness? That it stung me now, the thought of going to bed for the rest of my life not knowing if it was going to rain in the Urals?

I went into my room and unfolded my school uniform. It was too small. A new school year had just started but I, newly minted Zionist enemy, wasn't allowed to say goodbye to my friends. I pressed the dress to my face, inhaling its institutional reek. I didn't despise the smell as Mom did. From one pocket I fished out a fragment of Juicy Fruit in silvery foil. From another, my crumpled scarlet Young Pioneer tie.

Propelled by a sudden nostalgic patriotism I turned toward the door, ready to announce to Mom that I wanted to take the tie – but then stopped. Because I knew what she'd say.

Nyet, she'd say plainly.

Mom also said *nyet* to a farewell open house. And she wouldn't allow relatives at the airport – only Sergei. The plan was to bid goodbye to close family at my grandparents' house two nights before leaving and spend our last evening with Dad.

At our farewell dinner in Davydkovo, the Frumkin clan was in fine form. Babushka Liza had cooked her usual gloppy food for two days; Uncle Sashka got drunk, Aunt

Yulia was late, and Dedushka Naum, well, he bellowed and he raged – on and on.

'My own daughter – a traitor of Rodina!'

Then, shifting from accusation, he wagged an ominous finger: '*Nostalghia* – it's the MOST HORRIFYING emotion known to mankind!'

Naum had apparently confessed Mom's treason to his benefactor, the venerated Baltic commander Admiral Tributs. The World War II great man was reassuring: 'When she's over *there*, starving and cold, begging us for forgiveness, we will help her to return!'

Dedushka relayed this with glee. '*You'll come crawling back,*' he shouted, '*on your knees, across our Soviet border! You'll kiss our beloved black Soviet earth!*'

Cousin Masha and I kicked each other under the table: everyone knew that heavily armed men and snarling German shepherds patrolled the Soviet border. No, there was no crossing back.

Marring our intimate family tableau was a houseguest, Inna, a distant relative from Chernovtsy. Sixteen and pimply, Inna had two enormous black braids and a lofty desire to work for the KGB when she graduated from high school. As Dedushka calmed down and tears coursed along Babushka Liza's doughy cheeks, the KGB wannabe, who despite her ambitions was on the slow side, suddenly gasped in comprehension. She leapt to her feet and proclaimed that she could *not* share the table with a traitor! Then she barged out the door, braids swinging. On our way down we saw her on the landing, being groped by a non-sober neighbor.

But the true heartache was Baballa.

Mom concealed our departure from her until the very last month, and when Babushka Alla finally heard, she went pale as a ghost.

'All my life I've lost those I love,' she told Mom very quietly, lips trembling. 'My husband in the war, my grandma in the gulags. When Anyuta was born I got my joy back. She's the only thing I cherish in life. How can you take her away?'

'To save her life,' Mom replied gravely.

To avoid more heartbreak, Mother pleaded with Baballa not to see us off on our departure morning. Baballa was there all the same. She sat on a bench outside our apartment house, wearing her usual blue pencil skirt, striped blouse, and a hastily applied smear of red lipstick. She was fifty-seven, bleached blonde, six feet tall, and gorgeous. Hugging her, I caught her familiar whiff of Red Poppy face powder and Belomor cigarettes. Shyly she pressed a bottle of vodka and a tin of black caviar into Mom's hands.

As our taxi drove off I saw her sink onto the bench. That was my last image of her.

At customs we were prodded and questioned, our puny luggage turned inside out. They confiscated Mom's letters from Lucien, along with a green spray can of Jazmin, a classy imported deodorant.

'*That's* your luggage?' said the feral blond passport official, eyeing our two dwarf suitcases. '*Veyz mir,*' he taunted in a mock Yiddish accent.

I walked backwards for a few steps, waving to Dad, who stood on the other side of the chrome barrier. He was making a 'write me' sign with his hands. On the stairs leading up to the departure gate I caught another glimpse of him through the glass. He seemed small and hunched, suddenly, desperately gesticulating to Mom. I tugged at her sleeve but she just kept marching up – a five-foot, hundred-pound elf looking like a miniature sergeant in her hand-sewn khaki skirt suit. I thought of Orpheus, how he glanced back and screwed everything up, and I stopped looking at Dad.

On the plane I was on my ninth plastic tumbler of free Pepsi when they made the announcement. 'We have just left Soviet territory.' I wanted to sit there with Mom and ponder the moment, but my bladder was bursting.

★ ★ ★

Six months later. The elfin woman trudges along the edge of a highway, ahead of her girl, who's just turned eleven and is now the taller of the pair. Fordi, Pon-ti-aki, Chev-ro-leti. Woman and girl have been learning the names of the different cars that go roaring past, only catastrophic inches away. Apparently there are no sidewalks in Northeast Philadelphia. At least not on the road that leads from the Pathmark as vast as Red Square to their drab one-bedroom on Bustleton Avenue, its ceiling even lower than a *khrushcheba*'s, its wall-to-wall carpet the murky, speckled gray of crushed hope.

It's an obscure, foggy night – humid although it's almost December. The woman has on a flimsy hand-me-down parka, courtesy of her school friend Irina, who helped sponsor her American visa. The girl wears a little-old-lady-style belted coat with sleeves way too short and a bedraggled synthetic fur trim. Both woman and girl are panting, hugging the guardrail as they laboriously trudge. Their arms clutch a paper grocery bag each. Occasionally they put the heavy bags down, slump on the guardrail, and shake their tired arms. Lights glare poisonously through the fog. It starts drizzling. Then raining. The girl struggles with her coat to shield her grocery bag, but it breaks anyway. Squishy loaves of white bread and trays of thirty-nine-cent chicken parts tumble onto the road's edge. Cars slow down, honk – offering rides? The girl – me – is silently crying. For so many reasons, really. But my mother – the woman – stays cheerful, unperturbed, scrambling to snatch a box of blue-berry Pop-Tarts from the oncoming traffic and stuff it into her bag, which is still holding up, miraculously. Clasping the grocery bag with one arm for a moment, she shoots an awk-ward wave back at the honking cars, shaking her head 'no' to a ride. They can't see her smile in the dark.

'Come, isn't this an adventure, Anyutik?' she exclaims, trying to cheer me up. 'Aren't Americans *nice*?'

At this particular sodden moment, of the multitude of things I so sorely miss about Moscow, I miss our *avoska* bag more than anything else.

★ ★ ★

And the precious trusted mayonnaise jar – the one we bore to Vienna, then Rome, then Philadelphia? I've been missing it, too. Because that Mature Socialist totem has vanished from our lives forever, after Mom, almost straight off the plane, rushed me to see a world-renowned scleroderma expert.

The fancy American hospital where he worked turned

out to be barren of diversions and character: no instructive syphilis posters, no patients carrying matchboxes with stool samples and Provansal vessels with urine – along with chocolates and Polish pantyhose – to the bribe-expecting receptionist. No nurses screaming '*Trakhatsa nado menshe!*' (You should screw less!) at gonorrhea sufferers.

The scleroderma expert was himself an immigrant from far-away Argentina. When Mom detailed our desperate Soviet medical odyssey to him, he shocked her. By laughing. He even summoned his colleagues. The nurse, the new resident, the head of Dermatology – everyone shook with laughter, asking my bewildered mom to repeat again and again how Soviet doctors treated my scleroderma with penicillin and *moomiyo* goo and healing mud from gaudy Odessa.

Baring his big horsey teeth, the guffawing doc explained at last that childhood scleroderma was an entirely harmless version of this normally fatal disease. It required no treatment at all.

'Welcome to the free world!' the doctor congratulated my now-laughing mother and me as he escorted us to the foyer. When we stepped back out onto the humid Philadelphia sidewalk, Mom was still laughing. Then she hugged me and sobbed and sobbed. The mayonnaise jar, our indispensable socialist artifact, went into an outsize American trash can. Ahead of us was an era of blithely disposable objects.

And Pathmark.

My First Supermarket Experience was the anchoring narrative of the great Soviet epic of immigration to

America. Some escapees from our socialist *defitsit* society actually swooned to the floor (usually in the aisle with toilet paper). Certain men knelt and wept at the sight of forty-two varieties of salami, while their wives – smelling the strawberries and discovering they lacked *any* fragrance – cried for opposite reasons. Other emigrants, possessed by the ur-Soviet hoarding instinct, frantically loaded up their shopping carts. Still others ran out empty-handed, choked and paralyzed by the multiplicity of choices.

The Jewish Family Services office where we collected our meager refugee stipend resounded with food stories. The stories constituted an archive of socialists' misadventures with imperialist abundance. Monya and Raya complained about the flavor of American butter – after smearing floor wax on bread. The Goldbergs loved the delicious lunch meat cans with cute pictures of kitties, not suspecting the kitties were the intended consumers. Vovchik, the Odessa lothario, slept with his first American *shiksa* and stormed out indignant when she offered him Triscuits. Desiccated cardboard squares! Why not a steaming bowl of borscht?

Mom, who was smarter than Orpheus and never once looked back after heading up the ramp at Sheremetyevo Airport, roamed Pathmark's acres with childlike glee. 'She-ree-ohs . . . Ri-seh-rohonee . . . Vel. Vee. Tah . . .' She murmured these alien names as if they'd been concocted by Proust, lovingly prodding and handling all the foodstuffs in their bright packaging, their promiscuous, throwaway *tara*.

Meanwhile, I steered the supermarket cart behind her like a zombie. I hated the Pathmark of Northeast Philadelphia. It was the graveyard of my own *zagranitsa* dream, possessed of a fittingly funerary chill and an otherworldly fluorescence. Shuffling the aisles, I felt entombed in the abundance of food, now drained of its social power and magic. Who really wanted the eleven-cent bag of bananas if you couldn't parade it down Kalinin Prospect inside your transparent *avoska* after standing in a four-hour line, basking in envious stares? What happened when you replaced the heroic Soviet verb *dostat'* (to obtain with difficulty) with the banal *kupit'* (to buy), a term barely used back in the USSR? Shopping at Pathmark was acquisitioning robbed of thrills, drama, ritual. Where did *blat* come into play, with its savvy maneuvering of social ties, its camaraderie? Where was envy and social prestige? The reassuring communal *ochered'* smell of hangovers and armpits? Nobody and nothing smelled inside Pathmark.

A few weeks into our Philadelphia life, I began to suspect that all those cheery disposable boxes and plastic containers piled on Pathmark's shelves were a decoy to conceal the dark truth. That American food – I hesitate to say it – wasn't exactly delicious. Not the Pop-Tarts that Mom served cold and semi-raw because nobody told her about the toasting part. Not American *sosiski*, hot dogs sour from nitrates. Definitely not the yellow-skinned thirty-nine-cent chicken parts bandaged in plastic. These made me pine for the bluish, Pravda-swaddled chicks Baballa brought back from her elite canteen at Gosstroy. Those had graphic claws, a poignant comb, sad dead eyes, and stray feathers Grandma burned off with her clunky cigarette lighter, filling the house with a smell like burnt hair. We enjoyed the chicks once a month, as a *defitsit* treat.

When our Jewish Family Services stipend ended, Mom worked cleaning Philadelphia houses, a job she pronounced 'fascinating!' Then she landed work as a receptionist at a hospital, which required her to ride three separate buses. Her shift began at noon and brought her home past ten, when I was already in bed. Tactfully she spared me the details of standing in all weather at unshielded bus stops. I, in turn, never told her how I felt coming back to an empty, ugly apartment from the dreaded Louis H. Farrell Elementary School, with only our hand-me-down grainy black-and-white TV for company. When Dinah Shore came on, I wanted to howl. She was the human equivalent of the peanut butter and jelly sandwich that came with my free refugee school lunch. All squishy, pseudofolksy white-ness, with an unnatural, cloying coupling of sugar and salt.

I spent most of my first afterschool hours slumped on our shared mattress, nose in books from the two boxes of them Mom had had slow-mailed from Moscow. The bottle-green Chekhov, the gray Dostoyevsky – breaking off from their color-coordinated collected works, I tried to practice Tchaikovsky's *The Seasons* on the battered secondhand piano Mom had bought for me with a handout from Clara, her American aunt. But the notes under my fingers produced only tears, the wrenching reminder of our old Arbat life. And so I paced in dazed agitation, from the bedroom, past the TV to the piano, to the kitchenette and back. And yet not even in my worst homesick moments could I admit to missing Rodina with any *sincerity*. Sincerity, it seemed, had been bled out of us by the cynical Brezhnevian seventies. Which added a layer of denial to homesickness.

Rodina-Urodina. A Motherland that rhymed with 'ugly hag.'

A scarlet-blazed myth that flipped into an ironic gag. Historically the word – denoting one's birthplace, from the root *rod* (origin/kin) – had been the intimate, maternal counterpart to *otchizna* (fatherland), that resoundingly heroic, martially tinted noun. The Bolsheviks banned Rodina, suspicious of its folkloric entwining with nationalism. Under Stalin it resurfaced in 1934, aligned now with official *Soviet* patriotism. In World War II it was mobilized full force – feminized further – as *Rodina-Mat'*, literally 'motherland-mother,' to be defended to the last by its sons and daughters. Grassroots patriotism swept the nation. But by my childhood, like all 'meaningful' words, Rodina had acquired a cartoonish bathos. Even if treason to the motherland was a criminal offense.

Come to think of it, there wasn't a single word for the country we'd never see again that I could use with any authentic nostalgia. Soviet Union? Pining for anything with *Soviet* in it was politically incorrect since the word evoked the lumbering carcass of the official regime. Rossiya (Russia)? That too was tainted with the saccharine kitsch of state-certified nationalism: all those swaying birch trees and troika sleds. And so I resorted to *sovok* or *sovdep* – bitterly sarcastic slang for the land of the *Homo sovieticus*.

Such linguistic calibrations didn't concern Mother much. After all, she'd spent most of her adult Soviet life as a spiritual émigré, yearning for the imaginary Elsewhere she envisioned as *her* own true Rodina. Occasionally she'd admit to missing the tart-green *antonovka* apples, a fairly neutral Nabokovian gesture. And once, only once, when she heard a song about Arbat, our intimate old Moscow neighborhood, she burst into tears.

Myself, I had neither accepted nor rejected our socialist state. Instead I constantly played the angles, with its values and countervalues, its resonances. From this all-encompassing game I'd created my childhood identity. So now, along with the unmentionable Rodina I was mourning the loss of a self.

My name, for example.

Anna, Anya, An'ka, Anechka, Anyuta, Nyura, Niusha. What a menu of nuanced social meanings and linguistic attitudes available within my own single name. And now? I wasn't even Anna (my official passport name). I was a Philly-accented *Ee-ya-nna* – the sonorous, open Russian 'A' squished and rubberized like the Wonder Bread of our exile.

Bread. I missed Moscow bread.

Standing at the fridge, dragging a slice of Oscar Mayer bologna onto a slice of spongy whiteness, I'd mentally inhale the voluptuous sourdough tang of our neighborhood bakery by the tree-lined Tverskoy Boulevard. There, manipulating in my small grip a giant two-pronged fork attached by a grimy string to the wall, I'd poke and press, testing for freshness, the dark burnished loaves arranged on their tilted worn-wood shelves under a slogan: BREAD IS OUR SOVIET WEALTH – DON'T BUY MORE THAN YOU NEED!

✼ ✼ ✼

We had arrived in Philadelphia on November 14, 1974. A few weeks later, we noticed people appearing downtown in drab uniforms, singing and clanging bells beside red buckets under puzzling signs for a 'Salvation Army.' To this day,

'Jingle Bells' and 'Joy to the World' pierce me as the sound-tracks of émigré dislocation.

I had stopped believing in Ded Moroz (Grandfather Frost) when I was six and we still lived in Davydkovo. My neighbor Kiril and I stayed up past midnight waiting for the promised arrival of our Soviet New Year's version of Santa in his long flowing robe. I had on a tiara of snowflakes and a satiny costume gown Mom fashioned for the occasion from an old dress of hers. The doorbell rang at last. Ded Moroz himself swayed on our threshold, majestic and glassy-eyed. Then all six feet of him collapsed face-first into our *khrushcheba*'s tiny foyer. The next morning he was still there, snoring, still in his robe but with his beard now detached and crumpled under one cheek. A dead-drunk Ded Moroz wasn't the worst. The really awful ones screwed up the gifts parents had given them in advance – delivering rubber-smelling inflatable beach balls, for instance, to the family who'd bought expensive East German toy sets.

But I loved Soviet *novy god* (New Year's) anyway. The harsh scent of pine on our balcony where our tree awaited decoration. My small mom teetering on a tall wobbly stool to reach the high closet for the box of our New Year's orna-ments, swaddled in coarse pharmacy cotton. By the last week of December, the State dumped long-hoarded delicacies onto store counters. From Praga Dad carried home the white box of its famous chocolate layer cake; Mom's *avoska* bulged with sharply fragrant thin-skinned clementines from Abkhazia. And eagerly we awaited Baballa's holiday *zakaz*, the elite take-home package of *defitsit* goods from Gosstroy. You never knew what each year would bring. I prayed for the buttery *balik* (smoked sturgeon) instead of the prestigious but disgusting canned cod liver.

Philadelphia had no snow our first December. Worse, fellow émigrés gravely warned one another against putting up Christmas trees, since Jewish-American sponsors liked to drop in on their charges to deliver mezuzahs or bags of used clothes. Our generous sponsors went ballistic at the sight of an evergreen, sometimes even reporting the blasphemous refugees to Jewish Family Services. Many ex-Soviet citizens didn't realize that their Jewishness was now a religion, not simply the 'ethnicity' declared in the fifth entry of their surrendered red passports. The sponsors in turn had no clue that Christmas was banned in the USSR – that the trees, gifts, Ded Moroz, and general cheer were the secular socialist hooray to the new year.

Obediently Mom lit the alien Hanukkah candles on the menorah we'd been given. On the plywood shelf around it she heaped candies gooey with vile peanut butter, and charcoal-black cookies filled with something white and synthetic. A charcoal-black cookie! Would *anyone* eat such a thing? The candies remained unsucked, the cookies unwrapped. My eyes grew duller and more vacant each day – and Mom relented and bought a *yolka*, a holiday tree, from the five-and-dime store. Barely twelve inches tall, made of rough plastic, and decorated with out-of-scale red and green balls that cost nineteen cents a package, it didn't make me any happier.

For our first New Year's in America, instead of champagne Mom served the sticky-sweet Manischewitz wine our sponsors had urged on us. And she gave our celebratory salat Olivier a thorough Pathmark makeover! Mercifully, Mom didn't tamper with the potatoes and eggs.

But she replaced the proper fresh-boiled diced carrots with canned ones, swapped our *canned* peas for the bright-green frozen variety, devoid of the requisite mushiness. For protein, some evil force propelled her toward the gristly, vinegary Hormel's pickled pig's feet. Worst of all was the mayo. Instead of our loose, tangy-sharp vanished Provansal, it was Hellmann's now smothering Mom's Olivier in a cloyingly fluffy, infuriatingly sweet blanket.

At eleven p.m. Mom scooped the Pathmark Olivier into the two Czech bowls with pink flowers – the scant remnants of our past lives we'd carried inside our two tiny suitcases.

The bowls had been Baballa's present to us for our last Moscow New Year's. That night, right before suppertime, she'd stormed into our Arbat apartment, furiously stomping snow off her green wool coat, swearing in a voice raspy from cigarettes and cold. 'Your *present*,' she snorted bitterly, handing Mom a misshapen, rattling parcel inside an *avoska*. It *had* been a very desirable Czech dinner set. Except that after standing in line for it for most of the day, Baballa had slipped on some ice on her way over. We sat on the floor under our festive Soviet tree, picking through a wreck of broken socialist china. Only two bowls had survived intact. At the dinner table Baballa drowned her regrets in vodka, topping up my glass with champagne when Mom wasn't looking. After dessert and the turning-of-the-year tumult, she led us all out for a walk to Red Square.

It had just stopped snowing outside and the temperatures were plunging to minus twenty. And I was drunk. For the first time in my life. On Red Square! Thanks to the cold, the alcohol coursed through my bloodstream slowly, caressingly, warming my limbs as we tramped along. Beneath the floodlit tropical marzipan domes of St. Basil's Cathedral, we uncorked another bottle of Sovetskoye bubbly. It was 1974, the year of our emigration. My parents kissed on the lips while Grandma sang patriotic songs in disharmony with the other drunks on the square. Squealing with pleasure like a collective farm piglet, I rolled around in the fresh powdery snowdrifts, sending up silvery showers twinkling and dancing against the floodlights.

In Philly, as the clock struck 1975, Mom and I picked at our Pathmark salat Olivier and sipped the bubbleless Manischewitz from hand-me-down mugs. Far away, eight hours earlier, in another land, Dear Leonid Ilyich Brezhnev had once again adjusted his reading glasses, rattled his medals, thunderously cleared his throat, and then shuffled his papers in a desperate scramble to locate the first line of his New Year's address to the Rodina.

'Dear Compatriots!' The phrase no longer included us.

PART IV

RETURNS

Perestroika family reunion, 1989

CHAPTER EIGHT

★

1980s: MOSCOW THROUGH THE SHOT GLASS

At the start of the eighties, less than a decade into our American exile, I went to a *gadalka*, a fortune-teller.

Trudging up to her fifth-floor lair in New York's Little Italy, I murmured curses at every landing. This *gadalka*, Terri by name, charged a whopping ninety bucks for her readings – and I didn't even trust fortune-tellers. But an attack of professional angst had driven me there.

'I hear music.'

The *gadalka* Terri announced this on her threshold in a thick Italian New Yorkese.

I stared at her, panting and amazed. My angst involved my piano studies at Juilliard. How'd she know I was a musician?

But from here the reading went nowhere. Terri, in her thirties, sipped tea from a chipped *I Heart NY* mug, squinted and strained, conjured trivialities.

'Your cousin doesn't love her husband . . . In your mama's life there's a person named Bennett . . .' I nodded along. I felt the ninety bucks evaporating in my pocket.

Then came her big finale. 'Soon,' exclaimed Terri, waving her tea mug, 'soon you'll see your papa and the rest of your family!'

I handed over the cash and tramped back downstairs fuming, my angst unaddressed, my real question – *Will I become a famous pianist?* – unanswered. Outside I went and consoled myself with a jumbo cannoli.

My mother had by then followed me from Philadelphia to New York, where we shared a one-bedroom on a drab street in the mostly Colombian enclave of Jackson Heights, Queens. But still. After the doldrums of Philadelphia, immigrant multiculti New York felt like home. I loved how our hallway smelled of garlicky *pernil* and stewed beans. Salsa and cumbia blasted from every apartment, while our own was filled with the lofty, competing sounds of Beethoven and Brahms. Despite my career angst, generally, life was okay. Mom taught ESL at a nearby elementary school, and what's more, she'd rekindled her Moscow lifestyle of concerts, theaters, and endless ticket lines. She was even happier seeing me worship at the altar of High Culture. Ever since I at thirteen had begun taking the train up from Philly to attend Julliard's pre-college program – and then the college proper in 1980 – I'd lived and breathed piano. The keyboard completely took over my life, sustained me through years of immigrant dislocation, repaired my fractured identity.

'So? What did the *gadalka* say about your piano?' Mom wanted to know. I shrugged. I asked if she knew anybody named 'Bennett.' Mom nearly fell out of her chair.

'Mrs. Bennett? She's our Board of Education comptroller – I just saw her today!'

Amid the Bennett hue and cry I almost forgot Terri's last bit about our family reuniting. Mom slackened to a wistful smile when I remembered. It was her turn to shrug. Oh well . . .The Soviet State was eternal, intractable. Reunions just weren't in the cards.

And then they all began dropping dead.

In the Russian vernacular the early eighties are known as the 'pompous funeral era.' Or 'the three-coffin Five-Year Plan.'

'Got your funeral pass?' went a Kremlin guard joke.

'Nah,' replies the attendee. 'Got a season ticket.'

Most of the doddering Politburo were pushing seventy. The death of Alexei Kosygin, the sometime reformer, kicked off the decade. Dear Leonid Ilyich Brezhnev followed on November 10, 1982, three days after he'd been seen looking his usual self – a fossilized turtle – at the sixty-fifth anniversary of the revolution parade.

On Leonid Ilyich's death day, Soviet TV turned true to form – mysteriously weird. A droopy Tchaikovsky symphony instead of a much-anticipated hockey match? A didactic Lenin flick in place of the Militia Day pop concert?

The following morning, 'with great sorrow,' the Kremlin announced the passing of the general secretary of the Soviet Communist Party Central Committee and chairman of the Presidium of the USSR Supreme Soviet.

Nobody wailed.

Dear Leonid Ilyich, seventy-five, was neither feared nor loved. In the last of his almost twenty years ruling the

270-million-person socialist empire, he was a decrepit pill-popper who washed his sedatives down with zubrovka, a vodka flavored with buffalo grass. He'd survived strokes, a clinical death, and a jaw cancer that made mush out of his five-hour-long speeches. He still gave them – often. His *rezhim* clanked along, just as sclerotic as he, resuscitated somewhat by hard currency from soaring oil and gas prices.

This domino player had a nice life for himself. His cartoonish extravagance held a perfect mirror to the kitsch materialist epoch he led. Brezhnev adored foreign cars and bespoke jackets of capitalist denim. Right before dying he indulged in his favorite sport, killing boar at the Zavidovo hunting estate, where choice prey were brought in from all over the USSR and fattened on fish and oranges. The Politburo hunting party fattened itself on caviar straight out of sturgeons, steaming crayfish soup, and spit-roasted boar *au plein air*. It was an age of crony banquets and hyperelite food allocations, and Dear Leonid Ilyich was the empire's first epicure, with a habit of sending culinary souvenirs – a pheasant, a rabbit, a bloody hunk of bear – to favored friends. By many accounts he was a harmless, fun-loving man. Too bad about the Prague Spring, the torture of dissidents in psychiatric wards, the war in Afghanistan.

Above all Brezhnev loved baubles – which presented a peculiar funeral problem. Protocol required each medal to be borne behind the casket on its own velvet cushion. But Dear Leonid Ilyich had amassed more than two hundred awards, including a Lenin Prize for Literature for a fabricated ghostwritten autobiography. Even with several medals per cushion, the award-bearing cortège consisted of forty-four men.

Mom and I during all this sat glued to our TV in New York. But any wild flicker of hope from the *gadalka* Terri's prediction died when they announced the successor.

Yuri Andropov, the ex-KGB chief, a hunter of dissidents, was definitely *not* a nice man.

But though his heart was hard, Andropov's kidneys barely functioned. Thirteen months later men in shiny mink hats once again followed a coffin out of the mint-green and white Hall of Columns to the tune of Chopin's funeral march.

Andropov's successor's health was summed up by another joke: 'Without regaining consciousness, Comrade Konstantin Chernenko assumed the post of general secretary.' He lasted just over three hundred days.

'Dear Comrades,' went a mock news announcement, 'don't laugh, but once again with great sorrow we inform you . . .'

In March 1985 a barely known agricultural secretary who had been Andropov's protégé became the Soviet Union's newest leader. Mikhail Sergeevich Gorbachev was only fifty-four, vigorous, with functioning organs, a law degree from Moscow State University, a thick southern Russian accent, a pushy wife, and an emphatic manner that instantly seduced the Western media. Initially Russians didn't joke too much about the South America-shaped blotch on his bald scalp. The venom came later. Gorbachev was the sixth – and last – general secretary of the country known as the USSR.

It's become fashionable in Russia these days to glance backward through a mist of rosy nostalgia, particularly at the Mature Socialism of Brezhnev.

'We stole to our heart's content . . .'

'Oh, but still we were so *honest*, so *innocent* . . .'

'Families were *closer* . . . the ice cream more wholesome.'

From the Gucci-ed and Prada-ed to the miserably pensioned, Russians wax fondly today about lines; recall *defitsit* jokes; praise the flavor of the Stagnation Era kolbasa. I'm no different here in Queens. Is it not a special privilege, really, to possess such a rich, weird past? To have worn the Young Pioneer tie in that scarlet Atlantis known as the USSR? To savor such a bittersweet lode of socialist madeleines?

Then, over a couple of days in 2011, the violence of the historical reality bears down on me – *really*, for the first time in my adult life.

I'm sick and keeping to bed. Instead of the new Boris Akunin thriller, I have at my bedside an enormous squishy blue plastic bag Mom has lugged over from her apartment. The blue bag holds letters – two decades of correspondence from Russia from the seventies and eighties. Mom has kept it *all*, it turns out, crammed helter-skelter into folders, manila envelopes, shoeboxes. Despite the thirty-odd years that have passed, the USSR-issue graph paper and square envelopes with hammer-and-sickle airmail logos and sixteen-kopek stamps saying *Mir* (Peace) are barely frayed or yellowed. There are birthday cards with garish Soviet roses, and New Year's greetings featuring the snowy Kremlin we were certain we'd never see again.

Sipping lemon tea, I reach in.

Razluka. The faintly folkloric Russian word for 'separation' engulfs me.

This is the third new year we greet without you, my aunt Yulia's anarchic hand protests. *How long can this all last?*

In the slanted scrawl and sweetly screwy old person's grammar of my grandma Liza: litany upon litany of small daily laments to cover the existential pain of losing her daughter to exile.

Navsegda – forever. What was our emigration but death with the concession of correspondence?

But from Granddad Naum not one line in the crowded blue bag. Yulia recently told me that after Mom departed, he morally and mentally shriveled, his face a stony mask of Soviet-intelligence-worker denial. A longtime pal denounced him to the authorities, so that Naum, having escaped war bullets and Stalin's gulags, faced arrest for his daughter's 'treason to Rodina.' He was saved by Admiral Tributs, the World War II hero. Mother found this out much later and wept.

My beloved little swallow who flew away from me . . .

The words are Grandmother Alla's, a few days after we'd left her on a bench by our Moscow apartment. The biggest cache of letters is hers. Her round, emphatic script brings back her hoarse, tobacco-y laugh; as I read I can almost see her, there by her dim bedroom mirror, forcing metal hairpins into her bleached blonde bun.

Raw despair brims in her letters. A woman in her fifties who, after neglecting her son, poured all her latent maternal love onto a child who 'flew away.'

My last hope has been crushed, she writes – after months of fresh pleading with the OVIR visa office have ended yet again with the denial of a visit permit. *I have nothing to live for . . .*

In November 1977, not long after Grandma Alla's sixtieth birthday, there's a four-page letter from my dad.

I can barely lift a pen to write about what has come to pass, he begins.

Alla had been staying over with him when she felt a terrible burning in her chest. She moaned, threw up. *The ambulance took forty minutes to arrive. A haughty, very young doctor examined her. She was histrionic and the doc decided she was a hysteric — informed me so directly.* He injected her with a tranquilizer and left.

The next evening Sergei found his mother facedown on the floor. *This time the ambulance came fairly rapidly. But it was all over.* He sat the rest of the night stroking his mother's hair. *Her face was calm and beautiful.*

The autopsy showed an embolism: a piece of arterial plaque had torn off and gradually blocked the blood flow over twenty-four hours. In any other country Grandma Alla could have been saved.

Babushka loved you with total abandon, Anyuta, I read, blinking away the stabbing tears. *She lived for your letters, leaping twice a day to the mailbox.* She died in Brezhnev's Moscow on a Friday. On Sunday, Dad found my last letter to her, from 4,700 untraversable miles away in Philadelphia.

★ ★ ★

There are other letters from Sergei, but not many. Barely two dozen in the thirteen years we were apart. Another memorable one dates from May 1975. My first Philadelphia spring was in full, saturated azalea bloom. When Mom came home from work, her eyes were red, and it wasn't from hay fever. She'd opened Dad's letter at lunch.

Lariska, dear,

For the longest time I couldn't bring myself to write to you about 'everything.'
... What had happened to me is, I suppose, logical — and you yourself predicted it all back here in Moscow. I've realized soon enough that living alone is beyond me. The loneliness, the desire to be useful to someone (someone who, alas, is close by). In short, I've asked a certain Masha to live with me.

After a bit more Masha explaining, he announces: *God willing, in October we will have a child, and these circumstances force me to apply for a divorce.*

But apparently divorcing an émigré is extremely complicated. So would Larisa help by sending by registered mail, asap, a letter to the Soviet international court stating she has no objections?

My mother did object. She objected passionately. She'd been secretly hoping all along that Sergei would eventually join us. But being my proud, overly noble mom, she mailed the registered letter the following day.

Folded in Dad's letter I find now a response that was never sent. It's from a betrayed eleven-year-old — me:

Sergei. This is the last time you will hear from me. OK, you got married, but only a scumbag could write such a mean cynical letter to Mother. Then a coda in my still-shaky English. *OK, gud-buye forever. PS. I dont' have father any more. PPS. I hope your baby will be stupid and ugly.*

A year after Dad's treachery, a trickle of contact eked back between me and him – if *contact* applies to a very occasional letter and an annual birthday telephone call. Those static-tormented transatlantic conversations ruined the day for me. Dad sounded not entirely sober, both cocky and timid, tossing off thorny little insults. 'I got the tape with you playing Brahms. Hmm, you have a long way to go.' He fancied himself a classical music critic.

By the time I was finishing high school, Grandma Liza wrote to say that Sergei had left his second family – for a much younger woman. And that Grandma had gotten a call from Masha, the scorned second wife, warning that his secret plan was 'to reunite with his *first* family.'

At this news, Mom just gave a snide giggle. She had by then moved on with her life.

And the Rodina we'd left behind forever?

It appeared in dreams.

I dreamed all the time I was in the Arbat by our gray building there at the corner of Merzlyakovksy and Skatertny Lanes. A low, ominous sky loomed. I gazed up yearningly at our corner window, seeing the black space where I'd once broken the glass. Somebody would let me inside. I'd take the elevator to the fifth floor and push open our door. Ghostlike, I'd sneak along to our old multi-cornered balconied kitchen . . . where a strange woman stood pouring tea from our chipped enameled kettle into Dad's orange polka-dot cup. It was the kettle that had me waking up in a cold sweat.

Mom was tormented by the classic Soviet-émigré anxiety dream. Not about going back and being trapped behind the Iron Curtain. No, the one about finding herself back in

Moscow with her family – *empty-handed*, with nary a single present for them. She'd wake up seared with guilt and send more money, more gifts to Russia. Our fellow émigrés bought row houses, then semidetached houses, then split-level private houses with patios. Mom to this day owns nothing.

✳ ✳ ✳

It was the 1987 New Year's card from Grandma Liza that sounded the first genuine hope.

Consulted the OVIR about processing your invitation to Moscow. They don't anticipate any problems!!!

By then perestroika (restructuring), glasnost (openness), and the now-forgotten early-Gorbachev term *uskorenie* (acceleration) had become the new Soviet slogans.

'You wouldn't *believe* what's being said on TV,' breathless relatives cried in their crackly calls. 'But shhh . . . *it's not for telephone conversation!*'

Even my mom, bitterly wised up by the demise of the Thaw and cynical about any USSR leadership, was suddenly buying the Gorbachev optimism. The Radiant Future – perhaps it was finally coming. For real this time! Once again a utopian, fairy-tale Russia beckoned, where store shelves would groan with bananas, wheat bulge in the fields, and the borders swing open.

And the borders did open.

In the early fall of 1987, thirteen years after our departure from Moscow, shortly before my twenty-fourth birthday, Mom came home from the Soviet consulate in New York. 'Your *gadalka* Terri, the fortune-teller . . .' she muttered, shaking her head in wonderment. She displayed our blue American passports. Affixed to each was the official visitor visa to Moscow.

My mother's nightmares of returning to Rodina empty-handed set off a frenzy of gift buying, as though she were trying to pack all her years of guilt at leaving her family into the suitcases we were lugging back to the USSR.

What unbeautiful suitcases they were.

Four monster discount-store duffel bags, each resembling a lumpy black refrigerator on wheels. In the chaos of buying and packing I kept flashing back to our lean exodus with barely twenty pounds apiece. 'Madam Frumkin, you're a very wise woman,' a refugee greeter had complimented Mom in Rome in 1974.

Now we were hauling back half a warehouse.

What do you take to a country entirely deprived of consumer commodities? Seventeen packets of two-for-a-dollar panty hose, nude and black, as 'just in case' presents; instant coffee; eight batons of salami; ballpoint pens; wrist-watches; garish flashing cigarette lighters; heart medicine; calculators; shampoo – and anything with any American logo, for kids.

The specific requests from Moscow were simultaneously maddeningly particular and vague. *Hooded* terrycloth robes, *must be blue*. Two jumpsuits for a 125-centimeter-long baby of the nice *nomenklatura* physician treating Grandpa Naum. Knitting yarn – red with some golden thread – for a friend of a friend of someone who might one day help with admission to an exclusive health sanatorium. Door locks – because apparently perestroika unleashed criminals all over

Moscow. Disposable syringes. Because Russians had now heard of AIDS.

Requests for parts for Ladas and Zhigulis (Soviet autos) made Mom groan and gnash her teeth.

I for my part insisted that Dad get no presents. Mom counterinsisted on something neutral yet classy. She settled on a lavishly illustrated book about Proust.

Meanwhile, intent on a grand entrance to the country that scorned us for leaving, I outfitted myself with an extravagant vintage forties raccoon coat.

'Going back to visit *Soyuz* (the Union)?' asked the owner of the ninety-nine-cent store we'd emptied in Queens. He had a wise smile, a guttural Soviet-Georgian accent.

'How many computers you taking with?' he inquired.

None, we told him.

'You're allowed two!' he said brightly. 'So you'll bring *one* IBM!'

Which is how we got involved in a shady Georgian's black market transaction, in exchange for three hundred bucks and a ride to Kennedy Airport from his cousin. The broad-shouldered cousin arrived promptly in a dented brown Chevy. He clucked approvingly at our monstrous duffel bags.

A few miles along the Long Island Expressway he announced: 'First time on highway!'

It started pouring. We drove in tense silence. Then our dented, baggage-heavy Chevy skidded on the slippery road and, as if in slow motion, banged into a yellow cab alongside us. We felt our limbs; nothing seemed broken. The cops arrived and discovered the cousin had no driver's license and an expired American guest visa. The word *deportation* was uttered.

How we got to JFK I can't recall. I remember only the check-in lady at Delta informing us that while *we* might still catch the flight, our *bags* certainly wouldn't.

'My nightmare,' Mom bleated in a very small voice.

'They'll put the bags on the next plane,' a fellow returnee reassured us. 'Of course, Soviet baggage handlers slash bags. Or if your lock is shitty-discount they just stick a hand in. Anything valuable by the surface?'

Mom stayed awake the ten hours of the flight nervously trying to remember what exactly she'd put near the surface inside our duffel bags.

'Salami,' she finally said.

✫ ✫ ✫

And what is it like to be emigrants returned from the dead? To be resurrected in glasnost-gripped Rodina?

Your plane touches down right after a late-December snowstorm. There's no jetway or bus. You descend and tramp along the white-muffled tarmac toward the terminal. You tramp very slowly. Or so it seems, because the clock freezes when you enter another dimension.

The northern darkness and the sharp chill awaken a long-buried sensation from a childhood that suddenly no longer feels yours. For thirteen years you haven't smelled a true winter, but you're inhaling it now through the cloudy, warm cocoon of your breath. You keep tramping. In the eerily slowed time you hear your pulse throbbing in your temples, and the squeaking of snow amplified as if Styrofoam were being methodically crushed by your ear.

You glance at your mother; her face looks alien in the

poisonous yellow of the airport lights. Her lips are trembling. She's squeezing your hand.

With each loud, squeaky step you grow more and more terrified. Of what exactly you're not quite sure.

Normal time resumes in the chaos of the passport control lines.

The uniformed kid in the booth stares at my photo, then at my raccoon coat, then back at the photo, frowns, goes to consult with a colleague. I catch myself hoping that we'll be sent back to New York. But he returns, stamps my American passport, and asks, in Russian:

'So . . . you missed Rodina?'

I detect a familiar sarcasm in the way he says Rodina, but I muster my best American smile and nod earnestly, realizing as I do that everything I've missed will probably have vanished. The loss of the imaginary Rodina. Was that what terrified me in the snow on the way to the terminal?

From the baggage area through the glass pane, a distant heaving wall of greeters waves, gesticulates.

'*Papa!*' Mom shrieks.

'Dedushka Naum? *Where . . . where?*'

And then I spot them – Granddad's thick dark glass frames peering above a bouquet of mangy red carnations.

Wild with excitement, Mom is now waving frantically to her brother and sister. Standing next to them, also waving, is a man with a mane of gray hair and vaguely familiar features.

Something more familiar comes looming along the baggage carousel. They have arrived with us – our four epic duffel bags, with the Georgian's IBM carton trailing behind. Each bag sports a neat slash near the zipper.

'The salami . . .' murmurs Mom.

In the frenzy of hugging, crying, touching, I finally recognize the man with the thick gray hair. It's my father. But not the father I'd imagined from across the Atlantic – a romantically nihilist Alain Delon look-alike who abandoned us with cruel matter-of-factness.

The man now kissing me awkwardly is heavy and old, with polyester brown pants, shabby, square shoes with thick rubber soles, and a collapsed, sunken jaw.

This is Sergei, my father, I'm thinking. *And he has no teeth*.

'The salami, they stole our salami!' Mom keeps repeating, laughing madly, to Sashka, my gimpy uncle who wears a spiffy, furry karakul cap and seems jarringly, uncharacteristically sober.

'*Chudo, chudo* – miracle, miracle.' My aunt Yulia is wiping tears onto my raccoon coat.

Glancing sideways at Dad's toothless mouth, I realize this: I have forgiven him everything.

The anguished nights back in Davydkovo with Mom, waiting for his key to turn in the lock, the divorce letter, the horrible birthday calls. Because while Mom and I have prospered, even flourished, my father's life and his looks have been decaying. And I'm pretty sure this is true about Rodina generally.

A triumphant mini-armada of two Lada cars delivered us to our former apartment in Davydkovo. The squat USSR-issue Fiats, resembling soap dishes on wheels, proudly bore our epic duffel bags on their roofs. Their socialist trunks weren't designed for ninety-nine-cent U.S. abundance.

'The rich, they have their own ways . . .' snorted the pimply traffic cop who stopped us to extract the usual bribe.

The forty-meter *khrushcheba* apartment where Liza and the entire family tearfully awaited wasn't designed for our epic duffel bags either. Especially since my grandparents had invited two elephantine Odessa relatives to stay with them *while* we visited.

And then we were there, thirteen years after our farewell dinner, back around Liza's laden table.

Nobody missed our eight stolen batons of New York salami. We didn't realize this at the time, but 1987 was virtually the farewell year for the *zakaz*, the elite take-home food package Granddad still enjoyed, thanks to his naval achievements. Very soon the *zakaz* would vanish forever, along with most any sort of edible and, eventually, the USSR itself. I could still kick myself for not making a photo documentation of Babushka Liza's table. It was straight out of the 1952 *Book of Tasty and Healthy Food*. There were the vile, prestige cod liver conserves under gratings of hard-boiled eggs, the buttery smoked sturgeon *balík*, the Party-favored tongue, the inescapable tinned *saíra* fish in tomato sauce – all arrayed on Stalinist baroque cut-crystalware my grandparents had scored as fiftieth wedding anniversary gifts.

'Black bread!' Mother kept squealing. 'How I missed *our* black bread.' She squealed too about the *sushki* (dried mini-bagels), the *zefír* (pink rococo marshmallows), and the *prianíki* (gingerbread). That night, through my fitful sleep as we all bivouacked on cots in my grandparent's boxy living room, I heard the fizz of Mom's Alka-Seltzer tablet dissolving in water, drowned out by the droning legal soap operas of her deaf aunt Judge Tamara, up from Odessa.

'*Chudo, chudo, chudo* – miracle miracle.' Relatives tugged on our sleeves, as though we might be a mirage. Grandpa Naum was the happiest customer of all. His smile was wide, his tense intelligence worker's frown smoothed – as if thirteen years of shame and fear and moral dilemmas had magically slid away. His dogged loyalty to whatever regime was in power had paid off. All was ending well. The omniwise Gorbachevian State had magnanimously forgiven us prodigal traitors to Rodina. It was now fine even to openly condemn Stalinist crimes, a sentiment Granddad had bottled up for over three decades.

'If only Gorbachev would restore the navy to its former glory' was his one lament.

'Let's thank the Party,' he thunderingly toasted, 'for bringing our girls back to our Rodina!'

'Fuck the Party!' shrieked the young glasnost generation.

'Fuck Rodina!' the entire family chimed in unison.

★ ★ ★

Our Moscow fortnight passed in a blur. Never in our lives have we felt so desired and loved, been kissed so hard, listened to with such wild curiosity.

A demonic hospitality possessed Mom to invite people she barely knew to visit us in America. Because now they *could*.

'I'll send you a visa, stay with us a month, we'll show you *our* New York!'

I kept pinching her under the table. *Our* New York was a

small one-bedroom in Queens that Mom and I shared with my antique Steinway grand and my six-foot-three boyfriend, a haughty British poststructuralist.

'That first visit,' Aunt Yulia confided recently, 'we found you so adorable, so American in your fancy fur coats. And more than a little demented!' She giggled. 'How you loved *everything* about our shabby, shithole Rodina! Perhaps because of the snow?'

True. A fairytale white had camouflaged all the sores and socialist decay. To our now-foreign eyes Moscow appeared as a magical Orientalist cityscape, untainted by garish capitalist neon and billboards. Even my mother the Rodina-basher found herself smitten. With *everything*.

The store signs: RYBA. MYASO. MOLOKO. (Fish. Meat. Milk.) These captions formerly signifying nothing but empty Soviet shelves and unbearable lines were now to Mom masterpieces of neo-Constructivist graphic design. The metro stops – those teeming mosaic and marble terrors of her childhood, now stood revealed as shining monuments of twenty-four-karat totalitarian kitsch. Even the scowling pirozhki sales dames berating their customers were enacting a uniquely Soviet linguistic *performance*.

Mom for her part very politely inquired what coins one might use for the pay phones.

Grazhdanka, she was snarled at. 'Citizen, you just fell from *Mars*?' Me in my vintage raccoon coat? I was branded as *chuchelo*, a scarecrow, a raggedy bum.

In retrospect 1987 was an excellent year to visit. Everything had changed. And yet it hadn't. A phone call still cost two kopeks, and a three-kopek brass coin bought you soda with thick yellow syrup from the clunky *gazirovka* (soda) machine outside the maroon-hued, star-shaped Arbat metro station. Triangular milk cartons still jumbled and jabbed in *avoska* bags; Lenin's bronze outstretched arm still pointed forward – often to Dumpsters and hospitals—with the slogan YOU'RE ON THE RIGHT PATH, COMRADE!

At the same time, perestroika announced itself at every turn. I marveled at the new fashion accessory: a chain with *an Orthodox cross!* Mom couldn't get over the books. Andrei Platonov (Russia's Joyce, unpublished since the twenties), Mikhail Bulgakov's previously suppressed works, collections of fiery contemporary essays exposing past Soviet crimes – all now in handsome official hardcovers, openly devoured on the bus, on the metro. People read in lines and at tram stops; they read as they walked, drunk on the new out-pouring of truths and reassessments.

Along newly pedestrianized Arbat Street, we stared at disgruntled Afghan war vets handing out leaflets. Then gaped at the new private 'entrepreneurs' selling hammer-and-sickle memorabilia as ironic souvenirs. Nestling *matryoshka* dolls held a tiny Gorbachev with a blotch on his head inside bushy-browed Brezhnev inside bald Khrushchev inside (yelp) mustachioed Stalin – all inside a big squinty-eyed, goateed Lenin. We bought lots.

Back at the Davydokovo apartment, we sat mesmerized in front of Granddad's Avantgard brand TV. It was all porn all the time. Porn in three flavors: 1) Tits and asses; 2) grue-some close-ups of dead bodies from war or crimes; 3) Stalin. Wave upon wave of previously unseen documentary footage of the Generalissimo. Of all the porn, number three was the most lurid. The erotics of power.

✳ ✳ ✳

And there was another phenomenon, one that reverberated deep in our imagination: *Petlya Gorbacheva* (Gorbachev's Noose). The popular moniker for the vodka lines.

They were astonishing. Enormous. And they were blamed entirely on the Party's general (*generalny*) secretary, now dubbed the mineral (*mineralny*) secretary for his crusade to replace booze with mineral water. Even the abstemious leader himself would later amusedly cite a widespread gag from that very dry period.

'I'm gonna go kill that Gorbachev motherfucker!' yells a guy in the vodka line. Hours later he comes slumping back. 'The line at the Kremlin to kill him was even longer.'

The joke barely conveys the popular wrath over Gorbachev's antialcohol drive.

At a mobbed, shoddy liquor shop near our former Arbat apartment, Mom and I watched a bedraggled old woman with the bluish complexion of a furniture-polish imbiber. Theatrically she flashed open her filthy coat of fake fur. Underneath she was naked.

'*Píla, pyu i budu pit'!*' she howled. (I drank, I drink, I will drink!)

On the faces of fellow vodka queuers I noted that existential, sodden Russian compassion.

The trouble in the alcoholic empire had started in May 1985. Just two months in office, Gorbach (the hunchback) issued a decree entitled *On Measures to Overcome Drunkenness and Alcoholism*. It was his first major policy innovation – and so calamitous that his reputation inside the Soviet Union never recovered.

The mineral secretary was of course right about Soviet drinking being a social catastrophe. Pre-perestroika statistics were secret and scant, but it's been estimated that alcohol abuse caused more than 90 percent of the empire's petty hooliganism, nearly 70 percent of its murders and rapes, and almost half of its divorces – not to mention the extremely disturbing mortality rates. Perhaps a full-scale prohibition would have had some effect. Instead, Gorbachev promulgated the typical half measures that ultimately made him so reviled by Russians. In a nutshell: after 1985 drinking simply became more expensive, complicated, and time-consuming.

Vodka factories and liquor stores were shut, vineyards bulldozed, excessive boozing harshly punished. The sclerotic state sorely needed cash – among other things, to clean up the Chernobyl disaster – but it gave up roughly nine billion rubles a year from alcohol sales. Such sales, under the mineral secretary, took place only after two p.m. on workdays. Meaning the hungover workforce had to maneuver more skillfully than ever between the workplace and the liquor line.

Not the most efficient way to combat alcohol-related loss of productivity.

We had arrived in Moscow in late December. Getting booze for the holidays ranked at the top of everyone's concerns. New Year's festivities were about to commence, but store shelves were barren of that Soviet good-times icon: Sovetskoye champagne. Baking, too, was a wash: yeast and sugar had completely vanished, hoarded for *samogon* (moonshine). Fruit juices, cheapo *pudushechki* candies, and tomato paste had evaporated as well. Resourceful Soviet drinkers could distill hooch from anything. *Kap-kap-kap.* Drip-drip-drip.

Trudging around snowy, parched perestroika Moscow, Mom and I kept dropping into liquor lines to soak up alcoholic political humor. The venom poured out where vodka didn't.

At the draconian penalties for consuming on the job: *The boss is screwing his secretary. Masha, he whispers, go open the door — wide — so people don't suspect we're in here drinking.*

At the price hikes: *Kid to dad: On TV, they're saying vodka will become more expensive, Papa. Does it mean you'll drink less? No, son, says Papa, it means you'll eat less.*

At the effect of the antialcohol drive: *Gorbach visits a factory. See, comrades, could you work like this after a bottle? Sure. After two? Yup. All right, five? Well, you see we're working!*

* * *

To properly grasp the social and political disaster of Gorbachev's Noose, you have to appreciate Russia's long-soaked, -steeped, and -saturated history with vodka. So allow me to put our blissful family reunion into a state of suspended animation – befitting our fairytale visit – while I try to explain why our Rodina can only really be understood *v zabutylie* (through a bottle).

Booze, as every Russian child, man, and dog knows, was the reason pagan Slavs became Christian. With the first millennium approaching, Grand Prince Vladimir of Rus decided to adopt a monotheistic religion. He began receiving envoys promoting their faiths. Geopolitically, Islam made good sense. But it banned alcohol! Whereupon Vladimir uttered his immortal line, 'Drinking is the joy of the Rus, we can't go without it.' So in 988 A.D. he adopted Byzantine Orthodox Christianity.

The story might be apocryphal, but it puts a launch date on our Rodina's path to the drunk tank.

Originally Russians tippled mead, beer, and kvass (a lightly alcoholic fermented refreshment). Serious issues with *zeleny zmey* (the green serpent) surfaced sometime in the late-fourteenth century when distilled grain spirits arrived on the scene. Called variously 'bread wine' or 'green wine' or 'burnt wine,' these drinkables later became known as vodka, a diminutive of *voda* (water).

Diminutive in name, a permanent spring flood in impact.

Vodka's revenue potential caught the czars' eyes early. By the mid-seventeenth century the state held a virtual monopoly on distilling and selling, and for most of the nineteenth century, one third of public monies derived from liquor sales. Then came the First World War. The hapless czar Nicholas II put his empire on the wagon, fearful of the debacle of the Russo-Japanese War a decade earlier, a humiliation blamed on the sodden state of the military. Bad move. Nikolai's booze ban starved Russia's wartime coffers; the resulting epidemic of illicit moonshining destabilized the crucial grain market. Grain shortages led to hunger; hunger led to revolution. (Perhaps the mineral secretary in the twilight of his own crumbling empire might have paid closer attention to history?)

Even so, the Bolsheviks were no fans of vodka, and they initially kept up prohibition. Lenin, who occasionally indulged in white wine or a Munich pilsner while in exile, insisted the Russian proletariat had 'no need of intoxication,' and deplored his utopian State trading in 'rotgut.' The proletariat, however, felt differently. Deprived of vodka, it got blasted into oblivion on *samogon* supplied by the peasantry, who preferred to divert their scarce, precious grain and bread reserves to illegal distilling rather than surrender them to the requisitioning Reds. The samogon flood overwhelmed the sandbags. By the mid-1920s a full state liquor monopoly was once again in effect.

The monopoly's most ardent advocate? One Iosif Vissarionovich Stalin. 'Socialism can't be built with white gloves,' he hectored diffident comrades at a 1925 Party congress. With no other source of capital, liquor sales could and should provide a temporary cash cow. The 'temporary' ran on and on, financing the lion's share of Stalin's roaring industrialization, and later, military defense.

World War II descended; Russia boozed on. A classic fixture of wartime lore was the 'commissar's 100 grams' – the vodka ration for combatants (about a large glass) prescribed by Grandpa Naum's Leningrad protector, the bumbling commissar of defense, Klim Voroshilov. On the home front, too, vodka kept flowing. Despite massive price hikes, it provided one sixth of state income in 1944 and 1945 – the beleaguered empire's biggest single revenue source.

By Brezhnev's day our Rodina was in the collective grip of 'white fever' (the DTs). Or, to use our rich home-brewed slang, Russia was

kak sapozhnik – 'drunk as a cobbler'
v stelku – 'smashed into a shoe sole'

v dugu — 'bent as a plough'
kosaya — 'cross-eyed'
na broviakh — 'on its eyebrows'
na rogakh — 'on its horns'
pod bankoy — 'under a jar'
vdrebezgi — 'in shatters'

By this time national drinking rituals had long been set, codified, mythologized endlessly. The seventies were the heyday of the *pollitra* (half-liter bottle), priced at 3.62 rubles, a number with a talismanic effect on the national psyche. There was the sacramental *granenniy stakan* (the beveled twelve-sided glass); the ritual of chipping in *na troikh* (splitting a *pollitra* three ways); the obligatory 'sprinkling' to celebrate anything from a new tractor to a Ph.D.; and the 'standing of a bottle' (a bribe) in exchange for every possible favor, be it plumbing or heart surgery.

Vodka shimmered in its glass as Russia's poetry, its mythos, its metaphysical joy. Its cult, religion, and signifier. Vodka was a liquid cultural yardstick, an eighty-proof vehicle of escape from the socialist daily grind. And well, yes, a massive national tragedy. Just as significantly, before — and especially *during* — Gorbachev's antialcohol push, the *pollitra* served as a unit of barter and currency far more stable than the ruble, which was guzzled away anyhow. Vodka as cure? From the common cold (heated with honey) to hypertension (infused with walnut membranes) to whatever existential malaise afflicted you. In the bottom of the vodka glass, Russians found Truth.

And this Truth Mikhail Sergeevich Gorbachev was taking away.

To his credit, statisticians later established that male life expectancy rose during the mineral secretary's temperance drive. Then it plummeted. Between 1989 and 1994, well into Yeltsin's vodka-logged rule, death rates among males ages thirty-five to forty-four rose by 74 percent. But as Mayakovsky said: 'Better to die of vodka than of boredom.'

Boredom meaning . . . the clutches of sobriety. At a research institute where Dad worked-slash-imbibed before he joined the Mausoleum Research Lab, he had a *sobutílník* ('co-bottler,' the term for that crucial drinking buddy), a craggy old carpenter named Dmitry Fedorovich. After the first shot, Dmitry the Carpenter always talked of his brother. How this brother was near death from a kidney ailment, and how Dmitry Fedorovich had lovingly sneaked into the hospital with 'medicine': a *chetvertinka* (quarter liter) and a big soggy pickle.

The kidney sufferer partook and instantly died.

'And to think that if I hadn't gotten there on time he'd have died sober,' the carpenter sobbed, shedding tears into his beveled vodka glass. His co-bottlers cried with him.

To die sober. Could a Russian male meet a more terrible end?

* * *

Like all Russian families, mine has its own entanglements with the green serpent, though by the *Russian* definition of alcoholism – trembling hands, missed workdays, full-blown delirium, untimely death – only my uncle Sashka truly qualified. As an *alkologík* – a.k.a. *alkash, alkanaut, alkimist* – he was a figure of awe even among the most sloshed members of Moscow's intelligentsia. His status derived chiefly from the Accident, which happened when Mom was four months pregnant with me.

One day, Dad, who'd been mysteriously disappearing, telephoned Mom from the Sklif, Moscow's notorious trauma hospital.

'We wanted to spare you in your state,' he mumbled.

At the Sklif, Mom found her then twenty-two-year-old baby brother unconscious, every bone broken, a tube sticking out of his throat. The walls and ceiling were splattered with blood. She almost miscarried.

Several days before, Sashka had lurched up to the door of Naum and Liza's fifth-floor Arbat apartment, blind-drunk. But he couldn't find his keys. So he attempted the heroic route of alky bohemian admirers of Yulia, my femme fatale aunt. To win her heart they'd climb from the landing window to her balcony – a circus act even for the sober.

Not knowing that the busy balcony railing was loose, Sashka climbed out from the window.

My uncle and the railing fell all five floors to the asphalt below.

He landed right at the feet of his mother, who was walking my little cousin Masha. When the hospital gave Grandma Liza his bloodied clothes, the key was in his pocket.

After six horrific months at the Sklif, Uncle Sashka emerged a half-invalid – one leg shortened, an arm semi-paralyzed, speech impaired – but with his will to drink undiminished.

When we moved to our Arbat apartment, Sashka would often be dragged home unconscious by friendly co-bottlers or kind passersby. Or Mom and Dad would fetch him from the nearby drunk tank. He spent nights in our hallway reeking so badly, our dog Biddy ran away howling. Mornings after, I sat by his slumped body, wiping blood from his nose with a wet rag, waiting for him to come to and teach me a ditty in his rich and poetic alcoholic vernacular.

I particularly remember one song charting the boozer's sequence, its pungency alas not fully translatable.

In a day we drank up all the vodka
Then we guzzled *spirt* and *sa-mo-gon*!
Down our throats after which we poured
Politura and *o-de-kolon*!

From Dad I knew that two-hundred-proof industrial *spirt* (ethyl alcohol) was best drunk on the exhale, nostrils squeezed shut lest you choke on the fumes. *Samogon* I knew also from Dad, who sometimes distilled it in our small kitchen using Mom's pressure cooker and high-tech lab paraphernalia pilfered from Lenin's Mausoleum Lab. *Politura* (wood varnish) was clearly far grimmer stuff, and *odekolon* (cheapo eau de cologne) wasn't exactly fruit compote either.

Sashka and his ilk drank many other things besides, in those lushy pre-Gorbachev years. Down the hatch went *bormotukha* (cut-rate surrogate port poetically nicknamed 'the mutterer'), *denaturat* (ethanol dyed a purplish blue), and *tormozok* (brake fluid). Also BF surgical glue (affectionately called 'Boris Fedorovich'), ingeniously spun with a drill in a bucket of water and salt to separate out the good stuff. Like all Soviet *alkanauts*, Sashka massively envied MIG-25 pilots, whose airplanes – incidentally co-invented by Artem Mikoyan, brother of Stalin's food commissar – carried forty liters of the purest, highest-grade spirits as a deicer and were nicknamed the *letayushchy gastronom* (flying food store). That the planes crashed after pilots quaffed the deicer they'd replaced with water didn't deter consumption.

As a kid I found nothing deviant or unpleasant about Sashka's behavior. The best and brightest of Soviet arts, science, and agriculture imbibed likewise. Far from being a pariah, my limping, muttering uncle had a Ph.D. in art history, three gorgeous daughters, and a devoted following among Moscow intellectuals.

Our Russian heart, big and generous, reserved a soft spot for the *alkanaut*.

Lying dead drunk on the street he was pitied by women, the envy of men. Under our red banner he replaced Slavic Orthodoxy's *yurodivy* (holy fool) as a homeless, half-naked prophet who roamed the streets and spoke bitter truths. (Bitter – *gorkaya*, from *gore*, meaning grief – was the folk synonym for vodka.) For abstainers, on the other hand, our big Russian heart had nothing but scorn. They were despised, teased, goaded to drink, regarded as anti-Russian, antisocial, antispiritual – *Jewish*, perhaps! – and altogether unpatriotic.

And theirs was the poisoned cloak Gorbachev chose to march forth in.

The last time I saw Sashka was in the early nineties, when he came to visit us post-Gorbach in Queens. He spent *his* fortnight inside our Jackson Heights apartment, afraid to go into Manhattan lest skyscrapers fall on his head. During his stay, Grandmother Liza died. When he heard, Sashka guzzled the entire bottle of Frangelico hazelnut liqueur

Mom had hidden in a cupboard, except for the bit I managed to drink too. He and I sat sobbing until Mom came home from work and we told her the news.

He died prematurely a few years later, age fifty-seven, a true *alkash*.

'Are you NUTS?' demanded the Moscow morgue attendant, when his daughter Dasha brought in the body. 'Who brings in such unsightly cadavers? Beautify him a bit, come back, and then we'll talk.'

My grandma Alla was a happier drunk.

Alla drank beautifully. She drank with *smak* (savor), *iskra* (spark), and a full respect for the rituals and taboos surrounding the *pollitra*. She called her *pollitra trvorcheskaya* – the artistic one – a play on *palitra*, the painter's palette. I was too young to be a proper co-bottler, but I was hers in spirit. I soaked up vodka rituals along with grandmotherly lullabies. We were a land in which booze had replaced Holy Water, and the rites of drinking were sacramental and strict.

Imbibing solo was sacrilege numero uno.

Lone boozers equaled antisocial scum or worse: sad, fucked-up, sick *alkologiks*.

'Anyutik, never – never! – have I drunk a single gram without company!' Alla would boast.

'Alla Nikolaevna!' Mom would call from the stove with deep parental reproach in her voice. 'Any reason you're telling that to *a four-year-old*?'

When Alla drank with her girlfriends, she'd pour *limonad* into my own twelve-sided glass before apportioning vodka among real co-bottlers in exact fifty-gram rations. *Glaz-almaz* (eye sharp as a diamond) – the co-bottlers congratulated her pour.

Following their cue, I'd stare lovingly at my glass and bark an anticipatory *nu* (so) before the toasting commenced. Toasting was mandatory. Anything from an existential '*Budem*' (We shall be) to flowery encomiums for every dead relative. People from the Caucasus particularly excelled at encomiums.

Like the adults I'd exhale sharply – then tilt back my head. Down it all in one gulp, aimed right at the tonsils. Yelp '*Khorosho poshla*' (it went down well) and purposefully swallow an appetizer before properly inhaling again.

Drinking without a *zakuska* (a food chaser) was another taboo. Cucumber pickles, herring, caviars, sharp crunchy sauerkraut, garlicky sausage. The limitless repertoire of little extra-savory Russian dishes seems to have been created expressly to accompany vodka. In the lean post-war years Alla and the teenage Sergei grated onion, soaked it in salt, and smothered it in mayo – the *zakuska* of poverty. Men tippling at work favored foil-wrapped rectangles of processed Friendship Cheese, or a Spam-like conserve with a bucolic name: Zavtrak Turista (Breakfast of Tourists). Foodless altogether? After the shot you made a show of inhaling your sleeve. Hence the expression *zakusit' manufak-turoy* (to chase with fabric). Just one of the countless untranslatables comprehensible only to those who drank in the USSR.

Silence, finally, was also a despised drinker no-no. The Deep Truth found in a glass demanded to be shared with co-bottlers. In one of Alla's favorite jokes, an *intelligent* (intellectual) is harangued by two *allkogoliks* to chip in to make three. (Rounding up strangers to split a *pollitra* was customary; co-bottling always required a quorum of three.) To get rid of the drunks, the reluctant *intelligent* hands them a ruble, but they insist that he drink his share. He does. He runs off. His co-bottlers chase after him halfway around Moscow.

'What . . . *what* do you want from me now?' he cries out.

'A *popizdet'*?' Obscene slang roughly translatable as 'How about shooting the shit, dude?'

The fifty-gram gulps of moonshine, the herring, the pickles, the toasts – shooting the shit in a five-meter Moscow kitchen shrouded in smoke from coarse Yava cigarettes – these were what reestablished a fragile bond between me and my father, in the snow-mantled capital of perestroika.

We're back in December '87 once again, our visitor fairy tale reanimated.

This bond with Dad was, and would remain, unsentimental, a friendship, masculine almost, rather than one of those histrionic, kiss-kiss Russian kinships. And in future years it would be oiled and lubricated with vodka and *spirt* – *samogon*, too. Because as an offspring of the USSR, how to *truly* know your own father – or Rodina? – until you've become his adult equal, a fellow co-bottler?

It didn't take many hours of boozing with Dad to realize how wrong I'd been about him at Sheremetyevo Airport. I, a smiley American now, arriving from a country that urged you to put your money where your mouth was – I mistook Sergei's sunken mouth for the sign of a terrible life of decay.

He saw things differently. In the loss of his teeth he'd found liberation, it turns out – from convention, from toothpaste lines, from the medieval barbarism of Soviet dentistry. His first few teeth had been knocked out accidentally by his baby, Andrei; gum disease took the rest. With each new gap in his mouth my father felt closer and closer to freedom.

And women, they loved him regardless. Lena, the pretty mistress sixteen years his junior, waited five years while he 'sorted things out' with his second wife, Masha. Masha and Dad drank well together but sucked as a couple. That marriage officially ended in 1982 after Masha hit Dad on the head with a vodka bottle. Whereupon Dad and Lena got hitched.

Better even than no teeth, Sergei had no real employment.

Not having to report daily for *sluzhba* – the dreaded socialist toil – *this* was the unholy grail of slacker intelligentsia males of his generation.

Three years after we emigrated Sergei was expelled from his prestigious and classified job at the Mausoleum Lab. It took that long for the thick resident KGB stool to realize that Dad's first wife was a traitor to Rodina, and that Sergei co-bottled with dangerous dissidents. Under some innocent pretense Dad was summoned to the local militia office. The two KGB comrades greeted him warmly. With practically fraternal concern, they chided Dad for losing his footing in Soviet society. Hinted the hint: that all could be fixed if Comrade Bremzen agreed to inform on his dissident co-bottlers. My father declined. His nice mausoleum boss, teary-eyed, handed him resignation papers. Dad left the cadaver-crowded basement with a sense of dread, but also a certain lightness of being. He had just turned forty and no longer served Lenin's immortal remains.

Subsequent, briefer stints at top research centers intensified Sergei's disdain for socialist toil. At the Institute of Experimental Veterinary Science, the Ph.D.s got fat on bounty looted during collective farm calls. The head of the Bee Ailments section had amassed a particularly exciting stock of artisanal honey. Dad resigned again, though not before pilfering a Czech screwdriver set he still owns.

Full unemployment, however, was not a viable option in our righteous Rodina. To avoid prison under the Parasite Law, Dad cooked up a Dead Souls kind of scheme. A connection landed him fictitious employment at Moscow's leading oncology research lab. Once a month he came in to collect his salary, which he promptly handed over to his boss on a deserted street corner, keeping a small cut for himself. His only obligation? The compulsory collective-farm labor stints. Together with elite oncology surgeons Dad fed cows and dug potatoes. The outings had their pastoral charms. The bottle of medical *spirt* made its first appearance on the morning bus to the kolkhoz. Arriving good and pulverized, the leading lights of Soviet oncology didn't dry out for two weeks. When that 'job' ended, Dad got another, better 'arrangement.' His work papers now bristled with a formidable employment record; the state pension kept ticking. All the while he luxuriated Oblomov-like on his homemade *divan*, reading novels, listening to opera, snagging a few rubles doing technical translations from languages he barely knew. While his devoted wives toiled.

My romantic mom defied the Soviet *byt* (daily grind) by

heroically fleeing to *zagranitsa*. Dad beat it in his own crafty way.

But he wasn't simply a crafty do-nothing sloth, my dad.

* * *

The dinner invitation that December 1987 sounded almost like an awkward, weirdly formal marriage proposal.

'I would like to . . . er . . . *receive* you,' Sergei told Mom on one of our walks. He meant to infuse the stilted 'receive' with his usual irony, but his voice shook unexpectedly.

Mother shrugged. 'We can just drop by for tea sometime.'

'*Chai* wouldn't do,' my dad pressed. 'But *please* give me a few days to prepare.' The anxiety in his voice was so palpable, I accepted on Mom's behalf with a grinning American 'Thank you.'

'*Amerikanka*,' Father said, touching my raccoon coat with something approaching paternal affection. Ah yes, of course: *Russians* never dispense grins and thank-yous so easily.

For the visit Mom wore much more makeup than usual. And she too smiled, prodigiously, flashing a perfect new dental crown. At Dad's doorstep she managed to look ten feet tall.

Sergei had long since moved from our Arbat apartment to an atmospheric lane across the cement-hued Kalinin Prospect. His snug thirty-five-meter one-bedroom overlooked the Politburo Polyclinic. From his window I peered down on the lumbering silhouettes of black official Chaika cars – hauling infirm *nomeklatura* for some quality resuscitation.

I stared at the Chaikas to avoid the sight of the blond, Finnish, three-legged table. It was a relic from our old life together. Familiar to the point of tears, there was a scratch from my eight-year-old vandalism, and a burn mark from Mother's chipped enameled teakettle – the kettle of my American nightmares. On the heavy sideboard sat the pewter antique samovar Mom and I had found in the garbage dump one rainy April, carried home, lunging over the puddles, and polished with tooth powder. My insipid childhood watercolors were up on Sergei's walls as if they were Matisses. I noted one particularly anemic still life. The faux-rustic vase filled with bluebells had been painted by Mom.

'I think he constructed a cult of us after we left,' she hissed in my ear.

As Dad scurried in and out of the tiny kitchen in his slippers, his wife, Lena, prattled in a clear, ringing Young Pioneer voice. Unsettlingly, she had the same build and short haircut as my mother, but with a turned-up nose, far less makeup, and pale eyes of startling crystalline blue. In those crystalline eyes I saw flashes of terror. *She* was here: the dread First Wife. Resurrected from exile, returned in triumph, and now semireclining on Dad's maroon divan in the pose of a magnanimous Queen Mother.

'Lenochka,' Mother said to her, '*can't* you persuade Sergei to get dentures?'

We'd already unloaded the gifts. Proust for Dad, choice nuggets of ninety-nine-cent American abundance for Lena, plus an absurdly expensive bottle of Smirnoff from the hard currency store, where there were no enraged mobs.

To our swank, soulless booze my toothless father replied

with home brews of staggering sophistication. The walnut-infused amber *samogon*, distilled in Mom's ancient pressure cooker, suggested not some proletarian hooch but a noble, mysterious whiskey. In another decanter glimmered shocking-pink *spirt*. Steeped in sugared lingonberries, it was known (I learned) as *nesmiyanovka* ('don't-laugh-ovka') after Alexander Nesmiyanov, Russia's leading chemist, at whose scientific research facility the recipe had been concocted by his savvy associates. Miraculously the lingonberries softened the hundred-proof ethyl harshness, and in my stomach the potion kept on – and on – blossoming like the precious bud of a winter carnation.

'The canapés – weren't they your favorite?' cooed my dad, handing Mom on her divan a dainty gratinéed cheese toast.

'Friendship Cheese, cilantro, and, what, *adzhika* (spicy Georgian chili paste)?' she commented coolly.

'Made the *adzhika* myself,' noted Dad – humbly, almost abjectly – as he proffered another plate, a wonder of herring and egg thingies.

His next salvo was borscht.

It was nothing like Mom's old flick-of-the-wrist vegetarian version, that small triumph coaxed out of tired root vegetables and a can of tomato paste. My mother was a flighty, impulsive, dream-spinning cook. My deadbeat dad turned out to be a methodical, determined master crafts-man. He insisted on painstakingly extracting fresh juice from carrots and beets for his borscht, adding it to the rich rounded beef stock, steeping the whole thing for a day, then flourishing a last-minute surprise of pounded garlic and *shk-varki*, the crisp, salty pork crackling.

Dad's *satsivi*, the creamy Georgian walnut-sauced chicken, left me equally speechless. I thought of the impossible challenge of obtaining a decent chicken in Moscow. Of the ferocious price of walnuts at the Central Market near the Circus; of the punishing labor of shelling and pulverizing them; of the multiple egg yolks so opulently enriching the sauce. With each bite I was more and more in awe of my father. I forgave him every last drop there was still left to forgive. Once again, I was the Pavlovian pup of my childhood days – when I salivated at the mere thought of the jiggly buttermilk jellies and cheese sticks he brought on his sporadic family visits. This man, this crumple-mouthed grifter in saggy track pants, he was a god in the kitchen.

And wasn't this dinner his way of showing his love?

But all the juice-squeezing and pulverizing, the monthly budget blown on one extravagant chicken dish – it wasn't for me. It was not into *my* face Dad was now gazing, timidly seeking approval.

The living-slash-dining room suddenly felt stifling and overcrowded. I slipped off to the kitchen, where Lena was glumly chain-smoking Dad's Yavas. Her glass held pink lingonberry *spirt*. Unwilling to let her commit the cardinal sin of drinking alone, I offered a dog-eared toast.

"*Za znakomstvo!*' (Here's to getting to know you!)

'*Davay na brudershaft?*' she proposed. Drinking *na brudershaft* (to brotherhood) is a ritual in which two new friends interlace arms, gulp from each other's glass, kiss, and thereafter address each other as *ty* (the informal, familial form of you). We emptied our shot glasses, kissed. Lena's cheek had a gullible, babyish softness. We were now co-bottlers, Dad's new wife and me.

Pals.

Back in the living room I found Sergei murmuring away at Mom's side. 'In *those* days,' I overheard, 'food tasted better to me . . .'

Mom smiled the same polite but regal smile. It never left her face the whole evening.

We drank the last, parting ritual shot. '*Na pososhok.*' (For the walking staff.)

'Marvelous dinner!' Mom offered in the cramped hallway as Dad longingly draped the pseudomink rabbit coat over her shoulders. 'Who knew you were such a *klass* cook?' Then, with it's-been-nice-seeing-you American breeziness: 'You *must* give me your recipe for that beef stew in a clay pot.'

'Lariska!' muttered Dad, with barely concealed desperation. 'It was *your* recipe and *your* clay pot. The one I gave you for your birthday.'

'Da? Really now?' said my mother pleasantly. 'I don't remember any of this.'

And that was that. Her empty Americanized smile told him the past was past.

'Bravo, Tatyana!' I growled to her in the elevator. 'Stanislavsky applauds you from his grave.' Mom in her makeup gave a worn, very Soviet grin involving no teeth.

My 'Tatyana' reference was to every Russian woman's favorite scene in Pushkin's verse novel, *Eugene Onegin*. Tatyana, the ultimate lyric heroine of our literature, meets up again with Onegin, the mock-Byronic protagonist who'd cruelly scorned her love when she was a melancholy provincial maiden. Now she's all dressed up, rich and cold and imperious at a glamorous St. Petersburg ball. Encountering her after years, Onegin is the one who's dying of love – and Tatyana is the one who does the scorning. The sad part? She's still in love with Onegin! But she's now married, has moved on, and the past is the past. The sadder part for Mom? It was Sergei who was married.

From my cot in the overheated darkness of my grand-parents' apartment I thought I heard my mother crying, ever so quietly. As the relatives from Odessa snored on.

CHAPTER NINE

✦

1990s: BROKEN BANQUETS

A*bysta*, the bland Abkhazian cornmeal mush, comes alive with lashings of salty young local *suluguni* cheese. And so I tucked some *suluguni* into my Abkhaz gruel, then watched it melt.

It was Christmas Day, 1991 – a bit before seven p.m.

In the kitchen of a prosperous house in the winemaking countryside, women with forceful noses and raven-black hair tended to huge, bubbling pots. My boyfriend, John, and I had arrived a few days before in Abkhazia – a breakaway autonomous republic of Georgia one thousand long miles south of Moscow. Primal, ominous darkness consumed Sukhumi, the capital of this palm-fringed subtropical Soviet Riviera. There was no electricity, no drinking water. On blackened streets teenage boys waved rifles and a smell of catastrophe mingled with the salty, moist Black Sea wind. We'd come during the opening act of Abkhazia's bloody conflict with Georgia, unresolved to this day. But here, in the country house of a winemaker, there still lingered an illusion of peace and plentitude.

The women hauled platters of cheese bread into the

room, where dozens of men crowded around a long table. Innumerable toasts in our honor had been fueled already by homemade Izabella wine. Not allowed by tradition to sit with the men, the women cooked and watched TV in the kitchen. I dropped in to pay my respects.

At exactly seven p.m. my spoon of corn mush froze midway to my mouth.

A familiar man occupied the screen. The man wore a natty dark pinstriped suit, but exhibited none of his usual autocratic vigor. He seemed tense, spent, his skin tone a loony pink against the gray backdrop with a scarlet Soviet flag on his left. The contours of the birthmark blotches on his forehead looked drawn with thick pencil.

'Dear fellow countrymen, compatriots!' said Mikhail Sergeevich Gorbachev. It was six years and nine months since he'd assumed leadership of *Sovetsky Soyuz,* the Soviet Union.

'Due to the situation which has evolved . . .'

The *situation* being as follows: that August, a coup against Gorbachev had been attempted by eight extremely dimwitted Party hard-liners (some obviously drunk at the time). The putsch collapsed almost straightaway, but the pillars of centralized Soviet power were cracked. Boris Yeltsin, fractious new president of the USSR's Russian republic, went leaping in, emerging as resistance leader and popular hero. Gorbachev still hung on – barely: a wobbler atop a disintegrating empire.

'Due to the *situation* . . .'

My mouth fell open all the way as Gorbachev continued speaking.

Much had changed in my own *situation* since my first time back in Moscow in December of 1987. Returning to Queens, I'd sobbed uncontrollably, facedown on Mother's couch. '*There* everyone loves us!' I wailed. '*Here* we have nothing and nobody!'

I had other reasons to cry. No wonder *gadalka* Terri, the fortune-teller, was mute about my future as an international keyboard virtuoso. My wrist had become painfully disfigured by a lump the size of a mirabelle plum. I could barely stretch a keyboard octave or muster a chord louder than mezzo forte. The more I tortured the ivories, the more the plum on my wrist tortured me.

A stern-browed orthopedist prescribed instant surgery.

But a pianistic trauma guru had a different prescription. Because my technique was ALL WRONG. Unless I relearned piano from scratch, she inveighed, my 'ganglion' lump would just return. I postponed my Juilliard MA exam and signed up for her rehabilitation course. I'd been playing since I was six, starting on our Red October upright piano in Moscow. Into the sound I produced – *my* sound – I'd poured my entire identity. Now, at twenty-four, I was relearning scales with my plum-lumpy wrist. I still remember my face reflected in the guru's shiny Steinway. I looked suicidal.

To come up with her weekly wad of crisp bills I took translating gigs, using Italian mustily recalled from our refugee layover in Rome. A cookbook as hefty as a slab of Etruscan marble landed one day on my desk. Instead of *andante spianato* and *allegro con brio*, my life was now to be occupied by *spaghetti al pesto* and *vitello tonnato*. Glumly I transcribed recipes onto index cards, while in the same room

John, my boyfriend, was finishing his Ph.D. thesis – so rife with Derrida-speak that it was, to me, Swahili.

John and I had met in the mideighties when he arrived in New York on a Fulbright. Cambridge-haughty, he wrote for trendy *Artforum* and deconstructed obscure Brit punk bands. Me, I brooded over my Schumann and lived with my mom in an immigrant ghetto. But somehow we clicked, and soon he was colonizing my bedroom in Queens. The Derridarian, Mom christened him – a being from a mystifying other planet. 'And what do *you* do?' condescended John's post-structuralist pals. I stared at the floor. I labored at scales and translated recipes.

The idea came out of nowhere, a flicker that lit up my dismal brain.

What if . . . I *myself* wrote a cookbook? Russian, of course. But embracing more so the cuisines of the whole USSR, in all its multiethnic diversity? My resident Derridarian magnanimously volunteered himself as coauthor, to help with my 'wonky' immigrant English.

I remember our fever the day our proposal went out to publishers.

And their icy responses. 'What, a book about breadlines?'

Then, stunningly, a yes – from the publisher of *the* cookbook of the burgeoning new foodie zeitgeist, *The Silver Palate*.

Contract signed, I was drifting down Broadway when a heckler piped up in my dizzied head.

'You *fraud*! What're your credentials? Zero, a big fat Russian *nol*'!'

Sure, I'd learned some recipe-writing from my Italian job, cooked enthusiastically with my mom, occasionally even gawked at overpriced chevres at Dean & Deluca. But watching Julia or Jacques on TV or leafing through the glossy layouts in *Gourmet*, I felt the same émigré alienation that had gripped me during my first bleak Philadelphia winter. Some capitalists were boning duck for a gala to which I wasn't invited. This eighties 'foodie' world of pistachio pesto and mushroom duxelles – I was a rank outsider to it. A class enemy, even.

But in my floppy handbag rested our signed contract and the chicken I'd already bought for recipe testing.

By the time I finished the opening chapter, on zakuski, the lump on my wrist had disappeared. By chapter two – soups – my guru-directed fingers were effortlessly tossing off octaves. But somehow the desire was gone. The bombastic Rachmaninoff chords felt hollow under my hands. My sound wasn't *mine*. For the first time in my adult life, plumbing the depths of late Beethoven no longer claimed my heart. Well into salads I played my Juilliard MA exam (adequately), shut the lid on my Steinway, and have hardly touched the ivories since.

The all-consuming passion that sustained me all these years had been supplanted. By a cookbook.

I realize, gazing back across my Brezhnevian childhood, that two particular Moscow memories propelled me on my food- and travel-writing career. Two visions from the socialist fairy tale of abundance and ethnic fraternity.

A fountain. A market.

The fountain was golden! *Druzhba Narodov*, or Friendship of Nations, it was called – and it glittered spectacularly inside VDNKh (Exhibition of National Economic Achievements), that sprawling totalitarian Disneyland where in 1939 my five-year-old mother saw Eden.

Grandma Alla and I liked to sit on the fountain's red granite edge, cracking sunflower seeds as sparrows peeped and the water jetted fantastically among sixteen larger-than-life golden statues. They were of kolkhoz girls in ethnic costumes, set in a circle around a baroque eruption of wheat. The fountain was completed right after Stalin's death, and gilded (so people whispered) at Beria's orders. 'National in form, socialist in content' – a spectacle of the happy family of our Socialist Union republics. How could I *ever* confess to my anti-Soviet mom that I, a cynical kid exposed to samizdat, was utterly mesmerized by this Soviet imperialist fantasy? That in their wreaths, tiaras, hats, ribbons, and braids the golden maidens were my own ethnic princesses?

The friendship of nations . . .

The hackneyed phrase was one of the most powerful propaganda mantras of the Soviet regime. *Druzhba narodov*: it celebrated our empire's diversity. Compensated us for our enforced isolation from the unattainable *zagranitsa*. What comrade, went the official line, needed crap capitalist Paris when more than 130 languages were spoken inside his own borders? When to the east he could behold the tiled splendors of Samarkand; enjoy white, healthy lard in Ukraine; frolic on pine-fringed Baltic sands? Your typical comrade didn't make it past sweaty Crimean beaches. But oh, what a powerful spell the ethnographic myth cast over our Union's psyche!

Some Union, ours. To telescope rapidly: Russia, Ukraine,

Byelorussia, and the newly aggregated Transcaucasus formed the initial Soviet fraternity, bonded by the 1922 founding treaty. Soon after, Central Asia supplied five fresh socialist *–stans*: Uzbek, Tajik, Turkmen, Kazakh, and Kyrgyz. Come the midthirties, the Transcaucasus was split back into Georgia, Armenia, and Azerbaijan. All the carving and adding wasn't entirely neat, though. Samarkand, a predominately Tajik city, was given to Uzbekistan. The Christian Armenian population of Nagorno-Karabakh got trapped in Muslim Azerbaijan. The nasty seeds of future *un*-friendships were being sown across the map. By 1940 the Soviet family reached fifteen members when the three Baltic republics and Moldavia were dragged in, courtesy of the treacherous Molotov-Ribbentrop Pact. My gilded fountain's enigmatic sixteenth maiden? She was the happy Karelo-Finnish Union Republic, later demoted to a subrepublic of Russia.

So there we were: the world's largest country by far, one sixth of the planet's land surface; a seeming infinity pitched within 37,000 miles of the border, reaching from the Atlantic to the Arctic to the Pacific Oceans. Fifteen full Union republics – all founded, please note, on *ethno-national* principles, from behemoth Russia (population almost 150 million) to teensy Estonia. In addition: twenty autonomous subrepublics, dozens of administrative 'national' units, 126 census-recognized 'nationalities' (Sovietese for ethnicity) – more than fifty languages spoken *just in the Caucasus*.

Such was the bomb of diversity that began to explode in the last decade of the twentieth century.

322

Back in my childhood, though, the Party talk was all SOLIDARITY. Profound RESPECT for ALL republics. The great Soviet COMMITMENT TO ETHNIC EQUALIZATION! (Prolonged stormy applause.) The Bolshevik fathers created nations. Stalin for his part deported them. Under Brezhnev, the Union's original vision of federalism and affirmative action had been revived – as institutional kitsch. The Mature Socialist celebration of ethnic friendship produced a never-ending costume carnival of Dagestani metalwork, Buryat archery skills, Moldavian embroidery. As a kid I lapped it all up. And the barrage of state-sponsored multiculturalism left me in a tizzy of perpetual hunger for the 'cuisines of our nations.'

So I acquired the second of my Moscow memories – of the two-storied Central Market on the Boulevard Ring, in the company once again of my hard-living Babushka Alla.

The Tsentralny Market was the friendship of nations come to throbbing, screaming, haggling life. Instead of golden statues, shrill Uzbek melon matrons wiped juice-stained fingers on striped *íkat* silk dresses, while Tajik dames hovered witch-like over banks of radishes, their heavy eyes kohl-rimmed, their unibrows a sinister line. I wandered the market aisles, ravenous, addled by scents of wild Uzbek cumin and Lithuanian caraway. After the greenish rot of state stores, the produce here radiated a paradisiacal glow. Kazakhs hustled soccer ball-size crimson apples (Kazakhstan's capital was Alma-Ata: 'Father of Apples'). Fast-talking Georgians with Stalinist mustaches whistled lewdly at my blond grandma and deftly formed newspaper cones for their *khmeli-suneli* spice mixes, tinted yellow with crushed marigold petals. I was particularly agog at the

Latvian dairy queens. The Baltics were *almost zagranitsa*. Polite, decked out in spotless white aprons, these lady-marvels filled Grandma's empty mayonnaise jars with their thick, tangy *smetana* (sour cream). In contrast to state *smetana*, theirs was a *quality* product: undiluted with buttermilk-diluted-with-milk-diluted-with-water – the usual sequence of Soviet dairy grift.

★ ★ ★

I gushed, and gushed, about the Central Market – as spectacle, as symbol – in the introduction to our cookbook.

In the friendship of nations spirit, the very first recipe I tested was my dad's Georgian chicken with walnut sauce (with the bird from my handbag on Broadway). Georgia was the Sicily of the Soviet imagination – a mythic land of inky wines, citrus, poets, tree-side philosophers, and operatic corruption. I followed with Armenian dolmas, then on to Baltic herring rolls, Moldavian feta-stuffed peppers, Byelorussian mushrooms.

Even pre-revolutionary Russian cuisine reflected the span of the empire. With Mikoyan's 1939 *Book of Tasty and Healthy Food*, this diversity got *Sovietized*. As the decades progressed, our socialist cuisine merged into one pan-Eurasian melting pot. Across the eleven time zones, the state's food service canon included Ayzeri *lulya kebab* and Tatar *chebureki* (fried pies). In Moscow you dined at restaurants named Uzbekistan or Minsk or Baku. And singularly *Soviet* hits such as salat Olivier and the proverbial 'herring under fur coat' lent socialist kitsch to Uighur weddings and Karelian birthday parties.

This was the story I wanted to tell in our book.

Please to the Table came out at the end of 1990. With four hundred recipes on 650 pages, it was heavy enough to whack someone unconscious.

A couple of months after publication, a phone call startled John and me in the dead of an Australian night. (We'd moved to Melbourne, where my Derridarian taught art history.) It was our editor in New York, very excited. *Please to the Table* – if you please – had just won a James Beard Award.

The news was doubly shocking to me.

Because who could *ever* imagine a more ironic moment for a fat, lavish book celebrating the culinary friendship of our Soviet nations? It was the spring of 1991, and our happy Union was coming apart at the seams.

For a principal pair of reasons, arguably. One was Gorbachev's disastrous handling of ethnic conflicts and secessionist passions in the republics. The other: the piteous mess he was making of the Soviet economy, which left stores barren of almost *everything* edible.

✳ ✳ ✳

'Ha! Better publish it as a USSR tear-off calendar!' my Moscow friends had joked two years earlier, while I was still researching *Please to the Table*.

The first salvos were erupting from our brotherly republics.

Down with Russian imperialism! Russian occupiers, go home!

Thousands of pro-independence demonstrators marched under these sentiments in Tbilisi, Georgia, in early April 1989. The protests lasted five days. That summer John and

I went recipe-collecting in the romantic, mountainous Caucasus. Reaching Tbilisi, we found the histrionic Georgian capital still reeling in shock. On April 9, Moscow's troops had killed twenty protesters, mostly young women. Everywhere, amid balconies jutting from teetering houses and restaurants dug into cliffs around the Kura River, Tbilisians seethed with opulent rage, calling down terrible curses on Moscow. The Kremlin, meanwhile, blamed the massacre on local officials.

Our hosts in town were a young architect couple, Vano and Nana, I'll call them – flowers of a young liberal national intelligentsia. Their noble faces convulsed with hatred for Kremlin oppression. But to us Nana and Vano were Georgian hospitality personified. A guest thereabouts is revered as a holy creature of God, to be bathed in largesse. In our honor, *kvevri*, clay vessels of wine, were dug out from the ground. Craggy wands of *churchkhella* – walnuts suspended in grape must – were laid out in piles. Cute baby lambs had their throats cut for roadside picnics by the crenellated stone walls of an eleventh-century Byzantine monastery. We became more than friends with Nana and Vano – family, almost. I cheered their separatist, righteous defiance at the top of my lungs.

One evening we sat under a quince tree in the countryside. We were full of dark, fruity wines and lavash bread rolled around opal basil and cheese. I felt at home enough to mention Abkhazia. Formally an autonomous republic of Georgia, Abkhazia was making its own moves to secede – from Georgia. We'd all been laughing and singing. Suddenly Nana and Vano froze. Their proud, handsome faces clenched with reignited hatred.

'Abkhazians are monkeys!' sputtered Nana. 'Monkeys down from the hills! They have no culture. No *history*.'

'Here's what they deserve,' snarled Vano. He crushed a bunch of black grapes savagely in his fist. Red juice squirted out between his elegant knuckles.

It was a preview of what lay ahead for Gorbachev's *Soyuz* (Union).

✳ ✳ ✳

What lay ahead also was the furious rumbling of stomachs.

In trying to reform the creaking, rusting wheel of the centralized Soviet system, Gorbachev had loosened the screws, dismantled a part here, a part there, and ultimately halted the wheel – with nothing to replace it. Typical Gorbachevian flip-flops left the economy floundering between socialist planning and capitalist supply and demand. Deficits soared, output stagnated, the ruble plummeted. The economy was collapsing.

Starting in 1989, John and I began living part-time in Moscow and traveling around the USSR – this for another book now, one my Derridarian was writing himself. It was to be a dark travel picaresque about the imploding Imperium. We stayed during the winter months mainly, during his Aussie summer vacations. I loved our first arrival, after a twenty-hour flight from Melbourne, to Dad's and Grandma Liza's welcome spreads, touchingly, generously, improbably conjured out of thin air. Our second arrival a year later was different. In December 1990, Babushka Liza had only diseased boiled potatoes and sauerkraut. I remember the anguished embarrassment in her eyes. The 'foreigners' were at her table, and she had only *this* to offer.

'*Nichevo v magazinakh!*' she cried. 'There's nothing in the stores! *Pustiye prilavki* – empty counters!'

The socialist shortage vernacular always reached for hyperbole, so I didn't take her words literally. Counters might be empty of desiderata – instant coffee, bananas – but in the past you could always count on salt, eggs, buckwheat, coarse brown *vermishel*. The next day I went to a Davydkovo store. And came face-to-face with IT. *Nichevo* – nothingness. The glaring existential emptiness of the shelves. No, I lie. The *nichevo* was framed by castles and pyramids constructed from 'sea-cabbage salad' – canned seaweed that made you vomit on contact. Two bored salesgirls sat inside the barren store. One was drawling a joke about 'coupons for grade #6 dogmeat.' The joke involved fur, claws, and chopped wooden bits of the doghouse. The other was assembling a mini-Lenin mausoleum ziggurat from the cans.

'A tomb for socialist edibles!'

Her laughter echoed amid the empty counters.

On a TV concert that New Year's Eve, the big-haired pop diva Alla Pugacheva bellowed a song called '*Nyam-nyam*' (yum yum). Usually Pugacheva bawled about 'a million scarlet roses.' Not now.

'*Open your fridge and take out 100* taloni/ *Add water and salt, and bon appetite/ Yum yum/Ha-ha-ha. Hee-hee-hee.*'

Taloni (coupons) – one of many official euphemisms for the dread word *kartochki* (ration cards). Other evasions included the alarmingly suave 'invitation to purchase.' They only rubbed salt in the truth: for the first time since World War II, rationing was being inflicted on *Homo sovieticus*. What's more, Gorbachev's new glasnost meant you could now scream about it out loud. 'Glasnost,' explained a Soviet mutt to an American mutt in a popular joke, 'is when they loosen your leash, yank away the food bowl, and let you bark all you want.' The barking? You could hear it from space.

As centralized distribution unraveled, food deliveries often detoured into the twilight zone of barter and shady semifree commerce. Or stuff simply rotted in warehouses. There was something else, too, now: nasty economic un-friendship within our happy Soviet fraternity. Granted increased financial autonomy by Gorbachev, regional politicians and enterprises fought to keep scarce supplies for their own hungry citizenry. Georgia clung to its tangerines, Kazakhstan its vegetables. When Moscow – and scores of other cities – restricted food sales to locals, the neighboring provinces halted dairy and meat deliveries into the capital.

So *everyone* hoarded.

My dad's four-hundred-square-foot apartment, besides being overcrowded with me and my six-foot-three Brit, resembled a storeroom. Blissfully unemployed, Dad had all day to forage and hunt. In the torturous food supply game, my old man was a grossmeister. He stalked milk delivery trucks, artfully forged vodka coupons, rushed to beat bread stampedes. He made his own cheese, soft and bland. His ridged radiators resembled a Stakhanovite bread rusk-drying plant. The DIY food movement of late perestroika would awe modern-day San Franciscans. On the rickety balconies of my friends, egg-laying chickens squawked among three-liter jars holding lingonberries pureed with rationed sugar, holding cucumbers pickled with rationed salt – holding *anything* that could be brined or preserved. 1990: *the* year of sauerkraut.

To shuffle as John and I did between Moscow and the West in those days was to inhabit a surreal split-screen. Western media gushed about Gorby's charisma and feted him for the fall of the Berlin Wall, the end of the cold war. Meanwhile, in Moscow, the dark, frosty air swirled with conspiracies of doom, with intimations of apocalypse. Famine was *on its way*. Citizens were *dropping dead* from expired medicine in humanitarian aid packages sold by speculators. (Probably true.) 'Bush's Legs,' the frozen chicken parts sent by Bush père as relief aid had *surely* been injected with AIDS. The Yanks were poisoning us, trampling our national pride with their diseased drumsticks. Private kiosks sold piss inside whiskey bottles, rat meat inside pirozhki. Ancient babushkas – those kerchiefed Cassandras who'd seen three waves of famines – lurked in stores crowing, '*Chernobyl harvest!*' at the sight of any misshapen beet.

The histrionics of discontent possessed a carnival edge. A perverse glee, almost. Force-fed cheerful Rodina songs, Soviet society was now whooping up an anti-fairy tale of collapse.

It was during such a time – when deliveries were called off for lack of gasoline and newspapers shrank to four pages because of lack of ink; when the words *razval* (collapse), *raspad* (disintegration), and *razrukha* (devastation) echoed everywhere like a sick song stuck in the collective brain –

that the Derridarian and I journeyed around the USSR for his book of Soviet-twilight picaresques.

Picture sardine cans on ice: rickety Zhiguli cars were our means of transport, usually on frozen roads. Lacking official Intourist permits, we couldn't legally stay at hotels, so we depended on the kindness of strangers – friends of friends of friends who passed us along like relay batons in a Soviet hospitality race. Between summer 1989 (the Caucasus) and December 1991 (the Caucasus again) we must have clocked 10,000 miles, give or take another endless detour. We roamed Central Asia, jounced through obscure Volga regions where some old folk still practiced shamanism and swilled fermented mare's milk. We rambled the periphery of boundless Ukraine and the charmed mini-kremlins of the Golden Ring around Moscow.

HUNTERS IN THE WINTER! appealed a sign in the gauzy Ukrainian steppe. PLEASE ARRANGE TO FEED THE WILD ANIMALS.

Our first driver was Seryoga, my cousin Dasha's blond wispy husband, who'd fought in the Afghan war.

'So we're near Kabul,' went a typical Seryoga road tale. 'So this frigging muezzin's not letting us sleep. So my pal Sashka takes out his Kalashnikov. BAM! Muezzin's quiet. *Forever*.'

Seryoga taught me several crucial survival skills of the road. How to spray Mace, for instance, which we practiced on his grandmother's pig. Also bribery. For this you positioned an American five *baks* note so that its edge stuck out of a pack of American Marlboros, which you slid across the counter with a wink as you cooed: 'I'd be obliged, very *obliged*.' The bribing of GAI (traffic police) Seryoga handled himself. Not always ably. On one particularly grim stretch of

Kazan-Moscow highway we were stopped and fined 'tventi baks' exactly twenty-two times. It was the GAI boys' version of a relay.

The dizzying landscape diversity of our multicultural Rodina celebrated in poem, novel, and song? It was now obliterated by winter, dissolved in exhaust fumes, brown compressed snow, the hopeless flattening light.

Our departures from Dad's crammed Moscow quarters . . . Up in the five a.m. blackness to make the most of the scant daylight ahead. My dad in the kitchen in his baggy blue track pants, packing our plastic bags with his radiator-dried rusks. Broth in his Chinese aluminum thermos; a coiled immersion heater for tea. Rationed sugar cubes. Twelve skinny lengths of salami from the hard-currency store to last the trip. We embrace. Sit for exactly one minute in silence – a superstitious Russian departure rite.

Our arrivals . . . Whether in Hanseatic Tallinn or Orientalist Tashkent, the potholed socialist road always led to an anonymous Lego sprawl of stained concrete blocks – five, nine, thirteen stories – in identical housing developments on identical streets.

'*Grazhdanka* (citizen)!' you plead, exhausted, desperate, starving. 'We're looking for Union Street, House five, structure seventeen B, fraction two-six.'

'*Chavo* – WHA?' barks the *grazhdanka*. 'This is *Trade* Union Street. *Union* Street is . . .' A vague motion somewhere into snowy Soviet infinity.

No map, no public phone without the receiver torn out. No idea if your friends-of-friends hosts are still awaiting you with their weak tea and their sauerkraut. An hour slogs by, another. Finally the address is located; you stand by the sardine can on wheels in shivering solidarity, a half-petrified icicle, as Seryoga dismantles the Zhiguli for the night so it won't be 'undressed.' Off come the spare tire, the plastic canisters of extra gas, the mirrors, the knobs. The pathetic moron who relaxes his vigilance for even one night? He buys his own windshield wipers at a car-parts flea market, as we did the next day. I think Tula was where this road lesson occurred. Tula – proud home of the samovar and stamped Slavic gingerbread, where we nearly keeled over from a black market can of expired *saira* fish. Or was it in the medieval marvel of Novgorod? Novgorod, which I remember not for the glorious icon of a golden-tressed angel with the world's saddest twelfth-century eyes, but for the hostile drunks who spat at our license plates and pulled our wispy Afghan vet out of the car to 'tear open his Moscow ass.' Novgorod, where I got to use Mace on actual humans.

We'd stopped in Novgorod en route to the more civilized Baltic capitals – Estonian Tallinn, Lithuanian Vilnius, and Latvian Riga. It was the empty-shelves December of 1990; Gorbachev, floundering, had just replaced half his cabinet with hardliners. The previous spring, the Baltic republics had declared their independence. To which the Kremlin responded with intimidation tactics and harsh fuel sanctions.

And yet we found the Baltic mood uplifting, even hopeful.

In Vilnius we crashed with a sweet, plump, twenty-something TV producer with a halo of frizzy hair, a dusky laugh, and boundless patriotism. Regina was the fresh modern face of Baltic resistance: earnest, cultured, convinced that *now* was the time to right historic injustices. Her five-meter kitchen chockablock with birchbark Lithuanian knickknacks felt like the snug home branch of Sajudis, Lithuania's anti-Communist liberation movement. Boho types in coarse-knit Nordic sweaters came and went, bearing scant edibles and the latest political news – Gorbachev's foreign minister, Eduard Shevardnadze, had just resigned, warning about a return to dictatorship! Regina's friends held hands and prayed, *actually prayed* for the end of Soviet oppression.

I'd been to Vilnius when I was eight, on a movie shoot. To my dazzled young eyes, cozy 'bourgeois' Vilnius seemed a magical porthole onto the unattainable West. Particularly the local *konditerai* scented with freshly ground coffee and serving *real* whipped cream. The whipped cream drowned my sense of unease. Because, boy, the Lithuanians really hated us Russians. Later, Mom, ever eager to bust up my friendship-of-nations fantasy, explained about the forced annexations of 1939. This might have been my opening foretaste of Soviet dis-Union. I remember feeling terribly guilty, as if I myself had signed the secret protocol of the Motlov-Ribbentrop Pact handing the Baltics over to Stalin. So now I prayed along with Regina.

With Christmas approaching, Regina got a crazy idea. *Šakotis!*

Šakotis (it means 'branched') is the stupendously elaborate Lithuanian cake resembling a spiky-boughed tree. Even in bountiful times nobody made it at home: besides fifty eggs per kilo of butter, *šakotis* demanded to be *turned on a spit* while you brushed on new dripping layers of batter. Regina was,

334

however, a girl on a mission. If Vytautas Landsbergis – the soft-spoken, pedantic ex-musicologist who led the Sajudis movement – could defy the Godzilla that was the Soviet regime, *she* could make *šakotis*. Friends brought butter, eggs, and a few inches of brandy. We all sat in the kitchen, broiling each craggy layer of batter to be stacked on an improvised 'tree trunk.'

The *šakotis* came out strange and beautiful: a fragile, misshapen tower of optimism. We ate it by candlelight. Someone strummed on guitar; the girls chanted Lithuanian folk songs.

'Let's each make a wish,' Regina implored, clapping her hands. She seemed so euphoric.

Three weeks later she called us in Moscow. It was January 13, long past midnight.

'I'm at work! They're storming us! They're shooting—' The connection went dead. Regina worked at the Vilnius TV tower.

In the morning we tuned in Voice of America on Dad's short-wave radio. Regina's TV tower was under Soviet assault; tanks were rolling over unarmed crowds. The violence had apparently ignited the previous day when the Soviets occupied the main print media building. A mysterious Moscow-backed force, the 'National Salvation Committee,' claimed to have seized power. Huge numbers of Lithuanians kept vigil around their Parliament, defending it. Everyone sang, linking hands. Thirteen people were killed and hundreds injured.

'Hello, 1968,' Dad kept muttering darkly, invoking the Soviet crackdown of Prague. TAKE AWAY GORBACHEV'S

NOBEL PEACE PRIZE! demanded a slogan at a Moscow protest rally. Russia's liberal media, previously Gorby supporters, bawled in outrage – so he promptly reintroduced censorship. All the while insisting he hadn't learned about the bloodshed in Vilnius until the day after it happened. Was he lying, or had he lost control of the hardliners? That dark new year of 1991, all I could think of was Regina's cake. Smashed by tanks, spattered with blood. Our friendship-of-nations fantasy – where was it now?

I wonder if Gorbachev phrased the question this way himself. For he too must have bought into our anthem's gilded cliché of indomitable friendship – of the '*unbreakable* Union of Soviet Republics.' What Party ideologue hadn't?

And yet from its very inception this friendly vision of a permanent Union contained a lurking flaw, a built-in lever for self-destruction. In their nation-building and affirmative-action frenzy, the twenties Bolsheviks had insisted on full equality for hundreds of newly Sovietized ethnic minorities. So – on paper at least – the founding 1922 Union Treaty granted each republic the right to secede, a right maintained in all subsequent constitutions. Each republic possessed its own fully articulated government structure. Paradoxically, such nation-building was meant as a bridge to the eventual merging of nations into a single communist unity. More paradoxical was how aggressively the Party-state fostered ethnic identities and diversity – in acceptable *Soviet* form – while suppressing any *authentic* expressions of nationalism.

The post-Stalin leadership had generally been blind to the potential consequences of this paradox. Whatever genuine nationalist flare-ups occurred under Khrushchev and Brezhnev were dismissed as isolated holdovers of bourgeois national consciousness and quickly put down. The response of Gorbachev-generation Party elites to the national question was . . . *What* national question? Hadn't Brezhnev declared such issues solved? The Soviet people were one 'international community,' Gorbachev pontificated at a 1986 Party congress. 'United in a unity of economic interests, ideological and political aims.' Were this not his real conviction – so I ask myself to this day – would he have risked glasnost (literally 'public voicing') and perestroika (restructuring) in the republics?

'We never expected an upsurge of emotional and ethnic factors,' the supposedly sly Shevardnadze later admitted.

Unexpectedly, the floodgates burst open.

'Armenian-Azeri fighting escalating in Nagorno-Karabakh; Southern Ossetians clashing *again* with Georgians – twenty dead!' Our friend Sasha Meneev, head of the newly created 'nationalities' desk at the liberal Moscow News daily, would update us breathlessly during our times in the capital. 'The Gagauz – Christian Turkish minority in Moldavia, right? – seeking full republic status. Ditto Moldavia's *Slavic* minority. Crimean Tatars demanding repatriation; Volga Tatars threatening sovereignty over oil reserves . . .'

'Sooner or later,' one of Gorbachev's advisers bitterly quipped, 'someone is going to declare his apartment an independent state.'

True to form, the mineral secretary, caught between reformers and hardliners, vacillated, flipped and flopped. Tanks or talks? Repressions or referendums? Desperate to preserve the Union – at least as some species of reformed federation – Gorbachev would try them all. Without success. The biggest blow would come from his largest republic, specifically from his arch-nemesis, Boris Yeltsin, the Russian republic's populist renegade head. In summer 1990 Yeltsin announced Russia's sovereignty (not full independence, but close). Resigning from the Communist Party, he roused fellow republic leaders to 'take as much sovereignty as they could swallow.'

Now, in the wake of the bloodshed in Vilnius, Yeltsin – true to *his* form – rushed to Estonia's Tallinn to loudly support the breakaway Balts. In February 1991, another uproar. On live TV he called on the embattled Gorbachev to resign and transfer control to the collective leadership of the republics. So began Gorbachev's annus horribilis. And the political war between USSR and Russia. Moscow vs. Moscow.

Could politics get any more surreal?

Nevozmozhno/neizbezhno. Inevitable/impossible. *Nevozmozhno/ neizbezhno* . . .

This schizophrenic refrain about the prospects of the Union's explosion ticked through my tired brain as John and I traversed the empire in its last months – days? hours? years? – in 1990 and 1991.

What would happen? Ethnicities commandeered into

Soviet kinship by Bolshevik whims – would they go on slaughtering each other inside convoluted borders drawn up by early Soviet cartographers? Or would a tidal wave of Moscow tanks enforce happiness in the big Soviet family?

From one day to the next we couldn't imagine – any more than we knew whether at any particular nightfall we'd face rancid sauerkraut or be treated to a pathos-drenched feast by a clan of blood-baying nationalists. A world was coming unstitched. We felt helpless, bewildered, our sardine can on wheels caught up in history's centrifuge. And how different the foods of our fraternal republics tasted to me. The dishes I revered from my childhood's garish seventies recipe post-card collections on 'cuisines of our nations' now conjured not a friendship buffet but a witches' brew of resentments freshly stirred up by glasnost. Each family of the Soviet fraternity was unhappy after its own fashion. Each stop we made revealed the particular flavor of some tiny nation's past tragedy, the historical roots of the conflicts engulfing the empire. How little I, the award-winning cookbook author, *really* knew about our Union of cuisines.

Snapshot from Samarkand, winter of 1991. Everyone here fights over *palov* (meat pilaf), the Central Asian monodish. The deeper issue? Stunning Timurid-dynasty Samarkand, the tourist pride of Turkic-speaking Soviet Uzbekistan with its blue-tiled fifteenth-century mosques, is in fact a city populated mostly by Farsi-speaking Tajiks.

Pre-revolution this region was a bilingual khanate. People intermarried, ate the same pilaf, and called themselves Sarts.

Unlike the Lithuanians (theirs an actual, pre-Soviet country) neither the Tajiks nor Uzbeks ever had anything resembling a separate national consciousness. Not until Stalin, fearing a pan-Turkic insurgence in the late 1920s, split Central Asia (then known as Turkestan) into five Union republics. Obsessive Bolshevik social engineering supplied each with a semifabricated history, a newly codified written language, and freshly minted ethno-identity. Nifty nationhood package aside, Tajikistan got stuck with some scrappy mountains; Uzbekistan drew the gorgeous *Tajik* cultural centers of Samarkand and Bukhara. Uzbekistan also scored Amir Timur – a.k.a. Tamerlane the warrior king – who was designated an Uzbek national hero. Funny, since Timur was actually a Mongol who fought *against* the Uzbeks.

Along came glasnost, and old scores long muzzled by the Kremlin's heavy centralized hand were back, in full fury.

'Uzbek pilaf! Vile and greasy!' raged an elderly Tajik nationalist professor when we paid a call on him at his boxy low-rise apartment. The *Tajik* pilaf on his table – 'Delicate! Reflective of our ancient Persian heritage' – had been assembled into a cumin-scented mound by his gorgeous young unibrowed wife. Talking to the local Uzbek minority, we learned, of course, that Tajik pilaf was pathetic: 'Tasteless! Bland!' These declarations were completely bewildering, because the Tajik and Uzbek pilafs of Samarkand tasted identical.

Our hosts in Samarkand were an aged Bukharan-Jewish couple, Rina and Abram. '*Interesno*.' Abram squinted from his third-party perspective. 'Tajiks here listed themselves as Uzbeks on their passports when it helped with their careers. Now suddenly they remember their heritage?'

Rina and Abram had their own grief. 'When *they* finish killing each other,' hissed Rina, 'they'll turn on us Jews.' Rina sat by her mulberry tree weeping tears into a bowl of tannic green tea. She and Abram had applied for an exit visa to Israel. 'But how to leave *this* behind,' lamented Rina, gesturing at their palatial private house with a fully cemented backyard (a proud Bukharan-Jewish-Soviet tradition).

'Oi vai, oi vai,' cried Abram from the back door. 'Tajiks, Uzbeks, Jews – under Brezhnev we all lived as one *muhallah* (community/neighborhood). Gorbachev *bud' on proklyat* (be damned)!'

Spectacular wails and ululations awoke us our last Samarkand morning. The wailers were our hosts. Storming into our bedroom, they began frantically slashing the mattress on which we still lay. 'OI OI OI!' The decibels of their shock nearly cracked the palatial walls painted with crude rococo landscapes.

'VAI VAI VAI!' resounded the entire neighborhood.

Soviet tanks? I gasped. A Jewish pogrom?

'WORSE!' Rina screamed.

The morning's radio had just announced the government's latest economic shock measure. All fifty- and hundred-ruble banknotes were to be withdrawn from use. Citizens were given three days only to exchange their old bills – maximum amount, one thousand rubles. Some forty dollars at black market rates. In catastrophic silence we sipped our green tea as Rina and Abram slashed fake-rococo chairs and striped cushions. Their entire life savings fluttered around the rooms in a morning breeze. Most of it in banned fifties and hundreds.

Just another day on the road, 1991. On the crumbling Imperium's fringes.

Snapshot from Tashkent, Uzbekistan's capital, later that same winter. At the Alay Bazaar the January sun angled across mottled-green Kokand melons. Men in skullcaps thronged around carts piled high with indented *non* flatbreads the size and shape of soup bowls. The biggest trade this season? Little red horoscope booklets. The future. The future. What does the future hold?

At the bazaar I gravitated again and again to the rows of Korean ladies hawking their prodigious pickles: shredded carrots laced with garlic and coriander; fiery cabbage kimchi they called *chim-che*. The Koreans were socialist Central Asia's model farmers. At their prosperous, orderly kolkhozes with names like Politotdel (Political Department) they grew wonder onions and overfulfilled every Five-Year Plan by 500 percent. Koreans also farmed most of the rice for the pilaf Uzbeks and Tajiks argued about. But behind the Koreans' golden success story lurked another sort of tale . . .

After we'd bought several rounds of her pickles, Shura Tan, in her late sixties, told us her story. She spoke in halting Russian dotted with Uzbek words. When she got nervous she flattened her shredded carrots with a strangely shaped ladle and meticulously reassembled them into perfectly triangular mounds.

Like most Soviet Koreans of her generation, Shura was born in the Russian Far East. The diaspora had been there since the 1860s, swelling after refugees from the 1910 Japanese invasion of Korea crossed over to the future USSR. The Korean comrades grew rice and fished; the Bolsheviks gave them Korean-language schools, theaters, clubs. 'We Koreans were happy,' said Shura.

Then, in the fall of 1937, men in uniforms came to their kolkhoz. The Koreans were given three days to pack. Panic swept through their villages. Where were they being taken? Wrenched by despair, Shura's mother assembled a huge sack of rice and wrapped in cloth a handful of earth for her garden plot. 'Why take the earth?' protested the family. Shura's mother took it all the same. It was her earth.

The Koreans were told to bring food for a week, but the journey lasted a month, maybe longer. Packed into sealed cattle cars, the panicked deportees traveled almost four thousand miles west across frigid Siberia. Old people and babies died from hunger and illness, their bodies dumped from the moving train. All the way Shura wept. She was then a small child.

At last the train stopped. As far as the eye could see were reeds, mud, swamps – the endless plains of Central Asia. The Koreans began building mud huts, sometimes without window or doors

'Scorpions fell on my bed from our walls,' Shura recalled, raking her carrots. 'And black snakes as long as this' – she opened her arms wide. But the worst killer was the muddy, diseased swamp water – the only drinking water available. That's when Shura's mother remembered her earth. She filtered the poisoned water through it.

'And that's what saved us,' said Shura. 'The earth.'

Koreans became the first Soviet ethnicity to be deported

by Stalin in its *entirety*. More than 180,000 strong, down to the last child. Accusation: potential pro-Japanese espionage during Soviet-Japanese tensions over Manchuria, even though most Koreans hated Japan. Another motive for their deportation: the hard-toiling Koreans could farm the barren Central Asian steppes.

Between 1937 and 1944 these steppes served as Stalin's dumping ground for scores of other, smaller ethnicities he charged with treason. Sealed cattle cars – 'crematoria on wheels' – ferried in Chechens, Ingushi, Karachai, Kalmyks, and Balkars. Also Crimean Tatars, Volga Germans, Ingrian Finns, Kurds, Poles from the Ukraine. The Koreans assimilated and stayed. Others, like the Chechens and the Ingushi, returned to their Northern Caucasus homeland under Khrushchev's Thaw, only to find their houses occupied by Russians and neighboring ethnic minorities, and the stone tombs of their ancestors employed as construction material. Mountain nations venerate their ancestors. The insults were never forgiven. Gorbachev's glasnost reawakened the memories.

Nation builder and nation destroyer – simultaneously – is how the historian Terry Martin describes the Soviet State. As whole ethnic populations drew Stalin's black marks, the officious encomiums to Union minorities rang out undiminished. Propaganda reels after the Great Patriotic War showed happy Korean collective farmers at their glorious socialist toil. There were even well-financed Korean theater productions. A Korean-language newspaper – *Lenin Kichi* (Lenin's Banner) – was imposed on every Korean kolkhoz, representing yet another socialist irony.

Deprived of Korean schooling by Stalin, the generation

of Shura the pickle maker could no longer read *hangul* script.

'I know Russian, a little Uzbek,' sighed Shura. 'Korean? Nyet. No language – no homeland.' She sighed again. 'But at least we have this.' She pointed down to her pickles. After mixing some *kachi* red chile paste into a tangy salad of cabbage and peppers, she scooped some into my hand. The heat of her chiles left my face numb.

✳ ✳ ✳

Update: Moscow, August 19, 1991. Tanks rumble up the bombastic thrust of Kutuzov Prospect. Soviet TV plays *Swan Lake* . . . over and over. Party hard-liners announce control of the government. Gorbachev? Under house arrest at his Crimean dacha. Officially the 'state of his health' doesn't permit him to continue as president. The right-winger vice president Comrade Yanaev is taking over. Comrade Yanaev's hands tremble visibly at his press conference. Not quite sober for history's call.

Hello, *Avgustovsky putsch* – the August coup.

We stare at our television in a seaside suburb of Melbourne, where Mom happens to be visiting me and John from New York.

'*Vsyo, eto vsyo,*' Mom is crying. 'This is the end!'

I keep dialing my father in Moscow. And getting through.

'*Da, putsch, putsch* . . .' Dad giggles sardonically.

'Ma, Ma,' I keep reasoning, nine thousand miles away from the scenes. 'If things were that bad they'd have cut the international phone lines!'

They'd have cut Yeltsin's phone too. Instead, there he is in all his bearish populism, defiant atop a tank outside the

White House, the Russian parliament building. In popular elections that June he'd become Russia's first freely elected leader *in a thousand years*. Now he rallies Muscovites to resist the takeover. Crowds cheer him on. Citizens weep and complain openly for imperialist cameras. The plotters' script has been botched: Is this any way to run a *putsch*?

Over the next two days the coup goes phhht, and in such a pratfall style that to this day Russian conspiracy theorists question what *really* happened. Things move at shocking speed after this. Yeltsin bans the Communist Party. More republics head for the exit. Gorbachev clings on in this crumbling world, still devoutly for the Union, even in its now hobbled form. The friendship of nations: no longer only a cherished ideological trope for Comrade Gorbachev. Without it he's out of a job.

'I'm not going to just float like a lump of shit in an ice hole,' he informs Yeltsin in December, after 90 percent of Ukrainians icily vote to secede from his Union.

✳ ✳ ✳

That December of 1991 my Derridarian and I returned for our final road trip – south via Ukraine to the rebellious Georgian subrepublic of Abkhazia, wedged in between Georgia and the southern border of Russia. What with the chaos and gasoline shortage, nobody wanted to drive us. Finally we found Yura, a thirty-something geology professor with a Christ-like ginger beard. 'I refuse to give bribes – *out of principle*,' he informed us quietly. This was bad news. On the plus side: *his* rattletrap Zhiguli operated on both gas *and* propane, slightly increasing our chances of actual motion.

The propane stank up the car with a rotten-egg smell. On the road Yura pensively cracked pine nuts with his big yellow teeth; his cassette tape whined with semi-underground sixties songs about *taiga* forests and campfires. Geologists – they were their own sub-culture.

Yura's Zhiguli was a metaphor for the disintegrating state of our *Soyuz*. Innocent tourist side jaunts metastasized into days-long quests for accelerator components. Every fill-her-up of black market gas cost five monthly salaries. Meantime all around us they were renaming the landscape. Kharkov in Ukraine was no more; it was Kharkiv now, in Ukrainian. Lenin and Marx streets clanged into dustbins.

By the time we sputtered into Abkhazia's civil-war-torn Black Sea capital of Sukhumi, I no longer knew whom to side with in ethnic conflicts, whom to trust. I now put my faith in anyone who put out a hot meal. I trusted and loved the wiry young Abkhazian driver lent to us by the local writers' union to help fix our sardine can on wheels. The kid proudly took us to his parents' village house for a meal. We ate bitterish, gamy wild duck shot that morning – smothered in a thick, tomatoey, fiery sauce. It might have been the most memorable dish of my life. Then the excellent youngster stole Yura's last gas canister.

To Sukhumi we carried an introduction from our Moscow acquaintance Fazil Iskander, the greatest living Abkhazian writer. During an electrical blackout we called at the darkened flat of Alexei Gogua, chief of the Abkhazian Writers Union. We found the gray-haired Gogua writing in his pajama pants by a flickering candle. What terrible straits we'd landed him in! Abkhaz hospitality demanded a resplendent welcome. We were visiting foreign writers –

sent by Fazil, the Abkhaz Mark Twain. But Sukhumi's infra-structure was shattered. Which is how a Zhiguli convoy of separatist culturati accompanied us to the well-lit country house of a prominent winemaker.

Shortly before seven p.m. I slipped out to the kitchen.

'*Due to the situation which has evolved . . .*'

The inevitable/impossible was finally happening. At seven p.m. on Christmas Day, 1991, Mikhail Sergeevich Gorbachev was giving his resignation speech.

The *situation* had developed further and fatally for him. Several weeks earlier, his thorn-in-the-side Yeltsin had secretly met leaders of Ukraine and Byelorussia at Brezhnev's former hunting lodge in a Byelorussian forest. The troika's advisers and lawyers cooked up a devilish plan: As founding members of the 1922 Union Treaty, the three republics *had the power to annul it* – to simply dissolve the USSR! In its place they formed the Commonwealth of Independent States. Byelorussian herbal vodka lubricated the signing. Before bothering to inform Gorbachev, Yeltsin telephoned the news to George H. W. Bush. ('Dear George,' he addressed him now.) At a subsequent meeting in Kazakhstan, eight more republics went ex-Union. Clearly Gorbachev was finished.

And yet his TV announcement caught me by total surprise, there with my uneaten spoonful of Abkhazian corn mush. Reading from a paper, often awkwardly, the last leader of *Sovetsky Soyuz* spoke for ten minutes. He lauded his own democratic reforms. Admitted mistakes. Took credit for the elimination of a totalitarian system and for 'newly acquired spiritual and political freedom.' About the new freedom and such he wasn't fabulizing exactly, but the ladies around me gently waved him off. His phrases rang meaning-less, false – simply because after all his flip-flopping, who'd ever believe him?

The USSR's dying minutes still replay in my mind in dazed, elegiac slow motion.

I recall the exact words that Gorbachev mangled in his crass provincial accent (so at odds with his suave inter-national image). I taste the salty cheese in the corn mush, inhale the kitchen's garlicky pungencies; I hear the thudding splat of a pomegranate heavy with seeds that – another metaphor for the Imperium? – fell on the kitchen floor and cracked open.

The Abkhaz women had been watching impassively for the most part, chins propped in hands. But as the resignee thanked his supporters and wished his countrymen best, the lady of the house whispered:

'*Zhalko, a vse-taki zhalko.*'

'*Zhalko,*' echoed the others: 'A shame, a shame, in the end.'

'*Zhalko,*' I murmured along, not sure what we were wistful about. The sudden humanity of a tone-deaf reformer – hero abroad, villain at home? The finis, the *official, irrevocable* curtain falling on our fairy-tale communal lie, the utopian social experiment for which millions of lives had been brutally sacrificed – now signing off in the most undramatic fashion imaginable? Empires! They weren't supposed to gurgle away in ten badly colorized minutes. The locomotive carrying citizens into a brighter tomorrow wasn't meant to just run out of gas and die in the middle of nowhere, like one more woebegone Zhiguli.

As Gorbachev later wrote in his memoirs, he got no farewell ceremony, no phone calls from presidents of former

Soviet republics. *They* didn't believe in the friendship of nations. Were there any murmurs of 'a shame' from them at the end?

When the speech was over, the blazing red Soviet banner was lowered for the very last time in history, and a peppy Russian tricolor rose in its place.

A *new day in a new state*, said the announcer, and the TV reverted to regular programming. A cartoon, I think it was, or maybe a puppet show.

I know you'll wonder how it felt to wake up next day in a *new state*. Only I didn't wake up – not till two whole days later. My brain pounded violently against my temples. My blurred vision registered white-coated people bending over me with expressions of saccharine Soviet concern. 'How is our *golovka*, our little head?' they cooed, waving smelling salts under my nose. *Where was I?* Ah, yes . . . the only place in darkened Sukhumi with its own electrical generator. The Sanatorium of the Russian Armed Forces, where we'd been lodged on arrival by the hospitable Abkhazian writers. After the USSR ended on TV there'd been toasts, many toasts – flowery prodigies of Caucasian eloquence laboriously trans-lated from Abkhaz to Russian to English (for the sake of the Derridarian, who was now sprawled beside me, ghostly pale and grunting). Dimly I recalled the ritualistic pouring of homemade Izabella wine onto the roof of our decrepit sardine can around four a.m. The equally ritualistic guzzling down of a farewell *kantsi*, a horn filled with 1.5 liters of the same such Izabella. Gogua, the elderly writer-in-chief, collapsing softly into the arms of his secretary.

'*Golovka*, the little head, how is it?' pressed the white-coated people.

The *golovka* pounded and hammered and throbbed. Passed out from epic alcohol poisoning. That's how, since you asked, I greeted the dawn of a new historical era. Ah, Izabella.

Ah, dawn; historical hungover dawn . . .

The Zhiguli's engine finally expired somewhere near Kiev, and in exchange for a bottle, a GAZ truck towed Yura the Christ-like geologist eight hundred miles to Moscow. John and I took the overnight train with its red-carpeted corridor. Back in Melbourne again, where it was summer, we sat on a green hill leaning on our two massive suitcases, homeless and miserable – the sublet we'd arranged had fallen through. Soon I left my Derridarian in Australia and returned to New York. Our relationship sank under the strain of the USSR's dying days – though it took us a few more long-distance years (he moved to California) to break up officially. His travel book never came out.

Between 1992 and 1999, Yeltsin's *dermokratiya* (crapocracy) sent Russia into free-market shock. Rampaging inflation, pitiful salaries unpaid – the previous hungry years of sauerkraut were remembered as plentiful. Overnight, a giant sleazy fire sale of national resources spawned oligarchs out of former apparatchiks and gangsters. Lesser beings lost everything: identity, pride, savings, Crimean beaches, and the comforting rhetoric of imperialist prestige and power. Not to mention the Soviet state's social benefits. What's more, Boris 'Champion of Sovereignty' Yeltsin started a war to stop Chechnya from seceding, a conflict with horrors that fester to this day.

In 2000 an obscure midget with a boring KGB past was elected post-Union Russia's second president and started flexing his muscles. Authoritarian symbols and rhetoric were revived. Among them, the Soviet national anthem – the words 'Russia – our sacred power' substituted for 'unbreakable Union of Soviet Republics.' Under Putin's petrodollar kleptocracy, narcissistic consumerism began to bloom and boom. Money and glamour – Russified as *glamur* – swaggered in as the new state ideology (fretfully decried by the intelligentsia). These days Muscovites still order Georgian *kharcho* soup and Ukrainian *vareniki* dumplings at cute 'ethnic' restaurants. But mostly they enjoy carpaccio and sushi – at oligarch prices.

Recently, cleaning my office in Queens, I unearthed a box of recipe postcards from the seventies. Fifteen sets, each celebrating a Soviet republic's cuisine. Arranging them slowly on my dining table, I recalled the rain-washed autumn day four decades before when I scored these *defitsit* treasures at the big Dom Knigi bookstore and triumphantly carried them home. Poring now over the faded Technicolor close-ups of Moscow-designated 'national dishes,' I still twinged at their faintly fragrant Orientalist spell, their enticements to wanderlust. There was 'Azerbaijani' sturgeon salad, inexplicably smothered in *Slavic*

sour cream, pictured against socialist oil derricks rising from the blue Caspian Sea. Faux 'Kyrgyz' cakes, exotically called 'Karagat' though featuring black currants in no way native to arid Kyrgyzstan. Umpteen ethnic variations on salat Olivier and kotleti. National in form, socialist in flavor, exactly as the Party prescribed.

Why was it, then? Why, of all the totalitarian myths, had the gilded fairy tale of the friendship of nations stayed so deeply, so intimately lodged in my psyche?

Fearing the answer might expose my inner Soviet imperialist, I quit speculating. Instead I decided to throw a birthday dinner for Mom featuring the *real* dishes of our erstwhile republics. As celebration, as semi-expiation.

For a solid week I pulverized walnuts for Georgian chicken *satsivi*, folded grape leaves around scented Armenian lamb, fried pork crackling for my bonafide Ukrainian borscht. Proudly I set these out on Mom's birthday table along with Moldovan feta strudels and *abysta*, that bland Abkhazian corn mush of my farewell to the USSR. For dessert, a dense Lithuanian honey cake. And in tribute to the toasts at the dissolution of the Union Treaty, I even steeped a Byelorussian herbal vodka.

Mom was touched almost to tears by my handiwork. But she just couldn't help being herself.

'*Za druzhbu narodov* – To the friendship of nations!' She offered the dog-eared toast with a grin so sarcastic, it practically withered my edible panorama of the republics.

'Imagine!' she exclaimed to her guests. 'The daughter I raised on Tolstoy and Beethoven – she went gaga over the stupid gilded fountain at VDNKh!'

I was a little hurt by her words, I have to admit.

That Friendship of Nations fountain, by the way, has been freshly regilded in Moscow. Kids with their grandmas still circle around it. 'Babushka, Babushka, tell us what it was like to live in the USSR?' the kids want to know.

'Well, *once upon a time* . . .' begin the babushkas.

CHAPTER TEN

TWENTY-FIRST CENTURY: PUTIN ON THE RITZ

We landed in Moscow on Good Friday, 2011 – my mom, Barry, and I.

For the very first time ever, relatives weren't there to embrace us at the airport. They still loved us, they claimed, but life now was different. Busier. *Terríble* airport traffic.

Earlier that afternoon we'd been devouring an epic garden lunch under late-April cherry trees in Odessa. The city of my mother's birth, that gaudy, piratical Soviet port of my childhood seaside vacations, had been transformed into a charming, smiley, semiglobalized city in very foreign *Ukraine*. We'd stopped over in Odessa to do family research – only to discover that second cousin Gleb, our closest local relative, had a broken nose, a prison past, and complete alcoholic amnesia. So we researched Odessa's garlicky cooking instead, shopping up a storm at the boisterous Privoz market. Our suitcases bulged with wholesome Ukrainian lard, folkloric garlic-studded kolbasa, and buttery smoked *kambala* flatfish.

None of this was presents for family. A month in the world's fourth most expensive metropolis loomed ahead of us. We anxious American paupers stocked up on cheap, delicious Odessa edibles as if preparing for combat. Putin's Moscow: a battleground, not for the fainthearted and shallow-pocketed.

In the new millennium our visits to Moscow had been infrequent and brief. Mother and I stayed away altogether from 1991 to 2001, missing out on the booze-soaked get-rich-or-have-your-brains-blown-out anarchy of the Yeltsin years. Not by design; it just happened. My grandparents and Uncle Sashka were dead; our surviving relatives came to visit in New York. As for *rodina*, we no longer mentally spelled it with a capital R. From the irony, dread, and tangle of signifiers sprouting from the dead morass of Sovietese, the word had shrunk to a de-ideologized, neutered noun, denoting, simply, where you were born. I felt more at home elsewhere, traveling and eating for a living. I'd bought an apartment in Istanbul with a Bosporus view and had devoted my latest cookbook to frenetically hospitable Spain, after writing about the tastes of Latin America and the Pacific Rim.

Moscow?

'Dubai with Pushkin statues,' Barry, my boyfriend, pronounced it on our previous visit.

It was already late evening on this Good Friday when we settled finally into our rented 'highrise' flat.

'Highrise,' pronounced *khi-rize* in Russian, was the deluxe tag that Moscow4Rent, the rental agency, had concocted for our boxy two-bedroom apartment on Novy Arbat Avenue. The view made our jaws drop. From the twenty-second-floor windows we beheld 1) Hotel Ukraine, a showpiece of

Stalinist neo-Gothic gigantomania; 2) Novy Arbat Avenue, Khrushchev's swashbuckling slap at such feats of Stalinist ornamentalism; 3) the bulky Parliament White House, site of the 1991 attempted putsch that triggered the fall of the empire. Even at night the endless soaring construction cranes of Putin's gangster-corporate capitalism were still at it. Moscow's rapacious real estate schemes never sleep.

The *khi-rize* cost a small fortune. But leaning transfixed on a windowsill I gazed at the wide street below in breathless exhilaration at a long-ago childhood fantasy finally realized.

I had arrived!

In the early sixties bulldozers crushed a swath through crooked, archaic Old Arbat lanes, gouging out this massive, ruler-straight avenue then known as Kalinin Prospect. Strolling the renamed Novy Arbat of today, a foreigner might only see sleek BMWs cutting off sooty rheumatic city buses on a choked six-lane thoroughfare, with late-modernist towers hulking alongside, grubby-gray but with a certain brutalist je ne sais quoi. This foreigner might smirk at the tacky red-lettered globe on the tawdry Arbat center, frown at the ersatz steakhouses and yakitori joints sprawling westward and east.

Me? From the window I saw the boulevard of my young dreams.

I saw that now-tacky globe – year 1972. Magically blue it glowed inside its original wraparound logo: AEROFLOT: SPEED AND COMFORT. Rotating and flashing the locations of different mysterious foreign countries, it was a wonder cabinet of the latest Japanese electronics in Moscow. Below it shoppers in furry hats promenaded along Moscow's widest sidewalk, past Vesna department store, in the gleaming windows of which checkered Polish coats preened, never actually for sale inside. Black Volgas and Chaikas glided by imperiously in the two lanes reserved for officials. Some lucky Muscovites toted *defitsit* cornflakes boxes from the swishy, American-style self-service Novoarbatsky supermarket. I saw my young self there too, gaping up at the giant Times Square-style screen where cartoons and bright propaganda reels blazed. Kalinin Prospect was my mirage of the West, my vision of technology's march, my crystal ramp into the future. My Ginza and Broadway and Champs-Elysées packed into one.

As for our own *khi-rize*, it was one of four twenty-six-story prefab-concrete residential skyscrapers completed in 1968, only two years before I moved to an Old Arbat lane nearby. Strictly allocated to the *nomenklatura*, these towers fascinated me then with their sheer newness and geometricity. They were my own private, inaccessible residential utopia. I wanted to spend my life here at the very apex of late-sixties Soviet modernity – *right here* at the very spot where now in 2011 my mom is wrestling with the malfunctioning electric teakettle.

Memory likes its cruel tricks with the objects of our nostalgic yearnings. They usually turn out to be smaller, disheartteningly trite, when finally reencountered in real life. How miraculous then, I thought to myself, that not even thirty-plus years and a passport full of visa stamps could shrink the stature of ugly Kalinin Prospect.

Before collapsing onto our *khi-rize* Ikea beds, we snacked at our Ikea kitchen table on the sausage and pepper vodka we'd hauled with us from Ukraine. Mom and Barry too tired, I think, to parse the bounty of ironies, with the giant wedding cake of Stalin's Hotel Ukraine blazing floodlit across the Moscow River.

Next morning we left Mom with her telephone troika – global digital, local land line, Russian cell – and headed off for a nostalgic stroll along Boulevard Ring, the route I used to take with Grandmother Alla. The day was mid-spring-like and stunning. The sky gleamed cerulean blue, and in the suddenly balmy air the tulips flashed and pansies winked from their beds. *Anyutini glazki* (Anyuta's eyes – *my* eyes) is Russian for pansies, and I love them for it. My heart sang. The boulevard flora inspired a Nabokovian nostalgia for that 'hospitable remorseful racemosa-blossoming Russia.'

As for the fauna . . .

'Got a car for my birthday,' a six-year-old in an Abercrombie hoodie was telling his pal. 'Not a TOY, *kretin*. A car. With a chauffeur.'

On Nikitsky Boulevard, ladies young and old, belles and bêtes, hobbled along on sadistic ten-inch heels, like throngs of exotic giraffes. 'Look!' whispered Barry, gawking at a blonde in hot pants and vertiginous pink platform-stilettos. Pink satin ribbons fluttered from her absurdly teetering ankles.

But it wasn't *her* footwear attracting all the attention.

The Muscovite gaze, which blatantly sizes you up and down, assessing your clothes and accessories, piercing you with disdain or caressing you and yours with haughty approval – that collective gaze now fixed on my toes. They were bare. For our sentimental walk I'd worn sensible Adidas flip-flops, and in doing so had violated some code of Moscow propriety. Here in my old neighborhood, I suddenly felt self-conscious and foreign, as if trapped inside a 'naked in public' anxiety dream.

My bare toes were glared at inside some of the world's most expensive real estate: at the tea shop (ten dollars an ounce of 'white needle' Fujian leaves), at the bakery (ten dollars a wedge of tiramisu), at the florist (ten dollars a rosebud). These fine merchants all embodied the most cherished post-Soviet attributes: *eleet* and *ekskluziv*.

We fled off the boulevards onto Tverskaya Street, ducking into the more populist Contemporary Russian History Museum.

'Woman!' thundered a custodial babushka. 'Your toes will fall off from frostbite!' Outside it was well into the seventies. But instead of defending my flip-flops, I joined a debate between the frostbiter and a mothy spinster in charge of the room with the glamorized diorama of a Soviet communal apartment kitchen (!).

Who was Russia's best-ever ruler? bickered the babushkas. The alarmist said Brezhnev: 'Eighteen whole years of calm and prosperity!' The moth declared that she cried just thinking of what Bolsheviks did to poor, poor czar Nicholas II – and, in the same breath, pronounced *Stalín* the best-ever leader. 'Bless him for leading Russia to victory.'

'What about. . . er . . . all the people he killed?' I put in, uninvited.

The Stalinist waved me off philosophically. 'Cut a forest and splinters will fly.' It's a popular expression among Stalin apologists. We left the two of them grunting in agreement with each other (and most other Russians) about the country's worst-ever leader – Gorbachev! – and once more braved the boulevards.

'Your *shlyopki* (flip-flops)!' yelled an orange-haired hippo from a bench. 'People spit – and worse! – on the streets! Want a leg amputated?'

'But Moscow these days seems so *clean*,' I cravenly bleated, overwhelmed by how quickly my leisurely, nostalgic stroll had unleashed a present-day nightmare.

'Clean??' came the answer. 'When *churki* are doing the cleaning?'

Churki (logs) is a racial slur for Moscow's nonwhite migrant workers from our former fraternal republics. Even on this gorgeous pre-Easter Saturday when the heart yearned to sing and Muscovites were buying Dom Perignon for Easter brunch, workers from erstwhile Soviet Central Asia were out in force, sweeping sidewalks, unloading trucks, handing out leaflets promoting sushi bargains. Brushstroke by diligent brushstroke they were painting the historic pastel-hued mansions and the nouveau-riche antihistoric replicas. Suddenly I understood why Moscow center had the eerie fake sheen of a movie set.

Migrant workers in Moscow number anywhere from two to five million, possibly as much as a quarter of the capital's ballooning population. They've been flocking here since the midnineties, fleeing the post-Soviet Disasterstans. To be underpaid, abused by nationalists, harassed by police.

Beyond the hippo on her bench, a young Tajik street cleaner leaned on her broom. She gave a smile at my toes. 'Finally a beautiful day,' she sighed. 'Last week when it snowed, my shift started at four a.m.' Born in 1991, the year the Imperium ended, she had two babies back in Tajikistan.

Her brothers were drug addicts. Her parents, she said, remembered Soviet rule as paradise.

'*Moskva – zloy gorod*,' she concluded. 'Moscow – mean city.'

On Tsvetnoy, the last of the boulevards, finally it rose ahead, my sentimental journey's destination – the Central Market. The charmed food fairyland of my childhood was now a viciously expensive new mall with edgy international brands, artily designed by a British architectural firm. 'Very post-bling,' I'd been told.

Smiling stilettoed giraffes handed out outsize oranges by the entrance. 'Visit our Farmer's Market upstairs,' they cooed. Their gaze lightly brushed my toes and moved on.

Escalators ferried us aloft, past Commes des Garçons, Diesel, and Chloe, past puzzling conceptual art and hip displays of homegrown fashion genius.

The Farmer's Market held nary a farmer.

The buzzy-bucolic name had been cooked up by a local restaurant group for their organically minded epicurean food hall. We wandered this New Russian arcadia, ogling hundred-dollar boxes of Italian chocolates, farmhouse French cheeses, newfangled sashimi, and Iberico hams, all arranged under the dramatic sweep of the stainless-steel ceiling. Here was Moscow throwing down its Guccied gauntlet at storied food halls like Berlin's Ka De We and London's Selfridges.

A dewy-cheeked Kyrgyz Eve called out from a fruit aisle with a shiny red apple.

'*This*, dear madam, is honey-sweet,' she enticed. 'Just arrived from Bordeaux. Or perhaps something tart – a Pippin from Britain? Or here,' she sirened on, 'here's our *own* little apple!'

A bumpy, mottled-green specimen of the native Semerenko variety now reposed in her delicate hand.

'Looks homely,' I muttered.

'Oh, but the heavenly taste will transport you *straight* to your dacha childhood,' our Kyrgyz lovely promised, smiling ethereally.

I chewed on a wedge and grimaced. The apple was sour. Around us cute Central Asian boys in retro flat caps slavishly steered shopping carts for *ekskluziv* patrons. Somehow the sight didn't inspire old dacha reveries. And the whole au courant local-seasonal note rang hollow too – just another bit of imported post-bling bling. Not to mention that 'our' apple was crazy expensive.

'*Anya*,' I said, noting the Kyrgyz Eve's name tag. 'We're namesakes!'

'*Nyet*.' She suddenly went glum. 'Aynazik is my native name,' she murmured. 'But think anyone here would bother pronouncing it?

'*Moskva – zloy gorod*,' she whispered, holding out an apple for the next passing customer. 'Moscow – mean city.'

On the way out we received more free oranges, along with a lustrous onion from Holland. Boarding the trolley back to the flat, I felt extremely alienated from this new Moscow. I called Dad's wife, Lena, on my cell to ask if there were any affordable food shops in this city of Cartier-priced pippins. 'Not in the center, my dear!' Lena giggled. Non-elites no longer lived in the center. They sold or rented their flats and lived off the income in faraway suburbs rich in *diskaunt* outlets like Kopeechka (literally 'Little Kopek'). 'You can try taking a metro, then a shuttle bus to Kopeechka,' suggested Lena. 'But their produce is often rotten.'

We found Mom in the *khi-rize*, prattling on three phones at once.

'Moscow,' she was saying to someone. 'What a mean city.'

* * *

The Easter weekend's unsentimental journeys were over; the work week was upon us.

So just what brought me – you might wonder by now – to Putin's mean petro-dollar capital for an entire *month*? An incoherent jumble of motives, really. Seeing family. Resavoring flowering boulevards and dusty museums. Testing the scandalous scale of apple sticker shock. Fishing for socialist relics – my poisoned madeleines – amid the gleaming piers of Villeroy & Boch showrooms.

Beyond that? Beyond that I had one clear task on the agenda, and it was all Dasha's doing.

Dasha Hubova was a professor of cultural anthropology turned TV producer. We'd met by chance at a three-star chefs' conference in Madrid. I had read her article on the oral history of the 1932 Ukrainian famine. It was gut-wrenching stuff about the death of infants, cannibalism. Imagine my shock in Madrid when I learned that this very Dasha now ran Telecafé, the twenty-four-hour digital food channel owned by Russia's media giant, Channel One. From famines to round-the-clock food porn – such a New Russian trajectory, I thought.

Little realizing where that trajectory would intersect with mine.

'Come to Moscow, we'll give you a show,' tempted Dasha after filming me a bit in Madrid. She even agreed to a separate gig for my mother when I glowingly flacked Mom's credentials. ('Ace at historic meals! Chirps like a nightingale in lilting Russian, uncorrupted by post-Soviet Americanisms!')

Mom was ecstatic. Her luggage to Moscow held photogenic wardrobe ensembles and a thick folder of notes for her six-part show-to-be on historic cuisines. Sixty years after failing her drama school exams in Stalin's Moscow, my *mamochka*, Larisa Naumovna Frumkina, was finally getting her close-up. And her cooking had gotten it for her.

Each of us was assigned a chef and filmed in his kitchen. Mom's partner was Alexander Vasilievich, from a restaurant called CDL (the Russian acronym for Central House of Writers), part of the old Writers Union. One of Moscow's most flagrantly historic locations, its Gothic-romantic 1889 mansion was where Soviet literary elites gathered for legendary dinners and readings – all inaccessible, of course, to us mere mortals. Here the devil dined in Bulgakov's *The Master and Margarita*.

And here now, dropping in on Mom's shoot, I heard a director shout: '*Svet na geroinyu* – more lights on *the heroine!*'

Mom beamed, glowing, ever the 'heroine.' Her chef sidekick, on the other hand – middle-aged, painfully shy Alexander Vasilievich – seemed to want the floor to open and swallow him up.

I left them and headed to a retro-Soviet candy shop across the street. I had in mind an experiment. Under thick glass were arrayed sweets by the Red October Chocolate Factory – the pet confectionary of the food commissar Anastas Mikoyan, still in operation though now owned by a German concern. Earlier, among the nostalgic Little

Squirrel and Mishka the Clumsy Bear chocolates, I'd spotted the *ananas* – object of my dread, shame, torment, and triumph in kindergarten. Now I bought myself a candy and sucked on the crunchy chocolate shell, slowly licking toward the center, *exactly* as I had four decades before. I was trying, I confess, to manufacture a madeleine-esque moment. But the filling, so excruciatingly luscious to me once with its synthetic-exotic flavor of pineapple, now tasted simply . . . synthetic. Something feebly tried to stir in me, then faded. With a sigh, I went tramping back to the *khi-rize* as Moscow scowled at my flip-flops.

That night, I reluctantly changed into semi-stilettos – for dinner with oligarchs. Russia's nouveau riche are not the smug-faced gangsters in maroon velvet jackets they used to be. Now entering their post-bling stage, they send their kids to Oxford, donate to the arts, sometimes even forsake ritzy Petrus for old, noble Barolos.

And *who* of all people had become the biggest fan and friend of the oligarchs? My pauperist, antiestablishment mom! For some time, rich Russians had been falling madly in love with her when she squired them around the Metropolitan Museum of Art in New York. She responded with affection. 'They've become *cultured*,' she claimed. Occasionally she even entertained oligarchs at her cramped immigrant quarters in Queens. 'A hundred *million* dollars?' repeated one very nice oil man to my question about what constituted wealth in Russia. He chuckled good-naturedly, full of Mom's borscht. 'A hundred million's not even *money*.'

Now, in Moscow, our hosts were a charming fiftyish couple, veterans of my mother's tours of the Met. They had a family bank. We dined at a panoramic Italian restaurant at the newly renovated Hotel Ukraine; it was visible through binoculars from our *khi-rize*. From our roof terrace table we could almost touch the mammoth stone Stalinist stars and hammer-and-sickles at the base of the hotel's refurbished spire. Mr. Banker wore a Pucci-esque shirt; Mrs. Banker, *flat* shoes. She laughed heartily at my flip-flop adventures.

'No onions,' Mr. Banker told the waiter. 'No garlic or hot peppers.'

'You're . . . Buddhist?' I gasped.

'*Da, da,*' he acknowledged, ever so modest. 'We converted during the 2008 financial crisis. The stress.'

'Twenty years,' murmured Mrs. Banker into her forty-dollar garlic-free pizza. 'Twenty years since the USSR. *How* we've changed.'

Barry joked about all the Land Rovers and Bentleys in Moscow. Everyone laughed.

'Actually we have a *Range* Rover,' confessed Mr. Banker.

'And also a Bentley,' confessed his wife.

'What's a Bentley?' asked Mom.

✳ ✳ ✳

With Mom's TV shoot done and mine yet to come, we went for a family reunion out in Davydkovo. My cousin Masha lived there now, in our former *khrushcheba* apartment. Exiting the metro, I suggested a quick pre-reunion stroll in the woods. The Davydkovo pine woods, where Stalin's dacha still lay. Brooding, mysterious.

Him again.

The Father of All Nations had at least a dozen

government dachas. But the one behind the thirteen-foot green fence in Davydkovo by my ex-Central Committee kindergarten was his actual home for more than two decades. From the Kremlin to here was a twelve-minute trip in the Leader's armored black Packard. Hence the dacha's nickname, Blizhnyaya, the 'nearest one.'

A few years earlier, photos of the inaccessible Blizhnyaya started popping up on the Internet. I pored over the images of the neo-modernist green country house – all straight-lined functionality denounced by Stalinist ideologues but apparently privately favored by the Boss. Weirdly disturbing, his personal coat hanger; his dark, monastic bathrobes with the shortened sleeve for his withered left arm.

The Blizhnyaya, initially modest in size, had been built in 1934 by the architect Miron Merzhanov (arrested in 1943, released after his client's death) and surrounded with thick, trucked-in trees. The nature-loving Generalissimo took special interest in the planting of *belíye* (porcini) mushroom patches; in our harsh northern climate the heroic dacha gardeners even raised watermelons, which were sometimes sold to unsuspecting shoppers at the opulent Yeliseevsky food emporium on Gorky Street.

Churchill, Mao, and Tito all slept on the second floor added in 1943. Their ever-paranoid host, though, hardly ever used a bedroom. He'd doze off on one of the hard Turkish couches scattered about; on one such, on March 1, 1953, he suffered his fatal stroke.

A few years earlier, too, journalists were given an unprecedented tour of the secret green house. There were hints the dacha was being declassified; in Moscow now I hoped to pull some journalistic strings and at last penetrate that tall fence in the forest, behind which lay the presence that haunted my most impressionable childhood. With Barry and Mom along, I intended a little reconnaissance.

The pine trees seemed less majestic than I remembered. Along muddy paths, yummy mommies in skinny jeans and stilettos pushed strollers; vigorous pensioners speed-walked by, arm in arm. There it loomed at last: the dacha's fence. Two blond young guards in uniform stood by a side entrance, smoking. Unsmiling.

'The dacha . . . um . . . er . . . Stalin?' I mumbled.

'Classified object,' I was informed. 'No questions permitted.'

As if drawn by an inner force, I led us away to another, much lower fence. Beyond it, through evergreens, I could make out a low pale-brick building – my old kindergarten, where I gagged on *nomenklatura* caviar and sucked in ecstasy on the *ananas* candy. The sight of my former prison catapulted me back to my sad-eyed bulimic past with such violence that I clutched onto a sticky pine trunk, desperately gulping the resinous air. The madeleine had attacked.

I pulled myself together and we left the woods. A deluxe apartment complex towered ahead, gleaming and shiplike. STALIN'S DACHA announced the sign on the inevitable fence. APARTMENTS FOR SALE BY INVESTORS.

'People don't mind living in a building named after Stalin?' I asked an Uzbek guard, a fresh ripple of nausea stirring.

'Why?' He grinned. 'I'm sure they're proud.'

'How about a Molotov tennis court?' Barry asked, after we translated. 'Or a Beria swimming pool?'

'Beria?' puzzled the guard, catching the name. He looked confused.

We hurried off, late now to Masha's, and promptly got lost among Davydkovo's identical five-story sixties-era apartment blocks. The cracked concrete walls and laundry flapping from rickety balconies were depressing and slum-like, all too familiar. But no, this was Moscow 2011: Barry had to stop, several times, to fasten his tourist lens on a Maserati parked by a rusted fence or an overflowing hulk of graffiti-scrawled garbage bins.

We recovered a little around Masha's table. After dinner she took me into the bedroom and began pulling out small cardboard boxes from drawers and closets. I reached into one box and felt the cold metal heft of my grandfather's medals. Masha and I tipped the whole treasure onto the bed. Order of Lenin, of Victory, of the Red Banner. Just as we had decades ago, we pinned the medals to our chests and danced a little in front of the mirror. Then we sat on the bed, holding hands.

The following noon I plucked a grape from a ruby-red crystal pedestaled bowl, cranked a heavily lipsticked smile for the cameras, and thought a monstrous thought: one of history's bloodiest dictators likely touched this bowl I'm eating from.

Him again.

No, I hadn't slid into obsessional fantasy. I was on my TV shoot, an hour from Moscow at the super-bourgeois dacha of Viktor Belyaev, ex-Kremlin chef and my show partner.

Until a heart attack a few years before, Viktor had spent three high-stress decades cooking for the top Soviet hierarchy. From this lofty gig he'd inherited porcelain manufactured exclusively for Kremlin banquets, and a red crystal bowl set named Rubinovy (ruby, after the Kremlin star). The crystal's former owner? The mustachioed one himself. More astounding still, the bowls had come from the dacha – *that* green dacha. Date of issue: 1949, Stalin's seventieth jubilee year, celebrated so joyously, the entire Pushkin Museum of Art was commandeered as a giant display case for gifts to Dear Leader.

Viktor was disarmingly friendly and compulsively talkative. When Dasha the producer had originally said 'Kremlin chef,' I imagined a dour Party hack with a heavy KGB past. Instead, in his baby-blue cashmere sweater and discreet gold neck chain, Viktor suggested a relaxed clone of Louis Prima, the jazz man; he had a very jazzy Dodge Camaro parked in his driveway.

Bonding with him pre-shoot over a quick cigarette out on the porch, I was amazed to learn that Viktor had cooked at *the* dacha in 1991, right before Gorbachev's resignation. The mineral secretary had a residence on Blizhnyaya's grounds, which he never used and wanted to convert into a small hotel – for international *biznes* VIPs. Viktor was brought in to handle the food operation and do some catering in the main house.

'*Gorbach*,' huffed Viktor. 'Nobody's favorite boss! Half my staff quit because of Raisa – that harpy-from-hell, our First Lady. Now, Brezhnev's wife – *she* was *golden*.'

'Viktor,' I pressed. 'Please – the dacha!'

Viktor shuddered theatrically, fingered his gold chain. 'Horrifying musty smell of sinister history . . . moats and drawbridges everywhere . . . some of the pine trees even hollowed out with doors and windows – for guards!' Because the Generalissimo detested all food smells, a massive three-hundred-yard corridor separated Blizhnyaya's dining room from the kitchen. 'And his closet . . .' Viktor grimaced. 'I knew Stalin was short, but his clothes . . . *they were for a child – or a midget.*'

Viktor initially learned about the forbidding green dacha from his elderly mentor, a certain Vitaly Alexeevich (last name strictly secret), formerly one of Stalin's personal chefs. On March 6, 1953, Vitaly Alexeevich dutifully reported for his shift. He was met on the dacha porch by Valechka, the Generalissimo's loyal housekeeper and, possibly, mistress. She had a car waiting for him.

'Flee,' Valechka told him. 'Now! Drive as far as you can. Disappear!!' Stalin's death had just been announced.

The chef ran, while other dacha staffers perished at Beria's orders. He returned to Moscow the day of Beria's execution, and for the rest of his life laid flowers on the housekeeper's grave.

'Vitaly Alexeevich was a cook *ot boga* (God's talent),' sighed Viktor. 'He'd sing to his dough to help it to rise.' I thought of Mom's and my struggles to crack the mysteries of Slavic yeast dough for our kulebiaka. Crooning to it, as Stalin's chef had done – was that the secret?

'So was it *really* haunted, the dacha?' I wanted to know, thinking of all the times I slinked past the green fence during kindergarten, my heart hammering.

Viktor shuddered again.

At the end of his first night catering at Blizhnyaya, he was sitting alone in Stalin's old dining room. He leaned on the massively long wooden table, the one at which murderous

Politburo men gathered for their nocturnal banquets four decades before. An eerie silence . . . Suddenly Viktor heard footsteps . . . footsteps so ghostly, he bolted into the woods drenched in cold sweat. The same thing happened to the actor who played Stalin during a 1991 film shoot there. And when Stalin's old dacha guard was invited back for a documentary, he suffered a heart attack. '*His* boot leather—' stammered the guard at the hospital. 'I smelled it – his boot leather and the Karelian birch of *his* furniture!'

At this point we were summoned back inside. The TV cameras were ready for us.

The sight of Viktor's table almost gave me a heart attack myself.

For our shoot – on *Soviet* cuisine – my partner had conjured up a Technicolor fantasia out of *The Book of Tasty and Healthy Food* – Politburo dreambook edition. Dainty, open-faced *rasstegai* fish pies nestled inside Stalinist crystal; an elaborate beef roulade layered with a delicate omelet reposed on a Kremlin-issue porcelain platter. There was even a torte outfitted with caramel rockets, contributed by a generous ex-*nomenklatura* confectioner. *Polyot* ('flight'), the torte was called: a meringue relic from the sixties *kosmos*-mania era.

I stared transfixed at this culinary time capsule. At the jellied ham rolls under mayonnaise curlicues, in particular. Early September, 1974: Praga restaurant take-out shop. Me standing – for the very last time, I thought – in the gigantic line for our Sunday kulebiaka as Mom at home irons out final immigration formali-ties. I'm eyeing the jellied curlicued ham rolls my parents couldn't ever afford, thinking desperately: *Never in my life will I see them again.*

And now I learn that pre-Kremlin, Viktor cooked at Praga!

My Praga.

Was there some profound meaning in all this co-incidence? Had some god of Soviet Civilization sent Viktor my way to help me properly savor my childhood's treasures and reveal its mysteries?

Arriving in Moscow this trip I'd been crestfallen to learn that my Praga was closed. One of the city's last pre-Soviet great restaurants had been bought by the Italian designer Roberto Cavalli, to be converted, no doubt, into a post-bling elite playground. Seeing its iconic yellow facade disfigured by scaffolding at the head of Novy Arbat, I felt as if some dear old grandparent had died.

Viktor and I mourned the closure of Praga as the cameras rolled. 'A-plus,' hooted our young director. 'I'm loving you guys' chemistry!' Feeling relaxed at last, I prattled on about stalking diplomats by Praga's entrance and hawking Juicy Fruit gum at school. The mostly youthful, post-Soviet crew lapped up my socialist misadventures.

'More! More stories like this!' they cried.

When Dasha had originally suggested a show on Soviet cuisine – 'The topic is *hot*' – I'd been bewildered.

'But isn't Moscow full of people who remember the USSR a lot better than I do? I mean, I'm from New York!'

'You don't understand,' said Dasha. 'Here we have mish-mash for our memory. But an émigré like you – *you* remember things clearly!'

After the lunch, and before the *shashlik* (kebab) grill shoot by his dacha backyard swimming pool, Viktor clued me in on his time at the Kremlin kitchens.

Supplies were from their very own teeming farms. So damn rich was Politburo milk, truckers would loosely set deep metal lids on the milk buckets, and by arrival the clattering lids had churned up gorgeous thick, sticky cream. For instant pilfering.

I was astonished. 'You mean despite all the perks – elite housing, Crimean resorts, special tailors – Kremlin employees *still* stole?'

'And how!' chuckled Viktor. Soon after taking over he raided his employees' lockers and turned up sixty kilos of loot. '*And that was before noon.*'

There beneath the twenty-five-foot ceiling of the main old Kremlin kitchen he made other discoveries too:

A war-trophy forty-eight-burner electric stove belonging to Goebbels.
A massive mixer from Himmler's country house.
Czar's dog bowls from 1876.
Ivan the Terrible's former torture tunnel. With a slanted floor – to drain blood.

'Ready for the poolside shashlik!' announced the director.

After we wrapped and the crew headed home, I sat around with Viktor and his wife, eating leftovers. I was dazed by what I'd learned at his fantasy table. It was akin to discovering that Santa Claus was somehow, after all, real. The Soviet myth of plenty that my latter-Soviet generation had scoffed at? That fabled abundance so cynically, even existentially scorned?

How spectacularly it had flourished on Kremlin banquet tables.

The Politburo loved to stun foreign guests with Soviet opulence. Train convoys from all over the empire carried sausage from the Ukraine in porcelain tubs, lavish fruit from Crimea, dairy from the Baltic republics, brandies from Dagestan. Seven pounds of food per person was the official banquet norm. Black caviar glistened in crystal bowls atop 'Kremlin walls' carved from ice tinted with red beet juice. Lambs were boiled whole, then deep-fried; suckling pigs sported mayonnaise show ribbons and olives for eyes. Massive sturgeons reclined majestically on spotlighted aquarium pedestals aflutter with tiny live fish. Outside, we queued up for wrinkled Moroccan oranges in subzero winters; inside the Kremlin, there were passionfruit, kiwis, and, as Viktor put it tenderly, 'adorable *baby-bananchiki*.'

'Just imagine,' waxed Viktor. 'The colorful lights at Georgievsky Hall in the Grand Palace are finally lit, the Soviet anthem starts up, everyone's awestruck by all that glimmering china and glittering crystal . . .'

Putin's protocol guys dustbinned the glitter and glimmer.

I suppose in a city with the world's thickest swarm of billionaires – where a Pilates studio is never far away and sashimi is flown in daily from Tokyo – there wasn't much call for gastronomic Potemkin villages anymore. So the staged fairy tales of abundance had finally been retired – along with all that crystal and nonsustainable caviar. Instead of fifteen zakuski, Kremlin banquets now featured bite-size pirozhki, and small bowls of berries sat where receptacles piled with glowing fruit once towered triumphant.

Fairly recently Putin added a wrinkle: USSR nostalgia. 'Herring under fur coat,' meat brawn – current Kremlin chefs now served communal-apartment dishes in dainty individual portions alongside foie gras and carpaccio. Which struck me as a perfect expression of the New Russian pastiche.

Today's streamlined service made sense, Viktor conceded as he poured us a rare Masandra Port from Crimea. But he missed those days of yore, I could tell. Who *wouldn't* miss actually living inside a socialist fantasy? Me? Misty-eyed, I told Viktor that his table was the closest I'd ever come to the *skatert' samobranka*, the magic tablecloth of Russian folklore.

Viktor left the Kremlin after his heart attack and now ran a catering company and a restaurant. He headed the association of Russian restaurateurs, trying to promote native cuisine. That battle was lost, though, he thought.

'Young Russian chefs can do pizzas – but who remembers how to cook *our* kasha?' And he sighed a heartfelt sigh. He who had presided over the gleam of Kremlin walls carved out of red ice.

Back at the *khi-rize* I was reviewing my notes – *Gorbachev, per Viktor: Ate little. Drank even less. Left banquets after forty minutes. Yeltsin: Loved lamb chops. Lousy dancer* – when my email pinged. It was a message from another world, from El Bulli near Barcelona.

The world's most magical and important restaurant was about to close forever, and Ferran (the chef) and Juli (co-owner) wanted me to attend a farewell dinner. I'd known the two of them since 1996. Their Catalan temple of avant-garde cooking was an intimate part of my professional history. My first visit fifteen years before had transformed everything I thought and wrote about food. 'You're family,' Ferran always told me. And now here I was, stuck in mean, alien Moscow, ungrounded in past or present, fumbling with madeleines. My visa was single-entrance, so I couldn't even slip out to say a hurried farewell.

I slumped in my chair, stung by loss from my *real* life. *Queridos Amigos!* I started to type, *Estoy en Moscu cruel, muy lamentablemente no puedo* . . . A strange rumbling from below interrupted my Spanish. There was something world-devouring and cataclysmic to it, as if a tsunami were approaching. My desk began to vibrate.

We all ran to the windows. Way down below us tanks slowly rolled through the rainy night along deserted Novy Arbat. Missile launchers came prowling after them, then troop carriers, artillery.

The phone rang. 'Watching Victory Day rehearsal?' my dad chortled almost merrily. 'The *tekhnika* (hardware) should be passing you now – right under the big billboard for that movie *Malchishnik Dva (Hangover 2)*!'

'*Tanki i banki*, tanks and banks,' grumbled my mom. 'Welcome to Putinland.'

The great celebrations of Victory Day – May 9 – drew closer. Putinland's officious militaristic patriotism went into overdrive. To judge from the hype, the lollapalooza promised to out-wow even anything we'd seen under Brezhnev.

The airwaves overflowed now with the Great Patriotic War (VOV in abbreviated Russian). Forties black-and-white films, close-ups of *blokada* bread, piercing footage of a little girl playing piano with frozen hands in besieged

Leningrad – suddenly there was no escaping them. On buses old people and migrant workers hummed along to war songs piped over the sound systems. Helpful ads enticed cell phone users to dial 1–9–4–5 and get a free VOV tune as a ringtone.

In Brezhnev's time the State had co-opted the mythic traumas and triumph of the Great Patriotic War to reinfuse ideology into a cynical young generation. Russians had grown a lot more cynical since. In today's society, one so desperately lacking an anchoring national narrative, the Kremlin was once again exploiting the cult of VOV to mobilize what was left of national patriotism, to bring generations together in a tightly scripted rite of remembering. '*My narod pobeditel*' (We, nation victorious) – I now heard it ad nauseam, just as I had in my childhood. Unheard: the catastrophic official blunders costing millions of lives, the brutal post-war deportations of ethnic minorities. In case anyone *mis*remembered? A 'Commission for Countering Attempts to Falsify History to the Detriment of the Interests of Russia' had been established in 2009.

And who was it that had led Russia to its May 9 Victory?

Perhaps I'd finally slid into obsessional fantasy. The run-up to Victory Day appeared to my inflamed mind as a veritable Springtime for Stalin.

Men with rotten teeth and sour breath hawked sundry Staliniana at street stalls on cheesily pedestrianized Arbat Street, and even respectable bookstores did a brisk business in Stalin fridge magnets. The Kremlin had been careful about an open endorsement. Vernacular opinion, however, told a different story. Nearly half of all Russians polled saw Stalin in a positive light. A notorious 2008 TV survey had the Generalissimo rated third for 'most important Russian in history' – barely edged by Prince Alexander Nevsky of Eisenstein film fame, and Pyotr Stolypin, a reformist early-twentieth-century prime minister noisily admired by Putin. But everyone believed the results had been cooked to suppress the controversial truth.

I noticed that in the popular imagination his figure seemed split. The *bad* Stalin was the orchestrator of the gulags. The *good* Stalin was an ur-Russian brand projecting power and victory.

It was deeply distressing.

Amid all this ideological ghoulism and ahistorical mishmash the *khi-rize* became my refuge, the haven of my own pre-post-Soviet innocence. What a perfect comfort it was, easily idealized and yet so authentic. I got a lump in my throat every time I entered the woody, cozily modernist lobby. I loved the achingly familiar USSR reek of cat spray and acrid cleaning detergent. Loved the coarse blue oil-paint trim and the rotating gallery of very Soviet concierge babushkas.

Inna Valentinovna, my favorite babushka, was one of the *khi-rize*'s original residents. She had scored her prestige apartment during the late sixties for her scientific achievements and now whiled away her bustling, bossy retirement by concierging part-time. As May 9 drew nigh, she transformed our lobby into a maelstrom of veteran-related activity.

'How our *veterani* love this!' she enthused, showing me the forlorn state gift packages of buckwheat groats, second-rate sprats, and emphatically non-elite chocolates.

'Dusty buckwheat,' groused Mom. 'Putin's thank-you to those who defended his Rodina.'

Among our *khi-rize* VOV vets, I was particularly eager to meet a woman named Asya Vasilievna. She'd just completed a memoir, so Inna informed me, about her mentor and friend Anna Akhmatova, the great Russian poet of our sorrows after whom I was named. 'Wait,' Inna kept admonishing me in her lobby stronghold. 'Wait for her here!' But elderly Asya Vasilievna never appeared.

Victory Day dawned.

We watched the Red Square parade on TV. The Kremlin midgetry, Medvedev and Putin, commemorated the world's largest catastrophe (a.k.a. VOV) wearing vaguely fascistic black overcoats. Vigorous octogenarians shingled in medals surrounded them on the podium. 'Arise, Our Vast Country,' the solemn 1940s VOV anthem, blared as elite guards began the old Soviet-imperial goose step – dressed in weirdly czarist-looking uniforms thick with blingy gold braid.

'PPP,' scoffed my mom. 'Putin's Patriotic Pastiche.'

In the afternoon Inna Valentinovna shepherded us to a neighborhood parade on Arbat Street. The local vets looked much frailer than the heroes on Putin's podium. Some could barely walk under the weight of their medals; others wheezed and coughed in the wind. Muscovites watched the shuffling throng of veterans with indifference, whereas Ayzeri men in black leather jackets whistled and clapped with great feeling.

Inna Valentinovna pushed me toward one tall, sloped-shouldered, medal-hung nonagenarian. He had fought in the Baltic navy at the same time as my granddad. His gaze remained serene and absent even as schoolkids shoved big thorny roses into his leathery hands.

'I'm from New York,' I stammered, feeling suddenly shy. 'Perhaps you knew my grandfather – chief of Baltic naval intelligence Naum Solomonovich Frumkin.'

After an uncertain pause, a glimmer animated his pale, ghostly features.

'New York,' he quavered. 'Not even the Nazis matched the enemy we faced after the war. *New York! Vile imperialist America!*'

And with great dignity he walked away from me.

The reception was warmer in the bitterly cold shadows by Arbat's hulking Vakhtangov Theater, where Inna Valentinovna beckoned us over to a cordoned-off vets' VIP area of outdoor tables. A mock field kitchen was dispensing convincingly unappetizing wartime kasha from a fake cauldron and weak tea from a fake kettle. But the breaths around our wobbly plastic table reeked with reassuring eighty-proof authenticity. Our Styrofoam cups of tea were emptied and filled with vodka. A pickle materialized. Despite the droning, officious speeches, despite the sad spectacle of impoverished vets paraded around like stuffed dolls instead of receiving long-overdue benefits, a glow blossomed inside me. How precious, co-bottling in the cold with this crowd. How little time with them we had left.

I soggily proposed a toast to my granddad. Tears of remorse ran down my cheeks as I recalled how Mom and Yulia threw out his Sorge memorabilia, how Cousin Masha and I giggled when, for the umpteenth time, he reminisced about debriefing Nazis at the Nuremberg Trials. Now there were only fraying cardboard boxes of his medals and a yellowed German magazine cover on which Dedushka's high forehead and ironic eyes hovered over the puffy-faced Hermann Goering.

Next morning in the lobby I finally encountered the elusive Asya Vasilyevna.

The memoirist friend of Anna Akhmatova had dark, quick, intelligent eyes and sported a smart vest. Overwhelmed, I kept holding and stroking her ancient hand.

Asya Vasilievna met Akhmatova during their VOV evacuation in Tashkent.

Vets got to make free phone calls on May 9, and Asya had spent hers talking to the granddaughter of Nikolai Punin, Akhmatova's lover in the twenties and thirties. Punin brought Akhmatova into the Fountain House in St. Petersburg. There, in a dismal communal apartment carved out of a wing of that former palace, Akhmatova resided for almost three decades.

I once visited Akhmatova's movingly curated museum at the Fountain House. A copy of Modigliani's sketch of her hung on the wall of the monastically sparse room she once occupied. In this room Akhmatova had her epic all-night encounter with a young Isaiah Berlin from England, for which she was denounced by the state, her son sent back to the gulag. It was her bronze ashtray that brought me to tears. Knowing the apartment was bugged, Akhmatova and her friend and biographer, Lydia Chukovskaya, would utter loud trivialities – 'Autumn is so early this year' – while the poet scribbled a new poem in pencil and Chukovskaya memorized the lines. Then they'd burn the page in the ashtray.

'Hands, matches, an ashtray,' wrote Chukovskaya. 'A ritual beautiful and bitter.'

Now in our *khi-rize* lobby, unbidden, Asya Vasilievna launched into Akhmatova's poem 'Requiem,' dedicated to the victims of purges. She began with the blood-curdling preface: *In the dreadful years of the Yezhov terror I spent seventeen months in prison lines in Leningrad . . .*

She spoke as if in a trance, mimicking the low, slow, mournful recitation I knew from Akhmatova's recordings.

The stars of death stood above us,
and innocent Russia writhed . . .

'Let's go sit so you're more comfortable,' interrupted Inna Valentinovna, ushering us into a special vets' room – a tiny pink-walled cubbyhole off the lobby, plastered with photos of VOV heroes.

. . . and innocent Russia writhed
beneath the bloody boots

My gaze drifted across the gallery on the wall as Asya declaimed on. Marshal Zhukov. Voroshilov. Dashing Rokossovsky. And presiding over all, squinting his yellowish feline eyes . . .

HIM? AGAIN?

. . . beneath the bloody boots
And the Black Marias' tires . . .

In Germany you'd be arrested for displaying the visage of

Hitler, I thought. Here? Here a woman recited a searing dirge to those crushed in the purges – right beneath the executioner's portrait!

Something in me snapped. I wanted to howl, bang my head against the shiny Soviet-style table, flee from this insane asylum where history has been dismantled and Photoshopped into a pastiche of victims and murderers, dictators and dissidents, all rubbing sentimental shoulders together.

I did howl after Asya finished.

'Ladies!' I burst out. 'Have you lost your marbles? Akhmatova's testament to suffering ... here under STALIN's mustaches?'

I finished, mortified at my outburst. How could I be haranguing these frail survivors of a terrible era? What right did I have to wag my finger at women who'd endured and outlived the Soviet century? My lips were shaking. I wanted to cry.

The ladies seemed unoffended by my outburst. Asya Vasilievna's dark eyes flickered with some sly wisdom I couldn't grasp. Her half-smile was almost mischievous. Inna Valentinovna patted me warmly on the shoulder.

'*Iz pesni slov ne vykinesh*,' explained Inna Valentinovna, proffering an old Russian chestnut. 'You can't yank words out of a song.'

Meaning: the past was the past, just as it was. *Without executioners there would be no victims or poems.*

'What kind of logic is that?' I protested to my mother later. She pressed her hands to her temples and shook her head.

'I'm glad I'm leaving soon,' she said.

★ ★ ★

Our time in Moscow was drawing to a close. Mom was headed back to New York; Barry and I would leave a couple of days after her on a two-week magazine assignment in Europe. I looked forward to life again as I knew it: breathing Stalin-less air, perusing restaurant menus without going green at the prices, trundling around proud and free in my flip-flops.

Mom finally flew off. Without her prattling on three phones at once and feeding streams of ravenous visitors, the *khi-rize* felt lonely and empty. Mom, I realized, had been my moral compass in Russia, my anchoring narrative. Without her Moscow had lost its point.

Except for one last mission. The mission I'd been dreaming about most of the forty-plus years of my life – one of my secret reasons for coming here. Something I could never do with Mother around.

'*Mavzoley?* Mausoleum?'

'*Da, nu? Mavzoley,*' said the brusque voice answering the phone. 'Yeah, what of it?'

The voice sounded so disrespectful and young, I almost hung up in confusion.

'*Da! Nu?*' demanded the voice.

'Are, you . . . um, um . . . *open?*' I asked nervously, since some tourist websites suggested the V. I. Lenin Mausoleum was now closed on Sundays, and Sunday – *today* – was our last chance.

'Scheduled hours,' the voice snapped sardonically.

'What's the admission charge?'

'In Russia we don't charge for cemeteries!' cackled the voice. '*Not yet!*'

The mausoleum line was the shortest I'd ever seen it, a scant 150 meters long.

Lenin clearly wasn't enjoying Stalin's cachet; his days inside his *eleet* and *ekskluzív* Red Square real estate were numbered, I reckoned. Two-decades-old talk of burying him had flared up again. A prominent member of Putin's United Russia Party noted, almost ninety years after the fact, that Lenin's family had opposed mummification. Asked to vote at goodbyelenin.ru, 70 percent of Russians favored removal and burial. Only the Communist Party leadership yawped in outrage.

We lined up between a skinny Central Asian man and a gaggle of noisy Italians in cool high-tech nylon gear. Our Central Asian neighbor flashed us a pure gold smile. In Soviet days, I recalled, brothers from exotic republics put their money *right* where their mouths were, installing twenty-four-karat teeth instead of trusting *sberkassa* (the state savings offices).

Roughly my age, the man introduced himself as Rahmat. 'It means 'thank you' in Tajik – ever heard of Tajikistan?'

Mr. Thank You proved to be a font of flowery, heavily accented Soviet clichés. His city, Leninabad, bore the 'proud name of Lenin!' To visit the mausoleum had been his '*zavetnaya mechta* – cherished dream.'

'My dream, too,' I admitted, earning a round of twenty-four-karat smiles and ritual handshakes.

On entering the mausoleum's grounds you were made to surrender the works – wallets, cell phones, cameras. Photos were strictly forbidden.

Which was unfortunate.

Because something wildly, improbably, heart-stoppingly photogenic was taking place out in the center of cordoned-off Red Square. I heard bugles, drumbeats. Kids in white and blue uniforms were drawn up in ranks for their Young Pioneer induction ceremony. A big woman in polka-dots moved along the rows, tying scarlet kerchiefs around their necks.

'ARE YOU READY?' roared a loudspeaker.

'ALWAYS READY!' cried the kids, giving the Young Pioneer salute.

Was I hallucinating? Or were the girls really wearing the big Soviet white bows in their hair?

'Vzeveites' s kostrami sinie nochi . . .'

The relentless choral cheer of the Young Pioneer anthem filled Red Square. A scarlet myth blazed once more in the distance.

'My pioneri deti rabochikh,' Rahmat and I sang along. 'We're Young Pioneers, children of workers!' With no anti-Soviet mother there to tug at my sleeve, I sang at the top of my lungs.

'Frigging Young Pioneer Day,' a guard was explaining to someone nearby. 'Every frigging year, the frigging communists with this . . . Look! Zyuganov!' The brick-faced current Communist Party leader was up on the makeshift podium. *'Queridos compañeros,'* someone began shouting in accented Spanish. 'Welcoming comrades from shithole Havana,' grimaced the guard. 'And for this freak show, they close Red Square!'

We filed by the Kremlin Wall burial tombs where rest the noble remains of Brezhnev, Gagarin, the American John Reed, and, yes, *Himagain*.

'Us! Walking this holy ground!' Rahmat apostrophized behind Barry and me. 'This holy ground at the very center of our socialist Rodina!'

Such was his childish awe, I didn't have the heart to remind him that the 'proud four letters: CCCP' had been busted up twenty years ago, that in no way was Moscow *his* rodina.

'Scared?' I whispered to him as we descended into the mystery of mysteries of my childhood – the mausoleum burial chamber.

'Of what? Lenin isn't scary,' Rahmat assured me serenely. 'He is *svetly* (luminous) and *krasivy* (beautiful) and *zhivoy* (alive).'

Our face time with Vladimir Ilyich was barely two minutes, maybe less. Stony-featured sentries every ten feet in the darkness goaded us on a tight circuit around the glassed-in sarcophagus, where Object No. 1 lay, glowing, on heavy red velvet. I noted his/its polka-dot tie. And the extreme luminosity achieved by cunningly spotlighting his/its shining baldness.

'Why is one fist clenched?' Barry whispered.

'No talking!' a sentry barked from the shadows. 'Keep moving toward the exit!'

And then it was over.

I emerged into the Moscow Sunday confused and untransfigured. All these years . . . for what? Suddenly it felt deeply, existentially trivial. Had I really expected to howl with laughter at the ritual kitsch? Or experience anything other than the faintly comical anticlimactic creepiness I was feeling right now?

Barry on the other hand seemed shaken. 'That was,' he blurted, 'the most fascist thing I've ever experienced in my life!'

Red Square had reopened by now, and freshly minted Young Pioneers streamed past us. With profound disappointment I realized that the girls' big white Soviet bows were not the proper white nylon ribbon extravaganzas of my young days but small beribboned barrettes – fakes manufactured most likely in Turkey or China.

'I remember my pride at becoming a Young Pioneer,' Rahmat beamingly told a blonde squirrel-faced girl. She sized up his gold teeth and his third world pointy-toed shoes, then my flip-flops, and shouted, 'Get lost!'

We milled around with Rahmat for a while. He'd arrived in the capital just the day before and clearly hadn't yet learned the 'Moscow – mean city' mantra. He intended to look for construction work but, knowing not a soul, had come straight to the mausoleum to see Lenin's 'kind, dearly familiar face.' We smiled and nodded some more, with the vigorous politesse of two strangers about to part after a fleeting bond on a bus tour.

Two aliens, I reflected, a migrant worker and an émigré from her past, wandering Red Square beneath the gaudy marzipan swirls of St. Basil's Cathedral.

Finally Rahmat went trudging off to pay his respects to the Tomb of the Unknown Soldier. I felt a deep pang of sadness as I watched his slumped, lonely figure recede. My cell phone rang. It was Mom, calling at jet-lagged dawn from New York.

'Where are you?' she asked.

'Just walked out of the mausoleum,' I said.

For a while there was silence.

'*Idiotka*,' Mom finally snorted, then made a kiss-kiss sound and went back to bed.

PART V

MASTERING THE ART OF SOVIET RECIPES

A fantasy of abundance: the opening spread from the 1952 edition of *The Book of Tasty and Healthy Food*

KULEBIAKA

Fish, Rice, and Mushrooms in Pastry

Our decadent, farewell-to-the-czars fish kulebiaka layered with *blinchiki* (crepes) was probably the most spectacular thing Mom and I have ever made in our lives. And so time-consuming that I can't really recommend you try it at home. Instead, I offer here a far less laborious version – minus the complicated layers and blinchiki – that will still leave your guests gasping with awe. The soured cream in the yeast dough (Mom's special touch) adds a lovely tang to the buttery casing. Inside, the flavors of wild mushrooms, dill, and two types of fish all mingle seductively. Serve the kulebiaka for special occasions with a green salad and lemon-flavored vodka. Lots of it.

KULEBIAKA

Serves 6 to 8

60ml (4 tablespoons) warm milk

12g active dried yeast (or 2 sachets)

2 teaspoons sugar

1 large raw egg; plus 2 hard-boiled eggs, finely chopped

180ml soured cream

½ teaspoon kosher salt, plus more to taste

120g unsalted butter, cut into small pieces; plus 60g for the filling

300g plain flour, plus more as needed

3 tablespoons rapeseed or groundnut oil

225g boneless, skinless salmon fillet, cut into 2.5cm pieces

225g boneless, skinless cod fillet, cut into 2.5cm pieces

2 medium onions, finely chopped

200g small chestnut mushrooms, wiped clean and finely chopped

175g cooked white rice

3 tablespoons finely chopped dill

3 tablespoons finely chopped flat-leaf parsley

2 tablespoons vermouth or dry sherry

2 tablespoons fresh lemon juice

3 tablespoons chicken stock

1 pinch freshly grated nutmeg

Freshly ground black pepper, to taste

2 to 3 tablespoons dried breadcrumbs

Glaze: 1 egg yolk whisked with 2 teaspoons milk

1. MAKE THE PASTRY: In a medium bowl stir together the milk, yeast, and sugar and let stand until foamy. Whisk in the raw egg, 120g of the soured cream, and the salt. In a large bowl, combine the 120g of cut-up butter with the flour. Using your fingers, work the butter into the flour until the mixture resembles coarse breadcrumbs. Add the yeast mixture and stir well with your hands to make a soft dough. Wrap the dough in clingfilm and refrigerate for at least 2 hours.

2. Bring the dough to room temperature, about 1 hour. Grease a mixing bowl with a little butter or oil. Turn the dough out onto a floured work surface and knead, adding

more flour as needed, until smooth and no longer sticky, about 5 minutes. Transfer the dough to the greased bowl, cover with clingfilm, and leave in a warm place until doubled in size, about 2 hours.

3. MAKE THE FILLING: In a large skillet or frying pan heat the oil and 30g of the butter over medium-high heat. Add the salmon and cod and cook, turning once, until fish just begins to flake, about 7 minutes. Transfer the fish to a large bowl. Return the pan to medium-high heat and add the remaining 30g butter. Add the onions and cook until light golden. Add the mushrooms and cook until they are golden and the liquid they throw off has evaporated, about 7 minutes, adding more oil if the pan looks dry. Transfer the mushrooms and onions to the bowl with the fish. Add the remaining 60ml soured cream, the hard-boiled eggs, rice, dill, parsley, vermouth, lemon juice, stock, and nutmeg. Mix everything well with two forks, stirring gently to break up the fish. Season with salt and pepper. Let the filling cool to room temperature.

4. Preheat the oven to 200°C/400°F/Gas 6. with the rack set in the center. Halve the dough and form two logs. On two lightly floured sheets of greaseproof paper, roll each dough log into a 25cm x 40cm rectangle. Transfer one dough sheet to a large foil-lined baking sheet. Sprinkle with breadcrumbs, leaving a 2.5cm border. Spread the filling over the bread crumbs in a neat compact layer. Drape the remaining dough over the filling and pinch the edges to seal. Trim excess dough from the edges, and reserve scraps. Fold up the edges of dough and crimp decoratively. Let the kulebiaka rise for 15 minutes. Brush the top of the pastry with egg glaze. Roll out the dough scraps, cut into

decorative shapes, and press on top of the dough. Brush again with the egg glaze. Poke small holes through the top of dough for steam to escape. Bake until golden and beautiful, about 35 minutes. Let cool for 10 minutes, cut into slices, and serve.

GEFILTE FISH

Stuffed Whole Fish, Odessa-Style

Mom and I had our first-ever seder upon immigrating to Philadelphia in 1974. There we were, at the posh suburban home of our kind Jewish sponsors, being paraded around as 'heroic refugees' in our shabby Salvation Army clothes. Everyone stared and sang 'Let My People Go,' while Mom and I wept, from emotion mixed with embarrassment. To make matters worse, stammering out passages from the Haggadah in my still-broken English, I kept saying 'ten pleasures' instead of 'ten plagues.' Then came the gefilte fish. Flashing back to the red-haired sisters of my Odessa summer, I tucked into the neat American fish ball with great curiosity . . . and could barely swallow! The taste was so shockingly sweet, Mom and I later concluded that the hostess must have accidentally added sugar instead of salt. At our second seder the following night, the fish balls were *even sweeter*. Noticing our bewilderment, the host explained that *his* people come from Southern Poland, where Jews liked their gefilte fish sweet. 'You Russians, don't *you* make your fish peppery?' he inquired. Mom blushed. She'd never once made gefilte fish.

Now, many seders later, she and I know that Russian and Ukrainian Jewish babushkas usually cut the fish into thick steaks, remove the meat to grind with onions and carrots, then pack this stuffing (unsweetened) into the skin around the bones. The fish simmers forever with vegetables until the bones all but dissolve – delicious, though not very pretty. Perfectionists go a step further. Like those Odessa sisters, they stuff a whole fish. If you can find a submissive fishmonger willing to remove the skin in one piece – like a stocking, with the tail still attached – this is by far the most festive and dramatic gefilte fish presentation. The head is packed with some of the filling and poached alongside. At serving time, you reassemble the beast and get ready for compliments. If you don't have a whole skin, just make a loaf and lay a long strip of skin on top as a decoration. And of course, you can always prepare delicious fish balls from this mixture, in which case you'll need a good 3 litres of stock.

Back in 1920s Odessa my great-grandmother Maria prepared her gefilte fish with pike from the Privoz market. In America many émigré matrons use carp. My personal favorite is a combo of delicate whitefish with the darker, oilier carp. And while this recipe does contain a large pinch of sugar, it's the masses of slowly cooked onions that deliver the sweetness. With plenty of horseradish at table, please.

GEFILTE FISH

Serves 10 to 12 as a first course

4–5 tablespoons groundnut oil or pareve (or vegan) margarine, plus more as needed

2 large onions, finely chopped; plus 1 small onion, coarsely chopped

2 sheets matzo, broken into pieces

3 medium carrots, peeled; 1 carrot coarsely chopped, the other 2 left whole

1 whole whitefish, pike, or another firm freshwater fish, about 1.8kg, skinned (see headnote) and filleted (you should have about 650g fillets), head reserved; fillets cut into small pieces

650g carp fillets, cut into small pieces

3 large eggs

1 tablespoon ice-cold water

1 teaspoon sugar, or more to taste

2 teaspoons kosher salt and freshly ground white or black pepper to taste

1 litre fish stock (store-bought is fine) or chicken stock

Fresh watercress for decoration, if desired

Fresh or bottled horseradish, for serving

1. In a large skillet or frying pan heat the oil over medium-low heat. Add the 2 finely chopped onions and cook, stirring often, until softened, about 12 minutes. Let the onions cool for 15 minutes. While the onions are cooling, soak the matzos in cold water to cover for 10 minutes. Drain thoroughly, squeeze out the liquid, and crumble the matzo into a paste with your hands.

2. In a food processor, pulse the coarsely chopped raw onion and the chopped carrot until finely minced, and

transfer to a large mixing bowl. Working in 4 batches, pulse the whitefish and carp fillets, the sautéed onions, and the matzo until finely ground but not puréed, transferring the finished batches to the bowl with the onion and carrots. Stir in the eggs, water, sugar, 2 teaspoons of salt, and pepper to taste. Blend until the mixture is homogenous and a little sticky. To taste for seasoning, poach or sauté a small fish ball. If the mixture looks too loose to shape, refrigerate it for about an hour, covered with clingfilm.

3. Preheat the oven to 220°C/425°F/Gas 7. with the rack set in the center. Line a 45cm x 30cm foil roasting tray with a piece of foil. If using a whole fish skin with tail attached, lay it out on the foil and stuff with the fish mixture so it resembles a whole fish. With wet hands, shape any leftover mixture into oblong balls. If using a fish head, stuff it with some of the fish mixture, and add to the pan along with the fish balls. If making a loaf with a strip of skin as a decoration (see headnote), shape the fish mixture into a loaf approximately 40cm by 15cm on the foil and lay the skin along the top. Brush the top of the stuffed fish or loaf with a little oil. Bake until the top just begins to color, about 20 minutes.

4. While the fish bakes, bring the fish stock to a simmer. Add enough hot stock to the roasting tray with the fish to come two-thirds of the way up the side of the fish. If there is not enough, add a little water. Add the whole carrots to the pan. Reduce the oven temperature to 170°C/325°F/ Gas 3, cover the top of the tray loosely with foil, and continue braising the fish until set and cooked through, about 45 minutes. Baste it with the poaching liquid once or twice, and turn the fish balls, if using.

5. Allow the fish to cool completely in the liquid, about 3

hours, cover with clingfilm, and refrigerate overnight. To serve, using two large spatulas, carefully transfer it to a long serving platter, lined with watercress, if desired. Attach the head, if using, to the fish. Cut the carrots into slices, and use to decorate the top of the fish. Serve with horseradish.

KOTLETI

Mom's Russian 'Hamburgers'

Kotleti for lunch, kotleti for dinner, kotleti of beef, of pork, of fish, of chicken – even kotleti of minced carrots or beet-root. The entire USSR pretty much lived on these cheap, delicious fried patties, and when comrades didn't make them from scratch, they bought them at stores. Back in Moscow, Mom and I harbored a secret passion for the pro-letarian, six-kopek variety produced by the meat-processing plant named after Stalin's food supply commissar, Anastas Mikoyan. Inspired by his 1936 trip to America, Mikoyan wanted to copy Yankee burgers in Russia, but somehow the bun got lost in the shuffle and the country got hooked on mass-produced kotleti instead. Deliciously greasy, petite, and with a heavy industrial breading that fried up to a wicked crunch, Mikoyan factory patties could be scarfed down by the dozen. Wild with nostalgia, Mom and I tried a million times to recreate them at home, but no luck: some manufactured treats just can't be duplicated. So we always reverted back to Mom's (far more noble) homemade version.

Every ex-Soviet cook has a special trick for making juicy, savory patties. Some add crushed ice, others tuck in pats of butter or mix in a whipped egg white. My mother likes her kotleti Odessa-style (garlicky!), and adds mayo as binding instead of the usual egg, with delightful results. The same formula works with ground turkey or chicken or fish. Buckwheat kasha makes a nostalgic Russian accompaniment. Ditto thin potato batons slowly pan-fried with onions in lots of butter or oil. I love cold kotleti for lunch the next day, with some dense dark bread, hot mustard, and a good crunchy dill pickle.

KOTLETI
Serves 4

650g freshly ground beef chuck or braising steak (or a mixture of beef and pork)

2 slices stale white bread, crusts removed, soaked for 5 minutes in water and squeezed

1 small onion, grated

2 medium garlic cloves, crushed in a press

2 tablespoons finely chopped dill or parsley

$2^{1}/_{2}$ tablespoons full-fat mayonnaise

1 teaspoon kosher salt

$^{1}/_{2}$ teaspoon freshly ground black pepper, or more to taste

250g–350g fine dried breadcrumbs for coating

Rapeseed or sunflower oil and unsalted butter, for frying

1. In a mixing bowl, combine the first eight ingredients and blend well into a homogenous mixture. Cover with clingfilm and refrigerate for at least 30 minutes.

2. With wet hands, shape the mixture into oval patties

approximately 9cm long. Spread breadcrumbs on a large plate or a sheet of greaseproof paper. Coat patties in crumbs, flattening them out slightly and pressing down for the crumbs to adhere.

3. In a large skillet or frying pan heat 2 tablespoons of the oil with a pat of butter until sizzling. Working in batches, fry the kotleti over medium-high heat until golden-brown, about 4 minutes per side. Cover the pan, reduce the heat to low, and fry for another 2 to 3 minutes to cook through. Transfer to a plate lined with kitchen paper. Repeat with the rest of the patties. Serve at once.

KARTOCHKI

Ration Cards

As we started work on the 1940s chapter, Mother and I batted around various menu ideas for the decade. Maybe we'd bake millet, like my grandmother Liza did at the evacuation warehouse in Lenin's birth town of Ulyanovsk. Or we could improvise wartime 'pastries' – a slice of black bread with a barely there dusting of sugar. We even entertained recreating a banquet from the February 1945 Yalta Conference where the 'Big Three' and their entourage feasted on quail pilaf and fish in champagne sauce, while the battered country half starved.

In the end, we changed our minds: *cooking* just didn't seem right. Instead of a recipe I offer a photo of a ration card book. Place of issue: Leningrad. Date: December 1941, the third month of the terrible Siege, which lasted nine hundred days and claimed around a million lives. Temperatures that winter plunged to minus thirty. There was no heat, no electricity, no running water in the frozen city; sewage pipes burst from the cold; transport stood motionless. Peter the Great's imperial capital resembled a snow-covered grave-yard where emaciated crowds, so many soon to be ghosts, lined up for their ration of bread. By December 1941 the rations had fallen to 250 grams for industrial workers; for all other citizens, 125 grams – barely four ounces of something sticky and damp, adulterated with sawdust and cattle fodder and cellulose. But those 125 grams, those twenty small daily bites gotten with a puny square of paper, were often the difference between survival and death.

An image like this calls for a moment of silence.

Reproduction of a Rationing Card (ITAR-TASS/Sovfoto)

ЛЕНИНГРАД

С

КАРТОЧКА

НА ХЛЕБ

НА ДЕКАБРЬ 1941 г.

Фамилия ....

Имя, отчество ....

М. п.

Карточка при утере не возобновляется

CHANAKHI

Georgian Stew of Lamb, Herbs, and Vegetables

In Soviet times, without access to travel or foreign cuisines, Russians turned to the Union's exotic fringes for complex, spicy foods. Georgian food was Moscow's de facto haute cuisine, satisfying our northern cravings for smoke, herbs, garlic, and bright, sunny seasoning. If you can forget that this might have been Stalin's favorite dish, this soupy one-dish meal is a marvel. The Georgian penchant for masses of aromatic herbs is on captivating display, and the meat essentially braises in its own herbaceous, garlicky juices, along with tender aubergines, tomatoes, and spuds. By tradition the stew is baked in an earthenware pot called *chanakhi*. But enamel cast iron, such as Le Creuset will do just as well. All this stew needs is good hot flatbread to soak up the juices, and a sprightly salad of peppery greens.

CHANAKHI

Serves 6 to 8

2 bunches coriander, leaves chopped, plus more for serving

2 bunches basil, leaves chopped, plus more for serving

2 bunches flat-leaf parsley,
   leaves chopped, plus
   more for serving
12 large garlic cloves, finely
   chopped
Kosher salt and freshly
   ground black pepper, to
   taste
1 teaspoon paprika, plus
   more for rubbing the lamb
Large pinch of Turkish red
   pepper flakes, plus more
   for rubbing the lamb
1.3–1.5kg shoulder lamb
   chops, trimmed of excess
   fat and halved lengthwise
3 medium onions, quartered
   and thinly sliced
2 tablespoons olive oil
2 ripe plum tomatoes,
   chopped; plus 4 plum
   tomatoes, quartered
   lengthways
350ml tomato juice
2 tablespoons red wine
   vinegar
Boiling water as needed
3 slender long Asian
   aubergines (25–30cm
   long)
3 medium Yukon Gold or
   other waxy, yellow-
   fleshed potatoes, peeled
   and cut into wedges

1. Preheat the oven to 170°C/325°F/Gas 3. with the rack set in the lower third. In a mixing bowl combine the coriander, basil, parsley, and garlic. Toss the mixture with ½ teaspoon of salt, generous gratings of black pepper, paprika, and pepper flakes.

2. Rub the lamb chops with salt, black pepper, paprika, and pepper flakes. In a mixing bowl toss the lamb with the onions. Add a large handful of the herb mixture and the oil, and toss to coat.

3. Place the lamb and the onions as snugly as possible on the bottom of a very large enamel cast-iron pot with a tight-fitting lid. Set the pot over high heat and cook until steam begins to rise from the bottom, about 3 minutes. Reduce heat to medium-low, cover tightly, and cook until the lamb

is opaque and has thrown off a lot of juice, about 12 minutes. Turn the lamb, cover, and cook for 3 to 4 minutes longer. Add the chopped tomatoes, another handful of herbs, 240ml of the tomato juice, and 1 tablespoon of the vinegar, and bring to a vigorous simmer. Cover and transfer the pot to the oven. Cook until the lamb is tender, $1^{1}/_{2}$ to $1^{3}/_{4}$ hours, checking periodically and adding a little water if it looks dry.

4. While the meat cooks, place the three aubergines directly on three burners set over medium-high heat. Cook, turning and moving the aubergines until the surface is lightly browned and begins to char in spots but the flesh is still firm, 2 to 3 minutes total. Watch out for drips and flame sparks. Using tongs, transfer the aubergines to a cutting board. When cool enough to handle, cut each aubergine crossways into 4 sections. With a small sharp knife, make a slit in each section, and stuff some of the herb mixture into each slit. In two separate bowls, season the potatoes and the quartered tomatoes with salt and a little of the herb mixture.

5. Remove the lamb from the oven and stir in the potatoes, using tongs and a large spoon to push them gently under the meat. Add the remaining tomato juice and vinegar, another handful of the herb mixture, and enough boiling water, if needed, to generously cover the potatoes and meat. Scatter the aubergine sections on top, nestling them in the liquid. Cover and bake for 30 minutes longer. Add the tomatoes, scattering them on top without stirring, and sprinkle with the remaining herb mixture. Cover and bake for another 20 minutes.

6. Increase the oven temperature to 200°C/400°F/Gas 6.

Uncover the pot and bake until the juices are thickened, about 15 minutes.

Remove the stew from the oven and let cool for 5 to 10 minutes. Serve straight from the pot, sprinkled with additional herbs.

1960s

CORNBREAD FOR KHRUSHCHEV

Moldovan Cornbread with Feta

Say 'Khrushchev' and a Russian will laugh and immediately cry '*kukuruza!*' (corn) And so, in memory of Nikita 'Kukuruznik' (Corn Man) Khrushchev and his loony crusade to hook our Union on corn, Mom and I wanted to prepare a maize tribute. The notion of cornbread, however, struck Mom as odd. To a northern Slav, she insisted, bread made from maize sounded oxymoronic; it verged on sacrilege. Bread was sacred and bread was *wheat*. The bread-lines that sprouted during the 1963 crop failure helped push Khrushchev into early retirement, and after he'd gone, corn was either forgotten or recalled as an agricultural gag in northern parts of the Union. But not so in southwestern USSR, I reminded my mother. There cornmeal had been a staple for centuries. Georgians prepared it into *gomi* (white grits) or *mchadi*, griddled cakes to be dipped into stews. Western Ukrainians and Moldovans ate *mamalyga*, the local polenta, as their daily kasha (gruel).

I myself discovered the bounty of the Union's corn recipes when researching my book *Please to the Table*. And I fell in love with this fantastically moist, extra-savory Moldovan cornbread – enriched, local-style, with soured cream and tangy feta cheese. Recently, I made it for Mom. It came out so yummy that we ate it straight from the pan – warm and topped with fire-roasted red peppers. Mom recalled how in breadless 1963 she'd thrown out a bag of cornmeal someone had given her. *What am I to do with this yellow sawdust?* she'd wondered back then. Well, now she knows. Here's the recipe.

CORNBREAD FOR KHRUSHCHEV

Serves 6

2 large eggs, lightly beaten
500ml milk
90g unsalted butter, melted, plus more for greasing the pan
120ml soured cream
350g fine yellow cornmeal, preferably stone-ground, or fine polenta (not instant)

90g plain flour
1 teaspoon sugar
2 teaspoons baking powder
$^1/_2$ teaspoon bicarbonate of soda
340g grated or finely crumbled feta cheese
Roasted red pepper strips for serving, optional

1. Preheat the oven to 200°C/400°F/Gas 6. with the rack set in the center. In a large bowl, thoroughly stir together the first four ingredients. In another bowl sift together the cornmeal, flour, sugar, baking powder, and bicarbonate of soda. Whisk the dry ingredients into the egg mixture until smooth. Add the feta and whisk to blend thoroughly. Let the batter stand for 10 minutes.

2. Butter a 23cm x 23cm baking dish about 5cm deep. Pour the batter into the dish and tap to even it out. Bake the cornbread until light golden and firm to the touch, 35 to 40 minutes. Serve warm, with roasted peppers, if desired.

SALAT OLIVIER

Russian Potato Salad with Pickles

Sine qua non of socialist celebrations, this salady Soviet icon actually has a fancy, bourgeois past. The name? Derived from one Lucien Olivier, a French chef who wowed 1860s Moscow with his swank L'Hermitage restaurant. The Gaul's original creation, of course, had almost nothing in common with our Soviet classic. *His* was an extravagant still life of grouse, tongue, and crayfish tails encircling a mound of potatoes and cornichons, all doused with le chef's secret Provençal sauce. To Olivier's horror, Russian clients vulgarized his precious arrangement by mixing up all the ingredients on their plates. And so he retooled his dish as a salad. Then came 1917. L'Hermitage was shuttered, its recipes scorned. All Soviet children knew Mayakovsky's jingle: 'Eat your pineapples, gobble your grouse / Your last day is coming, you bourgeois louse!'

The salad gained a second life in the mid-1930s when Olivier's old apprentice, a chef known as Comrade Ivanov, revived it at the Stalin-era Moskva Hotel. Revived it in *Soviet* form. Chicken replaced the class-enemy grouse, proletarian carrots stood in for the original pink of the crayfish, and potatoes and canned peas took center stage – the whole drenched in our own tangy, mass-produced Provansal mayo.

Meanwhile, variations of the salad traveled the world with White Russian émigrés. To this day, I'm amazed to encounter it under its generic name, 'Russian salad,' at steakhouses in Buenos Aires, railway stations in Istanbul, or as part of Korean or Spanish or Iranian appetizer spreads. Amazed and just a little bit proud.

At our own table, Mom gives this Soviet staple an arty, nonconformist twist by adding fresh cucumbers and apple, and substituting crabmeat for chicken (feel free to stay with the latter). The ultimate key to success, though, she insists: chopping everything into a very fine dice. She also obsessively doctors Hellmann's mayo with various zesty additions. I think Lucien Olivier would approve.

SALAT OLIVIER

Serves 6

SALAD

3 large waxy potatoes, peeled, cooked and diced

2 medium carrots, peeled, cooked and diced

1 large Granny Smith apple, peeled and diced

2 medium dill pickles (dill-pickled cucumbers), diced

1 medium cucumber, cut lengthways, seeded with a teaspoon, peeled and finely diced

3 large hard-boiled eggs, chopped

400g tin peas, drained

4 tablespoons finely chopped spring onions (with 7.5cm of the green tops)

4 tablespoons finely chopped dill

340g white crabmeat, flaked; or crabsticks,

chopped (or substitute
chopped poached
chicken or beef)

Kosher salt and freshly
ground black pepper, to
taste

DRESSING

240g Hellmann's
mayonnaise,
or more to taste
80ml soured cream

2 tablespoons fresh lemon
juice
2 teaspoons Dijon mustard
1 teaspoon white vinegar
Kosher salt to taste

1. In a large mixing bowl combine all the salad ingredients and season with salt and pepper to taste.

2. In a medium bowl, whisk together all the dressing ingredients, season with salt, and taste: it should be tangy and zesty. Toss the salad thoroughly with the dressing, adding a little more mayo if it doesn't look moist enough. Adjust the seasoning to taste. Serve in a cut-crystal or glass bowl.

DAD'S ÜBER-BORSHCH

Borscht with Beef, Mushrooms, Apples and Beans

To my childhood *palate*, borshch (as Russians spell borscht) was less a soup than a kind of Soviet quotidian destiny: something to be endured along with Moscow tap water and the endless grayness of socialist winter. Our Soviet borshch took on various guises. There was the private borshch, such as Mom's frugal vegetarian version, endearing in its monotony. There was the vile institutional soup of canteens, afloat with reddish circles of fat. In winter we warmed our bones with limp, hot borshch, the culinary equivalent of tired February snow. In summer we chilled out with *svekolník*, the cold, thin borshch popularized here in America by Eastern European Jews.

Parallel to all these but ever out of reach was another soup: the mythical 'real' Ukrainian borshch we knew from descriptions in State-approved recipe booklets authored by hack 'gastronomic historians.' Apparently *that* borshch was everything ours wasn't. Thick enough to stand a spoon in, concocted in myriad regional permutations, and brimming with all manner of meats. Meats! *That* borshch represented the folkloric propaganda Ukraine, our wholesome Soviet breadbasket and sugarbeet bowl, envisioned as though never clouded by the horrors of famine and collectivization.

Not once during my childhood did I taste anything like this chimerical 'real' Ukrainian borshch. Neither was I that interested, really.

It was the dinner my dad, Sergei, prepared to impress Mom during our 1987 Moscow reunion that changed my mind. Convinced me that borshch could be something *exciting*. Never in my life had I tasted anything like Dad's masterpiece, with its rich meaty broth, the deep garnet color achieved by juicing the beetroot, the unconventional addition of mushrooms and beans, the final savory flourish of pork cracklings. Even after sampling many authentic regional versions on my subsequent trips to Ukraine, I still hold up Dad's borshch as the Platonic ideal.

Here's his recipe. My only tweak is to replace fresh beet-root juice with baked beetroot, which delivers the same depth of color. A rich homemade stock makes the soup special, but if the effort seems like too much, omit the first step, use a generous 2¹/₂ litres of store-bought chicken stock in Step 3, and instead of boiled beef, add about 500g of diced kielbasa (Polish sausage) or good smoky ham. Like most peasant soups, borshch improves mightily on standing, so make it a day ahead. A thick slice of pumpernickel or rye is a must. Ditto a dollop of soured cream.

DAD'S UBER-BORSHCH

Serves 10 to 12

1kg beef chuck, shin, or brisket in one piece, trimmed of excess fat

3.3 litres water

2 medium onions, left whole, plus 1 large onion, chopped

2 medium carrots, left whole, plus 1 large carrot, peeled and diced

1 bay leaf

Kosher salt and freshly ground black pepper

2 medium beetroots, washed and trimmed

25g dried porcini mushrooms, rinsed of grit, and soaked in 240ml hot water for 1 hour

2 slices good smoked bacon, finely chopped

1 large green pepper, cored, seeded, and diced

45g unsalted butter, plus more as needed

200g chopped green cabbage

1 teaspoon sweet paprika

3 medium waxy potatoes, peeled and cut into 1-inch chunks

400g tin can diced tomatoes, with about half of their liquid

1 small Granny Smith apple, peeled, cored, and diced

400g tin kidney beans, drained and rinsed

3 large garlic cloves, finely chopped

2 tablespoons finely chopped flat-leaf parsley

2 tablespoons distilled white vinegar, or more to taste

2 tablespoons sugar, or more to taste

For serving: soured cream, chopped fresh dill and thinly sliced spring onions

1. Combine beef and water in a large stockpot and bring to a boil over high heat. Skim and reduce heat to low. Add the whole onions and carrots and the bay leaf and season with salt and pepper to taste. Simmer partially covered, until the meat is tender, about $1^{1}/_{2}$ hours. Strain the stock, removing the meat. You should have $2^{1}/_{2}$ to $2^{3}/_{4}$ litres of stock. Cut the beef into 4cm chunks and reserve.

2. While the stock cooks, preheat the oven to 200°C /400°F/Gas 6. Wrap the beetroots individually in aluminum foil and bake until a small knife slides in easily, about 45 minutes. Unwrap the beetroots, plunge them into a bowl of cold water, then slip off the skins. Grate the beetroots on a four-sided grater or shred in a food processor. Set aside. Strain the mushroom soaking liquid and save for another use. Chop the mushrooms.

3. In a large, heavy soup pot, cook the bacon over medium-low heat until crispy. Remove with a slotted spoon and reserve. To the bacon drippings, add the chopped onion, mushrooms, diced carrot, and green pepper, and cook until softened, about 7 minutes, adding a little butter if the pot looks dry. Add the remaining butter and cabbage, and cook, stirring, for another 5 minutes. Add the paprika and stir for a few seconds. Add the stock, potatoes, tomatoes with their liquid, apple, and the reserved beef, and bring to a gentle boil. Skim off any froth, season with salt to taste, cover, and simmer over low heat until potatoes are almost tender, about 15 minutes. Stir in half of the grated beetroots and the beans, and add a little water if the soup looks too thick. Continue cooking over medium-low heat until all the vegetables are soft and the flavors have melded, about 25 minutes more. (The borshch can be prepared a day

ahead up to this point. Reheat it slowly, thinning it out with a little water if it thickens too much on standing.)

4. Before serving, use a mortar and pestle and pound the garlic and parsley with 1 teaspoon of ground black pepper to a coarse paste. Add to the simmering soup along with the reserved bacon, the remaining beetroots, vinegar, and sugar. Adjust the seasoning and simmer for another 5 minutes. Let the borshch stand for 10 minutes. To serve, ladle the soup into serving bowls, add a small dollop of soured cream to each portion, and sprinkle with dill and spring onions. Invite the guests to mix the soured cream well into their soup.

PALOV

Central Asian Rice, Lamb, and Carrot Pilaf

I never ate more bizarrely than I did during the Soviet Union's last winter in 1991. The economy was going to hell; food would be nonexistent in one place, then, thanks to some mysterious black-market forces, plentiful just up the road. Rattling around the collapsing empire in our ramshackle Zhiguli cars, my ex-boyfriend and I fasted one minute and feasted the next. Of the feasts, my favorites occurred in the Uzbek/Tajik city of Samarkand (where market forces have always been potent). There you could count on smoky kebabs from rickety stalls, ambrosial melons piled up in wagon beds, and at people's houses, *always* an aromatic festive *palov* mounded high on a blue and white ceramic platter. Outside, the world was coming unstitched; inside Samarkand homes we sat on low cushions sipping tannic green tea, scooped up delicious yellow rice (with the left hand, as tradition demanded), and nodded along politely to nationalist proclamations that Tajik pilaf was infinitely better than Uzbek pilaf — or vice versa. The proclamations didn't make sense. But *eating* the rice did.

A feast of cumin-spiced lamb and rice steamed together

until every spoonful is as eloquent as an Omar Khayyám quatrain, *palov* enjoys such ritual status in Central Asia that florid legends of its conception involve Alexander the Great or, in certain versions, Genghis Khan. The dish is prepared according to a strict code, traditionally by men (and often *for* men) and over an open fire. But it's also fabulous when made in a home kitchen, and super easy to boot. The soul of the dish is *zírvak*, a base of lamb and masses of onions and carrots. (To this mix feel free to add some cubed quince, a handful of raisins, and/or a few handfuls of cooked or tinned chickpeas.) The spices are spare and eloquent: doses of sweet and hot pepper, a whole bulb of garlic, and barberries, the tiny dried berries with a sharp lemony flavor. (Look for them at Middle Eastern markets.) Short- or medium-grain rice is then layered on top, and everything steams to perfection in a Turkic nomadic kettle called *kazan*, for which you can substitute any heavy pot with a tight-fitting lid.

Palov is best enjoyed with a couple of zesty, salady Central Asian sides. One is a coleslaw of shredded sweet daikon radish (also known as mooli) and carrots dressed with white vinegar, a touch of oil, and a pinch of sugar. For the other essential accompaniment, thinly slice 1 large onion, 2 large green peppers, and 3 large ripe tomatoes, and layer them in a shallow bowl, seasoning the layers with salt and pepper and sprinkling them with mild olive oil and red wine vinegar. Let the salad stand while the *palov* cooks. Tannic green tea, in small cup-bowls, is the classic Central Asian beverage, but we Russians also pour vodka.

PALOV

Serves 6 to 8

3 tablespoons rapeseed, sunflower or mild olive oil, or more as needed

1.2kg lamb shoulder with some fat and just a few bones, cut into 2.5cm chunks

Kosher salt and freshly ground black pepper, to taste

2 large onions, chopped

1½ tablespoons cumin seeds

1½ teaspoons paprika

Two large pinches cayenne

Large pinch of turmeric

3 to 4 tablespoons barberries (available at some Middle Eastern markets), optional

3 large carrots, peeled and coarsely grated

400g short- or medium-grain rice, rinsed in several changes of water and drained

850ml boiling water

1 whole bulb of garlic, outer layer of skin removed

See headnote for accompaniments

1. In a large, heavy casserole, preferably with an oval bottom, heat the oil until smoking. Rub the lamb generously with salt and pepper. In 2 to 3 batches, brown the lamb well on all sides, transferring the browned pieces to a bowl. Once all the lamb is browned, add the onions and a little more oil if necessary and cook, stirring until well browned, about 7 minutes. Return the lamb to the pot, reduce the heat to low, and stir in the cumin, paprika, cayenne, turmeric, and barberries, if using. Season generously with salt, cover, and simmer for 15 minutes, adding a little water if the lamb begins to burn. Thoroughly stir in the carrots and

cook for another 1 to 2 minutes. Adjust the seasoning.

2. Flatten the surface of the lamb mixture with the back of a large spoon. Pour rice over the meat and bury the garlic bulb in it. Place a small lid or a heatproof plate directly on top of the rice (so as not to disturb the arrangement of rice and meat when adding water). Pour in the boiling water in a steady stream. Being careful not to burn yourself, remove the lid or the plate. Taste the liquid and add salt if necessary. Cook the rice uncovered, without stirring, over medium-low heat until the liquid is level with the rice and small bubbles appear on the surface, about 15 minutes.

3. With a spatula, gather the rice into a mound and make 6 to 7 holes in it with the handle of a long wooden spoon for steam to escape. Reduce the heat to the absolute lowest, place a heat diffuser if you have one under the pot, cover tightly, and let the rice steam until tender, about 25 minutes. Check 2 or 3 times and add a little bit of water into the holes in the rice if there doesn't seem to be enough steam. Remove from the heat and let stand, covered, for 15 minutes.

4. To serve, spread the rice on a large festive serving platter, fluffing it slightly. Arrange the meat and vegetables in a mound over it, topping with the garlic bulb. Serve the grated radish and tomato salads alongside.

BLINI

Russian Pancakes with Trimmings

Finally the kitchen maid appeared with the blini ... Risking a severe burn, Semyon Petrovich grabbed at the two topmost (and hottest) blini, and deposited them, plop, in his plate. The blini were deep golden, airy, and plump — just like the shoulder of a merchant's daughter ... Podtikin glowed with delight and hiccupped with joy as he poured hot butter all over them ... With pleasurable anticipation, he slowly, painstakingly, spread them with caviar. To the few patches not covered with caviar he applied a dollop of sour cream ... All that was left was to eat, don't you think? But no! Podtikin gazed down at his own creation and was still not satisfied. He reflected a moment and then piled onto the blini the fattest piece of salmon, a smelt, and a sardine, and only then, panting and delirious, he rolled up the blini, downed a shot of vodka, and opened his mouth ...

But at this very moment he was struck by an apoplectic fit ...

— Anton Chekhov, from *On Human Frailty:*
An Object Lesson for the Butter Festival

Our book journey ended; the time came for our very last feast. Mom and I decided to hold an ironic wake for the

USSR. And what do Russians eat at commemorations and wakes? They eat blini. Coming full circle to our first chapter, we once again read Chekhov while a yeast sponge bubbled and rose in a shiny bowl on Mom's green faux-granite counter. Yeast for our farewell blini.

Blini has always been the most traditional, ritualistic, and ur-Slavic of foods – the stuff of carnivals and divinations, of sun worship and ancestral rites. In pre-Christian times, the Russian life cycle began and ended with blini – from pancakes fed to women after childbirth to the blini eaten at funerals. 'Blin is the symbol of sun, good harvest, harmonious marriages, and healthy children,' wrote the Russian poet Alexander Kuprin (*blin* being the singular of *blini*).

To a pagan Slav, the flour and eggs in the blini represented the fertility of Mother Earth; their round shape and the heat of the pan might have been a tribute to Yerilo, the pre-Christian sun god. Even in Soviet days, when religion was banned, Russians gorged on blini not only at wakes but also for Maslenitsa, the Butterweek preceding the Easter Lent. They still do. Religions come and go, regimes fall, sushi is replacing *seliodka* (herring) on post-Soviet tables, but blini remain. Some foods are eternal.

Authentic Russian blini start with *opara*, a sponge of water, flour, and yeast. The batter should rise at least twice, and for that light sourdough tang I chill it for several hours, letting the flavors develop slowly. Russian blini are the diameter of a saucer, never cocktail-size, and these days people prefer wheat to the archaic buckwheat. Most babushkas swear by a cast-iron frying pan, but I recommend a heavy nonstick. Frying the blini takes a little practice: 'The first blin is always lumpy,' the Russian saying goes. But after three or four, you'll get the knack.

The accompaniments include – must include! – soured cream and melted butter, herring, smoked salmon and whitefish, and caviar, if you're feeling lavish. Dessert? More blini with various jams.

BLINI

Serves 6 to 8

12g active dried yeast (or 2 sachets)
240ml warm water
60g sugar, plus 2 teaspoons
340g plain flour, plus more as needed
600ml full-cream milk, at room temperature
60g unsalted butter, melted, plus more for brushing the blini
2 large eggs, separated, yolks beaten
2 teaspoons salt, or more to taste
Rapeseed or sunflower oil, for frying
1 small potato, halved

For serving: melted butter, soured cream, at least two kinds of smoked fish, caviar or salmon roe, and a selection of jams

1. In a large mixing bowl, stir together yeast, water, and 2 teaspoons sugar and let stand until foamy. Whisk in 60g flour until smooth. Place the sponge, covered, in a warm place until bubbly and almost doubled in bulk, about 1 hour.

2. Into the sponge beat the milk, melted butter, remaining 280g flour, egg yolks, 60g sugar, and salt. Whisk the batter until completely smooth and set to rise, covered

loosely with clingfilm, until bubbly and doubled in bulk, about 2 hours, stirring once and letting it rise again. Alternatively, refrigerate the batter, covered with plastic, and let it rise for several hours or overnight, stirring once or twice. Bring to room temperature before frying.

3. Beat the egg whites until they form soft peaks and fold them into the batter. Let the batter stand for another 10 minutes.

4. Pour some oil into a small shallow bowl and have it ready by the stove. Skewer a potato half on a fork and dip it into the oil. Rub the bottom of a long-handled heavy 20cm nonstick skillet or frying pan liberally with the oiled potato. Heat the pan over medium heat for 1¹/₂ minutes. Using a potholder, grip the pan by the handle, lift it slightly off the heat, and tilt it toward you at a 45-degree angle. Using a ladle quickly pour enough batter into the pan to cover the bottom in one thin layer (about 60ml). Let the batter run down the pan, quickly tilting and rotating it until the batter covers the entire surface. Put the pan back on the burner and cook until the top of the blin is bubbly and the underside is golden, about 1 minute. Turn the blin and cook for 30 seconds more, brushing the cooked side with melted butter. If the pan looks dry when you are turning the blin, rub with some more oil. The first blin will probably be a flop.

5. Make another blin in the same fashion, turn off the heat and stop to taste. The texture of the blin should be light, spongy, and a touch chewy; it should be very thin but a little puffy. If a blin tears too easily, the consistency is too thin: whisk 30g more flour into the batter. If the blin is too doughy and thick, whisk in 60ml to 120ml water. Adjust the amount of salt or sugar to taste, and continue frying.

6. Repeat with the rest of the batter, greasing the pan with the oiled potato before making each blin. Slide each fried blin into a deep bowl, keeping the stacked cooked blini covered with a lid or foil (see note). Serve the blini hot, with the suggested garnishes. To eat, brush the blin with butter, smear with a little soured cream if you like, top with a piece of fish, roll up, and plop into your mouth.

NOTE

Blini are best eaten fresh. If you must reheat, place them, covered with foil, in a bain marie in the oven or in a steamer. Or cover a stack with a damp kitchen paper and microwave on high for 1 minute.

AUTHOR'S NOTE

This is a work of nonfiction, woven from family anecdotes and historical facts spanning ten decades of Soviet and post-Soviet experience. To the best of my knowledge, everything here is true, albeit filtered, at times, through the subjectivities of the protagonists. A handful of names have been changed; a few others might have been misremembered. For the sake of brevity and narrative drama some personal events have been compressed and rearranged slightly. I've done my best to check personal recollections and family myths against larger historical accounts, and to properly reconstruct dates, events, and political contexts. However, some of the people I portray are now elderly, while others are no longer with us, and I apologize for any undetected inaccuracies.

ACKNOWLEDGMENTS

I owe this book to Scott Moyers, who conceived it long before I did, gave it a name, found the dream editor for it as my agent, and continued to guide me even after his job profile changed. Comrade, my first *salut* is to you.

Since Scott left, Andrew Wylie has been a tower of inspiration, encouragement, and wise counsel every step along the way. Also at the Wylie Agency deep thanks to Jin Auh, and to Tracy Bohan for taking the book on its global adventure.

At Crown a boundless Slavic *spasibo* to editor-extraordinaire Rachel Klayman – for her passion, intelligence, rigor, and her deep, transforming empathy for the Soviet experience and this author's journey. Enormous gratitude to Maya Mavjee and Molly Stern for their publishing brilliance. At Transworld, huge thanks to Doug, Mads and Lisa.

Even while taking a book leave from journalism, I was still lucky to bask in the generosity and friendship of my extraordinary magazine family. At *Travel+Leisure* my deepest appreciations to our genius editor in chief, Nancy Novogrod, and the beautiful talented Nilou Motamed. At *Food & Wine* love and cheers to the always-inspiring Dana

Cowin and the awesome Kate Krader. An article about my mother's dinners for *Saveur* was one of the sparks that inspired the book. For this, and more besides, I thank James Oseland and the *Saveur* editorial team.

Suzanne Rafer and the late Peter Workman of Workman Publishing will always have a special place in my heart for launching me into the food writing world.

In Moscow I'm dearly indebted to Viktor Belyaev, ex-Kremlin chef and ur-raconteur; to Daria Hubova for putting me and Mom on TV; and to Irina Glushchenko and her indispensable book for educating me about Anastas Mikoyan.

My Russian clan has been a source of nurture and a joy: Dad, Sergei Bremzen, and his wife, Elena Skulkova; Aunt Yulia; *sestrichki* Dasha and Masha (and Masha's husband, Sergei), my brother, Andrei, and Nadyushka Menkova, the beloved von Bremzen family archivist.

On these shores *blagodarnost'* to Anna Brodsky (and Clava) for astute reads and precious communal apartment lore; and to Alexander Genis for his erudition and passion – and epicurean feats.

This book is imagined as a meal that spans decades of the Soviet experience. Our real meals wouldn't mean much without the company of Irina Genis, Andrei and Toma Zagdansky, and Alex and Andrea Bayer. A separate Sovetskoye Shampanskoye toast to Katerina Darrier, Maria Landa-Neimark; Innessa Fialkova; Elena Dovlatova; Isolda Gorodetsky; and Svetlana Kupchik for bringing Soviet past to such vivid life at Mom's table in Queens; and to Mark Serman for 'fables.' Among the non-Russians: huge hugs to Kate Sekules for *always* encouraging me; Melissa Clark for

Acknowledgments

being an angel; Mark Cohen for sharing his archival access; Peter Canby, Esther Allen, Nathaniel Wice, and Virginia Hatley for reading; Jonas and Ursula Hegewisch for their sparkle and style; and to all other pals in New York, Moscow, and Istanbul who fed me, listened to me, and lifted my spirits.

Larisa Frumkin is the soul and star of this book. *Mamulik*: you're my everlasting hero and role model. This book is yours.

Finally every word on these pages owes something to Barry Yourgrau, my partner, reader, editor, literary adviser, best friend, and true love. Without him this book would be a sad murky nowhere. Ditto my life.

SELECTED SOURCES

What follows is by no means an exhaustive list of the book-length nonfiction sources, both English and Russian, that I have consulted and/or quoted for this book, in addition to works of fiction, memoirs, magazine and newspaper articles, and reliable online materials. Sources that have been helpful to me across several chapters are cited in the earliest chapter. For the Russian titles I have relied on the standard Library of Congress transliteration system, which differs slightly from the more informal one used in the main text of the book.

CHAPTER I

Borrero, Mauricio. *Hungry Moscow: Scarcity and Urban Society in the Russian Civil War, 1917–1921*. New York: Peter Lang, 2003.

Giliarovskii, Vladimir. *Moskva i moskvichi*. Moscow: Moskovskii rabochii, 1968.

Glants, Musya, and Joyce Toomre. *Food in Russian History and Culture*. Bloomington: Indiana University Press, 1997.

LeBlanc, Ronald D. *Slavic Sins of the Flesh: Food, Sex, and Carnal*

Appetite in Nineteenth-Century Russian Fiction. Durham: University of New Hampshire Press, 2009.

Lih, Lars T. *Bread and Authority in Russia, 1914–1921.* Berkeley: University of California Press, 1990.

McAuley, Mary. *Bread and Justice: State and Society in Petrograd, 1917–1922.* Oxford: Clarendon Press, 1991.

Pokhlebkin, Vil'jam. *Kukhnia veka.* Moscow: Polifakt, 2000.

Suny, Ronald G., ed. *The Cambridge History of Russia, Volume 3: The Twentieth Century.* Cambridge: Cambridge University Press, 2006.

CHAPTER 2

Ball, Alan M. *Russia's Last Capitalists: The Nepmen, 1921–1929.* Berkeley: University of California Press, 1987.

Benjamin, Walter. *Moscow Diary.* Cambridge, MA: Harvard University Press, 1986.

Boym, Svetlana. *Common Places: Mythologies of Everyday Life in Russia.* Cambridge, MA: Harvard University Press, 1994.

Buchli, Victor. *An Archaeology of Socialism.* New York: Berg, 1999.

Elwood, Carter. *The Non-Geometric Lenin: Essays on the Development of the Bolshevik Party 1910–1914.* London-New York: Anthem Press, 2011.

Genis, Aleksandr. *Kolobok. Kulinarnye puteshestviya.* Moscow: Corpus, 2010.

Hessler, Julie. *A Social History of Soviet Trade: Trade Policy, Retail Practices, and Consumption, 1917–1953.* Princeton, NJ: Princeton University Press, 2004.

Kondrat'eva, Tamara. *Kormit' i Pravit': O Vlasti v Rossii XVI–XX Veka,* Moscow: ROSSPEN, 2009.

Martin, Terry. *The Affirmative Action Empire: Nations and Nationalism in the Soviet Union, 1923–1939.* Ithaca-London: Cornell University Press, 2001.

Massell, G. J. *The Surrogate Proletariat: Moslem Women and Revolutionary Strategies in Soviet Central Asia, 1919–1929.* Princeton, NJ: Princeton University Press, 1974.

Osokina, Elena. *Za fasadom stalinskogo izobiliya. Raspredelenie i rynok v snabzhenii naseleniya v gody industrializatsii, 1927–1941.* Moscow: ROSSPEN, 1999.

Tumarkin, Nina. *Lenin Lives! The Lenin Cult in Soviet Russia.* Cambridge, MA: Harvard University Press, 1983.

Viola, Lynne. *Peasant Rebels under Stalin: Collectivization and the Culture of Peasant Resistance.* New York: Oxford University Press, 1996.

CHAPTER 3

Balina, Marina, and Yevgeny Dobrenko, eds. *Petrified Utopia: Happiness Soviet Style.* London & New York: Anthem Press, 2009.

Fitzpatrick, Sheila. *Everyday Stalinism: Ordinary Life in Extraordinary Times: Soviet Russia in the 1930s.* New York: Oxford

University Press, 1999.

Glushchenko, Irina. *Obshchepit: Anastas Mikoian i sovetskaia kukhnia.* Moscow: GUVShE, 2010.

Gronow, Jukka. *Caviar with Champagne: Common Luxury and the Ideals of the Good Life in Stalin's Russia.* New York: Berg, 2003.

Kniga o vkusnoi i zdorovoi pishche. Moscow: Pishchepromizdat, 1939, 1952, 1953, 1954, and 1955.

Korenevskaya, Natalia, and Thomas Lahusen, eds. *Intimacy and Terror: Soviet Diaries of the 1930s.* New York: New Press, 1995.

Mikoyan, Anastas. *Tak bylo. Razmyshleniia o minuvshem.* Moscow: Vagrius, 1999.

Petrone, Karen. *Life Has Become More Joyous, Comrades: Celebrations in the Time of Stalin.* Bloomington: Indiana University Press, 2000.

CHAPTER 4

Berezhkov, Valentin. *Stranitsi diplomaticheskoi istorii.* Moscow: Mezhdunarodnye otnosheniia, 1987.

Glantz, David M. *The Siege of Leningrad: 900 Days of Terror.* London: Brown Partworks, 2001.

Jones, Michael. *Leningrad: State of Siege.* New York: Basic Books, 2008.

Lur'e, V. M., and V. Ia. Kochik. *GRU dela i liudi.* St. Petersburg: Olma-Press, 2003.

Moskoff, William. *The Bread of Affliction: The Food Supply in the USSR During World War II*. Cambridge: Cambridge University Press, 1990.

Murphy, David E. *What Stalin Knew: The Enigma of Barbarossa*. New Haven: Yale University Press, 2005.

Pleshakov, Constantine. *Stalin's Folly*. Boston: Houghton Mifflin, 2005.

Plokhy, Serhii. *Yalta: The Price of Peace*. New York: Viking, 2010.

Salisbury, Harrison E. *The 900 Days: The Siege of Leningrad*. New York: Avon Books, 1970.

Snyder, Timothy. *Bloodlands: Europe Between Hitler and Stalin*. New York: Basic Books, 2010.

CHAPTER 5

Djilas, Milovan. *Conversations with Stalin*. Harmondsworth: Penguin, 1963.

Medvedev, Roy, and Zhores Medvedev. *The Unknown Stalin: His Life, Death, and Legacy*. New York: Overlook Press, 2004.

Montefiore, S. S. *Stalin: The Court of the Red Tsar*. London: Weidenfeld & Nicolson, 2003.

Nikolaev, Vladimir. *Sovetskaia Ochered' Kak Sreda Obitaniia: Sotsiologicheskii Analiz*. Moscow: INION RAN, 2000.

Rappaport, Helen. *Joseph Stalin: A Biographical Companion*. Santa Barbara: ABC-CLIO, 1999.

Zubok, Vladislav. *Zhivago's Children: The Last Russian Intelligentsia.* Cambridge: Harvard University Press, 2009.

CHAPTER 6

Carlson, Peter. *K Blows Top: A Cold War Comic Interlude Starring Nikita Khrushchev, America's Most Unlikely Tourist.* New York: Public Affairs, 2009.

Castillo, Greg. *Cold War on the Home Front: The Soft Power of Midcentury Design.* Minneapolis: University of Minnesota Press, 2010.

Crowley, David, and Susan E. Reid, eds. *Socialist Spaces: Sites of Everyday Life in the Eastern Bloc.* Oxford: Berg, 2002.

Khrushchev, N. S. *Vospominaniia. Vremia, liudi, vlast'.* Vols. 1–4. Moscow: Moskovskie novosti, 1999.

Taubman, William. *Khrushchev: The Man and His Era.* New York: W. W. Norton, 2003.

Vayl', Petr, and Aleksandr Genis. *60-e: Mir sovetskogo cheloveka.* Moscow: Novoe literaturnoe obozrenie, 1996.

CHAPTER 7

Ledeneva, Alena. *Russia's Economy of Favours: Blat, Networking and Informal Exchange.* Cambridge: Cambridge University Press, 1998.

Yurchak, Alexei. *Everything Was Forever Until It Was No More:*

The Last Soviet Generation. Princeton: Princeton University Press, 2006.

CHAPTER 8

Herlihy, Patricia. *The Alcoholic Empire: Vodka and Politics in Late Imperial Russia*. New York: Oxford University Press, 2002.

Transchel, Kate. *Under the Influence: Working-Class Drinking, Temperance, and Cultural Revolution in Russia, 1895–1932*. Pittsburgh: University of Pittsburgh Press, 2006.

White, Stephen. *Russia Goes Dry: Alcohol, State and Society*. Cambridge: Cambridge University Press, 1996.

CHAPTER 9

Felshman, Neil. *Gorbachev, Yeltsin and the Last Days of the Soviet Empire*. New York: St. Martin's, 1992.

Kahn, Jeffrey. *Federalism, Democratization, and the Rule of Law in Russia*. Oxford: Oxford University Press, 2002.

Kapuscinski, Ryszard. *Imperium*. New York: Knopf, 1994.

Moskoff, William. *Hard Times: Impoverishment and Protest in the Perestroika Years*. Armonk, NY: M. E. Sharpe, 1993.

Nekrich, A. M., trans. George Saunders. *The Punished Peoples: The Deportation and Fate of Soviet Minorities at the End of the Second World War*. New York: W. W. Norton, 1978.

O'Clery, Conor. *Moscow, December 25, 1991: The Last Day of the*

Selected Sources

Soviet Union. New York: Public Affairs, 2011.

Remnick, David. *Lenin's Tomb: The Last Days of the Soviet Empire.*
New York: Random House, 1993.

Ries, Nancy. *Russian Talk: Culture and Conversation During
Perestroika.* Ithaca, NY: Cornell University Press, 1997.

Suny, Ronald G. *The Revenge of the Past: Nationalism, Revolution,
and the Collapse of the Soviet Union.* Stanford: Stanford
University Press, 1993.

Von Bremzen, Anya, and John Welchman. *Please to the Table:
The Russian Cookbook.* New York: Workman, 1990.

CHAPTER 10

Devyatov, Sergei, Yu. Shefov, and S. Yur'eva. *Blizhnyaya dacha
Stalina: Opyt istoricheskogo putevoditelya.* Moscow: Kremlin
Multimedia, 2011.